**ALBERT EINSTEIN, HANS ADOLF KREBS,
BRUNO WALTER, KURT WEILL,
ARNOLD SCHÖNBERG, MAX LIEBERMANN,
RICHARD TAUBER, MARC CHAGALL . . .**

Even today the fullest extent of the outcome is not known. True, we know that millions of people have been murdered, but even here actual numbers can only be estimated. Today we know the crude outlines of the extent of human suffering that was evoked, and at least we have an inkling that, beyond the terrible injustice, something more happened, something irretrievable was lost to both the Jews and the Gentiles of Europe. Now German culture is to all intents and purposes "cleansed of Jewish influence," just as Goebbels and his friends had wished. At the same time, we must realize that the promised gains have eluded us; instead an indefinable loss seems to have set in—a loss at best only felt, possibly estimated. How could such loss ever be measured?
—From *Germany Without Jews*

BERNT ENGELMANN was born in Berlin in 1921. He served in the Luftwaffe during the first three years of World War II, mostly in France. Due to his work with the French resistance and German anti-Nazi groups, he was arrested twice by the Gestapo and sent to Dachau concentration camp. He was freed when the camp was liberated by the U.S. Army in April 1945. Today Engelmann is acclaimed as one of West Germany's leading journalists and writers, with over thirty books to his credit. He lives with his wife and four children in Rottach-Egern in Upper Bavaria.

Bantam Books of Related Interest
Ask your bookseller for the books you have missed

CHILDREN OF THE HOLOCAUST by Helen Epstein

DAWN by Elie Wiesel

THE LAST JEWS IN BERLIN by Leonard Gross

NIGHT by Elie Wiesel

AN ORPHAN IN HISTORY by Paul Cowan

THE WAR AGAINST THE JEWS by Lucy S. Dawidowicz

GERMANY WITHOUT JEWS

Bernt Engelmann
Translated by D.J. Beer

BANTAM BOOKS
TORONTO · NEW YORK · LONDON · SYDNEY · AUCKLAND

GERMANY WITHOUT JEWS
A Bantam Book / October 1984

PRINTING HISTORY
First printed in Germany April 1979

ISBN 0-553-24445-0

Published simultaneously in the United States and Canada

PRINTED IN THE UNITED STATES OF AMERICA

O   0 9 8 7 6 5 4 3 2 1

Author's Acknowledgments

The author wishes to thank all those who in one way or another have helped in the preparation and completion of this work. Special thanks are due Mr. Ludwig Lazarus, Hanover, for his extreme helpfulness in gathering material and finding sources; to the editors of the Jüdischer Pressedienst (Jewish Press Service); to Dr. H. G. van Dam, Secretary General of the Central Committee for Jews in Germany, and to Mr. Paul Spiegel, for their willingness to help and their loyal support; to Mrs. Mary Tucholsky for helpful suggestions and her generous permission to use materials from the Kurt Tucholsky Archives in Rottach-Egern; to Dr. Frank Arnau for important facts and documents; to Dr. Victor Weidtman for his very generous advice in difficult questions of statistics; to Mr. Karl Dieling for his help in preparing the Appendix; to Ellen Reuter and other associates of the publishers, Franz Schneekluth; to Heinz Stuckenbrock and his unionized co-workers at Mohndruck, Gütersloh; to Mr. Hans Uhlig for careful proofreading and for compiling the Table of Contents and the Bibliography; to Rita van Endert for her help concerning the technical production of the manuscript and numerous suggestions; and most especially to my friend Moses Gercek, who encouraged me actually to write the book I had been planning and researching for years.

Yes, we love this country.

And now I want to tell you something: It is simply untrue that those who call themselves "national" and are nothing more than middle-class nationalists took out an exclusive lease on this country and its language.

Neither the government official in his frock coat nor the tenured high-school teacher, nor even the ladies and gentlemen of the "Stahlhelm" are the only ones who make up Germany. We are here too.

They open their mouths wide and shout, "In the name of Germany . . . !" They shout, "We love this country—only we love it." It is not true.

. . . And just as the nationalist organizations beat the drum along the roads—with the same right, with exactly the same right we, we who were born here, we who write and speak German better than most of those national jackasses—with exactly the same right we lay claim to the rivers and forests, the shores and homes, the clearings and the meadows: It is our country.

. . . Germany is a divided nation. We are a part of it. And in all contrasts remains—unshakably, without banners, without the blare of hurdy-gurdies, without sentimentality and without drawn sword—the silent love of our homeland.

Kurt Tucholsky, 1929

Contents

GERMANY
WITHOUT
JEWS

Introduction

A New Perspective

Almost forty years have passed since the spring of 1945, which witnessed the total defeat and complete collapse of the once powerful German Reich. With these events came the end of the Jewish persecution, which had been initiated by the German government and escalated to mass murder organized and carried out by the state. Much has been said and written about the martyrdom of the victims, the scope of the annihilation, and the barbaric methods used. The complex moral aspects of this terrible historic occurrence have also been addressed. But the main point of all these considerations is the undeniable slaughter of millions, termed euphemistically by the leadership of the Reich "the final solution."

The death of the "Third Reich," coming after the deaths of so many Jews is commonly interpreted metaphorically as a surprisingly swift and just punishment imposed on the Germans. The more obvious possibility of a concrete connection of cause and effect linking the persecution of the Jews to the absolute defeat of Germany has seldom been considered, let alone investigated.

The disgust, horror, and dull thuds of guilt awakened by

the "final solution"—by now almost in a kind of historical retrospective—have blocked unbiased and objective consideration. There has been no scrutiny into whether Hitler's so-called Jewish policy—aside from the intended extermination of the Jews—might not also have been a cause of the total collapse of his regime and the resulting German catastrophe. It may, in fact, have been the primary cause. In retrospect this realization would turn the familiar Nazi slogan "The Jews are our misfortune" into a macabre prophecy. No one has attempted to imagine what could have happened and what kind of a world we should have today had there been no persecution of the Jews in Germany. And yet such speculation is not idle; it gives us a basis for arriving at a critical judgment of a policy that is normally dismissed with the term "fatal," spoken either in unthinking sentimentality or in cold opportunism.

There is no doubt that Hitler's policies were fatal for the Jews.

But to this day we know far too little about whether it was, or had to be, disastrous for the Germans. And yet the question arises whether the policy could or did yield any benefits—even if we include the persecutors' own narrow conceptions of what constitutes a benefit. Any advantages perceived by this bias would have to be screened objectively.

Let us try to imagine that German anti-Semitism had pursued its objectives in a different, somewhat less cruel manner, perhaps by forcing the Jews into exile. In that case Germany today would also be practically free of Jews, but without the memory of violence, destruction, gas chambers, and mass executions. Under those circumstances, and perhaps without quite the same crippling guilt, it would be possible to discuss what benefits or losses came to Germany and the Germans as a consequence of their "gentle" deliverance from the late, if undesirable, Jewish minority. It would also be possible to examine to what extent the aims of the champions of the anti-Jewish policy had been achieved. Today, after the passage of some decades, the permanent consequences of eliminating the Jews are gradually becoming clearer. Whether these can in any way justify the anti-Semitic objectives is another question.

The results of such strictly objective weighing of the pros and cons of a policy started fifty years ago would certainly be of great value, not only for the Germans themselves, but also for the Jews who were exiled and for their descendants. It would also enable other people to form a clearer judgment concerning the usefulness of a similar policy in their own countries, and may throw some light on the value of anti-Semitic and other racist theories in general.

If an objective discussion derives considerable value under the mere hypothetical supposition that there were no mass murder, how much more relevant it becomes when we recall the blood spilled and the tears shed, and the millions of human lives exacted by that policy!

Let us then, within the context of this study, put aside our abhorrence, horror, and guilt. Let us overcome the taboo that has prevented us until now from examining more closely the causes and consequences of the Jewish persecution that culminated in the mass murders of the 1940s. Instead, let us adopt the necessary impartial approach essential for getting at the truth. Finally let us recognize that modern anti-Semitism is no longer primarily founded on religion, but just as much on politics and race. It was neither the invention nor the monopoly of Hitler—and sadly is by no means extinct with him; it would be dangerous and naive to place all responsibility on him for everything that happened and followed.

Let us try instead to sort out all available records, enter them correctly, and compile a balance sheet, regardless of the outcome, in the firm belief that we can learn from our most dreadful mistakes if only we are able to recognize them.

Bernt Engelmann

Chapter 1

Germany Without Jews . . . ?

Germany without Jews—impossible. Even now, the assertion that there are no longer any Jews in those states that make up the German geographic and cultural area will be met with skepticism and rebuttal. In the Federal Republic, in East Germany, and in Austria there are untold thousands of native and foreign nationals who are practicing Jews, not including the countless others who, twenty-five years earlier, would still have been classified as Jews.

However, we are not concerned with their mere existence, but with quite another sort of presence, which needs to be examined. For about two thousand years followers of Judaism have lived in the area which became known as Germany. Long before there was a German language, a German culture, or even Germany as a geopolitical concept, Jews were firmly established in the Germanic provinces. As full-fledged and often dominant citizens of Roman towns along the Rhine, Mosel, Main, and Danube rivers they contributed richly to Germany's cultural, political, and spiritual development.

The oldest manuscript to document the presence of a significant number of permanent Jewish residents within the walls of a town later classified as German can be found in an edict issued by the Emperor Constantine. Dated December 11,

321 A.D., it deals with honorary municipal offices awarded the Jews of Cologne.

During the eventful first thousand years of the Christian era—which witnessed the migration of nations, the fall of Rome, the formation of Germanic states, the rise of the Holy Roman Empire, and the colonization of northern and central Germany—Jews became a significant element in the urban life of central Europe. They were freeborn, with the right to bear arms and to acquire land: they participated in community affairs with clearly defined rights and obligations; they were merchants, artisans, doctors, artists, lawyers, and clerks. Alone or with the help of slaves they cultivated their gardens, fields, and vineyards. The relationship with their Christian neighbors was often a very amicable one including even joint business ventures. These relationships flourished in spite of various attempts by the church councils to restrict these contacts.

The Jews were present in large numbers, occasionally in leading positions, among the pioneers of the earliest German settlements along the rivers Elbe and Saale, as documented in the Worms uprising on the side of Emperor Henry IV. This was the first independent intervention by a German town that concerned the political fate of the nation, and the Jews of Worms participated decisively. The consequent treaty, concluded in the year 1074 A.D. between Emperor and town, opens with the words, "Judais ceterisque civilibus Wormsae" ("With the Jews and other citizens of Worms") in contrast to the more usual phrasing, "Our beloved citizens of Worms, both Christians and Jews".

Christians and Jews stood shoulder to shoulder in defense of their hometowns against assailants. Together they celebrated their victories or mourned their defeats. They played chess together and sang the same songs to lute accompaniment. They caroused together and jousted together, wielding shiny lances and bestriding noble steeds. Even in the art of love they did not pay undue attention to the difference in faith, and church prohibitions had to be invoked to prevent shared use of bathhouses.

Finally, those Jews from the towns along the Rhine, Main, and Danube—many of whom were propertied and educated—belonged to those social classes that helped create German literature. The Jews transcribed German into the Hebrew alphabet of their religious writings, just as the Christians employed not runic characters, but the Latin letters used by the church fathers. Not incidentally, the oldest extant version, and the only one in Middle High German, of the Gudrun epic, recently discovered and now in the library of Cambridge University, is recorded in vocalized Hebrew script. In addition, there are German legends, old German fairy tales, early medieval Rhenish folk songs, and even a courtly verse romance called the Book of Bovo, that have survived in Yiddish to the present day. The famous illustrated Mannesse manuscript has preserved some of the lyrics of a Jewish minstrel from Franconia, Susskind von Trimberg, who worked around 1250 A.D.

How closely and on the whole peacefully—even more important, how tightly linked by destiny—Christian and Jewish citizens lived together in German towns during the centuries that saw the emergence of what is called Germany, is symbolized in the oldest town hall of Cologne, erected "inter Judeos"—smack between the homes of the Jews and next to their bathhouse. During the early Middle Ages, Cologne was the most outstanding city in the Empire; many surviving documents show that Christians and Jews living within the same walls structured a practical and legal community that on occasion prevailed over the bond of a common faith with outsiders. This can be seen, for example, in the Letters of Defiance dated March 17 and April 11, 1401. In them, the knight Otto von Bellinchaven, the citizens Reynolt and Roloff von Coevoerde, as well as twenty-four other Christians of the Lower Rhine, formally declared hostilities against the city of Cologne because of alleged injustices suffered by "the Jew, Selichmann, son of Schaeff," at the hands of other Cologne Jews. Evidently the protesters considered Selichmann a good friend.

With the dawning of the second millenium of Christian-Jewish relations in Germany, life grew decidedly less harmonious and peaceful. The period of the waning Middle Ages and the onset of modern times were dominated by the growing secular power of the Church, religious fanaticism, feudal exploitation, intolerance, and superstition. The Jews of Germany were among those who suffered the consequences. The majority of Germany's inhabitants lived subhuman lives, in servitude and deprived of the right to bear arms. History books tend to dwell on the habits, intentions, successes, and occasional defeats of the rulers, with only an occasional hint about the lives of the ordinary citizen. Be that as it may, in those dark centuries of European history many groups— including the Jews, now expelled from the Christian community—were repeatedly hunted down, subjugated, robbed of all possessions, arbitrarily expelled or prosecuted, tortured, and brutally murdered. Besides Jews, victims at various times included peasants, miners, and artisans who attempted to organize in order to improve their unbearable living conditions; Cathars, Albigensians, Anabaptists, Hussites, the Gueux, Beguines, and numerous other "heretics," who threatened, not only accepted dogmas, but also the social order; and groups suspected of reverting to heathendom—the people of Dithmarschen, Lower Saxony, Prussia, and the Wends. Furthermore, entire provinces were laid waste by forays and punitive raids on the part of the feudal lords, mass executions were a response to failed popular uprisings, and there was constant persecution of witches.

In short, if the case of the Jews is not viewed as distinct, as is common, but in the context of the social evolution and the situation of other groups, it is seen that they were not the most harshly persecuted, let alone the only victims of the arbitrary power exerted by medieval rulers. Rather, they shared the fate of most other Germans of that period, indistinguishable in everything but faith from the millions of those who were suppressed, exploited, and persecuted.

Their faith, however, subjected them to vicious bloodbaths, the outcome of efforts at conversion, most of them unsuccessful; the worst butchery was perpetrated by the Crusaders moving to the Rhine from France. Many German Jews therefore migrated to the East, primarily to Poland, where the kings received them—like German Christian immigrants—with open arms. They were granted all rights and liberties because the emerging Polish towns needed tradesmen and artists.

Legal restrictions were imposed on those Jews who remained in Germany, severely limiting their choice of work and residence. Consequently they were confined to the newly established ghettos, and almost the only occupations open to them were commerce and money lending. Although there were a number of Jewish physicians and scholars, men of the cloth and clerks, artisans and domestics, their activities were concentrated in the ghetto, while business relations with the Christian community were restricted to trade and money lending. Thus tensions arose on the business level in addition to the tensions arising from religious differences.

Again, it would be a mistake to view this situation as unique to the Jews. At least at the outset, the Christian lower middle classes could, strictly speaking, be said to have lived in "ghettos," subject to laws governing residence and work, curfews, dress regulations, and guild statutes. They lived in small towns whose gates were locked at night and heavily guarded by day, constantly supervised by church and state. They were subject to tolls and other equally arbitrary fees. In short, the Christian masses of the late Middle Ages were almost as deprived and disenfranchised as the Jews.

Conversely, though Jews found themselves almost compelled to practice usury, so that it soon became their most important source of income, they hardly had a monopoly on it. Many devout Christians, both Germans and other nationals, not excluding cardinals and bishops and abbesses, mastered the art of lending money at high rates of interest.

The Jews were, in any case, the favorite "lightning conductors" to discharge the accumulated wrath of the people; since this outlet deflected any potential danger to the ruling powers, they looked on tolerantly. In cases of catastrophe, such as plagues and famine, Jews could simply be blamed for having defiled the Holy Wafer, poisoning the wells, or ritually murdering a Christian child. Thereupon the people were allowed to take ruthless "revenge" on the "Christ killers"—or at least their descendants—and in the process fill their pockets just a bit.

In one respect, though, the Jews were better off than were the other suppressed, exploited, and persecuted groups or classes. They had a way—even, objectively speaking, a quite simple way—out of their misery: baptism. "Heretics" who "repented" could at most hope for a less painful death. "Confessing" witches and sorcerers who broke under torture could trade their acquiescence only for a more rapid end to their agony at the stake. After a failed uprising neither vows never to rise against their masters again nor contemptible betrayals of their "accomplices" would avail repentant workers and peasants; they had to die anyway, and in an extremely cruel manner, calculated to stifle any thought of renewed disobedience within the widest possible circle.

However, Jews willing to turn Christian were received into the church with open arms, rewarded into the bargain, and safeguarded against further discrimination from the secular rulers, who joined in the jubilation. And the universal rejoicing was all the greater as such conversions were none too common.

It was precisely this growing isolation in a world of increasing hostility and deepening religious fanaticism that confirmed the members of the Jewish communities in Germany in their faith, producing the "obstinacy" that so infuriated many a Christian divine. Even the most dire misery and the most stringent oppression were able only in exceptional instances to induce the German Jews to change their religion. Beginning in the seventeenth century, Jewish refugees, who had left the Rhineland to settle in Poland and other Eastern countries, were subjected to still more heinous persecution.* They were as steadfast as other religious minorities under pressure. But what oppression could rarely achieve was frequently brought about by absence of pressure. The chronicles of the early and late Middle Ages record numerous cases in which Jews voluntarily—and presumbly out of conviction—agreed to baptism. In Cologne alone several dozen such conversions are documented, most commonly of educated and well-respected Jews, and it seems reasonable to suppose that the total number was much greater. A fair estimate of German Jewish families who converted to Christianity before 1800 would be several thousand.

Conversely, a far smaller number of Christians converted to Judaism. But such conversions did occur, even among prominent churchmen. Both Bodo, the Alemannic deacon at the court of Louis the Pious, and Wezelin, confessor to Emperor Henry II became Jews, to the great consternation of Christendom.

This brings us to a question that was of no importance until the late nineteenth century and assumes acute relevance in

---

*One exception was the mass conversion of Polish Jews to Roman Catholicism under the leadership of Jakob Frank (1726–1791). Frank's daughter, Eva (d. 1817 in Offenbach), succeeded her father as head of the Frankists.

the twentieth—what determines Jewishness? Does descent rather than religious affiliation decide who is Jewish?

This question was exploited, manipulated, distorted, and exaggerated in the Third Reich, with an extremism to the point of absurdity and with catastrophic consequences. History makes us reluctant to entertain it at all; but perhaps it contains a kernel of validity. Following centuries of social segregation on the basis of religion, German Jews were naturally united by a bond that went beyond religious affiliation. Until their destruction they not only shared Germany's fate and contributed substantially to it, but also had a distinct group identity: Their restriction, voluntary or otherwise, to certain urban professions; the different customs and habits required by their religion; their stronger drive toward education and learning; the unremitting defensiveness necessitated by the generally hostile conduct of the Christian world; and last but not least, the limited number of suitable marriage partners—all these and more combined gradually to effect the evolution of shared attitudes and traits. When a family left the Jewish community by converting or emigrating, these characteristics went with them, and it naturally took generations for the influence of a new group or environment to extinguish them.

It is this vague sense that underlies and supports the thesis of a more or less clearly definable Jewish group existing, independently of the religion. This leaves the question—categorically rejected by the anti-Semites of the late nineteenth and the twentieth centuries—whether the German Jews were not first and foremost Germans, differing from other Germans no more than, say, Catholic winegrowers in the Mosel region differed from Protestant businessmen in Hamburg. It must be remembered that all regional and class differences were originally far more pronounced, having begun to blur only in the last fifty years or so as a result of greater mobility, an upsurge in tourism, and the homogeniety brought about by the mass media. Opposed to this view is the anti-Semitic doctrine according to which Jews are members of a foreign "Semitic" race from the near East and therefore, for reasons other than religion, "alien to the species" of interrelated German tribes. Germans, the argument goes, with their predominantly "Nordic-Germanic" racial traits, share "blood kinship" that must be protected against mixing with the alien "inferior race," since any intermingling "inevitably leads to degeneration."

If we begin by examining the alleged "Semitic" origin of German Jews, we immediately encounter a mass of confused concepts. The term "Semitic" applies only to the *language* group of which Hebrew—the language of the Bible, of theology, and of the Jewish liturgy—is a member. But to call Jews *Semites* for that reason is absurd; one might just as easily call all Catholics "Latins" or "Romans." The supposed source of all that is Jewish in the near East is true only for the religion of Moses and to those believers in one invisible God who, expelled by the Romans or abducted as slaves in the first century A.D., spread the Law of Moses to the farthest corners of the known world. To therefore summarily designate the Jews—and particularly those living in Central Europe during the nineteenth and twentieth centuries—as Near Eastern and thus "alien to the species" is as senseless as calling all Western Christians simply "Levantines". After all, Christian teachings also began nearly two thousand years ago along the coasts of Asia Minor, and were propagated by apostles who were descended from the mixed populations of the Levant. The vast majority of the Jews living in the medieval towns along the Rhine—towns that had begun as ancient Roman settlements—were by no means pure descendants of the People of the Book. They were certainly no more homogeneous than the local disciples of Christianity, a Jewish sect also exported from Judea, which had been raised by the Romans to the position of state religion. The original Jewish tribes had, at any rate, formed only a very small community, and their heroic struggles against the Roman colonizers came near to wiping them out. The Jews along the Rhine may at most have had a "non-Aryan" great-grandmother who had found favor in the eyes of a Gallic or Germanic legionnaire; or they were simply descendants of Celtic, Germanic, or other converts, no different from converted Christians. It is patently obvious that only a minute fraction of the several hundred thousand Jews who settled in the German towns during the period of the Merovingians up to the first Crusades, could be descended from Judean exiles. These are the same people who later moved eastward, becoming the forebears of the many million Russian and Polish Jews.

None of the anthropological measurements and other research procedures—beginning with those of Rudolf Virchow, through those of Fishberg and of the Nazi racial researchers, up to comparisons of blood groups and the Rh factor undertaken by UNESCO—has succeeded in establishing any kinship between European Jews and Oriental peoples, or a link with Jews of the Yemen or Buckara. But there is clear proof of membership in the western mix that counted as Aryan during the Third Reich. The Nazi persecution of Jews, therefore, was obliged to ascertain "race" merely on the basis of parents' and grandparents' religious affiliation. The lack of any other established characteristics gave rise to a wonderful lack of logical reasoning: they claimed at the same time that it was not religion, but only "blood" that determined the worth or worthlessness of a human being.

In fact German Jews—who differed as much from those of distant countries and continents as did other Central Europeans—had intermingled to the same considerable extent with neighbors, conquerors, fugitives, and slaves as the Christians. (Two special cases are represented by Sephardic Jews and Khazars. The former, a Spanish-Jewish group, consisted of a small portion of the Jews expelled from the Iberian peninsula in the late fifteenth century. The Khazars, a group of Jews from eastern and southeastern Europe, arose in the middle of the eighth century, when the king and nobility of the Khazars, an ancient Turkish people originally settled between the Black and Caspian Seas and converted to Judaism.)

The Jews and Christians of Cologne may serve as an illustration. During the late-Roman period they made up only two of five competing religious groups. Originally at odds with the state religion of the Romans and with the slightly Romanized cult of the native Ubians, a mixed Celtic-Germanic population. But in the end the Ubians were supplanted. Besides Christianity and Judiasm, there was Mithraism, from Persia, preferred by the garrison soldiers; the cult of Isis, imported from Egypt, initially considered too lascivious but eventually powerful enough to gain official recognition (and possibly the basis of the Cologne carnival); and finally, the cult of Jupiter Dolichenus, brought from Syria, with its own temple in Cologne.

The diversity of these cultic forms, all transposed from the East, gives some indication of the motley mix of people that made up the Roman colony of Cologne. Greeks, Syrians, Phoenicians, Egyptians, Palestinians, and Persians lived alongside slaves and freedmen and freedwomen of every nationality, soldiers and veterans from the regiments garrisoned in the town, including not only Germans and Gauls, but also members of the Nubian legion—tall black men from Africa. The city was further peopled by sailors and officers of the *Classis Germanica*, the Roman Rhine fleet—some of them Batavians from the Rhine estuary, others seamen from Cyprus; according to the gravestones, some came from such distant parts of Asia Minor as Phrygia and Mysia. Most of them were married to local women, of predominantly Celtic-Germanic descent. In all, the city's population has been estimated at thirty to forty thousand people. Of these, at most a few hundred—legionnaires, freedmen and women slaves, who came from Frisia—were blond and blue-eyed. Five hundred years later the Nazi "race" fanatics seized on these traits and raised them to the level of an ideal, though they themselves could not for the most part meet these criteria.

The transition from Cologne's Roman rule to control by the Frankish kings was almost entirely peaceful. No one was expelled or displaced as an "undesirable alien." In fact, the mixture of races and populations grew even more motley with the medieval influx of still more Germanic tribes and the invasions of Huns and other central and East Asian people. They considered it their inalienable right to rape all the women and girls they could lay their hands on—a custom observed by conquerors to this day. Volumes could be filled with lists of all the peoples whose men passed through Cologne as warriors or traders, often leaving offspring behind. The women of just as many tribes came to Cologne, where they often settled permanently. They came as slaves or prostitutes in the trains of conquerors or as booty of returning crusaders. They also established themselves as market women and as artists of some kind. In modern times new blood keeps arriving as forced labor and as foreign workers.

In short, at one time or another Cologne was occupied by every European nation, by almost all African and Asian peoples, and of course, in 1945, by the victorious United States Army. This last power included such a variety of ethnic groups that it is to be compared only with the Roman army. And all the different occupying troops stayed long enough, at least, to join with the women of Cologne in bringing forth a sizable number of children.

This illustration demonstrates that all the talk of "purity of blood" in German districts and in Europe altogether might have some minimal validity when applied to only the most remote and inaccessible areas (specific valleys high in the Alps might qualify for this dubious distinction after centuries of inbreeding). Thus, we can safely ignore the rather vague concept of the reputedly predominant "Nordic-Germanic blood."

But what is true for the Gentile Germans must also be true for German Jews. It would be naive in the extreme to suppose that as the numerous foreign conquerors came and went for two thousand years, exercising their privileges as victors with greater or lesser force, they made rigorous distinctions between baptized and nonbaptized women. Nor can it be assumed that when Jews proselytized a heathen land, receiving the slaves they freed into the Mosaic community or when converting pretty serving maids to Judaism before marrying them, they always respectfully bypassed people of "Nordic-Germanic blood." Even the most rabid Jew haters were not presumptuous enough to claim "racial" differences between Jews and Christians.

As such, Jews shared in the lot of all religious and other minorities in the German Empire. Whoever constituted the majority at any one time judged others on their individual traits. When these were seen pejoratively, they were attributed to the whole group; when positive qualities manifested themselves, they were judged exceptional. As late as 1801, the Field Marshal Josef Count de Ligne (1735–1814), a liberal and enlightened nobleman basically well disposed toward the Jews, issued a disparaging generalization about the "ten million Hebrews in Europe." By this number he meant chiefly the Jews of Germany and of the Bohemian, Hungarian, and Polish territories belonging to Austria; he explicitly excluded only the upper class of wealthy and educated Jews from his summary judgment.

After such a positively abysmal summary—not even intended to express anti-Semitism—we cannot help but wonder what allowed the highly educated and aristocratic count to arrive at his opinion. Mainly we wonder how de Ligne thought the Jews of Germany and Austria who were not in the millionaire class should have been fashioned in order not to be seen as "cowardly, deceitful, and mean-spirited." Would the Count de Ligne, himself a distinguished officer, only have been satisfied with smart horsemen, outstanding swordsmen, and intrepid strategists?

It was absurd to expect courtly behavior from a half-starved proletariat, cut off from Western education and civilization, but as early as the Middle Ages in Germany, enough Jewish jousting masters existed to make those Jews more than exceptional cases. The Mansfeld Chronicle mentions the famous Jewish tournament at Weissenfels (1384), "where the Jews did thrust and parry, that the lists were adjourned." In a thirteenth-century legal opinion Rabbi Meir of Rothenburg mentions the Jewish swordsmen and stresses the importance of jousting. A 1443 manuscript from Gotha commends a Jew, one Ott, for having developed the art of wrestling, which had formerly been one aspect of jousting, into an independent discipline. Albrecht Dürer's famous depiction of wrestling is based on Ott's book of instruction, and Ott himself became the fencing and wrestling teacher for the Habsburg princes. Andreas and Jacob Liegnitzer were other celebrated German-Jewish fencing masters. The older brother, known as Andres Jud, was the author of a manual, *Das Fechten mit dem Schwert* [Fighting with the Sword]. Emperor Rudolf II issued several prohibitions on fencing matches between Jews and Christians as well as training of Jews by anyone other than Jewish swordsmen.

The predilection for fencing expressed by German Jews and the Bohemian, Polish, and especially Hungarian Jews of German origin survived well into the twentieth century. Had he lived 120 years later, the Count de Ligne would have been agreeably surprised. In six of the Olympic Games held between 1908 and 1936, ten Jewish men and two Jewish women (most of them Hungarian-Germans) won a total of thirteen gold and three silver medals in fencing with foils and sabers.

The same century that saw the well-meaning Count de Ligne give his all-embracing opinion on the Jews of Germany and Austro-Hungary also brought distinction to one of the most expert horsemen of the imperial German army, the Prussian Cavalry General Walter von Mossner. An officer of "full-blooded Jewish" descent, his preeminence was undisputed after he twice won the Great Army steeplechase.

A few months after the death of the Count de Ligne, on October 7, 1815, a Jewish lieutenant in the Imperial Austrian Army Engineers, Ignatz Wetzlar, successfully stormed the bridgehead of Macon, for which he was awarded the Knight's Cross of the Order of Maria Theresa medal and was made a peer. Two of his "full-blooded Jewish" descendants, the Barons Heinrich and Gustav Wetzlar von Plankenstern, held the rank of lieutenant general in the Austrian military.

In 1894, eighty years after the death of de Ligne, the Imperial Austro-Hungarian army had no fewer than 2,179 Jewish officers, including at least seven lieutenant field marshals, nine major generals, and two commanding generals, most of them from the same Galician and Carpatho-Ukranian villages and small towns in which the Count de Ligne had made his regrettable and repulsive observations. All these smart and dashing imperial officers, born to Jewish families, would surely have been surprised and ultimately embarrassed by the recommendations that flowed from the pen of their comrade-in-arms, de Ligne. "The Jews should be dressed in long Oriental robes with matching attractive, colorful caps. They should be provided with work suited to their propensities. Then their teeming throngs, which resemble the vermin visibly crawling through their reddish hair and repulsive garments, will be transformed into healthy, clean, handsome, and useful people."

Leaving aside the exaggerations and romantic notions peculiar to the style of the period, it becomes clear that the Count did not consider the dirt, the ugliness, and the alleged character flaws of the Jewish masses he describes as "racial" traits. He took them to be the results—easily remedied—of their living like pariahs, with social isolation, cruel persecution, ruthless elimination from all respectable professions and decent housing, constant humiliation, and indescribable poverty.

So much is already made clear by a sentence in the introduction preceding the Count de Ligne's *Abhandlung über die Juden* [Treatise on the Jews]: "The poor Jews may seem to be ridiculed in my humble work, but I am merely ridiculing those who ridicule them. Our Capuchin monks sport beards that are no less long, they also bring nasal sounds to their sacred chanting, and their dislike of the arts is no less pronounced." Finally, the person to whom the treatise was addressed and the enthusiastic description de Ligne gives of her prove that the Count considered the Jewish question purely as an economic and social problem. The treatise was written for Baroness Sophie Grotthus, née Meyer, whom he apostrophized as "Pupil of Amalia, inspired by the Great Frederick." Not only was Sophie Grotthus, née Meyer, a member of the inner circle of the witty and artistic Duchess Anna Amalia of Saxe-Weimar, mother of Carl August, and an intimate of Goethe; more importantly, she and her better-known sister, Marianne von Eybenberg—secretly married to the Imperial Austrian ambassador to Prussia, Count Henry XIV of Reuss, and at one time Goethe's mistress—were the daughters of a Berlin banker and born and reared in the Jewish faith.

The emancipation of the Jews was gradually realized in Western, Northern, and Central Europe in the train of the Enlightenment, the Declaration of the Rights of Man, and the liberation of the Third Estate. Soon it became impossible for the citizens of the German states and those in the western sections of the Austrian monarchy to seriously doubt that despite centuries of oppression, their Jewish fellow citizens were at least just as patriotically German, and with the same justification, as their Gentile neighbors. Their contribution to every social area, their participation in the struggle for a unified Germany, and their part in Germans' being recognized in the tribute as "the nation of poets and thinkers"— these were all far greater than might have been expected according to their number, their economic standing, and their historical position.

The first and probably most important single contribution was made by Moses Mendelssohn. A short, deformed, and sickly fourteen-year-old, the victim of childhood privations, he arrived in Berlin in 1743, having walked all the way from Dessau. Having taught himself all he knew, he soon became renowned as a scholar, the closest friend of Gotthold Ephraim Lessing, and eventually gained fame as the "German Socrates." He enabled the Jews—excluded from the larger society centuries earlier and doomed to a largely medieval way of life—to rejoin the intellectual and cultural life of the common country. He taught his coreligionists as well as the Gentiles, who had earlier neglected their prose literature, a "correct, clear, and graceful German." Thus he became the first world-renowned German author of the Jewish faith.

No less an authority than Johann Gottfried Herder, in his *Fragmente über die neuere deutsche Literatur* [Fragments Concerning Recent German Literature] wrote of Mendelssohn, "Socrates introduced philosophy to mankind. Moses is our nation's writer of philosophy, which he enhances with beauty of style; yes, it is he who knows how to set forth clearly his philosophy, as if inspired by the muses themselves."

The patriotic and military activities of German Jews, particularly those of Prussia, during the wars of liberation will be discussed below. The intellectual influence of some Jewish women was even greater, however. Rahel Levin, who was married to the Prussian diplomat and historian, Karl August Varnhagen von Ense, was the hostess of a salon frequented by the Humboldts and the Schlegels, Johann Gottlieb Fichte and Friedrich Gentz, Jean Paul and Adalbert von Chamisso. Shortly before his tragic end, Heinrich von Kleist called on Rahel, as she was universally known, and, Prince Ludwig Ferdinand of Prussia, a man of genius idolized by the people, who fell in battle at Saalfeld in 1806, was among her close friends. She was widely praised for her "magnetism of the mind and the heart."

It was thanks to Rahel that the appreciation of the writings of Privy Councillor Johann Wolfgang von Goethe spread from her salon throughout the whole of Germany, creating the cult of Goethe. Thus a minor poet of limited popularity grew into the Olympian recognized as such by the educated middle classes. It was a great day, not only for Frau von Varnhagen and her friends, but also for the visitor from Weimar, when the two at last met face to face during a surprise morning call on Rahel by Goethe.

Henriette Herz, a beautiful Jewish woman, widow of the Berlin physician and philosopher, Marcus Herz, also had an influential salon. Friedrich Schleiermacher was her very good friend. The Humboldts were devoted to her all their lives. Concerning her private circles and reading parties, it is no exaggeration to quote "that in those days in Berlin there were no men or women who distinguished themselves at a later date who had not belonged to these circles for a longer or shorter period, depending on their station in life."

In the Vienna salon of Baroness Fanny Arnstein, daughter of the Jewish banker Daniel Itzig of Berlin, the hostess brought together the great men of politics and the leaders of German art and literature, especially during the Congress of Vienna. Dorothea, the favorite daughter of the great Moses Mendelssohn, is a further example of the extraordinarily strong intellectual and cultural influence exerted by Jewish women, most notably at the beginning of the Jewish emancipation in Germany. The mother of Philip Veit, the painter, Dorothea inspired a whole new school of painting, the so-called Nazarenes. Her second husband, Friedrich Schlegel, published her novels, collections of songs, and translations under his own name, so that Dorothea can be claimed as the cofounder, at least, of German Romanticism in literature. Her nephew Felix Mendelssohn-Bartholdy, the most famous of the many gifted grandsons of the "German Socrates," was not only responsible for reviving an interest in amateur music recitals; it was also to his credit, as he once timidly joked, "That it had to be a young Jew" who returned "the greatest of all Christian music" to the people—Bach's St. Matthew Passion.

Berthold Auerbach was another member of this generation. Born in 1812, the son of a poor Jewish peddler in Nordstetten, (a village of Upper Baden) he became, in Paul Landau's words, "the originator of the German village story, the interpreter of peasant life, the most influential German popular poet, and the most popular writer of the period from, roughly, 1850 to 1870."

Fanny Lewald, born in 1811 in Königsberg (now Kaliningrad), originated the German women's novel and was a pioneer of feminism. She was descended from the same distinguished Jewish family that boasted two outstanding statesmen of the period: her cousin Heinrich Simon, a brilliant lawyer and fiery speaker, Liberal member of the first German parliament and of the National Assembly convened in the Paulskirche in Frankfurt; and Eduard von Simson, who had the honor of presiding over every parliament of the German constitutional struggle, from the meeting in the Paulskirche through the Reichtag (Imperial Diet) of 1871.

At the age of twenty, Simson had received the blessing of

the eighty-year-old Goethe. He was also instrumental in offering the imperial crown to two German kings—to Friedrich Wilhelm IV in vain, to Wilhelm I successfully. Finally, he became president of the newly created Court of Justice and founded the Goethe Society, which he headed until his death.

The period that stretched from the "German Socrates," Moses Mendelssohn, to Eduard von Simson, the "born president," gave the Jews in Prussia and other German states, if not the achievement of full equality, at least grounds for some satisfaction. They had finally become recognized by most educated Christians as valuable and indispensable members of the German nation.

In Austria there was a similar development. Its onset is also marked by a Jewish scholar, though not a philosopher but a "professor of public finance and police science." Josef von Sonnenfels was the baptized son of Jewish parents and the grandson of a Berlin rabbi. Sonnenfels was the "beacon of Austrian enlightenment." Listing Baron Sonnenfels' many and various accomplishments, his contemporary, Franz Gräffer, called him "the man who has banished inhumanity, bad taste, the Rococo, torture, buffoonery (though we may mourn the last!); the man who reformed the written language and business speech, a genius at administration, the man who shaped our most distinguished public servants and educators."

Vienna also had its culturally significant Jewish salons. Besides the one presided over by Baroness Fanny Arnstein, there was an important circle headed by her sister, Cecilie von Eskeles. Her daughter, Marianne, married the Imperial Austrian general of the Ordnance, Count Franz von Wimpffen, and for two decades she was at the center of Viennese intellectuals and artists. Incidentally, she and her aunts gained social approval for the Christmas tree, which was until then scorned by the "better class of people."

It was in the house of the (Jewish) Baron Karl Abraham Wetzlar von Plankenstern that Wolfgang Amadeus Mozart not only enjoyed the hospitality of a patron of the arts, but also met his (equally Jewish) librettist, Lorenzo da Ponte. Ludwig van Beethoven was another famous musical guest in the Plankenstern residence. The composer was also a close friend of another Jewish music lover, the merchant, Josef

Hönig Edlen von Henikstein, father of the Austrian chief of staff, Alfred, Baron von Henikstein.

The idol of all Viennese, high-born and low, the "darling of the country and the realm" (in the words of Ludwig Speidel), was Adolf Ritter von Sonnenthal. In his day he was surely the most famous actor in Germany. A Jew, he had started life in a tailor's shop in the town of Pest. Also of poor Hungarian Jewish descent were the "waltz kings," Johann Strauss the father and Johann Strauss the son.

These are merely a few examples from the nineteenth century. If none of them—not Mendelssohn's "Songs Without Words," Auerbach's stories, the Goethe cult of Rahel Varnhagen, the endeavors of Moses Mendelssohn and Josef von Sonnenfels to revivify German prose, the "Radetzky March," or the "Emperor Waltz"—is enough to demonstrate German thoughts and attitudes, we need think only of the poet who, though not in his own country, nevertheless in the eyes of the world ranks with Goethe: Heinrich Heine.

It was near the close of the nineteenth century that a controversy arose in Düsseldorf—was the outstanding son of the city entitled to be honored by it despite the fact that he was born a Jew and had died in "French exile"? Thereupon Germany's greatest, and in those days most popular, statesman, Otto von Bismarck, voiced his opinion: "Why shouldn't we erect a statue to Heine? He is, after all, a German with whom only Goethe can be mentioned in one breath." However, Düsseldorf refused to erect the donated statue, although eventually the monument did find an honored location—in New York.

Another Heine monument was erected to the poet she worshiped by the Austrian Empress Elisabeth on the isle of Corfu, her favorite haunt. It was removed at the instigation of Emperor Wilhelm II of Germany, her successor to this island residence. In response, Thomas Theodor Heine, "Germany's Daumier" and one of the leading political cartoonists of the day (also from a Jewish family, though distantly, if at all, related to the poet), attacked this barbarous act in the pages of *Simplicissimus*, a Germany humor magazine. This act of criticism earned him six months imprisonment for lèse-majesté.

Does it therefore follow that Wilhelm II and the citizens of Düsseldorf were anti-Semites, while Bismarck and *Simplicissimus* were kindly disposed to Jews? Matters are not so simple. The Düsseldorf councillors had no objection whatever, for example, when Friedrich Wilhelm von Schadow skillfully guided the Düsseldorf art academy to worldwide recognition, even though his mother, Marianne Davidels, was the daughter of a Jewish jeweler. Neither did they object when his brother-in-law, Eduard Bendemann, the son of a Jewish banker, became Schadow's successor as director of the academy. Bendemann's son, Felix, an admiral in the Imperial German Navy, was granted hereditary nobility. There was also no objection when Gustav Lindemann, descendant of a Jewish family from Danzig, and his wife, Luise Dumont, founded the municipal theater and ran it most successfully for over a quarter of a century. Nor were any objections raised when a Jewish physician, Artur Schlossmann, an outstanding pediatrician and social-hygiene expert, obtained the chair as professor for children's diseases at the medical academy of Düsseldorf and was made director of municipal pediatric services.

Nor was Emperor Wilhelm II a thorough anti-Semite. Among the Emperor's closest friends were some outstanding Jewish business leaders, such as Albert Ballin, chairman of the board of the Hamburg-Amerika Line; his advisers included Walther Rathenau, at that time head of the German Edison Company, and the venerable and semiblind Gerson von Bleichröder, who had been personal banker to Wilhelm I. Another confidant of the Emperor was Privy Councillor August von Simson, president of the Berlin Chamber of Advocates and the board of directors of the Krupp works in Essen. He was a son of Eduard von Simson, who, for many years was president of the Diet and later on of the imperial supreme court. Finally, Emperor Wilhelm even had a "full-blooded Jewish" aide-de-camp in the person of Walther von Mossner, already celebrated for his equestrian feats, who was to become commander of the exclusive cavalry of the guards.

On the other hand, at the beginning of his career, Otto von Bismarck was neither inclined to be friendly to Jews nor even willing, for reasons of common sense or justice, to support their emancipation. His attitude changed, however, not least because of his relationships with a number of friends, acquaintances, and associates of Jewish origin.

There was, for example, Hermann Barschall, who married Franziska von Puttkamer, a cousin of Bismarck's wife. As an influential right-wing conservative, he had smoothed the way for Bismarck's entry into the Prussian Diet. While he was Prussian ambassador, Bismarck repaid his cousin by marriage and the supporter of his career by pushing through the appointment of Barschall as district president of Thorn. This was the first occasion that a citizen of Jewish origin became a high-ranking Prussian administrator. Then there was Ferdinand Lassalle, Barschall's cousin. He organized and headed the first (and, until 1869, the only) Social Democratic organization of German workers. Remarkably enough, Bismarck's relationship with him was a very good one; he liked to confer with him and made use of Lassalle's support in the constitutional conflict of 1862.

Bismarck also had two ministers of Jewish descent—Heinrich von Friedberg and Rudolf Friedenthal. Friedberg, for many years Prussian Minister of Justice, was one of the authors of the unified penal code for the German empire; and Friedenthal was cofounder of the Free Conservative National Party. Under Bismarck he served as Prussian Minister for Agriculture and, intermittently, as Minister of the Interior. He participated extensively in drawing up the 1871 Reich Constitution that granted Jews full equality, at least *de jure*.

Bismärck's bankers and financial advisers were Gerson von Bleichroder, Robert von Mendelssohn, and his son, Franz von Mendelssohn. In 1884 Bismarck assured the latter emphatically, "I am no enemy of the Jews and like dealing with Jews. . . ."

Then there were the Hahn brothers, sons of the mathematician Elkan Marjus (subsequently, Ernst Moritz) Hahn. Ludwig Hahn, the eldest, achieved the post of Minister of the Interior by way of the Prussian Ministry of Education, after a career as a right-wing conservative journalist. From 1862 he headed the so-called Literary Office of the government—Bismarck's press and propaganda headquarters. For two decades Hahn (generally called "Press Hahn") was "Bismarck's enthusiastic herald and assistant. . . . Many an official speech by Wilhelm I, many a significant government memorandum flowed from his pen," according to Misch. Ludwig Hahn also composed an official, progovernment pious *Geschichte des preussischen Vaterlandes* [History of the Prussian Fatherland] which went through no less than twenty-three printings by 1893—forty-eight in an abridged version. He was also the author of a four-volume biography of Bismarck—not only a superb public-relations effort, but also the first detailed biography authorized by the "Iron Chancellor."

The younger brother of "Press Hahn," Karl, also a member of the ultraright wing of the Prussian Conservatives, had elected a career on the bench. Ultimately he presided over the Supreme Court in Berlin. At the time many fair-minded citizens considered it a rather dubious procedure that he, the brother of the press chief of the government, should be superintending the lawsuit Chancellor Bismarck was bringing against the insubordinate ambassador, Harry, Count Arnim.

Oscar Hahn, the third brother, was a councillor at the Prussian Higher Administrative Court. From 1870 to 1893 he was almost continuously a member of the conservative factions in the Reich Diet and the Prussian Diet. Furthermore, he was on the board of the archreactionary Protestant Ecumenical Synod as well as a close friend—and probably a like-minded partisan—of the court chaplain, Adolf Stöcker, leader of the "Christian-Socialist" anti-Semites.

As early as 1880 Bismarck expressed his unequivocal opposition to the anti-Jewish tendencies of the "Berlin Movement" headed by Stöcker—"I disapprove strongly of hostile actions against the Jews, both when they are directed at religion and especially where they discriminate on the basis of descent," the Chancellor declared in a conversation with Moritz Behrend. In point of fact, Stöcker's anti-Semitism could be based only on descent, since it was not directed against the Jews as a religious group, but against alleged "Jewish influence in politics and business" by people who, though of Jewish descent, had long ago converted to Christianity.

Specifically, the chaplain and his friends maintained that both liberalism and socialism were Jewish and dangerous— dangerous because they tended to undermine state and church; and Jewish because the founders and leaders of the liberal parties and of the Social Democrats were "almost without exception of Jewish descent," from Ludwig Bamberger and Eduard Lasker to Ferdinand Lassalle and Karl Marx. What Stöcker and his anti-Semitic followers conveniently ignored was the fact that their idea—not new even then—of a rigorously governed "Christian-authoritarian" state with a Prussian conservative character was the brain child of a Jew, Friedrich Julius Stahl from Munich. A student of Schelling and an active member of a fraternity, he became professor of natural

and canonical law at Berlin University, a pioneer of monar-
chism, and originator of the Prussian Diet. King Friedrich
Wilhelm IV made him a life member of the Diet, as well as
legal counsel to the crown. He headed the Conservative
Party, which until his leadership had been no more than a
splintered faction.

Even such a sketchy survey of the nineteenth century,
when the Jews of Germany and Austria realized almost total
emancipation, distinctly reveals at least two circumstances.
First, there was no foundation whatever for the belief that
the Jews were unfit for numerous activities in a state developing into a modern industrial society, though even such seemingly benevolent thinkers as the Count de Ligne held that
view. Rather, the reverse was true; those hindered for so
long from freely developing their talents proved to be actually overefficient, as if eager to make up within one generation for everything denied their forebears for centuries. Second,
a new and unexpected process made itself felt. Many German
and Austrian Jews—in particular those whose education and
wealth placed them in the upper middle class, especially in
the larger cities—suddenly gave up the religion of their fathers,
to which they had tenaciously clung through centuries of
persecution. Some dropped their opposition to conversion
and even their strong feeling of solidarity, formed in the
course of the hardships that had characterized their destiny as
a group. Remarkably enough, this change set in as soon as
outside pressure slackened and diminished the danger in
belonging to a religious minority.

In fact, most of the "Jews" who exerted a crucial influence
on culture and society in the nineteenth and early twentieth
centuries, some of whom were mentioned above, sooner or
later abandoned the religion of their fathers. Nevertheless,
they and their descendents must continue to be regarded as a
special group, as German Jews, in apparent contradiction of
the argument that the Jews of Germany were Germans and
did not belong to a foreign race, nation, or people. Even the
question of whether one or another among them was or
became a dissenter—Protestant or Catholic—is of minor importance for this investigation. And this special view is required
by the history of German anti-Semitism. In the early nineteenth century all baptized German Jews were separated
from the Jewish community at least insofar as they were no

longer subject to group oppression. This situation gradually changed with the rise of anti-Semitism based on "race." Within a few decades, new attitudes ironically led the majority of the converted back to the old group under state duress. Even the children and grandchildren of the converted were cast out of the (German) "national community"; and apart from exceptional cases, Germans of total or partial Jewish origin were faced with difficult alternatives. They could accept enforced affiliation with a group the legal status of which became more and more eroded, incurring the risk of becoming the defenseless victim of state-organized mass murder. Or they could flee the country where they felt at home while they still could.

The very fact that only a very few immediately chose the second route indicates how the Jews of Germany felt about their country of birth or adoption. Even with all the boycotts, pogroms, ever new humiliations, and rapidly increasing danger to life and limb, directed against an unpolitical group persecuted only for its Jewish religion or descent, most German Jews remained or escaped only at the last minute. The reluctance to emigrate is a measure of the depth and strength of the Jewish ties of loyalty to their country, so ardently denied by anti-Semites. Thousands of examples illustrate this close bond, which could not be weakened even by ten years or more of exile in remote corners of the earth and by awareness of the horrors of Hitler's reign. One example is particularly touching and gripping: a few lines taken from the epic poem *An die Deutschen* [To the Germans] by a German Jew, Karl Wolfskehl (1869–1948), perhaps the greatest, certainly the most original of the disciples of Stefan George. He composed it during his exile in New Zealand, and when he finished it on April 3, 1944 he appended a few remarks. "The poem contains everything I—together with my nephew, son of my brother, who died in a concentration camp, the last scion of the oldest Jewish lineage from the Rhine—have to say to the people who gave birth to the poets, the seers—and Hitler."

Wolfskehl, born in Darmstadt, had obtained his degree with a dissertation on Germanic courtship myths. He distinguished himself not only as a poet, but also as a brilliant translator of Old and Middle High German verse. We have to thank the German Jewish scholar, Ludwig Lazarus, who returned to Hanover after his exile, for discovering a further curious fact—that on his mother's side Wolfskehl was a descendant of Jente von Hameln, sister-in-law of Glückel von Hameln (1645–1724). The latter, a widowed mother of eight, wrote an autobiography that continues to be of interest for students of cultural history. What is remarkable about her work is that it was written at a time when her Jewish coreligionists had nearly as low an opinion of education, not to mention literary scribblings, for women as did the Christian Germans.

Lazarus has shown that Wolfskehl was by no means the only descendant of Glückel's sister-in-law Jente to contribute to German literature. He is only one of a whole army of significant minds active in every sphere of German culture.

To begin with, there are the poets and authors among Jente's descendants. Heinrich Heine is one of them, as are the recipient of the 1910 Nobel Prize for literature, Paul Heyse; Carl Sternheim, known for his delightful comedies and slightly less successful dramas; and the distinguished Protestant hymn composer, Karl Johann Philipp Spitta. Other descendants of Jente von Hameln include Eduard Gans, a renowned professor of jurisprudence; Gustav Droysen, a historian; the composer Felix Mendelssohn-Bartholdy; Richard M. Meyer, a literary historian; the Nobel Prize winner in chemistry Adolf von Baeyer; the philosophers Theodor Lessing and Leonard Nelson; Max J. Friedlander, an outstanding art historian; Friedrich Hitzig, the influential Berlin architect; Carl von Weinberg, a captain of the chemical industry; the satirist, caricaturist, and conservative politician of the right Johann Hermann Detmold; and Aby M. Warburg, cultural patron of the arts, and founder of the library named for him, which he established in Hamburg and which was later moved to London.

Finally, the women of the family include Fanny von Arnstein and Cecilie von Eskeles, who, along with their children and grandchildren, played such an important social and cultural role in imperial Austria. Others are Klara Kugler, wife of the poet and art historian Franz Kugler; Martha Bernays, wife of Sigmund Freud; and Charlotte Hensel, who married Werner Bergengruen, the writer. Even Martha Doss, wife of the geopolitician Karl Haushofer, whom the National Socialists exalted as one of their greatest ideologists, was one of Jente's descendants. Albrecht Haushofer, the son of this union, was professor for political geography and an official in the Foreign Office; he was shot by the Gestapo in 1945. He was also known as a poet and dramatist.

These examples should suffice to dispel any lingering doubts about the extent of the integration of the German Jews with the cultural representatives of their nation. The process was already well advanced by the mid-nineteenth century; the fusion was mainly of the upper-class Jews and the Christians of the "educated classes," including considerable segments of the nobility. Many Jewish families secured an "entrance ticket to European society," to quote Heine's mocking formulation, by getting baptized. By the late nineteenth century even those German Jews who adhered to their faith had become almost completely integrated, even in remote country districts.

The general flight from the countryside and the rapid cooling of religious fervor in the larger cities and industrial centers contributed to a steady lowering of the barriers between Christians and Jews, which had been based mainly on the difference in religious belief. Even before the First World War, so-called mixed marriages accounted for one-third of all Jewish marriages within the German Reich.

The enormous decline in birth rates was another symptom of the rapid disintegration of the Jewish community, once so tightly structured. Among the "Israelites," as they were officially called in the German Reich, the number of newborns decreased from 34.7 per thousand during the period 1841–1866 to 23.7 in 1888–1892 and to only 4.3 per thousand by the time the First World War broke out. It was only the influx of Eastern Jewish immigrants, mainly from Russia, that accounted for a slight increase in the total number of Jews in Germany at the turn of the century. In 1888 roughly 560,000 Israelites lived in Germany, of whom 15,000—or barely 3 per cent—were aliens. In 1910 the total had risen to 615,000, with 79,000—or nearly 13 per cent—from abroad. The number of German Jews had therefore already decreased slightly instead of, as might have been expected, showing a strong increase.

In 1911 Felix Theilhaber published a work of political economy, *Der Untergang der deutschen Juden* [The Decline of the German Jews] which predicted their "extinction" within the next generation as a result of the drop in the birth rate, the many Jews who abandoned their religion, and steady emigration to the United States, Palestine, and other countries by those Jews who held fast to their faith. Though the influx of Jews from the East continued, by 1925 the total number of Jews in Germany had indeed dropped to 564,000, including 108,000—or more than 19 per cent—of foreign birth. By 1933 only about half a million remained. Their proportion of the total population had decreased continuously, from 1.25 per cent in 1871 to 1.04 per cent in 1890; 0.95 per cent in 1910; 0.93 per cent in 1925, and 0.77 per cent at the start of the fateful year 1933. If foreign-born Jews are deducted from these minimal percentages, the result leaves a scant 0.5 per cent of professing Jews with German citizenship in the total population near the end of the Weimar Republic.

But even these figures do not disclose the full extent of what some have called, with regret, "the extinction of the German Jews," and others, with conceivable relief, have described it as the final "voluntary and peaceful absorption of a religious minority into Christian German civilization." In fact, during the first third of the twentieth century only a very few German citizens—somewhat less than 400,000—who professed the "Israelite creed" were Jews in the sense that they attended religious service with any regularity and not merely on the High Holy Days, much less observed the religious laws concerning the Sabbath, kosher food, and others. The great majority of Jews confined themselves to a certain reverence, a few cultural traditions, and frequent acts of charity, endeavoring to compensate for the lack of religious adherence to the laws before their conscience and before the Jewish community.

In some respects a typical example of the enlightened, cultured, and completely assimilated German Jewish citizenry—down to the celebration of Christmas with a tree and a Nativity scene—is furnished by Walter Rathenau. As Egmont Zechlin, the Hamburg historian, put it in his book, *Die deutsche Politik und die Juden im Ersten Weltkrieg* [German Policy and Jews in the First World War], Rathenau professed:

> a Christian way of thinking, and he repeatedly stated that it was "based on the ground of the gospels." With equal fervor, however, he persistently rejected conversion to Christianity. He further noted that the overwhelming majority of German Jews "were imbued with

one national consciousness only: the German." For him, it was "firmly established as a matter of course" that "any national consciousness other than the German has no reality for an educated and civilized Jew." A Jewish people or a Jewish nation no longer existed: "To me, Eastern Jews count as Russians, Poles, or Galicians as viewed by other Germans, while Western Jews are Spaniards or French. My people are the German people. My home, the German nation!" He determined affiliation to a people or nation as being solely dependent on "shared soil, experience, and spirit," along with "heart, mind, attitude, and soul!" At the same time he defined himself as "a German of Jewish stock." He shared with Riesser and Fuchs* the view that the German Jews were a Germanic tribe, similar to the Saxons, Bavarians, or Wends. He placed them "approximately between Saxons and Suabians; to me, they are less close to me than the people of Brandenburg or Holstein classes, perhaps somewhat closer than Silesians or Lothringians."

Prior to 1933, Germany contained within its borders roughly 525,000 Germans, stateless people, and resident aliens of the Jewish faith; in Austria the number was over 300,000; the Saar territory, Danzig, and Memel together held approximately 20,000 religious Jews. If at least 120,000 Jews in areas detached from Germany and Austria by the Versailles Treaty are added, the total comes to roughly 1 million people, or almost 1.2 per cent of the population.

To these citizens, clearly defined as Jews by their religious affiliation, should also be added those who abandoned the Jewish faith in the period preceding but were nevertheless declared to be "non-Aryans" by the Nazi racial laws beginning in 1933. Such legislation was originally restricted to Germany proper and later became extended to annexed and conquered territories. The precise number depends on differing estimates, even on guesswork; nevertheless, a reasonable total, including the million or so professing Jews, would be roughly 2.5 million

---

*Gabriel Riesser, vice president of the first German National Assembly in Frankfurt's Paulskirche, champion of emancipation; Eugen Fuchs, one of the intellectual and spiritual leaders of the Central Union of German Citizens of the Jewish Faith.

in the "Greater German Reich" and the "Protectorate" of Bohemia and Moravia.

Today there are approximately 21,000 members of Jewish communities in the Federal Republic of Germany, roughly 6,000 in West Berlin, and barely 1,000 in the German Democratic Republic. In addition, there are 8,000–10,000 Jews who do not belong to any community. Altogether, then, 36,000–38,000 persons of the Jewish faith are living in present-day Germany.

In the Austrian Federal Republic, there are today, mainly still in Vienna, up to 10,000 Jews, of whom less than half belong to Jewish communities. Besides this, an estimated 10,000–12,000 Jews live in the western section of the Czechoslovak Soviet Socialist Republic and in the former German western zones of the People's Republic of Poland. All in all, in that part of Central Europe that was once the "Greater German Reich," where there had been roughly one million Jews in 1933, most of them Germans, there are now barely 60,000—a decrease of 94 per cent.

Even these figures do not fully illuminate the actual situation. In other respects as well radical changes have occurred since 1933. First, the partitioning of Central Europe has almost completely cut off the few Jews still remaining in the western sectors of Poland, in Prague, and in other Bohemian communities from contact with other Germans, though many of them still consider themselves Germans.* Theirs is, as it were, a lost cause; in any case, they belong to a generation that will be all but extinct in the next few years. The younger ones have either already emigrated or are waiting for an

---

*Some years ago, the author had an encounter in Prague that may serve as an illustration. An elderly gentleman described himself in faultless unaccented German as "a Czechoslovakian citizen of Jewish persuasion and German nationality." Born before 1914, he had grown up in a small Bohemian town, was a student at the German high school, studied at Prague University, and completed his studies in Berlin. During the German occupation of Prague, where he practiced as a highly esteemed medical specialist, he was drafted. He therefore survived the Third Reich, while his wife and three children, parents, brothers, and sisters, all other relatives, and every friend had all become victims of the "final solution." In spite of these and other horrible experiences, he had—I am quoting him literally—"not ceased for a minute to be a German."

opportunity to leave Europe, or they have long ago abandoned both their German allegiance and their Jewish faith.

In the DDR the tiny Jewish communities reestablished in a few of the larger cities after 1945 play no significant part in public life. The eighteen or so prominent Communists of Jewish origin* who returned after the war and participated in establishing the new state have lost practically all influence. Most of those surviving have no more links with the German-Jewish tradition.

Nor do the few German Jews remaining in Austria and those who returned have any influence worth mentioning. The very few influential persons of Jewish origin, such as Austria's most eminent statesman, Bruno Kreisky, have almost completely severed their ties to Judaism.

We now come to the German Federal Republic (or West Germany), the most important of the successor states of the "Greater German Reich," by population, economic potential, and political status. West Germany presents the most likely case for doubt regarding the proposition that there is a "Germany without Jews," since today the nation boasts over 20,000 Jews—35,000 if we include West Berlin and non-professing inhabitants. But even the Jewish segment of the West German population, reduced to a bare 0.06 per cent, cannot convey a correct impression of the true extent of the catastrophe that hit the German Jews. They were afflicted precisely where they had been acclimatized for the longest time and could feel most closely connected with the local culture—not to mention the magnitude of the contribution they made.

A few figures may illustrate this situation. In the early summer of 1945, after the liberation of Germany from the Nazi rule of terror, the four occupation zones contained barely more than 10,000 people who had lived within the borders of the Reich, as Germans of Jewish faith, before 1933. Most of these owed their survival to an "Aryan" husband or wife who had remained loyal. A few hundred of them were also aided

---

*These include, Alexander Abusch; Gerhart Eisler, head of the information service until 1952; his brother Hanns Eisler, composer of the DDR national anthem; Professor Albert Norden; Friedrich Kaul, a lawyer; and such writers as Anna Seghers and Arnold Zweig.

by courageous men and women who had risked their own lives by hiding them "illegally." Roughly half of these survivors, in a condition of extreme physical and psychological stress, left Germany as soon after the war as they could. Among those forced laborers shipped into Germany during the war who survived, there were also roughly 90,000 foreign Jews from Eastern, Southeastern, and Southern Europe. Since there were no immediate possibilities for emigration, and since they were exhausted, starved, and ill, they were housed in camps as "displaced persons" (DPs). In the first few years after the war approximately 200,000 additional Eastern Jewish fugitives, who had somehow escaped extermination, arrived in Germany. Out of this total of nearly 300,000 Jews from Eastern Europe who filled the Western zones' reception camps during the early postwar years, not surprisingly more than 95 per cent emigrated as quickly as possible—primarily to Israel after the founding of the state, and earlier, mostly illegally, into the British Mandated Territory of Palestine; some also went to the United States and other overseas countries.

The relatively few DPs who remained in the Federal Republic stayed for various reasons. Some did not feel in good enough health to face the rigors involved in beginning a new life; others saw little opportunity for their particular line of work outside Europe; still others had married German women, established families, and found good livelihoods, which they were unwilling to exchange for an uncertain future; finally, there was a residue incapable of being rehabilitated or who had already fallen into a way of life that was at least semicriminal.

In the early 1950s the remnants of German Jewry were joined by some thousand German Jewish emigrants who returned from all parts of the world. Predominantly the elderly, after some initial hesitation, chose to spend their declining years in the country of their origin. During the years of exile most of these had adopted foreign citizenship, mostly that of the United States and Great Britain. This return movement continues, though the numbers decrease rapidly. A few thousand refugees from the Eastern Bloc countries added their quota to the Jews from Eastern Europe who had remained behind after the war and in most instances had acquired German citizenship. Most of these soon departed for Israel.

In addition, a significant number of foreign businessmen settled in the Republic, attracted by the "economic miracle." Some of the former DPs returned after meeting with failure in Israel or elsewhere.

On the other hand, many of the skimpy next generation of the newly founded Jewish communities in the Federal Republic emigrated to Israel. The resulting rise in the ratio of older people to the total Jewish population is even more marked than before 1933, when the "extinction" of the German Jews was already predicted. Though in the intervening years the average age has fallen slightly to 46.3 years, the figure is practically meaningless in view of the fact that the young people continue to move to Israel as soon as they are old enough to leave the nest.

Only about one-third of the Jews living in West Germany are gainfully employed. Close to 25 per cent live on modest pensions; about 40 per cent are dependents who have to be fed as well. Only a very few of those who do work still practice professions once typical for the educated class. For instance, there are only 70 to 80 Jewish doctors, no more than two dozen high-school teachers, most of them just about to be pensioned, only 2 or 3 private bankers, and—according to the magazine *Der Spiegel*—not a single budding lawyer. Only the number of elderly Jewish lawyers—150—is still relatively high. Most of them will retire soon, especially since the restitution cases in which they have specialized are almost all settled; there is no one to replace them.

The cited figures do not include those Jews who live in Germany only for a time, such as Iranian businessmen and their families, settled mainly in Hamburg, comprising a group of 150, or roughly 10 per cent of the Jewish community. Other transient residents are Israeli nationals in Germany as government officials, on business, or as students; Jewish citizens of the United States who are members of the American forces, correspondents, business representatives, or performers; some Eastern European Jews for whom West Germany is only a waystation on the road to Israel, at least for their children. Leaving these aside, the remnants of German Jewry—mainly aged and inactive individuals—leave little hope for any renewal, despite efforts on the part of some men who have expended admirable energy and surprising optimism in the attempt. The leadership is in the hands of the capable and vigorous Central Council of the Jews in Germany, headed since 1950 by Dr. Hendrik George van Dam, its secretary general. Despite his Dutch name, he is a genuine Berliner, descended from the upper middle class of German Jews that contributed so much to intellectual, artistic, and economic growth in Germany.

The reason why chances of such a regeneration are hardly promising is the complete drying up of a once inexhaustible source, from which German Jewry was always able to restore itself. This was the influx of millions of oppressed Eastern European Jews, reduced to misery and thus therefore frequently the objects of disgust to the highly civilized Central Europeans. These descendants of German Jews who, once upon a time, were forced to flee from the banks of the Rhine, Mosel, Main, and Danube, returned in the nineteenth and early twentieth centuries by the tens of thousands from the little towns and villages of Poland and Galicia, Lithuania, and the Ukraine. It took only a very short time for the returning generation to be assimilated into the nation, the language of which they had faithfully preserved during the centuries of exile (though this Yiddish sounded very strange in the ears of Germans, and even more so in the ears of the German Jews). The new arrivals aroused the resentment of the "established" Christians and Jews; old-timers observed the burning ambition of "Eastern Jews," true adherents to the faith even while they thirsted for the Western culture and civilization they had so sorely missed, and they interpreted the newcomers' behavior as pushy, if not worse, and judged them very harshly. From the ranks of these new citizens, often despised and subjected to great difficulties and obstacles in their social advancement—and more importantly, from the ranks of their sons and daughters—rose many of the most distinguished German scientists and artists.

This reservoir has run dry. Millions fell victim to Himmler's "special commandos" or were gassed. Those who fled to the Soviet Union have very little chance to emigrate and wherever the remaining Jews of Eastern Europe have found and used escape routes, these no longer lead to Germany.

Before we start drawing a balance sheet to examine what effect the annihilation of German Jewry and its potential reservoir has had on present-day Germany, we must address the question of what happened to those who had ceased being Jews long before 1933, who did not even have any recollection of their Jewish origin, but who were nonetheless declared to be "non-Aryans" in Hitler's "Third Reich."

A very considerable portion of this group left Germany in the 1930s and did not return after 1945. It can even be stated that those slightly less hard hit by the Nazi "racial" persecutions generally also felt slightly less attachment to their native land—perhaps because, once they were abroad, they immediately ceased to be Jews and therefore had it easier. Perhaps also for reasons expressed in an anecdote concerning the novelist Erich Maria Remarque, author of *All Quiet on the Western Front.* Questioned after the war about whether he wished to return to Germany, he is said to have replied, "But I'm not a Jew, that I should feel homesick."

An equally large proportion of those who did not go into exile died as victims of the persecution or on active service "for Führer and Fatherland." Hitler had no scruples about considering the so-called "second-degree half-castes" as well as many half-Jews as just useful enough for cannon fodder.

Of the remainder—comprising those who did not seize the chance, during the first difficult postwar years, to use their status as "politically untainted" to gain admittance to the United States or other lands of promise—a few thousand reverted to the faith of their fathers (or mothers), some even taking the initiative in reestablishing the Jewish communities. However, the majority turned their backs once and for all on the community of fate to which Hitler had forced them to return. Nevertheless it is worth noting that an astonishingly large number of this group of people, once discriminated against and disqualified as "half-castes," hold leading positions in all ranks and social spheres of the Federal Republic today. It would be ridiculous to ascribe this fact solely to the circumstance that these people, through no wish of their own, had enjoyed the advantage of not having been in any Nazi organization. The undeniably frequent preference for men with a strong Nazi past, most especially in the civil service and in business, but also at some universities and in a few publishing houses, would seem to indicate the opposite.

When testing anti-Semitic theories for their validity, we will have to deal with many important persons from the group that was completely, or largely, alienated from Judaism. (Those on the far right of the political spectrum must be prepared for some surprises on this score.) But at this point it is more important to draw attention to another aspect. Though not German Jews in the sense sketched above, this other group, observing both Christian and Jewish traditions, will also become extinct. And yet it was these people who were of such extraordinary importance to the Christian-Jewish symbiosis on German soil, which very nearly succeeded.

Why this extinction occurred, and with what consequences for both sides, this investigation will show. It should also answer the question repeatedly raised—and not only in Germany— about the advantage or disadvantage of tolerating or destroying a minority that is, at various times, thought to be more or less disturbing to the majority.

Chapter 2

Can Cultural Losses Be Measured?

"Certainly the Jew is also a human being; none of us has ever doubted thàt. The flea is also an animal—but not a pleasant one. Since the flea is not a pleasant animal, we are committed neither by duty nor conscience to care for it, to protect it, or to let it thrive. Rather it is our obligation to destroy it. So it is with the Jews. . . . Out with that scum! For our German people, we want a German culture free of Jews."* These remarkable statements and demands originated with Dr. Joseph Goebbels, who was to become Hitler's "Minister for the People's Enlightenment and Propaganda."

More than fifty years have passed since these hate-inspired opinions and demands were recorded and published. Even when writing his pamphlets, Goebbels could not foresee that his theory of "Jewish-cultural vermin" would soon be elevated to state doctrine and that his cry of "Out with that scum" would become official policy. Far less could anyone foresee the result of the greatest Jewish persecution in world history, waged by the National Socialists with the aid of all the instruments of power at the disposal of a modern indus-

---

*Joseph Goebbels, *Der Nazi-Sozi* (1929), p. 8,. *Das Buch Isidor* [The Book of Isidore] (1928), p. 165.

trial state. Even today the fullest extent of the outcome is not known. True, we know that millions of people have been murdered, but even here actual numbers can only be estimated. Today we know the crude outlines of the extent of human suffering that was evoked, and at least we have an inkling that, beyond the terrible injustice, something more happened, something irretrievable was lost to both the Jews and the Gentiles of Europe. Now the German culture is to all intents and purposes "cleansed of Jewish influence," just as Goebbels and his friends had wished. At the same time, we must realize that the promised gains have eluded us; instead an indefinable loss seems to have set in—a loss at best only felt, possibly estimated. How could such loss ever be measured?

A single illustration from the arts—painting—will serve. In the decades prior to 1933 a considerable number of distinguished painters of Jewish origin lived in Germany, and even more of them in the European nations to which Hitler later extended his persecution of the Jews. Some had already died when art became fettered in Germany, requiring among other things "proof of Aryan stock" as a precondition for a government license to paint. For instance, Franz Marc, offspring of a Jewish family from Arolsen, enlisted during the First World War and died at Verdun in 1916. Lesser Ury, a German Impressionist, died in Berlin in 1931. Emil Orlyk, an outstanding graphic artist and painter, who was named a professor at the Berlin Kunstschule [Art Institute] in 1905, was also spared the indignity of being expelled as a Jew; he died in the autumn of 1932.

Some others escaped deportation by fleeing in time. Among them were Jankel Adler, whose home had been in Düsseldorf, and Charlotte Berend, student and later wife of Lovis Corinth, who was able to emigrate to the United States. Marc Chagall, for many years resident in Berlin, moved to Paris; from there he fled to the United States ahead of the advancing Germans.

Some remained but died a natural death before the Nazis could do their worst. One of these was Max Liebermann who was eighty-six when the "Third Reich" began. (His commentary on the event was, "It's impossible to eat as much as we have to throw up.") He died in 1935, but not before Hitler had banned his paintings.

Other distinguished Jewish painters—and some undistinguished ones as well—perished in concentration camps, their lives ended in gas chambers, or fell victims to Himmler's special commandos. One of the most talented of the German Post-impressionists, Matisse's prize pupil, Paul Levy, was nearly seventy when the Gestapo dragged him from his home in Florence and took him to Dachau, where he perished. He is only one illustration of the fate met by innumerable outstanding artists, mourned by the world.

Many others were not granted the time to develop their gifts and achieve fame before they were murdered. We cannot know whether the Jews deported from Holland did not include a second Joseph Israels; those from Italy, possibly a new Amadeo Modigliani; the Jewish victims of the special commandos in Eastern Europe, talents as great as that of Marc Chagall or Mané-Katz.

Consequently the attempt to measure the loss the world—or even Germany alone—has suffered in this area is bound to fail. It is even more impossible to evaluate accurately the loss from works that were never produced or to capture it in percentages or pin it down to particular countries.

Nevertheless, let us make one more attempt to establish the loss caused by the persecution of Jews. We will examine a totally different area, one of the sciences, where for various reasons it seems easier to arrive at some accuracy in both quantity and quality of the loss caused by the persecution of the Jews.

Early in 1933 Germany had roughly 8,000 Jewish professors, researchers, and practitioners of medicine, roughly half of them in Berlin, about 2,500 in other major cities, and only about 1,500 in the medium-sized and smaller towns and villages. The total figure of medical men affected by the "Aryan legislation" in Germany proper was undoubtedly considerably higher. If we add to these all "non-Aryans" in the subsequent territories of the "Greater German Reich," we arrive at a figure of at least 20,000 medical men of Jewish origin—or with some Jewish ancestors—within the borders of Greater Germany.

It may be that this crude estimate needs correction. The important fact is that the German Federal Republic, where most Germans live today, contains, as we know, less than a hundred Jewish doctors. Even if West Berlin, the DDR, and Austria, are added, along with the remnants of Jewish German stock in the western sectors of today's Poland, in Prague, and in the rest of Bohemia, it will be difficult to discover more than a total of 250 Jewish men of medicine. The arithmetic reveals a loss of approximately 99 per cent.

Also disturbing is the realization that the mere loss in numbers—brought about through the emigration or the murder of Jewish doctors, researchers, and professors and by the absence of succeeding generations of Jewish medical men—has long been redressed. In the Federal Republic the gap has been completely closed. In West Germany alone there are now nearly 100,000 doctors—more than there ever were in the whole of Germany. If there is occasional talk of a shortage of doctors, the cause lies elsewhere and is unconnected—except perhaps indirectly—with the loss of "non-Aryan" medical men forty or so years ago.

On the other hand, a different kind of loss to Germany itself is the immediate consequence of the persecution of the Jews: a considerable loss in international prestige. Of course such a claim, embarrassing to German medical men, requires proof, and proof shall be forthcoming. For now, it may be sufficient to call attention to one bit of circumstantial evidence and to delay the more detailed examination.

The Nobel Prize for medicine is a distinction of the highest international repute. From 1901, the first year the prizes were awarded, through 1932, a total of thirty-two scientists* were accorded the honor. They comprised six Germans and two Austrians, five Englishmen, four Frenchmen, three Danes, two Dutchmen, two Canadians, two Americans, and one Russian, Italian, Spaniard, Swiss, Belgian, and Swede each. During this period Germany and Austria provided the most leaders in medicine. Their superiority is even more evident when we realize that six of the non-German (and non-Austrian) Nobel Prizewinners received all or some of their medical training in Germany; that one of the two Americans, Karl Landsteiner, a naturalized citizen, was born in Vienna and studied in Würzburg and Munich; and finally—and a further proof of the worldwide reputation of German medicine—some of the laureates who were neither born nor trained in Germany or Austria nevertheless published their works in German.

---

*In some years the Prize was shared by two recipients; Nobel Prizes were not awarded in 1915–1918.

Even if, for various reasons, we omit the Swiss, we are left with not less than nine out of thirty-two Nobel Prizewinners, or roughly 28 per cent, with a German background: six German nationals, two Austrians, and one American born in Vienna and trained at Bavarian universities. A further six, or close to 19 per cent, had studied in Germany.

From 1933 to 1969, a total of sixty-nine Nobel Prizes for medicine were awarded. Thirty-eight went to citizens of the United States, ten to citizens of Great Britain, four to Germans, three each to Swiss and French, two each to Australians and Swedes, and one each to an Italian, Dutchman, Dane, Austrian, Hungarian, Portuguese, and Argentinian. Thus the share of Germans and Austrians shrank considerably, to a mere 7 per cent, if the Austrian scientist, a naturalized American, is included, but only 5.8 per cent if the four Germans alone are counted. This is close to a quarter of the share prior to 1933. Instead, the English-speaking medical men, in particular the Americans, have taken an overwhelming lead.

The fact is that a considerable number of the Nobel Prizewinners for medicine, today residing in Anglo-Saxon countries, not only studied in Germany or Austria; these are also the countries where they were born and gained professional prominence. Special circumstances led these German scientists and professors to become American or British, so that they were no longer Germans when they received their Nobel Prizes. These special circumstances were their affiliation with German Jewry and their official persecution as "non-Aryans" after 1933, so that they were forced to emigrate.

Sir Ernst Boris Chain, for example, a British subject, shared the 1945 Nobel Prize in medicine with Sir Alexander Fleming and Sir Howard Walter Florey "for the discovery of penicillin and its therapeutic effect on various infectious diseases." Chain was born in Berlin in 1906. His parents, both Jewish, had emigrated from Russia and settled in Germany. Their son had been a student at a Berlin secondary school, and studied chemistry and physiology at the local university. After graduation, he had turned to biochemistry and eventually worked at the well-known Charité hospital until 1933, when he was kicked out. A short time later he found a new workplace in England. His special distinction lies in his contribution to the discovery of the chemotherapeutic effects of penicillin to synthesizing antibiotics.

Another British Nobel Prizewinner is Sir Hans Adolf Krebs, knighted in 1958, who was born in Hildesheim, Germany. After studying at the universities of Göttingen, Freiburg, Munich, and Berlin, he was on the staff of the Kaiser Wilhelm Institute for Biology from 1926 to 1930, before joining the faculty at the university of Freiburg in 1932. The following year he was forbidden to teach because he was Jewish. He emigrated to England, where he was able to lecture, first at Cambridge, then at Sheffield. During the war he carried out important research on nutrition for the British government, and in 1945 he was named to the Medical Research Council. He was proposed for the Nobel Prize as early as 1952, for his discovery of the citric acid cycle—"one of the most ingenious biochemical achievements ever," according to Hans Hartmann in his *Lexikon der Nobelpreisträger* [Encyclopedia of Nobel Prize Winners]. However, the decision went in favor of the American professor Selman Abraham Waksmann, also a Jew, born in 1888 in Priluka near Kiev, but whose mother tongue was German. He was the discoverer of streptomycin, the first antibiotic effective against tuberculosis.

The following year Krebs was the recipient. He shared the prize with Fritz Albert Lipmann, professor of biochemistry at Harvard University, who was singled out for "his discovery of the coenzyme A and its importance for intermediary metabolism." Lipmann, a former research assistant at the Kaiser Wilhelm Institutes of Berlin and Heidelberg, was a German Jew who had emigrated to America.

In 1964, Konrad Bloch of Harvard University was awarded the Nobel Prize for medicine, jointly with the Munich researcher Feodor Lynen "for the discovery of the mechanism and the regulation of the metabolism regarding cholesterol and fatty acids." Bloch, a German Jew, was born in the town of Neisse in Silesia. Of the sixty-nine scientists awarded the Nobel Prize for medicine from 1933 to 1969, no less than sixteen were of Jewish origin.* Nearly all of them were born

---

*In the order in which they received the Prize they are: Otto Loewi, professor of physiological chemistry and pharmacology at the University of Graz from 1909 to 1938; Josef Erlanger, an American of German-Jewish descent; Ernst Boris Chain; Hermann Josef Müller, an American

in Germany or other German-language areas, or had their education and training there, or were the offspring of emigrants.

The surprising fact that nearly a quarter of all Nobel Prize laureates for medicine in the period 1933–1969 are of Jewish descent—and the majority of these of German-Jewish descent, should not, however, lead to the erroneous conclusion that Germany lost two-thirds of its masterminds in medicine through Hitler's maniacal "racial" theories. Some of the exodus took place much earlier, in response to nineteenth-century anti-Semitism, which afforded unbaptized Jews few chances at university appointments, no matter how outstanding the individual talent. Even Paul Ehrlich, the founder of chemotherapy, though he was showered with decorations, given the title Excellency and considered "Germany's most brilliant research scientist in the realm of medicine" after he received the 1908 Nobel Prize, remained an honorary professor without any appointment, not even in an associate capacity.

On the other hand, the number of Nobel Prize laureates in medicine who left Greater Germany because of the persecution of Jews in the "Third Reich" is far larger than can be gauged from the list of the period 1933–1969. A number of laureates of earlier years left Germany and Austria when the persecution started. These include Otto Meyerhof from Hanover, who shared the prize in 1922 and until 1938 headed the Kaiser Wilhelm Institute for Physiology in Heidelberg. In 1940 he joined the faculty of the University of Pennsylvania and died in Philadelphia in 1951. Others who had accepted temporary appointments at foreign universities before 1933 chose not to return, as they might have done had Hitler not emerged. One such scientist was Robert Barany, lecturer in

---

of German-Jewish descent; Gerty Theresa Cori, née Radnitz, an American of German-Jewish descent, born in Prague, who emigrated with her husband, Carl Ferdinand Cori, to the United States and shared with him the 1947 Prize "for their discovery of the process of the catalytic glycogen metabolism"; Tadeus Reichstein, born in Wloclawek, Poland, professor at the university of Basel and a Swiss citizen, who received the Prize in 1950; Selman Abraham Waksmann; Sir Hans Adolf Krebs; Fritz Albert Lipmann; Joshua Lederberg, an American of Eastern Jewish origin; Arthur Kornberg, an American of German-Jewish descent; Konrad Bloch; François Jacob, André Lwoff, and Jacques Monod, three French medical men of Jewish descent; and S. E. Luria, an Italian who fled to the United States.

otology at the University of Vienna, his place of birth, and recipient of the Nobel Prize in 1914, during his captivity as a prisoner of war. Subsequently, he accepted an appointment at Uppsala University, where he remained until his death in 1936. Karl Landsteiner, laureate for medicine in 1930 "for the discovery of human blood groups," was also born in Vienna and was active at the Rockefeller Institute in New York from 1922 onward.

Otto Heinrich Warburg, descendant of a famous German-Jewish family that produced several distinguished scientists, was the son of Emil Warburg, the great physicist and long-time president of the Physical-Technical National Institute. Though Otto Warburg managed to survive the "Third Reich" in Germany, during the twelve years of Hitler's rule all official recognition of his achievement was denied the man who had been awarded the 1931 Nobel Prize "for the discovery of the nature and function of the respiratory enzyme."

The persecution of the Jews also drove non-Jewish scientists from Germany or prevented their return. One of these was Professor Max Delbrück; in 1937 he left Berlin, where he had been working with Warburg, Otto Hahn, and Lise Meitner. After settling in the United States, he was awarded the Nobel Prize in 1969 for his work in molecular biology— "his contribution to biology is the most important one of this century."* This category also includes Carl Cori, husband of Gerty Cori and her corecipient of the Nobel Prize.

All these names, however, can give only an understanding of the unusually high percentage of Jewish—and especially German-Jewish—men of medicine who ranked high among the elite of their profession throughout the world, at least as measured by Nobel Prizes. Of the total of 101 Nobel laureates in medicine between 1901 and 1969, 22, or close to 22 per cent, belong to the Jewish minority which in that particular period constituted no more than 1 per cent of the world population (and today is down to 0.4 per cent). Of the 22 laureates, 11 were born and raised in the German cultural area. Another 2,

---

*Delbrück, however, is also of Jewish ancestry. A forebear on his mother's side was the founder of German agrarian chemistry, Justus von Liebig (1803–1873), who was descended from a Jewish woman from Darmstadt who converted to Christianity.

of Eastern Jewish origin, worked in Germany for some time. Among the rest, 5 are second- or third-generation Americans with German surnames; 1 fled from Italy; and of the 3 who are French, one hails from Lothringen, another from Poland.

All these data, however, merely indicate an accumulation of marked special capabilities, in particular for medicine, among the descendants of those German Jews who in the early Middle Ages formed an important element among the citizenry of the German towns, many of whom subsequently migrated to the East, mainly to Poland. In fact, a number of distinguished physicians can already be found among the medieval Jews. Zedekias, personal physician to Emperor Charles the Bald, was considered a veritable magician because of his many successful cures. Emperor Frederic III held his personal physician, Jakob Loans, in such high esteem that he raised him to the peerage. The bishops also frequently entrusted themselves to Jewish doctors—a fact showing that the German Jews must have been extraordinarily skilled physicians: Christians were strictly prohibited from being treated by Jewish healers, "because it was better for a Christian to die than to owe his life to a Jew." Such and similar guidelines were promulgated and justified at the Church Assemblies of Béziers (1255) and Vienna (1267), the Synods at Avignon (1326) and Bamberg (1491), and by the Protestant faculties of the universities of Wittenberg and Rostock.

Apparently the fear of excommunication, with all its consequences, was less pronounced than the fear of pain, suffering, and premature death caused by illness. Reports from every century confirm the great medical skills and knowledge of numerous German Jews, and their practice flourished— much to the chagrin of Christian barber-surgeons and medicos, who saw themselves threatened by the frighteningly successful competition of the Jews.

Martin Gumpert and Alfred Joseph see the cause for the predominant position of the Jews in the field of German medicine during the Middle Ages and after as founded in the fact "that the Jews were relatively free from the superstitious and mystical ideas of their time and that they had a remarkable command of languages. They were thus in a position to acquire a great degree of medical knowledge and skills, particularly through the study of old Arabic works, which they were the first to make available to the West in translation."*

Beginning in the late fifteenth century, it was mainly Jewish fugitives from previously Arabic Spain who gained medical fame in Germany, such as Rodrigo de Castro, who settled in Hamburg around 1585. Many German sovereigns, as well as the king and queen of Denmark, sought his advice. De Castro was renowned primarily as a gynecologist, and he is said to have introduced the Caesarian section to Germany. He also wrote numerous important works on women's diseases. His son Benedict (1597–1684) was also a doctor and personal physician to Queen Christina of Sweden. After her abdication she took up residence in his house. A third member of this Jewish family of doctors, Jakob de Castro-Sarmento, discovered the healing properties of Peruvian bark (quinine) against fevers. Other famous physicians among the Spanish Jews who fled to Hamburg are Mussafia and Rosales. The latter was accorded the rank of count palatine by the Emperor himself—"unheard of since days immemorial!"

According to Gumpert and Joseph, "Many Jewish physicians were granted privileges by their sovereigns, such as relief from taxes and custom duties, freedom to travel, and residence permits in cities otherwise closed to Jews. In some cities Jewish doctors were even engaged at fixed annual salaries to serve as doctors to the community. In the late fourteenth century Salomon Pletsch was municipal surgeon in Frankfurt am Main, and he was succeeded by Master Isaak Friedrich. The elector's surgeon Baruch was active in Dresden, a Jewish municipal physician worked in Thorn, and the famous Moses (1511) is recorded in Aschaffenburg. Jewish women doctors were also not uncommon."**

---

*Foremost among these are the works of a genius, Moses Maimonides (1135–1204), which are still remarkably topical. Personal physician to the sultan in Cairo, this Jewish physician, equally famed as a philosopher, teacher of law, and theologian, may be considered the greatest medical man of the Middle Ages. He was centuries ahead of his time, denouncing all superstition and advocating athletics, care of the body, fresh air, and sun; he called for disinfection, was the first to establish the connection between bodily and mental well-being, and considered sexual satisfaction indispensable for both men and women.

**"Medizin" [Medicine], in *Juden im deutschen Kulturbereich* [Jews in the German Culture Area], compiled by Siegmund Kaznelson. The author is indebted to this work for various significant facts.

In view of this special standing of Jewish physicians in medieval and early-modern Germany, it is not surprising that they also played a considerable role in establishing and developing modern medicine. It seems clear that the emancipation of the Jews following the Enlightenment, with the result that more than merely isolated cases won admission to the universities, contributed crucially to the development of medicine as a modern science free from mysticism and superstition. It is as if Germany's reputation in medicine, beginning in the nineteenth century and ceasing so abruptly in the 1930s, is due largely to the achievements of German-Jewish scientists.

It must be remembered how minute was the proportion of Jews to the total population during that century; even one Jew among three dozen Christian celebrities would be sufficient proof of the fact that the small minority, suppressed until then, contributed in a disproportionate measure to the progress of medicine. Even a superficial examination, however, is enough to show that the comparison for the German-Jewish pioneers of modern medicine is far more favorable than a simple 1 to 36 ratio. It is generally agreed that the enormous progress of medicine during the last century and a half is largely due to the relatively young science of bacteriology, the originator of which was a Jewish botanist from Breslau, the first professor at a Prussian university not to be baptized, Ferdinand Julius Cohn.

This statement may surprise younger readers in Germany, who will never have heard of Ferdinand Julius Cohn (1828–1898). Even a multi-volume encyclopedia, such as the 1950s edition of the large *Brockhaus*, will not list the founder of bacteriology. They would have to turn to a German encyclopedia printed before 1933 or, better yet, the far more reliable *Encyclopaedia Britannica*, which is not tainted by anti-Semitism. Incredible as it may sound, the "eradication" of Jewish scientists and other major figures whose names could not be mentioned during the "Third Reich" has been reversed only in part in the *Brockhaus*, and that in a most unsatisfactory manner. Only about half of the German-Jewish medical experts have been restored. Anyone using this West German standard encyclopedia will learn no more of Maimonides than that "he also wrote several medical works."

Ferdinand Julius Cohn was the first to recognize bacteria as a form of life. He described them accurately, including their importance as the source of disease and the cause of epidemics. As head of the Physiological Botanical Institute in Breslau, he championed his brilliant student, Robert Koch (who was not Jewish). Without Cohn's research, Koch's work would hardly have been possible, no more than Louis Pasteur's, who also built on the results of another scientist whose background also hints at Jewish origins: the "savior of mothers," Ignaz Semmelweis from Ofen.

Apart from Cohn, three other famous German-Jewish scientists were present in the Breslau Institute when Koch demonstrated his first results concerning anthrax-causing bacteria. They assured him enthusiastically that he had made "the greatest bacteriological discovery of all times." The first was Julius Cohnheim (1839–1884), who had the reputation of being the most distinguished student of Rudolf Virchow. His reputation was founded on a revolutionary theory completely differing from the orthodox opinion of the day. It claimed that the migration of leukocytes through the capillary walls characterizes inflammation.

The second was Leopold Auerbach (1828–1897), who became equally famous as a neuropathologist and physiologist. The third, Carl Weigert (1845–1904), has two distinctions to his credit. One is his significant discovery that local irritations of various kinds result in localized tissue necrosis. He also developed staining techniques for distinguishing different tissue sections.

His younger friend and colleague was the great German scientist of Jewish origin, Paul Ehrlich (1854–1915). Together those two pioneered the continuous development of new chemical dyes and staining methods, used to distinguish even the tiniest particles of the human body.

Paul Ehrlich, one of the first to receive the Nobel Prize for medicine, eventually succeeded in perfecting differential staining of the various blood cells. He thus became the founder of hematology, which has become just as indispensable a diagnostic tool as is the Diazo reagent for urinalysis—another contribution by Paul Ehrlich to modern medicine.

Apart from a number of other important discoveries and pioneering work in a variety of areas, Ehrlich, together with the Japanese researcher Sahachiro Hata, succeeded in discovering arsphenamine—known as Salvarsan—a complex organic arsenic compound. It was Salvarsan that first supplied an effective means of combating syphillis. With this, Paul Ehrlich also became the actual founder of modern hemotherapy.

The battle against syphillis is also linked inseparably with the name of another great German-Jewish physician: August von Wassermann. Before Salvarsan and the ensuing chemotherapy, culminating in modern antibiotics, syphillis had been a terrible scourge for humanity; today it is no longer linked with fear and horror. Together with two Jewish dermatologists, Neisser and Bruck, he developed a blood test for syphillis, the so-called Wassermann test, which became vital in diagnosing and curing this fatal disease.

Hundreds of outstanding physicians and research scientists of Jewish origin brought German medicine to the pinnacle of worldwide recognition from the late eighteenth century until Hitler caused mass flight.* Three further examples will suffice here.

Friedrich Gustav Jakob Henle (1809–1885) belonged to an established Jewish family from Fürth, which converted to Christianity in the nineteenth century. Several of its descendants gained distinction, among them a Bavarian legal adviser to the crown, a Catholic bishop, and today's head of the Klöckner combine, Günter Henle. Friedrich Gustav Jakob Henle is considered one of the outstanding modern anatomists, compared by medical historians with Vesalius.

Benedict Stilling (1810–1879), though merely in general practice in Kassel, gained worldwide fame in anatomy and physiology. He also pioneered surgical techniques far ahead of his time.

Finally, there is Sigmund Freud, born in 1856 in the Moravian city of Freiberg. Trained as a neurologist, he published findings on hysteria, the neuroses, and mental pathology that revolutionized the field. Except in Germany—where he is still largely undervalued—he is considered the most significant physician of his time, the "Einstein of medicine." This is especially true in the whole Anglo-Saxon world. Vilified, derided, already suffering from a fatal cancer, deprived of his property after the Nazi annexation of Austria, he succeeded, with British help, in escaping to London, where the Royal Society made him a member and the British government granted him sanctuary for life.

---

*For complete lists, see Appendix.

Even Fritsch's anti-Semitic *Handbuch der Judenfrage* [Handbook on the Jewish Problem] admits, "It is an undeniable fact that now and again the Jews have produced capable scientists. At the same time, there can be no doubt that their significance, as in the arts, relied heavily on taking over the results of others. We see only a very limited number of great creative minds."

Then the author of the particular section, M. Staemmler, grants the achievements of the Jew, Paul Ehrlich, the grade of "very good," and those of the Jews Cohnheim, Weigert, Henle, Fränkel, and Besredka* "good on the whole." There follow a half-dozen additional Jewish physicians who are given the grade of "satisfactory." Then the author continues, "The basic question must be put differently. 1. Can one imagine German medicine without Jews? Would it lose something essential, would it be a loss to German medicine if the Jews disappeared from it? 2. Are the praiseworthy achievements of individual Jewish men of medicine negated by such serious damage caused by Jews that they offset, or even outweigh, these achievements?"

These allegedly pertinent questions are not, as might be expected, followed by a thorough and detailed examination. Concerning the first, it is settled with a simple assertion, without further comment. "The first question is to be answered in the sense that exclusion of Jews would not prove harmful to medicine." The second question is approached with nonsensical generalizations about Sigmund Freud (misinterpreted) and some other Jewish sexologists, including Magnus Hirschfeld, who considered sexual intercourse as natural even between unmarried individuals under twenty-one years of age. "Here we have the main danger of Judaism in medicine. Here the poison is inserted in the food intended for the destruction of the German soul," the author concludes.

---

*Fränkel may refer to the laryngologist Bernhard Frankel (1836–1911), a close friend and associate of Robert Koch and a pioneer in the movement to establish tuberculosis sanatoriums; or to Albert Fränkel (1848–1938), who introduced intravenous strophantin treatment for cardiac patients; or, finally, Albert Fränkel (1848–1916), who discovered the agent causing pneumonia. Besredka refers to Alexander Besredka (1870–1940), native of Odessa, a serologist who made important contributions in the battle against tuberculosis.

All that the handbook on the "Jewish problem" has to offer is generalized resentment, summary judgment lacking any foundation, prefaced by grudging praise for a few Jewish geniuses, as window dressing to mask nonexistent objectivity, and finally an appeal to the prudery of the petit bourgeoisie. That is all the thirty-second revised edition of 1933 has to say under the heading, "Judaism in medicine," as "proof" that "exclusion of Jews would not prove harmful to medicine."

We will have to dig considerably deeper in order to arrive at a well-founded judgment concerning potential damage to German medicine. It is indeed true that the expulsion and extermination of the Jews caused more than a temporary loss. Viewed in a historical perspective, we must investigate the qualitatives effects of a quarter-century of abrupt quantitative loss.

It would be a different matter if we could make comparisons by drawing on all scientific publications in the field of medicine; but such an investigation would require a special institute and years of work by a staff of highly trained scientists. And even so, an ideal examination might do no more than document with a fair amount of accuracy certain realignments, perhaps in favor of American research, and one of its probable causes, namely the mass immigrations during the 1930s of German-Jewish medical men into the United States of America.

Nevertheless, there are alternate techniques, though admittedly far cruder. One method that would furnish a practical starting point for assessing how much modern medicine is indebted to Jewish research scientists from Germany would consist of checking certain standard condensations of medical science to discover who has accomplished what to gain scientific fame and researching the possible German-Jewish origin of each of these scientists.

But since this method would also be immensely time-consuming, we must limit our investigation to an extract of some statistical reliability, allowing us to ascertain the percentage of German-Jewish scientists represented in thousands of medical procedures and discoveries named for their originators.

Fortunately a current work is available in Germany. *Die klinischen Eponyme—Medizinische Eigennamenbegriffe in Klinik und Praxis* [Clinical Eponyms—Medical Surnames in Clinic and Praxis], published in 1968. Its compilers, Professor

Bernfried Leiber (Frankfurt) and Dr. Theodor Olbert (Düsseldorf), note in a preface, "Roughly 100 years ago it was mainly neurology that began to identify diseases and syndromes, as well as certain symptoms, reflexes, tests, and other procedures with personal names. Since that time the practice has taken hold in all areas of medicine to such an extent that many thousands of eponyms are in current use in the clinical vocabulary. Whether we like it or not, we must live with these names, which increase from year to year in daily medical work. Just as in ancient Greece the "Eponymos"—the name giver—was the high official after whom the year of his rule was named, the medical eponym of modern times is usually the physician who discovers those clinical manifestations linked to his name, first describes them, first recognizes their importance, or has at least crucially contributed to their discovery."

Of the more than 1300 clinical eponyms—from "Aaron's sign" to "Zweifel's maneuver"—a selection of barely 10 per cent of the total was chosen as a representative sample, being as careful as possible to eliminate error. Many of the procedures listed in the handbook are named after more than one researcher, so that the 1300 entries honor roughly 2000 distinguished luminaries. With the aid of experts 193 eponyms of honored medical men were selected for further research. Reliable encyclopedias were consulted to determine whether each of the names was that of someone of Jewish origin, whether the person was born and raised in or around Germany, and whether the particular scientist emigrated.

Before we are astonished at the result and, depending on our basic outlook, are pleased, horrified, or only slightly surprised, it must be added that the outcome was rechecked by referring to the *Klinisches Wörterbuch* [Medical Dictionary] compiled by Professor Willibald Pschyrembel—a familiar resource to every physician. In this instance, we had available the newly revised and enlarged edition of 1969. The "Pschyrembel," as it is known for short, contains a great many eponyms along with a profusion of brief biographies of eminent scientists. Because there are so many more entries in the "Pschyrembel," the selection from this volume was limited to approximately 3 per cent. The result deviated only slightly from that of the more detailed investigation and can therefore be considered a confirmation. Surprisingly, there was very little overlap—that is, names that appeared in both samples.

Now for the result. Roughly one-quarter—24.8 per cent of the first sample; 26.2 per cent of the second—of the scientists listed in both works for a specific achievement or a scientific reputation were or are Jews. Nearly all—more than 92 per cent—of these came from the German-language area, by birth or by parentage, or were emigrants from czarist Russia who felt so closely connected to the German language and culture that it is safe to assume that, had it not been for anti-Semitism in Germany, they would have moved there instead of to more distant countries. In addition, of course, a considerable number of the Eastern-Jewish physicians worked and lived in Germany or Austria, at least for a time.

Finally, the sources revealed that, with a single exception, all those who were living under Hitler's rule during the "Third Reich" either emigrated or perished—in concentration camps, by suicide, or perhaps, as one case is literally reported, "of a broken heart."

The results of these samples agree in large part with those concerning the origin of Nobel Prize laureates. The areas of agreement prove to be so great that we can now risk an assessment that will be a careful analysis, not based on mere assumptions, but founded on precisely evaluated evidence.

Within the impressive list of achievements of international medicine, the share contributed by the Jews is a large one, quite out of proportion to what might have been expected. It seems to stand at precisely 25 per cent. This figure includes not only outstanding achievements rewarded with the Nobel Prize, but also lesser contributions, all of which go to make up current medical knowledge.

On the basis of our investigation we can also conclude with a high degree of probability that four-fifths of this sum of Jewish physicians and scientists come from the German area or at least from its Eastern-Jewish reservoir. Their contributions have benefited other countries, primarily the United States, overwhelmingly since the 1930s, but to some extent even earlier, as a result of the nineteenth-century migrations.

These facts are supplemented by our findings as to the almost total absence of Jewish physicians in present-day Germany, the precipitous decline of Germany's and Austria's share in medical progress—only hinted at by the distribution of Nobel Prizes—and the steep rise in the American share. We may be permitted some certainty in believing that all these charges are in large part attributable to German anti-Semitism and its closely related all-pervading small-minded stubbornness.

Quite simply, if Germany has ceased to be the most important center of medical research and scholarship, the decline is directly due to and is a consequence of maniacal racism. If the United States has assumed the leadership previously located in Germany and has taken it to new peaks, this preeminence, too, is closely related to the fact that the United States was the country that admitted the greatest number of the fleeing, persecuted victims from Central Europe.

We do not wish to enlarge on the enormous contribution to the current state of medicine in the United States made during the nineteenth and early twentieth centuries by Jewish immigrants from Central or Eastern Europe or by their American-born sons and daughters. It is sufficient to remember the many Nobel Prize laureates and to add a few names. First place goes to Jonas Salk, discoverer of the polio vaccine. But equally important is the father of American pediatrics, Abraham Jacobi (1830–1919). A resident of Baden, Jacobi took part in the Revolution of 1848 in Germany and was a close friend of Carl Schurz.* In 1910 he was president of the American Medical Association. Then there is Simon Flexner (1863–1946), the organizer and first director of the famous Rockefeller Institute for Medical Research, which he headed for two years. A leading bacteriologist, Flexner also made many contributions to our knowledge of the transmission of infectious diseases and developed a serum for meningitis. Helen Taussig was a respected pediatrician and professor at the Johns Hopkins University in Baltimore from 1927 to 1963, where, together with Alfred Blalock, she performed the first so-called blue-baby operation on a child's heart. We should also men-

---

*Translator's note: Carl Schurz (1829–1906) was a colorful non-Jewish historical figure with a distinguished career. Active in the Revolution of 1848, he escaped from Germany in 1850. After arriving in the United States in 1852, Schurz fought on the Union side in the American Civil War with the rank of general. After the war he worked as a journalist, was elected to the Senate, and from 1877 to 1881 served as Secretary of the Interior. In his later years he was an active editor and author in the muckraking tradition.

tion Bela Schick, a pediatrician from Graz, Austria, and professor at New York's Columbia University since 1923. He contributed significantly to the control of diphtheria with his discovery of the so-called Schick test.

Apart from these and many hundreds more individual contributions, America is also indebted to Jewish refugees from Central Europe, and most particularly from Vienna, for a medical specialty: psychoanalysis, and everything connected with it. The exodus of this discipline, spurned in Hitler's realm and even today leading a comparatively shadowy existence in Germany, has had a more far-reaching effect for the United States than might have been expected. Laura Fermi, the widow of the Italian nuclear physicist and Nobel Prize laureate Enrico Fermi, devotes the longest chapter of her book *Illustrious Immigrants: The Intellectual Migration from Europe, 1939/41* (University of Chicago, 1968) to the impact of psychoanalysis. It was Jewish practitioners from Germany and Austria who brought the new therapies to the United States and there perfected them.

She arrives at astonishing conclusions concerning the profound changes occasioned in the United States by psychoanalysis, from the transformation in treatment of young children through efforts to reduce individual aggression to a national willingness to deal with guilt, inferiority, and other complexes. This sketchy indication of the enormous gain for the new world power, the United States, and the corresponding loss for Germany and the Germans (who are in greater need today than ever before of treatment for their complexes), makes clear that the total loss suffered by German culture cannot, when all is said and done, be accurately calculated, let alone qualitatively evaluated. The loss applies to the expulsion or annihilation of so many professors, researchers, workers, and practitioners that it is beyond the reach of arithmetic, even when only a single area, such as medicine, is under scrutiny. Over and above the careful compilation of itemized figures, there are further aspects beyond the reach of any calculation.

We do know now that German medicine has suffered a considerable qualitative loss through the persecution of the Jews. But what about any possible gain? According to the opinion of the "anti-Semites' Bible"—as Theodor Fritsch's *Handbuch der Judenfrage* was called at one time—such gains would be found mainly in the area of sexual morality. However, despite the almost completely successful "elimination" of all Jewish physicians, even the most fanatical anti-Semites cannot claim that present-day German youth is "protected" against the influence of men of medicine who represent the view that "natural sexual intercourse, provided there is no compulsion from either party, is no sin nor dishonorable for young people between the ages of eighteen and twenty-one." Such "protection" is hardly advocated nowadays, even by conservative churchmen.

Another anti-Semitic attack was focused on contraception. Even among healthy young couples it was widely claimed that the practice jeopardized all of Germany, which therefore had to be "freed" from the yoke of the Jewish doctors. In fact, however, only a very few "non-Aryan" physicians of the time dared to advocate birth control openly, even for the economically weaker classes. Most of the Jewish doctors either expressed conservative views or avoided the subject. In the light of current practices, with increased use of the ever more popular "pill," few "gains" can be recorded here from the absence of Jewish influence.

The handbook touted another certain gain for German medicine if all Jewish doctors were "eliminated": the alleged growing commercialization of the medical profession would be halted. Today Jewish doctors—blamed for the supposed situation—are practicing in Germany only in isolated instances. According to the authors of the handbook, commercialization consisted of Jewish general practitioners' or internists' referring patients to specialists—oculists, ear, nose, and throat men, skin specialists, or gynecologists, as well as surgeons, neurologists, and psychiatrists. "Once the patient has fallen into the hands of a Jew, he will be unable to extricate himself." The handbook points out that "it is, of course, always a Jewish colleague who is recommended."

Medical specialization continues to increase even in Germany, though less so than in the United States. Therefore, since the exodus of Jewish physicians, referral to specialists has certainly not decreased. But even the heavy increase has not led to the so-called commercialization of the medical profession. The suspicion is now justified that it was not so much consideration for the welfare of the people and the state or morality that guided the pens of the anti-Semitic

German doctors who wrote such articles for the handbook, but at best, narrow-mindedness; at worst, pure envy.

Our examination has now reached a stage where we must go beyond the field of medicine. We are ready to trace the true motives of anti-Semitism and to question its justification.

Chapter 3

A Playbill

At the time Adolf Hitler became chancellor of Germany, a large proportion of German physicians were Jewish. A further number were of Jewish origin, meaning that they or their parents had at one time been members of the Jewish congregation.

An anti-Semitic source—a compilation by Karl Hoppmann published in 1931 by the press of the German student fraternities—gave percentages of Jewish doctors in various cities of Germany and Austria. They were as follows: Berlin, 52 per cent; Beuthen, 36 per cent; Chemnitz, 17 per cent; Danzig, 13 per cent; Dürkheim, 37 per cent; Glogau, 36 per cent; Hamburg, 25 per cent; Hanover, 12 per cent; Hildesheim, 10 per cent; Kassel, 13 per cent; Cologne, 27 per cent; Küstrin, 16 per cent; Mainz, 28 per cent; Meiningen, 23 per cent; Nuremberg, 50 per cent; Saarbrucken, 10 per cent; Stettin, 23 per cent; Vienna, 80 per cent; Worms, 30 per cent. Although the accuracy of these figures is open to doubt, since they seem the result of an individual poll conducted with inadequate methods, we may take the figures to be more or less correct. What matters is the irrefutable fact that the Jews furnished a far higher number of doctors than would have corresponded to their proportion among the total population. This was (and in retrospect often still is) considered brash, damaging, arousing of misgivings, and even from the point of view of the Jews themselves, unwise. The argument was roughly as follows: the Jews, as a small minority, should be quiet and humble without "pushiness"; minorities should not raise any claims, since they are only tolerated out of kindness.

"Jewish pushiness," however, was not limited to the medical profession or the medical-school faculties in Germany, though at the University of Berlin they made up over 50 per cent, in Breslau 37 per cent, and in Göttingen 34 per cent of the lecturers. The situation was similar for other academic professions. The lawyers in Berlin and Vienna, as well as in Breslau, Frankfurt am Main, and Nuremberg were mainly Jewish. The faculties of law and of economics included a high percentage of Jewish professors and lecturers, their journals featured a far larger number of Jewish authors than would have been "proper" for their proportion within the total population. Furthermore, in the social and artistic life of the large cities, the Jews played such an important role that they overshadowed any comparable group.

A 1929 playbill for a Berlin production spotlights this situation, more revealing than any long dissertations of the role played by the Jews in the cultural and social life of Germany's capital city. These were the years considered the most glamorous in the history of Berlin, which at the time surpassed Paris, London, and New York in the performing arts.

The playbill reflects a unique event, a special performance of Frank Wedekind's *Marquis von Keith*, a commemoration for Albert Steinrück, an actor (almost forgotten today) who had recently died. In his short lifetime Steinrück had achieved extraordinary success as a character actor in Berlin, Munich, and again in Berlin; he was closely identified with works by Wedekind. He had also been a prominent painter.

To honor their late fellow actor, almost everyone with any name and reputation in the German theater world took part in the performance of March 28, 1929. It was scheduled for a late hour, so that all the actors could fulfill their regular obligations. Even including extras, every part was assigned to a star. The honorary committee was a cross section of Berlin's leading citizens.

STAATS- THEATER

SCHAUSPIELHAUS AM GENDARMENMARKT

Donnerstag, den 28. März 1929, abends 23 (11) Uhr

Albert Steinrück

Gedächtnisfeier
Gedenkworte gesprochen von HEINRICH MANN

Einmalige Aufführung
„DER MARQUIS VON KEITH"
Schauspiel in 5 Akten von FRANK WEDEKIND
Unter Leitung von LEOPOLD JESSNER

Konsul Casimir	Werner Krauss	Ein Dienstmädchen	Fritzi Massary
Hermann, sein Sohn	Carola Neher	Simba	Käthe Dorsch
Der Marquis von Keith	Heinrich George	Metzgerknechte	Alexander Granach
Ernst Scholz	Lothar Müthel		Fritz Kortner
Molly Griesinger	Eleonore v. Mendelssohn		Victor Schwannecke
Anna, verw. Gräfin Werdenfels	Tilla Durieux		Paul Wegener
Saranieff, Kunstmaler	Jakob Tiedtke	Packträger	Rudolf Forster
Zamrjaki, Komponist	Conrad Veidt		Kurt Gerron
Sommersberg, Literat	Max Pallenberg		Veit Harlan
Raspe, Kriminalkommissar	Max Hansen	Dienstmänner	Paul Bildt
Ostermeier, Bierbrauereibes.	Hermann Vallentin		Hans Brausewetter
Krenzl, Baumeister	Otto Wallburg		Walter Janssen
Grandauer, Restaurateur	Albert Florath		Eduard v. Winterstein
Frau Ostermeier	Gisela Werbezirk	Bäckerweiber	Trude Hesterberg
Frau Krenzl	Rosa Valetti		Tilly Wedekind
Freifrau v. Rosenkron	Mady Christians	Kellner	Hans Albers
Freifrau v. Totleben	Maria Bard		Ernst Deutsch
Sascha	Elisabeth Bergner		Kurt Goetz

Gäste des Marquis v. Keith:
Roma Bahn, Sibylle Binder, Marlene Dietrich, Gertrud Eysoldt, Käthe Haak, Else Heims, Leopoldine Konstantin, Maria Koppenhöfer, Hilde Körber, Till Klokow, Lina Lossen, Lucie Mannheim, Renate Müller, Martha Maria Newes, Asta Nielsen, Maria Paudler, Henny Porten, Hannah Ralph, Frieda Richard, Dagny Servaes, Agnes Straub, Erika von Thellmann, Irene Triesch, Elsa Wagner, Ida Wüst, Alfred Abel, Ferdinand von Alten, Alfred Braun, Julius Falkenstein, Walter Franck, Max Gülstorff, Paul Grätz, Fritz Kampers, Arthur Kraußneck, Otto Laubinger, Hans Leibelt, Theodor Loos, H. C. Müller, Paul Otto, Johannes Riemann, Albert Patry, Dr. Max Pohl, Emil Rameau, Heinrich Schnitzler, Heinrich Schroth, Ernst Stahl-Nachbaur, Herrmann Thimig, Hans Wassmann, Mathias Wiemann, Wolfgang Zilzer.

Hilfsinspizient: Karlheinz Martin   Bühnenbild: Emil Pirchan   Bühnenmusik: Weintraubs Synkopaters
Bühneninspektor: Karl Rupprecht   Souffleuse: Marg. Krüger   Bühnenmeister: Franz Kaiser

Nach dem dritten Akt findet eine Gesellschaftspause von 45 Minuten statt.
Die Gemälde Albert Steinrücks sind im Islandsaal ausgestellt.

EHRENAUSSCHUSS:
Dr. h. c. Georg Graf von Arco, Kultusminister Professor Dr. Becker, Landtagspräsident Bartels, Victor Barnowsky, Professor Georg Bernhard, Oberbürgermeister Böß, Professor Albert Einstein, Jakob Goldschmidt, Direktor Herbert Gutmann, Victor Hahn, Intendant Gustav Hartung, Generalintendant Professor Leopold Jeßner, Generaldirektor Ludwig Katzenellenbogen, Dr. Paul Kempner, Dr. Robert Klein, Generaldirektor Ludwig Klitzsch, Hans Lachmann-Mosse, Generalkonsul Eugen Landau, Professor Max Liebermann, Reichstagspräsident Paul Löbe, Präsident Franz von Mendelssohn, Direktor Heinrich Neft, Professor Max Reinhardt, Professor Dr. Eugen Robert, Professor Edwin Scharff, Werner F. von Siemens, Generaldirektor Dr. Müller Sobernheim, Direktor Emil Georg von Stauß, Dr. Franz Ullstein, Generalmusikdirektor Professor Bruno Walter, Präsident Karl Wallauer, Dr. Erich Wienz, Theodor Wolff, Arthur Wolff.

ARBEITSAUSSCHUSS:
Erich Burger, August Dörschel, Norbert Falk, Alfred Fischer, Albert Florath, Heinrich George, Prof. Leopold Jeßner, Werner Krauss, Dr. Kurt Pinthus, Dr. Günther Stark, Hermann Vallentin, Richard Wilde, Dr. Fritz Wendhausen.

Preise der Plätze: Parkett u. I. Rang 60 Mk., II. Rang 40 Mk., III. Rang 20 Mk., Galerie 10 Mk.

This event offers us a rare opportunity to use the real world, as it were, rather than mere abstract statistics, to examine the part played by the Jews in pre-Hitler Berlin. In particular, we are able to see, on the one hand, their participation in the theater world of the metropolis, which could claim international leadership in stagecraft, and, on the other, their representation among the cultural leaders of the German capital.

Let us start with the performers who graced the stage on this memorable evening, which has become a part of theater history. The principal and secondary roles were filled by thirty-six actors, and a further fifty stars—most of whom are remembered even today, over fifty years later—did the walk-ons. Thus the stage held eighty-six outstanding stage and screen performers popular throughout Germany and well known far beyond its borders.

Only a few years later twenty-two of them, or more than one-quarter, were barred from working in German theater and film for no other reason than their Jewish descent. Among them were Elisabeth Bergner, Sybille Binder, Lucie Mannheim, Fritzi Massary, Eleonore von Mendelssohn, Irene Triesch, Rosa Valetti, and Gisela Werbezirk, as well as Ernst Deutsch, Julius Falkenstein, Kurt Gerron, Alexander Granach, Paul Grätz, Max Hansen, Fritz Kortner, Max Pallenberg, Dr. Max Pohl, Heinrich Schnitzler, Ernst Stahl-Nachbaur, Hermann Vallentin, Conrad Veidt, and Otto Wallburg. The actor and producer Kurt Gerron—remembered for his role as the producer in a cheap music hall in *The Blue Angel*—remained in Germany; he was transported to Auschwitz, where he was killed. Otto Wallburg also lost his life in Auschwitz. Most of the others were able to flee abroad even after 1933. Many other theater people who were not included in that memorable evening also went into exile, one that is particularly harsh for performers. Siegfried Arno, Albert and Else Bassermann, Curt and Ilse Bois, Felix Bressart, Maria Fein, Franziska Gaal, Therese Giehse, Ernst Ginsberg, Ilka Grüning, Dolly Haas, Peter Lorre, Paul Morgan, Grete Mosheim, Lilli Palmer, Camilla Spira, Szöke Szakall (who was renamed S. Z. Sakall in Hollywood), and Adolf Wohlbrück are a few of the best known among these. There were also the sopranos Gitta Alpar and Erna Sack and the tenors Jan Kiepura, Josef Schmidt, and Richard Tauber.

Some of the non-Jews—the so-called Aryans—who performed on that special occasion also turned their backs on Germany after 1933. Marlene Dietrich, for example, was able to pursue a triumphant career in the United States. She never deserted her German-Jewish colleagues in their hour of need; without her timely aid Richard Tauber would have starved to death.

Tilla Durieux was able to flee with her Jewish husband. War separated the couple, and she eventually learned of his arrest in Saloniki and his death in Germany. Nevertheless she remained in voluntary exile until after the end of the "Third Reich."

Their great popularity saved others from professional exclusion. Hans Albers, for instance, refused to divorce his "non-Aryan" wife, the actress Hansi Burg. In a similar position, Joachim Gottschalk committed suicide together with his wife and child. The final gesture of this celebrated actor was to bequeath his skull to the German theater "as a prop for Hamlet."

The director of the theatrical event, the great Leopold Jessner, manager of the national theater in Berlin and, until 1930, general manager of the Prussian state theaters, was also Jewish and forced to emigrate. We thus begin to see that the persecution of the Jews in the "Third Reich" had graver consequences for theater in Germany than merely the loss of one or another participant. Before we turn our attention to this question, however, we must take a closer look at the "honorary committee."

As would be expected within this setting, the names listed under this heading on the playbill represent a selection of prominent persons closely connected with either the theatrical or cultural life of Berlin. In all, the committee was made up of thirty-four names, including the (non-Jewish) public officials, from the president of the Reichstag, Paul Löbe, and the Prussian legislature, one Bartels, through the minister for cultural affairs, Dr. Becker, to Mayor Böss of Berlin. Of this total, more than a few were to become victims of "racial" discrimination some years later.

We have already mentioned Leopold Jessner, who was also a member of the "honorary committee." Two other members, both of Jewish origin, Victor Barnowsky and Max Reinhardt, were of the utmost significance in German theater history.

Barnowsky, born in 1875 in Berlin, managed all leading Berlin theaters from 1905 on. In 1933 he was forced into retirement and soon afterward had no choice but to emigrate. He died in New York in 1952.

Max Reinhardt, born in Baden near Vienna in 1873, moved to Berlin in 1894. According to the dramatic critic Fritz Engel, "As if waving a magician's wand, he gave everything to the theater—yes, even more than it demanded." His name is closely associated with the leading theaters in Berlin, the Salzburg Festival, and Vienna's Theater in der Josefstadt. In 1933 Max Reinhardt was forced to flee from Germany and in 1938 from Austria, having previously handed his favorite company over to "the German people," as he put it in a letter addressed to Hitler's propaganda minister, Dr. Joseph Goebbels. Reinhardt died in New York in 1943. Along with Max Reinhardt, the German theater lost an outstanding "Aryan" actress, Helene Thimig. She was Reinhardt's wife and accompanied him into exile.

Two lesser-known luminaries from the world of the theater joined Barnowsky and Reinhardt on the board of the "honorary committee"; they were Dr. Paul Klein and Dr. Eugen Robert, both Jews, as were the two representatives of the arts within this circle, Professor Bruno Walter and Max Leibermann.

Liebermann, a painter and at that time president of the Prussian academy of arts, was discussed earlier. Bruno Walter (original name, Bruno Walter Schlesinger) was born in 1876 in Berlin. Even as a young man he was a conductor at the Berlin royal opera house before conducting at the court opera in Vienna. He returned to Berlin by way of Munich and London, then went to Leipzig, where—with an international reputation—he led the Gewandhaus orchestra until he was dismissed and enjoined from working in his profession "on racial grounds" in 1933. He fled first to Austria, then to the United States. The New York Metropolitan Opera received him with open arms, as the celebrated interpreter of both Mozart and Gustav Mahler, who had been his teacher. He conducted many American orchestras, some already famous, others made famous by him. He also wrote music of his own as well as books, among them *Von der moralischen Kraft der Musik [On the Moral Power of Music]*, *Gustav Mahler*, and his autobiography *Themes and Variations*. He substituted for Otto Klemperer, whose health forced him to give up conduct-

ing the Los Angeles Philharmonic, before he died in 1962 in
Beverly Hills.

Otto Klemperer, born in 1885 in Breslau, was famous as a
conductor and composer. He began his career in Cologne,
then became conductor and general musical director of the
Berlin Kroll opera house, and finally headed the equally
prestigious national opera at Unter den Linden. In 1933 he
fled the racial mania of the "Third Reich" and took refuge in
the United States. The Nazi *Lexikon der Juden in der Musik*
[Encyclopedia of Jews in Music] devotes two full columns to
him, including the following remarks:

> His last abomination in Berlin was a performance of
> *Tannhäuser*, summarized in Alfred-Ingmar Berndt's *Gebt*
> *mir vier Jahre Zeit!* [Give Me Four Years] (Munich 1937)
> under the heading, "Pilgrims' Choir as Football Team":
> "We must point out as particularly characteristic that as
> late as February 13, 1933—after Hitler's seizure of
> power—the Jewish musical director Klemperer had the
> impertinence to proceed with a production in the Berlin
> state opera commemorating the fiftieth anniversary of
> Wagner's death that must be considered an intentional
> insult to the great German master* and a slap in the
> face to everyone still in possession of a shred of healthy
> feeling."

Bruno Walter and Otto Klemperer were not, however, the
only major conductors and composers lost to German culture
through the anti-Semitism of Hitler and his followers. Leo
Blech, born in Aachen in 1871, became a conductor at the
Berlin state opera in 1913; he remained as musical director,

---

*Even that great German master, Richard Wagner—who was, accord-
ing to Hitler and the National Socialists "the greatest exponent of true
Teutonic-German music"—should have added his luster to the list of
proscribed artists in the Nazi encyclopedia—his entry typographically marked
with a cross to signify "those musicians whose Jewish descent can be considered as firmly established, though in the absence of an unbroken chain of
documentary proof." Richard Wagner, who began by calling himself
Geyer (the name of his official stepfather, a Jewish actor) subsequently
told his friend, Friedrich Nietzsche, that he knew Ludwig Geyer to be
his biological father. Various investigations, among others those of Ernest
Newman and Leon Stein, confirm Wagner's Jewish origins.

until 1936, protected by Göring. He emigrated to Stockholm, where he became conductor at the royal court. Arnold Schönberg, born in Vienna in 1874, until 1933 led a master class at the Berlin conservatory. The pioneer of the twelve-tone system, he accepted an appointment in Boston. Kurt Weill, born in 1900, a native of Dessau, famous as the composer of *The Threepenny Opera*, and other works with Bertolt Brecht, also went to the United States; he died in 1950 in New York. Paul Hindemith, the great composer and musical scholar, a professor until 1933 at the Berlin conservatory, at first emigrated with his non-Aryan wife to Turkey, then to the United States. He taught at Yale University and conducted his own works with the New York Philharmonic.

Bruno Walter, Otto Klemperer, Leo Blech, Arnold Schönberg, Kurt Weill, Paul Hindemith, Arthur Schnabel, Leonid Kreutzer—all of them and their works, esteemed in the rest of the world, were banished and expunged from German musical life. Many others, less famous, shared this fate.

Many composers of operettas, movie music, musicals, and popular songs fell victim to ostracism, from Oscar Straus, Jean and Robert Gilbert, Emmerich Kalman, Leo Fall, Paul Abraham, and Victor and Friedrich Hollander to Rudolf Nelson, Willi Rosen, Mischa Spoliansky, Frederick Loewe (who composed *My Fair Lady* in New York), Paul Dessau, and Werner Richard Heymann (who had written the music to such films as *Congress Dances*).

On the other hand, Richard Wagner and the "Waltz Kings," the elder and younger Johann Strauss, were by no means the only "non-Aryans" whose Jewish origins were ignored or even—in the case of the Strausses—falsified with forged documents* by the "Third Reich." Otherwise the ban on the works of "non-Aryan" composers, already felt to be regrettable and troublesome by musicians and audiences, would have been unbearable for the people and their Führer. That the music of Felix Mendelssohn-Bartholdy, Jacques Offenbach, Giacomo Meyerbeer, Jacques Halévy, and Fritz Kreisler could not be performed the citizens had "hardly grasped"—as noted in a lament by the authors of an article in the official encyclo-

---

*Documentary proof of official falsification is found in Hanns Jager-Sustenau, *Johann Strauss, der Walzerkönig und seine Dynastie* (Vienna, 1965).

pedia of Jews in music. Now, along with several thousand other works, two and a half closely printed columns were added to the proscription lists containing many hundreds of popular dances by the imperial court ballet master, Emil Waldteufel (real name, Levy). On the other hand, Georges Bizet passed as "racially pure" despite his Jewish origins and the fact that he was Halévy's son-in-law; to do otherwise would have meant depriving the people of *Carmen*.

In order to comply with the musical whims of the Führer, it was necessary occasionally to turn a blind eye to an operetta, a film score, a popular song. Hitler's favorite operetta, for instance, was *The Merry Widow*, written by Franz Lehar, who had a Jewish wife, with a libretto by two Jews, Viktor Léon and Leo Stein. Hitler's intimate, Albert Speer, notes with obvious chagrin in his memoirs that "Every evening a crude projector was set up to show . . . one or two movies. . . . Revues with lots of big display were sure to please" Hitler. It was, of course, impossible to comply with such an insatiable demand without smuggling at least a few indispensable "racially alien" film creators into the ranks of the German film producers that had been so severely decimated by the "racial laws."

It could be considered a miracle that any German films continued to be produced at all, after nearly 40 per cent of the stars and starlets had been legally barred from working, along with more than half of all producers and directors.

Erich Pommer, for instance, head of production at UFA, the studio he had helped to make famous, was forced to leave Germany and went to Hollywood, where he died in 1966. Born in Hildesheim in 1889, he was no less successful in America than he had been in Berlin, where he had produced many of the greatest German films of the 1920s, from *The Cabinet of Dr. Caligari* and *Dr. Mabuse* through the monumental *Die Nibelungen* to *The Blue Angel* and *Congress Dances*.

Fritz Lang, born in Vienna in 1890, directed *Dr. Mabuse* and *Die Nibelungen*. He fled to Hollywood in 1935. E. A. Dupont was born in Zeitz in 1891. In Germany he directed *Variety* among others. Joseph von Sternberg, born in Vienna in 1894, gained worldwide fame with *The Blue Angel*. In Hollywood he directed other outstanding movies with Dietrich, such as *Shanghai Express* and *Blonde Venus*.

Ernst Lubitsch, who deserves first place among the German-

Jewish movie directors, had gone to Hollywood even before 1933. He was a native of Berlin, born in 1892, and a student of Max Reinhardt. He made it possible for some of the actors and directors driven out of Germany to establish themselves quickly and successfully in Hollywood.

The younger generation—men and women who were not yet so well established when their careers in Germany abruptly ended "on racial grounds" in 1933—included Max Ophuels and Robert Siodmak, but especially Billy Wilder. Born in 1906 in Krakow, Wilder had his first great success in Berlin in 1931 as director of *Emil and the Detectives*, based on the children's story by Erich Kästner. In 1934 Wilder moved to the United States. He achieved world fame in Hollywood with the script for *Ninotchka*, among others, and the direction of *The Lost Weekend*, *Sunset Boulevard*, *Witness for the Prosecution*, and many other prize-winning films.

This brings us to another area where noticeable gaps were inflicted after 1933 by the racial preoccupation of the rulers: the materials for movies, and their authors. The decrees of the "Third Reich" allowed neither Wilhelm Speyer nor Carl Zuckmayer to be published, let alone performed or filmed, no more than Vicky Baum (*Grand Hotel*), Alfred Döblin (*Berlin Alexanderplatz*) and Stefan Zweig (*Brennendes Geheimnis* [Burning Secret]). Walter Hasenclever and Ernst Toller, who together had written the script for the film *Menschen hinter Giltern* [People Behind Bars] were no longer active. The particular script writers of "non-Aryan descent" were lost to German film, among them Carl Mayer (author of *The Cabinet of Dr. Caligari*, *The Last Laugh*, and *Sunrise*); Albrecht Joseph (*Peter Voss*); Franz Schulz (*Zwei Herzen in Dreivierteltakt* [Two Hearts in Three-Quarter Time] and *Drei von der Tankstelle* [Three from the Filling Station]); Adolf Lantz and Ossip Dymow (*Rasputin*); Heinz Goldberg (*Affäre Dreyfus*); Friedrich Raff (*Der Stolz der dritten Kompanie* [The Pride of Company Three]; and Irmgard von Cube and Anatol Litvak (*Ein Lied für dich* [A Song For You]). Foremost, however, were Robert Liebmann and Norbert Falk.

Robert Liebmann, born in Berlin in 1890, wrote the script for many movies, most of them highly successful. Among others, he collaborated on *The Blue Angel*. Norbert Falk wrote the scripts of Lubitsch's major films.

Norbert Falk, born in 1873 in Weisskirchen, brings us back

to our starting point, the playbill for Thursday, March 28, 1929. His name is listed as a member of the working—not the honorary—committee. To do justice to this subject, we must mention a few others on this committee, who helped the arts, and certainly the theater, to reach their highest stage. Among these patrons there were several "non-Aryans" as well; a few years later they were not even permitted to enter the theaters they had done so much to support.

In first place is Franz von Mendelssohn (1865–1935), senior head of the old Berlin banking house of Mendelssohn & Co., and president of the Berlin Chamber of Commerce and Industry from 1914 on after serving as its vice president from its foundation in 1902. In 1902 he was also appointed to the college of the elders of the Berlin merchant guild, where his great-grandfather and father had already presided. Until 1913 he was the Royal Consul General for Belgium in Berlin and felt under an obligation to quit this post, when appointed a member to the Prussian Upper Diet by Emperor Wilhelm II. After 1921 he presided over the German Convention for Industry and Commerce, and in 1931 he became president of the International Chamber of Commerce.

Franz von Mendelssohn donated a number of valuable masterpieces to the public art collections of his native city, including a painting by Hieronymus Bosch; an outstanding benefactor of the theater, he was also one of the founders of the association for the prevention of cruelty to children, as only one example of his philanthropic activities. But soon enough none of these counted any longer. As early as 1933 the banking house, founded in 1795, was liquidated and taken over by the Deutsche Bank [Bank of Germany], which had already been "Aryanized," even though Ludwig Bamberger had been instrumental in establishing it. The Mendelssohns left the city after five generations of the family had taken such a great part in its economic and cultural development. To be precise, they had been active ever since the memorable day in 1743 when a pale, small, and deformed boy from Dessau was permitted entry into Berlin through the Rosenthal gate. The pigtailed guard on duty noted in his official journal first the exact number of cattle and pigs herded into the town on this particular day, before listing: "1 Jew"—namely Moses Mendelssohn. No other individual did as much to convert insignificant winter quarters, where the military and bureaucracy set the tone, into a city of intellect and culture.

Among the other patrons of Jewish origin on the "honorary committee" of the remarkable Berlin performance of 1929 Jakob Goldschmidt, the banker, must be noted. Born in 1882 in the village of Eldagsen near Hanover, Goldschmidt had worked his way up from the humblest of circumstances and was considered one of the shrewdest heads in the world of German banking. Two special achievements assured him a place in the history of German economics: the reconstruction of the Stinnes concern, which saved tens of thousands of jobs; and the merger of the Darmstädter Bank and the Nationalbank für Deutschland into the Danat Bank. German industry worshiped Jakob Goldschmidt as a hero, and he enjoyed an authority second to none. But his death in New York in 1955 went practically unnoticed.

An art collector and patron like Goldschmidt, but the scion of a very wealthy and highly regarded family, was Eugen (Baron von) Landau, born in Breslau in 1852. He and his older brothers proudly refused to use the title awarded their father, Jacob Landau. They also refused to be baptized. Landau's many contributions included his works as a banker, businessman, and philanthropist. Over eighty years old in 1933, he refused to leave Germany. In 1935 he died in Berlin.

Several other Jewish businessmen sat on the "honorary committee." Herbert Gutmann, well known in Berlin society, was the successor to his father, Eugen Gutmann, who had guided the Dresdner Bank to the level of an institute of world repute. Ludwig Katzenellenbogen, husband of Tilla Durieux, founded the business concern combining the Schultheiss-Patzenhofer brewery with the Ostwerke, which fell victim to the world economic crisis. Victor Hahn was known as an art collector and a patron. Walter Sobernheim, stepson of Eugen Landau, president of the board of the Schultheiss-Patzenhofer brewery, steered it safely through all crises; he was also a member of the national association of German industry and of the executive committee of the International Chamber of Commerce. Finally, Consul General Dr. Paul Kempner, son-in-law and partner of Franz von Mendelssohn, a brilliant legal mind, was the scion of a very distinguished Jewish family which had numerous other highly talented individuals to its credit.

His father, Privy Councillor Maximilian Kempner (1854–1927) was a well-known lawyer and industrialist as well as head of the national potash council. More distant relatives included Lydia Rabinowitsch-Kempner (1871–1935), bacteriologist and close associate of Robert Koch. She was the first woman university professor in Prussia, and, until 1933, director of the bacteriological laboratory of the Berlin-Moabit hospital. Her son, the lawyer Robert M. Kempner, was one of the American prosecutors at the Nuremberg War Crimes Trial. Friederike Kempner (1836–1904) attained unwanted celebrity through her poems, which were touchingly funny but were meant to be serious. In social work she was outstanding, contributing in large measure to the abolition of lifelong solitary confinement and to legal measures to prevent the burial of corpses only seemingly dead. Finally, there is her nephew, the famous drama critic and essayist Alfred Kempner, who used the name Alfred Kerr. He promoted the early work of such dramatists as Gerhart Hauptmann and Henrik Ibsen. We can be certain that Kerr (1867–1948) was present at that august theatrical occasion in 1929. Unlike the newspaper publisher for whom he worked, however, Kerr did not sit with the members of the "honorary committee" in the special box reserved for them. Kerr's employer, Hans Lachmann-Mosse, was publisher of the *Berliner Tageblatt*, in which Kerr's harsh critical reviews appeared until 1933; its editor in chief, Theodor Wolff, who headed the paper from 1906 until 1933, also one of the "honoraries," died in 1943 from injuries received in the Sachsenhausen concentration camp. Though over seventy, he had been deported there from his exile in France. Other editors and publishers who filled the seats reserved for the "honorary members," included the representatives of Mosse's competition, the publisher Dr. Franz Ullstein (born in Berlin in 1860, died in New York in 1945) and Georg Bernhard, editor in chief of the *Vossische Zeitung*. Bernhard, born in 1876 in Berlin, narrowly escaped from France and died in New York in 1944.

Alfred Kerr, the critic who was both feared and admired, naturally sat in one of the front rows of the orchestra, pad and sharpened pencil at the ready just like his colleagues, Bernhard Diebold of the *Frankfurter Zeitung* and Monty Jacobs of the *Vossische*. Both these men were also of Jewish origin. The same can be said of practically all the outstanding German drama critics in the decades prior to 1933, from Siegfried Jacobsohn (1881–1926), founder of the *Schaubühne* and *Weltbühne*, called by Fritz Engel (another well-known critic who fits into this list) "the most fervent advocate of a theater free of all dross," through Alfred Polgar (1875–1956), Fritz Mauthner (1849–1923), and Friedrich Gundolf (1880–1931), the great literary historian and member of Stefan George's circle, to Maximilian Harden (1861–1927), who, as publisher of *Zukunft* [Future], was also of considerable political significance. This is not to mention such older critics as Julius Stettenheim, Ludwig Fulda, and the great Otto Brahm.

The pre-Hitler German theater would therefore seem to be a theater of Jews for Jews, with predominantly Jewish authors, directors, actors, musicians, critics, and presumably also mainly Jewish audiences. Was Goebbels correct, then, when he spoke of a "nearly total Jewish contamination" of the German stage?

Objectively speaking, it cannot be denied that the theater of the years before 1933—though certainly not subject to "nearly total Jewish contamination"—was nevertheless strongly influenced by leading theatrical people and critics of Jewish origin in becoming the period in German stage and film that enjoyed the greatest international reputation. It nurtured the greatest variety of outstanding talent—including, of course, many non-Jews. Most of them had been trained by Max Reinhardt, Victor Barnowsky, or Gustav Lindemann, the (Jewish) founder of the Düsseldorf playhouse. It was their craftsmanship on which the "Third Reich" was able to subsist for a while.

Even people who would never call themselves anti-Semites, and would strongly refute such a label, are apt to raise an argument. Despite their admiration for individual Jewish directors, actors, or musicians, they claim that there were simply *too many* Jews. Then, as often as not, they will point out that the Jews only harmed themselves by being too pushy with too little caution, so as to provoke anti-Semitism.

Before examining these crucial questions in an attempt to clarify them, the final "non-Aryan" members of the "honorary committee" for the memorial performance must be noted. We will begin with Dr. (honorary) Georg Count von Arco, whose mother—Gertrud, née Mossner—was the sister of the "full-blooded Jewish" Prussian cavalry General Walter von Mossner, mentioned above. Count von Arco, born in Grossgorschutz near Ratibor in 1868, served in the army before turning to physics; a pioneer of radio, he constructed the wireless tower at Nauen, invented the high-frequency machine for the production of electric waves, and founded the Telefunken company which he headed from 1903 to 1933. He too belongs to the history of the theater for his contribution in opening up new media for both art and artists. Branded a "half-Jew," he died in 1940 in Berlin.

The last but certainly not the least of the twenty-two "non-Aryans" among the total of thirty-four members of the "honorary committee" of the evening is Professor Albert Einstein. At this stage, we do not wish to regard him as the great scientist and philosopher, lecturer at Berlin University, director of the famous Kaiser Wilhelm (today: Max Planck) Institute for Physics, and Nobel Prize laureate—nor as the arguably greatest scientist of our time, who decisively changed the picture of the universe, laying the foundations that allow the human mind to explore the universe and turning philosophical speculation into new paths. Nor do we want to consider him as the great art and music lover and the excellent violin player he was.

Rather, we prefer to deal with a few incidents in Einstein's life that illuminate in one way or another the maniacal racism of the Nazis, hoping that they will clarify the question whether the attacks on the Jews were meant to destroy something totally different from merely a small, bothersome religious or perhaps "racial" minority. The militant anti-Semites sang, "When Jewish blood spurts from the knife, then life is twice as good!" While people who considered themselves free of prejudice were merely of the opinion that, in the interest of the Jews, themselves, it would be best if Jewish influence were reduced to a level they were apt to call "bearable."

On May 10, 1933, on the square outside the main building of Berlin University, an evening "festivity" of a special kind took place. In the presence of the new national minister for propaganda and the enlightenment of the people, Dr. Joseph Goebbels (appointed to "purify German culture" from all Jewish and other "corrosive influences"), a huge bonfire was lit. To the accompaniment of the jeers of fanaticized students, books and writings of various kinds were burned. Among these were writings by Einstein—a few short essays and his principal work of sixty-four pages, *The Foundations of the General Theory of Relativity*.

Beginning on August 23, 1933, the *Deutsche Reichs und Preussischer Staatsanzeiger*, a party organ, published a series of notices, always opening with the words, "By virtue of Paragraph 2 of the law concerning the cancellation of grants of citizenship and the disavowal of German nationality of 14th July 1933 (EGBI 1S.58), I declare in unison with the foreign minister the following subjects to have lost their German citizenship because they have damaged German interests by behavior in conflict with duty and loyalty to the Reich and the people." Among those thus denaturalized there was also "Einstein, Albert, born March 14, 1879."

Finally, in the autumn of 1933 a traveling exhibit opened in Berlin before touring throughout Germany; all school children were obliged to visit it. It was intended to serve "the enlightenment of all national comrades about the enemies of the German people." Among the objects exhibited there was also a greatly enlarged photo of the greatest modern German scientist with the caption, "Einstein. Invented a highly controversial theory of relativity. Was greatly celebrated by the Jewish press and the innocent German people. Displayed his gratitude with lying atrocity propaganda against Adolf Hitler abroad. (So far has escaped the gallows)."

Were all these manifestations merely the aberrant outgrowth of racial mania? Certainly that was not all; among the writers whose works were publicly burned outside Berlin University there were also a number of "Aryans." Goebbels began by exhorting the assembled crowd "against impertinence and arrogance! For respect and veneration to the immortal German spirit of the people! Devour, flames, the writings of Tucholsky and Ossietzky!" Of these two, Kurt Tucholsky—an incomparable essayist, poet, and critic, one of the great names of German literature—was indeed of Jewish origin. The courageous pacifist, Carl von Ossietzky, however, was of "pure German stock," at least according to the Nazis' "racial theories." Hitler issued a furious decree forbidding him to accept the Nobel Peace Prize, awarded to Ossietzky while he was already languishing in a concentration camp, where he died in

1938. Many other well-known writers whose books were consigned to the flames on that occasion were not Jews nor even of partial Jewish descent. They included Erich Kästner, Erich Maria Remarque, Bertolt Brecht, Klabund, Heinrich and Thomas Mann (though the latter, Nobel Prize laureate of 1929, was the son-in-law of the well-known Munich mathematician of Jewish origin, Professor Alfred Pringsheim), Theodor Heuss, August Bebel, and Friedrich Wilhelm Förster, not to mention the many foreign authors, such as James Joyce, Jack London, Maxim Gorki, John Dos Passos, Ernest Hemingway, Upton Sinclair, Salvador de Madariaga, and Jaroslav Hasek, author of *The Good Soldier Schweik*.

The German Jews could merely claim that they, a tiny minority, furnished the major share of distinguished writers on that occasion. And not only in Berlin, but also in Frankfurt, Dresden, Munich, Breslau, and in many other German cities were the book-burning bonfires lit. The flames were fed not only with many, many books which had spread the fame of German literature throughout the world, but also some with a lasting impact that is becoming clearly evident only today, despite Goebbels and his auto-da-fé. From the philosophical writings of Moses Mendelssohn to the plays and poems of Erich Mühsam—who had prophesied as early as January 1933, "We, who are now going into exile, into the prisons, to the scaffolds," and was himself sadistically killed a year later in a concentration camp—they included such historical works as *The Communist Manifesto*, written by Karl Marx and Friedrich Engels; Rosa Luxemburg's *Letters from Prison* ("freedom is always the freedom of those who think differently"); works by Kafka and Freud; and Einstein's proof of the identity of matter and energy, which was then understood by only a few.

The lists of denaturalization also contained, apart from the names of famous and less famous German Jews, those of numerous "Aryans." The same list that named Georg Bernhard, Alfred Kerr, Ernst Toller, and Kurt Tucholsky also featured the names of non-Jewish pacifists, such as Friedrich Wilhelm Förster, Hellmut von Gerlach, and Otto Lehmann-Russbüldt; Professor Albert Einstein appeared with a whole series of "Aryans" who were deprived of their citizenship, such as the writers Frank Arnau, Theodor Plievier, and Oskar Maria Graf. The gallery of honor depicting the alleged enemies of

Germany—meaning honest adversaries of the Hitler regime—featured not only the photographs of the "father of the theory of relativity" and other famous scientists of Jewish origin, but also a series of pictures showing politicians, scientists, artists, and journalists of the most varied stamp. Ernst Thälmann—who was subsequently murdered on Hitler's instructions along with the socialist leader Rudolf Breitscheid in the concentration camp where both were interned—was the "purebred Aryan" head of the German Communists. The Social Democrat, Otto Wels, had displayed great courage early in 1933, when he refused to grant the consent of the Social Democratic Party to the "enabling act" demanded by Hitler. "We are defenseless, but not without honor," he said, thus incurring the hatred of those in power. Others were liberal journalists and Christian moral theologians.

"The soul of the German people can now regain self-expression"—thus spake Joseph Goebbels. At an earlier time, as a student in Berlin, he would have been happy if the literary historian at the University of Heidelberg, the famous and "non-Aryan" Friedrich Gundolf, had accepted him as a doctoral candidate. Now, confronting his brainchild, the burning of books he had organized, he continued, "These flames throw their light, not only on the end of a vanished era, but also on the beginning of a new one." The new era now starting brought extraordinary changes in all aspects of culture. In painting alone, nearly all modern works were removed from German art galleries, including works by Max Liebermann and Marc Chagall along with those by Paul Klee, Gauguin, Picasso, Cézanne, Matisse, and Van Gogh. A "true German" style was advocated. For the "House of German Art" roughly 1,500 works were submitted, of which only 900 were presented for final selection to the "Führer" himself. As Goebbels put it in his diary, Hitler was by no means satisfied with what he was shown. Not only did he have some of them removed from the walls and banned as "degenerate"; he even singled out one or the other work and crushed it with the heel of his boot. What remained was seen by William L. Shirer, who was present at the opening of the "House of German Art" in Munich. He called it the "greatest kitsch" he'd ever seen anywhere.

A similar situation existed in architecture. The Bauhaus in Dessau was closed. There was henceforth no meeting place in

Germany for the greatest architects, and not only for the Jews among them, such as Erich Mendelssohn or Richard J. Neutra, but also for such "Aryans" as Walter Gropius and Ludwig Mies van der Rohe. The barbarism did not even stop at destroying "species alien" buildings; the Ephraim Palace, a pearl of Berlin rococo, fell victim to the pickaxe.

Max Ophuels vividly sketched events in the theater world: "Thus the next day I went to the theater. It was ten minutes past ten. Traditionally Berlin actors are wont to turn up slowly and sleepily at about eleven. When I stepped on the empty stage, there was a man at the prompter's box, a complete stranger. He looked young, gaunt, energetic, and not well nourished—he could have been an out-of-work engineer, or a plain clothesman in the criminal police. He said in a tight-lipped manner, 'I am the new director. Herr Barnowsky will resign from his job in a day or two. I represent him. Yes, I repre . . . I just wish to settle one thing. From now on, rehearsals start at ten. Whoever comes after ten—whether talented or not—is no longer of interest. Please tell that to your actors. And by the way, this ruling also applies to you.' I went to the backstage telephone booth and called my wife. I said, 'Pack!' Valetti felt the same way; she said, 'When the stationmasters take over the stage, it's time.' "

Casting no aspersions against genuine stationmasters in their proper place—but, Rosa Valetti, the great "funny old girl" of stage and screen before 1933 had hit the nail on the head. From now on, art, like everything else in Germany, was at the mercy of individuals in uniform, who were always on "duty" with an outstretched right arm, communicated with each other by means of whistles, and aimed at "coordinating" everything with their own narrow-mindedness. Instead of the free development of achievement, spirit, talent, and genius, an ever more brutal terror set in, coupled with proof of "Aryanism," a dull philistine mentality, pseudonationalistic kitsch, and a Byzantine cult of the "Führer."

Hatred and envy by the unsuccessful and the failures directed at those who excelled or were successful took over. Feelings of resentment toward everything that deviated from the philistine norm, ever dormant in the souls of the petit bourgeoisie, were now fanned into full consciousness and aggravated. At long last they were given a fairly clear target: the Jews.

Until this time, especially in the large cities, only certain fringe Jewish groups had aroused the displeasure of the petit bourgeoisie. They were difficult to distinguish from the other members of hated groups—such as the snobbish parvenus in the crowd of predominantly non-Jewish refugees who arrived in Germany after 1918 from Eastern and Southeastern Europe, or those sons and daughters of the old established aristocracy who called attention to themselves by nonconformity, as leftist intellectuals, through promiscuity, or a preference for jazz, abstract painting, and other unusual fashions. Now, however, a new high authority, legitimized by Fieldmarshall and Reich President Paul von Hindenburg, proclaimed that there was a basic difference between "masters" and "subhumans," between "noble Nordic Aryans" and "species alien" scum from Asia Minor that called itself Jewish unless it was camouflaged through all kinds of tricks, such as baptism.

Thanks to Hitler, most simple, ignorant, narrow-minded Germans could now see themselves as noble. In exchange—though with mixed feelings—they were willing to put up with the government's making pariahs of a few families whom they knew more or less well and whom they had not until then found particularly objectionable; or with the fact that their always helpful and skilled family doctor was no longer permitted to practice; or with the remarkable incident that the respected, strongly nationalistic high-school teacher with the war wound who lived on the ground floor, should suddenly commit suicide.

They only found it somewhat confusing that so many Jewish things were now banned—the songs of Mendelssohn–Bartholdy, Heine's "Lorelei," even Charlie Chaplin, the clown Grock, and the popular leading man, Conrad Veidt, even their favorite operetta, *The White Horse Inn*—while a lot of things that had seemed despicable now turned out to be "pure Aryan."

But Dr. Goebbels knew how to resolve the dilemma. Since all Jews were "species alien," even though this was frequently not felt to be so, everything "species alien" must, of course, be particularly "Jewish." The identity claimed by Hitler between Judaism and Marxism served as a basis and model for all further equations. Jews had a "corrosive" effect, as did jazz; jazz was therefore Jewish. Jews speculated; the quantum theory was too speculative for "Aryans"; therefore its non-Jewish advocates were "spiritual Jews." The Jews wished the Germans to "degenerate"; modern painting was "degenerate art"; therefore modern art was the work of Jews. Usury, rape, pornography, as well as bargain prices, homosexuality, nudism—all were Jewish schemes for subjugating and exploiting the German "Aryans." Therefore, all those of "German stock" who occupied themselves in such or another "species alien" manner were "white Jews." Thus members of the aristocracy who did not become SS leaders despite thirty-two generations of purely "Aryan" forebears were, according to Heinrich Himmler, "not much better than the Jews"; after the final victory they should be denounced by Goebbels as spies or sex criminals and publicly hanged in the largest Berlin park.*

As shown by these examples, one was not fussy in the choice of means for declaring everything to be Jewish that was either despicable or merely out of favor. Regarding the definition of "the Jew in his antithesis to the Aryan," one was even less finicky. On the one hand, it was preached that creed was unimportant, "race" alone being the criterion. However, as proof of "Aryan" stock, it was sufficient to produce baptismal certificates showing all four grandparents to be "Aryans." Conversely, the Jewish creed of one ancestor, even if he had only temporarily converted to Judaism, "immediately"** led to the conclusion of a non-Aryan origin for his descendants—with all the implied precarious, occasionally fatal consequences—without ever permitting any counterevidence. Elizabeth Taylor, Marilyn Monroe, Norma Shearer, and the Swedish May Britt, to mention just four world-renowned actresses who converted to Judaism, would have been considered "non-Aryans" in the Third Reich and their descendants, without more ado, would have been branded Jews or half-breeds, though no "racial" justification could have been produced.

---

*"The princes should be made to march down Unter den Linden. The Labor Front would supply the masses to line the route, to spit at the princes, and thus express the fury of the people." So read notes made by Himmler's personal physician and masseur, Felix Kersten, of a conversation with Himmler.

**Compare the extract from the commentary concerning the so-called Blood Protection Laws in the Appendix.

At the same time there was no hesitation to declare some people Jews who, according to the Nazis, must be Jews but who actually were not. Occasionally extremely silly attempts were made to obtain proof for such assertions. Hitler's official photographer, Heinrich Hoffmann, reported after the war that the "Führer" had him travel to Moscow with the foreign minister, Joachim von Ribbentrop, for the signature of the German-Soviet agreement of alliance. He was to take a close-up photo of Stalin's earlobes! Hitler wished to ascertain whether they might not, after all, adhere to the skull and thus be "Jewish."

If, over and above pure propaganda, there was any meaning in this state-decreed hatred of Jews, which spread to everything else, good or bad, that deviated from the petit-bourgeois norm, it was contained in the desire for "coordination," which was to embrace not only administrative, but all spiritual, artistic, and cultural areas. The upright Jewish citizens, even more so the mass of middle-class citizens and proletarians of Jewish faith or of merely non-Aryan origin, might have been a matter of complete indifference to Hitler and his henchmen. Fundamentally, they probably were. These people fell victim to an overall judgment, executed by means of totalitarian measures, that was really directed against others, Jews and non-Jews.

For instance, if Albert Einstein had by chance not been a Jew, he would still have had to be ostracized and—from the point of view of the Nazis—rendered "harmless," along with a few thousand other scientists, artists, journalists, and teachers. For in order to make anti-Semitism as attractive as possible, it had to be turned against every free and progressive spirit, against everything bordering on genius and excellence, and anything that might arouse the mistrust and especially the envy of the ignorant petit bourgeoisie.

We are still faced with the question of how it came about that among the German Jews, and among those classified as such by means of the "racial laws," there were so surprisingly many outstanding personalities in the most diversified fields—far more than could have been expected from their numbers as a small proportion of the total population.

Chapter 4

Good-bye, Professor!

Until the early nineteenth century many of the German cities and minor states tended to keep out anybody of a different faith. This provision did not apply merely to Jews, but also referred to Christians of a denomination different from the local official religion.

Thus, for example, the Old Town of Hanover admitted only Lutherans from the compulsory reformation of 1533 to the beginning of the nineteenth century. Huguenots, Catholics, Jews, and other "nonbelievers" were tolerated only beyond the town walls. These had neither guild privileges nor full civil rights, were barred from membership on the city council, and were forbidden to enter the city proper outside hours precisely stipulated by regulations.

The archbishopric of Salzburg was an independent state with roughly 200,000 inhabitants dominated by the Jesuits. In the autumn of 1731 it was decided to expel all Protestants, whose congregations were overwhelmingly comprised of peasants working at semifeudal labor. Whoever had not renounced Lutheranism under oath by the day of the reformation and had not repented with conversion to the Roman Catholic faith had to leave the state within a week. Depending on the size of immovables to be relinquished, owners of houses and real estate were granted a reprieve of up to three months. The number of these refugees can be gauged by considering that the Kingdom of Prussia alone accepted 15,508 of the Salzburg exiles. The remainder emigrated to Sweden, Denmark, and Holland. The residence ban for non-Catholics remained in effect until the archbishopric was secularized in 1802.

The Palatinate may furnish the last of hundreds of possible examples. Here the followers of Calvin were favored in every way after the Reformation and until 1576, while Catholics and Lutherans were deprived of their civil rights and some of them were expelled. This state of affairs was followed briefly by the suppression and expulsion of the Calvinists. Under two further electors, the Reformation doctrine was raised to a state religion, and those of different denominations were banished. Around 1700, after the Peace of Ryswyk, sovereignty passed into the hands of the Catholic minority, unleashing persecution of Calvinists and followers of Luther. No one who was not a Catholic was permitted to hold office, and many non-Catholics had to leave their homes in one or another city and take refuge in neighboring villages.

Shortly after the Reformation, Berlin proceeded in a far more magnanimous manner, dictated by necessity and not based on charitable motives. In the early seventeenth century the metropolis of the Brandenburg Electorate, including all outlying districts, could boast of an imposing total of close to 14,000 inhabitants; by mid-century, at the end of the Thirty Years' War, this number was reduced by slightly less than half. The outlying districts had been demolished on orders from the elector in order to improve the city's defensive capacity. In the town itself, no fewer than 147 of 874 houses stood empty. Therefore the sovereign, later known as the Great Elector, in order to stop the decline of his capital and to revitalize the economy, brought in numerous foreigners, even if they did not hold to the "correct faith" as established in Brandenburg. Many of these were French Huguenots, who were subject to shockingly cruel persecution in their own country. In Berlin the new citizens from France were termed "the colony." To the great annoyance of the old settlers, they were awarded numerous privileges, including exemption from taxes for a period of years, their own courts, and permission to build a large church, where every other Sunday a Reformed service was given in French. They also had their own schools.

By 1700 Berlin was a flourishing city with more than 20,000 inhabitants. Roughly 8,000 of these—or at least one-third— were of Huguenot origin. But most of the other Berliners were also immigrants—principally Protestants from the Palatinate, Switzerland, and Salzburg, as well as Polish Catholics. Wends from the Lausitz and the Spree Forest worked as porters, maids, and wet nurses in middle-class homes. And finally there were the Viennese.

In 1671 fifty families had been carefully selected and recommended for settling in Berlin by Andreas Neumann, the Great Elector's Viennese agent. A generation later, this Viennese colony consisted of close to two thousand people, including some who had arrived without letters of safe conduct— servants, private tutors, clergymen, doctors, and their families.

In 1705 this group—still known as "the Viennese"—paid the exact sum of 117,437 talers in excise duties—compared with 43,865 talers from all the other old established merchants. The newcomers from Vienna were allowed to acquire houses and real property; they were also free to establish new industries and enjoyed various other privileges. But, unlike the Huguenots, they were not granted their own house of worship—for a very simple reason. The new citizens from France were at least Christians, while the Viennese were not: they had been forced to leave Austria because of their Jewish faith.

If Berlin and the whole of the Brandenburg-Prussian state were able to escape the economic ruin that threatened after the Thirty Years' War and again in the eighteenth century, following the immensely costly campaigns of Frederic the Great, it was due in the first instance to the Jewish and Huguenot citizens. In Berlin and Prussia their elite played a role similar to that of the Portuguese-Spanish Jews in the development of Hamburg, while the Jewish fur dealers and, subsequently, the book merchants from Poland did the same for Leipzig.

In Berlin the colony of Huguenots and the descendants of the Jews who had arrived from Vienna in 1671 grew into the cultural and economic elite. Except for them, the higher officials and officers belonging chiefly to the nobility were the only ones to play a significant role. They formed a caste strictly separated from the Jews and initially also from the Huguenots. However, entry into this caste through civil-service and army careers was open to members of the French nobility among the French colony and, later on, to aristocratic refugees who arrived in Berlin after the Revolution of 1789, as well as to Polish, Scottish, and other aristocrats living in exile in Prussia. For the Jews, it remained barred on religious grounds for another half-century. Even in the course of emancipation was membership in this caste only grudgingly granted. The Jewish middle class concentrated all the more on the professions, on banking, and on industry and commerce. Privately they cultivated the arts and sciences; the universities were still closed to them.

In the course of the Enlightenment the social barriers between Prussian nobility and the Jewish upper middle class gradually fell away. The Jewish upper class—most of its members baptized and fervently patriotic—soon also mingled with the Huguenots, who considered themselves Prussians. We have already mentioned the salons of Rahel, Henriette Herz, and Dorothea Schlegel and their profound influence on the literature and on the arts of the early nineteenth century and the numerous marriages between educated and wealthy Jewish women and members of the nobility. By the middle of the nineteenth century there was hardly a noble family in Berlin and subsequently in the rest of Prussia that did not have ties of one kind or another with a Jewish family, Prussian royalty not excluded.

For example, a nephew of King Frederic Wilhelm III, Prince Adalbert of Prussia, admiral and commander-in-chief of the royal navy, married a Jewish woman. The lady of his choice, Therese Elsler—a sister of the celebrated dancer, Fanny Elsler—certainly did not become a Prussian princess, since a so-called morganatic marriage did not fall within dynastic regulations. Nevertheless, a royal decree conferred on Therese Elsler the title of Baroness von Barnim. A son of the Prince and the Jewish baroness was able to join the elite officers corps of the Dragoon Guards as Baron Adalbert von Barnim.

King Friedrich Wilhelm III also raised the morganatic consort of Prince August of Prussia, the Jewish middle-class Maria Arend, to the status of Prussian nobility. She and her seven children were given the name von Prillwitz. One of the daughters, Elise von Prillwitz, married Count Harry von Arnim. A son, Ludwig, married Countess Georgine von Moltke. Her daughter, Wanda, married Hans von der Marwitz. The numerous children of the youngest daughter, Klara von Arnim, all married members of well-known Prussian aristocratic families.

However, as noted above, liaisons in Prussia between aristocratic Christians and members of the Jewish middle class were by no means limited to royalty. The Prussian minister of finance and later administrator of Silesia, Friedrich Count von Bülow, married the Jewish Jeannette Schmucker, daughter of a merchant, in 1804. Her descendants became connected with the baronial families Koenigsmark, Bassewitz, Wartensleben, von der Schulenburg, Schwerin, and Hardenberg. Frédéric Count von Limburg-Stirum married a member of the Jewish middle class, Johanna Ebers, who was born in Berlin in 1808. She was a granddaughter of Veit Ephraim, the court banker, who in his day was the elder of the Berlin Jews and the builder of the once famous palace bearing his name. The son of this marriage, Count Friedrich Limburg-Stirum, was for many years leader of the Prussian Conservatives. Emperor Wilhelm II, annoyed that Limburg-Stirum headed a reactionary aristocratic action group opposing the emperor's policy, saw fit to send off a furious telegram in which he called the count an "impertinent Jewboy." As the last of many hundreds of possible examples we may cite some of the children and grandchildren resulting from the marriage of Prince Elector Friedrich Wilhelm I of Hesse with a Jewish merchant's daughter, Gertrude Falkenstein, later known as Countess von Schaumburg and Princess von Hanau. The eldest daughter, Princess Auguste von Hanau, married Prince Ferdinand Maximilian zu Isenburg-Büdingen, a hereditary member of the Prussian Upper House. Their son, Prince Ferdinand, married Margita Countess von Doenhoff. As regards the other children, Princess Alexandrine married Prince Felix von Hohenlohe-Öhringen; her sister Gerta married Wilhelm Prince zu Sachsen-Weimar-Eisenach; another sister, Princess Marie, married Prince Wilhelm von Hessen-Philippsthal; and Prince Wilhelm von Hanau married first a Princess von Schaumburg-Lippe and then a Countess von Lippe-Weissenfels. He was the seventh of eleven children, progeny of the Prince Elector and the Jewish merchant's daughter.

These examples show the intimate link between the Prussian nobility as well as Germany's top ranking aristocracy and the German-Jewish upper class. However, this does not apply only to the elite: the daughter of a Jewish tailor, who earned his living by making alterations, was a countess and later the first "Princess" von Henckel-Donnersmarck. Blanche Lachmann was born in Moscow, and neither there nor in her later life in Paris could she claim to belong to the upper class. When she died in 1884 in Castle Neudeck, however, the widower Count Guido "Prince" Henckel-Donnersmarck— hereditary member of the Prussian Upper House, member of the Prussian state council, and one of the richest men in Germany—declared that his family owed a debt of gratitude to his dearly beloved Blanche, who had regrettably died too soon. He stated that their enormous wealth was in a large measure due to her prudence, enterprise, and fairness in all dealings.

Did the Jews push their way into the aristocracy? Or was the nobility inspired by the desire for middle-class Jewish daughters' dowries, which were often substantial? Both may have been true in individual cases, and at the time many anecdotes made the rounds in Berlin that seemed to prove one or the other.

But there was a trend of greater significance than these alliances between the "vons" and the "funds," as they were jocularly known, and which occurred as well between aristocrats in need of money and daughters of lower-middle-class non-Jewish citizens who had grown rich. More importantly, in the first decades of the nineteenth century the German Jews had become again what they had been before the Crusades in towns along the banks of the Rhine, Main, and Donau, and for a few centuries thereafter in Poland—an essential middle-class component of the large cities, principally Berlin, Vienna, Prague, Frankfurt am Main, Hamburg, and Breslau. The politically and intellectually most emancipated among them, together with many Christians and enlightened aristocrats, constituted the civilizing social elite.

This emergence out of the darkest Middle Ages into modern times was extraordinarily surprising, even to the Jews themselves. Many people simply could not grasp what was happening. These included not only many members of the lower middle class, some ignorant country squires, and not least the greater part of the Christian clergy as well as many orthodox rabbis.

But was this metamorphosis really so surprising? Here was a group of unassuming, despised creatures, crawling like caterpillars, often brutally trodden underfoot, who suddenly emerged into the light of day as colorful butterflies. And yet the great mass of Germans had undergone a similar transformation in the wake of the French Revolution after their delivery from centuries-long suppression. Until that time the Christian scholars and artists of the "lower orders" had been dependent on the whims of masters who were not always gracious. They had been penned in by guild rules and a most petty system of regulations exacted by spiritual and secular authorities; all this, it was said, was according to the will of God.

For once the Jews of Germany should have been examined not as exotic creatures, but simply as that part of the nation's inhabitants that was the only one successfully to have withstood conversion to Christianity. For this obduracy they paid an enormous toll in blood, suffering, and expulsion. For centuries Jews were forced to live as pariahs. It is therefore only logical that after the causes of their suppression were finally removed thanks to the rapid spreading of the Enlightenment, they seized the wonderful opportunity to participate again, still with some constraints, in the life of the nation. This they did to an extent corresponding with their capabilities that had been disregarded for so long.

Viewed from this angle, it was neither remarkable—nor, as the reactionaries saw it, an impertinence—for the German citizens of the Jewish faith to begin to play a substantial and often leading role in all social spheres. Nor did they assume more than a proportional share of certain academic, artistic, and other professions, as becomes evident when the usual and still popular religious prejudices are set aside and the percentages are calculated, not on the basis of the total population, but of the intelligent middle-class citizens who had for centuries been prevented from freely developing their capabilities. In the past the German Jews had been an integral component of this group, and they desired to resume that place now that the worst obstacles had fallen away.

Naturally they tended to choose those routes, as we shall see, that afforded them the best chances and the least difficulties. But, like all other liberated people, they also did not hesitate to accept those risks that their sense of civic responsibility demanded from them. This includes volunteering to the colors at the beginning of the Napoleonic wars of liberation. It also meant active support of the bourgeois Revolution of 1848, which struggled to oppose the reactionary restitution of the old conditions and the abolishment of hard-gained civic liberties.

At least 20 of the total of 230 citizens of Berlin who lost their lives in the cause of justice and freedom during the revolt of March 1848 were Jews. All the 230 lay in state. The king was forced by the populace to honor the dead—"pale and uneasy he stood" is the description of this scene in the song by Ferdinand Freiligrath. After this, all of them were buried in a common grave as a symbol of the abolition of differences between citizens of different religions.

The supraparliament created by the Revolution of 1848, the German National Assembly in St. Paul's Church in Frankfurt, also included several deputies of Jewish origin. The historian Johannes Hohlfeld, writing during the period of the Weimar Republic, claims that only one Jew, Eduard Simson, was at the convention in St. Paul's Church and that he was unchallenged in retaining the seat of president; whereas in the National Assembly of Weimar in 1919 more than a dozen Jews occupied deputies' chairs—a typical indication of the Jewish element's unwarranted "pushiness."

In truth, the Jewish citizens of Germany were more heavily represented in St. Paul's Church, with fifteen deputies, than in subsequent parliaments. Furthermore, they initially provided the two vice presidents. After the president, Heinrich von Gagern, had been given the mandate to form a commonwealth ministry, one of them, Eduard von Simson, took over the presidency; the other, Gabriel Riesser, remained vice president. Of the remaining thirteen Jewish deputies—either members of Jewish congregations or born Jews who converted to Christianity—the majority belonged to the moderate liberal center, as represented by Simson and Riesser. Others belonged to the most extreme right wing, including Wilhelm Stahl and Johann Gustav and Wilhelm Moritz Heckscher from Hamburg, as well as Johann Hermann Detmold, the son of a court physician, who was a lawyer in Hanover.

A physician from Königsberg, Johann Jacoby, belonged to the extreme left of the Paul's Church parliament. His famous publication of 1841, *Vier Fragen, gestellt von einem Ostpreussen* [An East Prussian Poses Four Questions], had been immediately confiscated. Jacoby had to endure a lawsuit "for arousing displeasure, arrogant criticism, scoffing at the laws of the land, lèse-majesté, and high treason." He was eventually acquitted by the supreme court in Berlin. King Friedrich Wilhelm IV refused to give the St. Paul's Church deputation a hearing, and one of its members, Johann Jacoby, challenged the monarch in the words that have since become part of the storehouse of German quotations: "It is the misfortune of kings that they refuse to listen to the truth!"

More than twenty years later during the Franco-Prussian war of 1870, Jacoby, not yet a member of the Social Democrats, was taken into protective custody by an overzealous member of the military for a pronouncement protesting annexation of French territory. His popularity among the common people of his East Prussian homeland afforded no protection. From a fortress near Lötzen the prisoner wrote to Bismarck, and—lo and behold—the letter reached the chancellor. Despite the war against a greater power and the very imminent foundation of the empire, Bismarck found time to reply to Jacoby personally and very politely. Shortly thereafter, the subject of protective custody was discharged from prison despite his avowed intention to continue with his energetic opposition to national policy.

It is a historical fact that the liberal, radical-republican attitude of Johann Jacoby was the exception among the Jewish deputies of the first German National Assembly. A progressive deputy, Franz Ziegler, wrote to his constituents in Berlin, "While we were all still living in political obscurity, Johann Jacoby emerged from the dark, poised, clear, brilliant, and courageous, becoming the leader of the political life of Prussia!"

A much more typical example of the attitude of the Jewish deputies of the St. Paul's Church parliament was Moritz Veit. He was descended from a Berlin family of the upper middle class that had been among the first Viennese to be brought in by the Great Elector. Veit was a publisher, and the firm he

founded issued the words both of Goethe and the French
refugee and Prussian patriot, Adalbert von Chamisso. Subsequently it merged with the publishing house of Walter de
Gruyter, which is still active. It was Veit who said that as a
Jew he had never met obstacles from his Christian fellow
citizens, "but again and again at the hands of the ruling
princes and their servants."

In *Juden im öffentlichen Leben Deutschlands* [Jews in the
Public Life of Germany] Ernest Hamburger writes,

> Therefore it is readily understood that the Jews should
> consider their interest best served by combatting royal
> absolutism and in the development and realization of the
> liberal state concept. Their will to fight was all the more
> pronounced and strong because they had to struggle for
> rights already granted other citizens. They advocated the
> acknowledgment of civil and human rights. They hoped
> for a salutary political effect from the extension of the
> sphere of personal freedom and from securing freedom
> of the press and of assembly. The defense of equality
> before the law was for them a matter of vital importance.
> They endeavored to increase the effectiveness of parlia-
> mentary institutions—as opposed to the executive—which
> they viewed as support or potential support against arbi-
> trary authoritarian power.

On the other hand, with their middle-class position, the
majority of German Jews were averse to all radical tendencies.
As liberals, they were not in favor of abolishing the monarchy
but in strengthening parliament. They were German patriots
with a national, not an international, attitude.

Ernest Hamburger commented,

> The Jews were not interested in petty state particularism.
> While to many German citizens it appeared the expres-
> sion of traditional loyalty and a protective wall for various
> material interests, to the Jews it had been merely the
> source of many disappointments. . . . Consequently by
> far the greater majority of them was to be found among
> the ranks of those favoring the unification of the nation.
> For this reason they also found their way to German
> liberalism. Since the latter advocated the particularist

solution, the Jews of Prussia were able to combine their liberal attitude with their attachment to the Hohenzollern monarchy. They felt more secure under its protection than in many another German state.

In 1861 the left wing of the liberals constituted itself as the German Progressive Party, demanded a German federated state under the leadership of a Hohenzollern, and proclaimed a moderate and liberal antirevolutionary program. Thereupon the majority of the Jews of Prussia and of the other German states identified themselves with these aims. They supported the Progressives with their votes, and they had a fair number of deputies within the factions of the party.

As had been the case in the National Assembly, the great majority of these Jewish deputies were members of the professional classes: doctors, lawyers, writers, and journalists. Most of the others were manufacturers, bankers, or simply rich men living on their inheritances and indulging in unpaid scholarship.

Wilhelm Beer may serve as a typical example of the latter category. He was a brother of the dramatist Michael Beer and of the composer Giacomo Meyerbeer. His father, the well-known banker Jacob Herz Beer, had been known as "the Croesus of Berlin" because of his many charitable donations and his patronage of local artists and writers. After his father's death, Wilhelm Beer continued the family enterprises, comprising the banking house and several manufacturing concerns. However, his principal occupation was astronomy, in particular research on the moon. He had the reputation of being one of the most important scientists working in this special branch. From 1846 on he was a member of the Prussian First Chamber, later called the Upper House. Despite his progressive attitude, he occasionally voted for highly reactionary proposals, such as the use of the Christian religion as the basis of all education in state schools and similar institutions.

Besides Beer and Stahl, two other men of Jewish origin sat in the Prussian First Chamber, both of them bankers and estate owners—Siegfried Guradze and Martin Magnus. The example of the Magnus (originally Meyer) family, long-time residents of Berlin, demonstrates impressively what the anti-Semites meant when they talked about the Jews as "pushy," especially in the sciences and the arts, and of the "alienation" of German universities. It will become very clear that this view, with its anti-Jewish bias, grew out of a peculiar premise quite incapable of withstanding objective examination and representing no more than lower-middle-class or provincial prejudices.

Anton Baron von Magnus was born in Berlin in 1821, the son of the Jewish banker, Friedrich Martin Magnus, owner of a baronial estate and deputy to the Prussian First Chamber. After he had been baptized and had studied law and political science, he entered the Prussian foreign service. In 1853, at Bismarck's instigation, he was raised to the nobility and was Prussian—later imperial—ambassador in The Hague, St. Petersburg, Mexico, Vienna, and Copenhagen.

His uncle, Eduard Magnus, born in Berlin in 1799, became one of the most popular and distinguished painters of the Biedermeier period. In a long series of solidly crafted portraits, he depicted the celebrities of his native city and many visitors to Berlin: Felix Mendelssohn-Bartholdy, old Marshall Friedrich Wrangel, the sculptors Bertel Torwaldsen and Christian Daniel Rauch, and the young Adolf Menzel, not to mention all the Prussian rulers of his time. In 1837 he became a member of the Prussian Academy of Arts; in 1844 he was finally appointed a full professor.

The painter's younger brother was the chemist and physicist Heinrich Gustav Magnus, born in Berlin in 1802. After studying in Berlin, Stockholm, and Paris, he joined the faculty of Berlin University in 1831 as a lecturer in technology and physics; he became an assistant professor in 1834 and a full professor in 1845. Hermann von Helmholtz, the great scientist, eulogized his colleague, in an 1870 obituary: "At a time when Berlin offered the chemistry student wholly insufficient opportunities for practical training, Magnus made his private laboratory available to gifted students and supported them most selflessly." Magnus's most significant scientific achievement in physics is considered to be the discovery of the so-called Magnus effect. It explains the phenomenon of deflecting forces in bodies freely rotating in the atmosphere—for instance, shells leaving the gunbarrel with a "spin." Gustav Magnus also distinguished himself in physiology. Science owes him the important discovery that all tissues "breathe"—that is, take in oxygen and emit carbonic acid.

Rudolf Magnus, born in 1873, another member of this family, gained scientific renown as a physiologist, pharmacologist, and zoologist. He discovered the positioning and stoppage reflexes of vertebrates as well as their dependence on the function of the inner ear and the cerebellum—facts that explain the establishment of equilibrium in the higher animals. His last appointment was as professor of physiology at Utrecht University.

Privy councillor Paul Wilhelm Magnus was associate professor for botany at Berlin University. He made a name for himself in the study of algae, and participated in several scientific expeditions.

This one family gave birth to seven other university professors. Still other descendants include a translator with a worldwide reputation (Erwin Magnus), a physician and research physiologist (Adolph Magnus-Levy), a radio pioneer (Kurt Magnus), an economist and banker (Dr. Ernst Magnus), and an outstanding jurist (Julius Magnus).

While the Magnus family contributed so many distinguished artists, scholars, and authorities in a variety of fields in one century, it was only one of several dozen similarly outstanding families belonging to the old established Jewish elite of Berlin—not to mention the rest of Prussia and the other states in Bismarck's nation as well as—or especially—Vienna, Prague, and Budapest.

With special reference to Berlin, however, exactly the same can be shown to be true for at least two other groups that had arrived between the late seventeenth and early nineteenth centuries. Together with the Jews, they formed the cultural elite of the city, which they helped to raise to the rank of a metropolis. These were fugitives from France—Huguenots and refugees of 1789—and Prussian, as well as Swedish, Polish, and Scottish noblemen who joined the middle classes to the extent that they abandoned their traditional pursuits, turning instead to the arts and sciences, literature, and commerce, banking, or other branches of the economy.

As these groups sought erudition, development of their talents, political influence, or merely acquisition of wealth, their success did not elicit crude invective against "foreigners" or "country squires" from even the most narrow-minded petty bourgeois. It was not even suggested that they had arrogated too many places in universities, hospitals, art associations, head physician jobs, or boards of directors.

This situation would appear to be all the more remarkable since in Berlin that sector of the nobility that had penetrated the ranks of the cultured middle classes merged with the "upper circles" of the French "colony" and of the Jewish community, forming a culturally productive new upper layer. The union was also made more intimate through inumerable marriages across all borders of origin and descent.

Among the descendants of Moses Mendelssohn and their marriage partners alone we find over forty names of nobility (excluding Jewish families raised to the nobility, such as the "von Simsons"). We also find the names of roughly a dozen French—mainly Huguenot—old families.

Of course the descendants of Moses Mendelssohn were also linked with most of the established "good" Jewish families of Berlin; the mixture coincided almost exactly with that of the Berlin social register.

The descendants of Moses Mendelssohn and their spouses also accurately reflected the professional pursuits of the upper middle classes. We find among them a number of distinguished bankers and industrialists; a few high officials and judges; a dozen professional officers and as many large estate owners; a few prominent engineers; a number of publishers and some outstanding educators; several social workers, including three nuns; numerous renowned writers, musicians, actors, and artists; many doctors and several lawyers; and a total of thirty-one university professors in every possible field, including at least six scholars with worldwide reputations.

Surely only one conclusion can be drawn from this example. The "pushiness of the Jews and their hangers-on," as the anti-Semites never tired of putting it, into the academic posts at German universities at least seemed partly based on fact—but the number of professors of purely Jewish origin, and especially of the Jewish faith, was not quite as high as was often asserted and was already declining before 1933. Moreover, the alleged "pushiness" was nothing more than the safeguarding of legitimate claims by people who had at long last been granted their civil rights. And again, these claimants were acting exactly like the other members of their social level, though possibly showing a little more restraint and caution as the result of bitter past experience. Only by believing that the entire educated bourgeoisie of the nineteenth and early twentieth centuries had been too ambitious and had striven too greedily for the prestigious posts of university lecturers, can we blame the Jewish segment of this class for not having remained modestly in the background while others prospered.

It might be argued, all evidence to the contrary, that the Jews nevertheless acted imprudently and had been "too pushy," if for no other reason than because people considered them "aliens," even if they were not in fact foreigners.

A qualified response to such an argument arises from the inadmissible generalization at the root of this argument. In the nineteenth century those German citizens of Jewish origin who pursued university careers could not be considered aliens, since they were not, as a rule, in any way distinguishable from citizens of non-Jewish origin. The typical "Jewish" professor of that epoch came from a solid middle-class family, was baptized, and had frequently changed the family name to one that would not remind anyone of his Jewish origins. His observance of a patriotic attitude, correct dress, cultivated speech, and strict "morality," as current codes of behavior would have it, was indistinguishable from that of his "Aryan" colleagues.

Nor did the typical assimilated German-Jewish professor differ in appearance from his "Aryan" colleagues, all legends to the contrary. Had such external features existed, the Nazi "race" researchers would happily have applied such distinguishing marks. Instead, they were obliged to seize upon parents' and grandparents' faith as the sole, if absurd, criterion to determine "race."

Conversely, embarrassing surprises often resulted from the attempt to select Nordic-Germanic prototypes from a larger circle of groups, using external features as guidelines. Only Nordics, it was held, would be of heroic size, with narrow skulls, fair hair, blue eyes, and straight noses, giving the impression of courage and "boundless honesty"—according to Adolf Hitler's definition of the "Aryan" in *Mein Kampf*. The female counterpart to this masculine ideal was a sweet maiden with honey-colored braids, a trusting glance from light-blue eyes, and a maternal, not sensual, mouth.

In the autumn of 1933 the Reich's propaganda ministry went to the trouble of going through a heap of photographs portraying youths and maidens of Nordic-Germanic appearance and picking out an ideal representative of each. These two were to be united, even if only for the purposes of a poster. The choice fell upon a young girl who worked as a technical assistant in the propaganda ministry. It so happened that her name was not Kriemhilde, as in ancient Germanic folklore, but Maria; her surname, however, was that of one of the most prominent Nazis (who incidentally, did not in the least resemble an "Aryan"). The selected young man was an athletic secondary-school student from the Mecklenburg nobility. Dr. Goebbels personally approved the choices. At the last minute, however, replacements had to be found for both young people, since both refused to cooperate on different pretexts. Understandably, both concealed their true reasons: the ideal young woman was of Jewish origin through both parents, though she herself was a baptized Protestant; the young man's mother was a baptized Jewish woman, and his father had a "non-Aryan" grandmother.

To return to the hypothetical objection. Of course these two were not considered "foreign," certainly not in appearance or manners. Nor were several hundred thousand other German Jews—though only a few of them may have resembled the "Nordic-Germanic type"—who in no way differed by any outward token from the various other types to be found among the German population. They were looked upon as German by their fellow citizens, just like the Huguenots or the Salzburg Protestants. Only a reminder about the difference in religious faith—when it survived and became known—could arouse old prejudices. The same reaction was extended to Protestants in Roman Catholic groups and to Roman Catholics in Protestant circles.

However, one important factor did have some negative influence on the generally benign position of German Jews. Unlike the Huguenots and the Salzburg Protestants, whose numbers had not increased for many generations, from roughly 1870 on the Jewish population because of the arrival of coreligionists from the East. These immigrants were descendants of Jews long ago exiled from Germany. When Jews were liberated in the Western nations, they became unwilling to endure the misery and growing suppression within czarist Russia. For many of them—the very poorest—Germany was only a waystation on the road to the United States—the free country on which all their hopes centered. Some, however—chiefly the sons and daughters of the well-to-do, unable to study at Russian universities or able to do so only under degrading conditions,* streamed to the German universities. Another group tried to prosper by engaging in trade within the flourishing German nation. Still others sought employment in industry, the crafts, or agriculture. Finally, the antisocial and criminal dregs concentrated on petty thievery, various kinds of fraud and shady dealings. As a result, the existing minimal percentage of German Jews in the general population registered a sudden rise—noted uneasily by Jews and Christians alike. However, even under these new conditions the Jewish share of punishable offenses was in line with that of other populations; though slightly higher than the Protestants' share, it was lower than that of the Roman Catholics.

This aspect, however, was only one of the consequences of the heavy migration from Eastern Europe, and not the most important by far. While the young intellectuals among the Eastern-Jewish newcomers adjusted quickly to conditions in Germany, and discarded their "foreign ways," the least educated and poorest among the refugees were not able to do so. And because they clung to their manner of speech—which sounded peculiar to ears accustomed to the High German vernacular—to their old-fashioned dress, and to their religious and other customs, the people they had come to live with could not recognize them for what they really were—compatriots, fellow citizens from the medieval German towns, exiled a long time ago and now at last returned. Since the end of the eighteenth century their old homeland had developed along lines very different from those experienced by these people in Russian ghettos. While the inhabitants of Western and Central Europe had for some time been enjoying the benefits of their newly won rights, the Eastern Jews had continued to live in deepest misery and under the most cruel suppression. They could sustain themselves only by their religious belief, frequently transfigured with mystical

---

*In order to obtain residence permits in the university towns where they wished to study outside their area of residence, young Jewish women eager for higher education, for instance, had to register with the Russian police as prostitutes—and this as late as the turn of the century.

overtones, and by strict adherence to a complex code of religious laws. The enlightened residents of the large cities found this way of life equally odd. After all, they had freed themselves from church interference in their private lives, and they looked upon such piety not as a virtue, but as superstition.

Under these circumstances it was almost a miracle that the nonintellectuals among the Eastern Jews—though often not until the next generation, which grew up in Germany—were able to adjust to an environment that was so completely new and occasionally beyond comprehension. Up to that point, they were seen by their new neighbors, Christians and Jews alike, as being both peculiar and alien. It was as if today a barefoot scruffy hermit, wearing a soiled habit, were to come down from a distant Alpine valley into a modern, bustling city, demanding in the supermarket goat's milk, wild honey, and flax for his spinning wheel.

In fact the influx of Eastern Jews did much to revive the anti-Semitism that, by 1870, had been kept alive mainly by a few fanatics. Now, however, the petit bourgeoisie finally had a new target for derision and scorn: a miserable heap of defenseless strangers—coreligionists, to boot, of those they were forced to look upon with envious respect.

Among these petit bourgeois filled with a new hatred against the Jews were some Germans of Jewish origin. How could it have been otherwise? Most of these were from the lower middle class and feared for their own livelihood. But some were highly educated people, including even one or two reputable scholars. However, narrow-mindedness is by no means rare among specialists, whether Jews or Christians, and it is possible that their aversion to the Eastern Jewish immigrants was in part an expression of selfishness and instinctive professional anxiety. Perhaps they already had a presentiment that the ranks of the despised and hated "late returnees" would give birth to a remarkable number of luminaries in science, who would attain the highest level of fame in Germany and later also in the United States.

The enormity of the loss to German civilization from the fact that countless thousands of disappointed Eastern Jews packed their bags and emigrated further afield, mostly to the United States and other overseas countries, would be revealed only much later. For the present let us examine the consequences of another unique procedure—the "cleansing" of the German universities accomplished by ousting all academics of Jewish, or even partly Jewish, origin. It was carried out in 1933 by a band of adventurers, failed careerists, misfits, and petit-bourgeois run amok, who had risen to power as a result of the world economic crisis, the panicky fear of Communism, and other unsettling circumstances.

The action began with the enforcement on April 7, 1933, of the "Law for the Restoration of the Professional Civil Service, " which deprived Hitler's political opponents as well as some of the civil servants of "non-Aryan" descent of their jobs. The law also affected employment in German universities and institutions of public law. Exempted from immediate dismissal were only "non-Aryan" active veterans who had seen active service in the First World War; officials who had started their civil service careers before August 1, 1914; and the fathers and sons of men who had died in that war.

Two years later, on November 14, 1935, the government decreed the dismissal of all "non-Aryans" still employed in the civil service and nullified the original exemptions. A further two years later, on January 26, 1937, the order came to dismiss even those officials whose spouses were not of "German or related stock." Helge Pross wrote in the first section, "Deutsche Ausgangssituation 1933" [The German Starting Position, 1933], of her *Die Deutsche Akademische Emigration nach den Vereinigten Staaten 1933–1941* [The German Academic Emigration to the United States 1933–1941]:

> Judging by the most reliable estimates, the number of those dismissed by the winter semester of 1934–1935 in accordance with the new laws amounted to 1,145, or 14.34 per cent of the total faculties of the universities and technical institutes during the winter semester of 1932–1933.
>
> If to this figure are added the assistants, the staffs of independent scientific or semiscientific institutes, such as state libraries, the figure rises to 1,684. "Natural departures," such as normal retirement or death are not included.
>
> However, these figures give only an incomplete pic-

ture of the National Socialist dismissal policies as far as
they affected the universities. After the winter semester
of 1934–1935 . . . but especially after the regulations of
November 14, 1935 went into effect, an additional number of teachers in institutions of higher learning were
victimized. According to a 1938 estimate, one-third of all
teaching personnel at universities and colleges were
dismissed, forcibly pensioned off, or transferred. By 1939,
presumably 45 per cent of all university positions were
newly filled or otherwise reassigned.

In his work *The Rescue and Achievement of Refugee
Scholars*, Norman Bentwich gives the number of university
lecturers dismissed during the first two years of the "Third
Reich" as roughly 1,200. But even these figures tell us very
little. The loss of a single professor with an international
reputation can considerably lower the scholarly level of a
university. The elimination of a whole number of leading
lights can make a laughingstock of a university faculty or
worse, allow it to dwindle quietly into oblivion.

William L. Shirer reports:

> In the University of Berlin, alone, where so many great
> scholars had taught in the past, the new rector, a storm
> trooper and by profession a veterinarian, instituted
> twenty-five new courses in *Rassenkunde*—racial science—
> and by the time he had really taken the university apart,
> he had eighty-six courses connected with his own
> profession.
>
> The teaching of the natural sciences, which in Ger-
> many had been so pre-eminent for generations, deterio-
> rated rapidly. Great teachers such as Einstein and Franck
> in physics, Haber, Willstätter and Warburg in chemistry,
> were fired or retired. Of those who remained, many
> were bitten by the Nazi aberrations and attempted to
> apply them to pure science.

Professor Wilhelm Röpke, himself dismissed from the University of Marburg in 1933, remarked, "It was an act of
prostitution, a mark of infamy staining the honorable history
of German education." And Julius Ebbinghaus, looking back
on that sinister period in 1945, commented, "While there

was still time, the German universities failed to oppose publicly and with all their might the destruction of scholarship and of the democratic state. They failed to nourish the flame of freedom and justice during the night of tyranny."

This failure proved very costly. By 1939, the number of university students had dropped from 127,920 to 58,325. Registrations dropped even more sharply at the technical colleges, which at one time had produced some of the best engineers and technicians in the world. Their numbers shrank from 20,474 to 9,554.

One sentence reveals far more graphically than any statistics the true situation of the German universities and institutes after the expulsion of "the Jews and their hangers-on" and their replacement with anti-intellectualism. At a banquet given by the University of Göttingen in honor of Bernhard Rust, the Nazi minister of culture, whose special area was "German science," he asked with concern whether the famous mathematical institute had really suffered from the legislated changes in personnel. The venerable professor David Hilbert replied drily in his East Prussian dialect, "Suffered? Nay, Mister Minister, it has ceased to exist."

Chapter 5

The Nobel Prize and the Order of Merit

What could have caused David Hilbert to claim that, after the expulsion of the Jews, his institute had practically ceased to exist? Apart from Hilbert himself, were there no other distinguished mathematicians of "Aryan" descent at this "queen of universities" (a term coined by Georg Christoph Lichtenberg)?

We may assume that Hilbert did not intend to have his pessimistic judgment of the condition and future of his institute understood in such a narrow sense. A considerable number of very distinguished mathematicians had been obliged to leave Göttingen University pursuant to the "racial" laws. For example, Paul Bernay had accepted an appointment in Zurich.

It was not, however, merely the loss of a number of distinguished university professors that Professor Hilbert was alluding to. Rather, it was the obvious intellectual desolation that resulted from the absence of any exchange of ideas between those who remained and their associates and friends of long standing. The fruitful stimulation from spirited discussions was sorely missed, as was contact with alert minds throughout Germany, men and women at home in the arts and sciences, whose main link with the universities had been through the expelled Jewish colleagues.

One such was Richard Courant. Not only Hilbert, but other scholars as well, had agitated unsuccessfully, of course—on his behalf. In contrast to all the theses of the anti-Semitic "racial" fanatics, he was the leading "practician," who had extended Hilbert's theories to develop the "direct" method. Courant had also been the actual organizer of the teaching of mathematics in Göttingen. His great contribution lay in increased emphasis on applied mathematics. Finally, he was coauthor of two important textbooks. One—*Funktionstheorie*—was written in collaboration with Adolf Hurwitz (1855–1919), the (Jewish) teacher of Hilbert; the other, *Methoden der mathematischen Physik*, was the joint effort of Hilbert and Courant.

Emmy Noether was the daughter of another mathematician, Max Noether of Göttingen (later Erlangen), praised by Nietzsche in his letters to Franz Overbeck. Apart from her own voluminous and distinguished work, she had been an important link with other faculties and universities. Her brother Fritz taught mathematics, electrotechnology and mechanics at the Breslau technical college. Both brother and sister were on friendly terms with a number of professors and artists—such as Felix Hausdorff, a (Jewish) professor of mathematics in Bonn, who, as a philosopher using the pseudonym Paul Mongré, was one of Nietzsche's friends and supporters. Another was Alfred Pringsheim, well-known collector of Italian pottery, professor of mathematics in Munich, and father-in-law of Thomas Mann.

Paul Bernay primarily tackled the foundations of mathematics along Hilbert's lines, for years cooperating closely with Hilbert, and contributed to the spread of his friend's ideas with a joint publication, *Grundlagen der Mathematik*, [Foundations of Mathematics].

These examples could go on and on, but the few may suffice to illustrate what David Hilbert meant when he declared that his own institute had ceased to exist. And the erosion did not apply only to Hilbert's field, mathematics; all of the most outstanding physicists on the Göttingen faculty had been expelled, including James Franck, the first Göttingen professor to receive the Nobel Prize in physics, and Max Born, who was awarded it after he had left Germany. Born was one of the leaders of the Göttingen school of physics and philosophy from which half a dozen Nobel Prize laureates emerged: Wolfgang Pauli, Werner Heisenberg, Paul Dirac, Maria Goeppert-Mayer, Enrico Fermi, and Otto Stern. Also at Göttingen was the future "father of the hydrogen bomb," Edward Teller.

The forced emigration of Max Born robbed Göttingen and Hilbert of further contact with Albert Einstein. It was Born who maintained a fascinating and productive correspondence with him. Until 1933 Hilbert himself had been in contact with Einstein at least once a year—at the annual meeting in Berlin of a distinguished group of artists and scientists, the members of the so-called peacetime generation of the Prussian Order of Merit (*pour le mérite*).

Albert Einstein had been admitted to the order in 1923, along with the painter Max Liebermann, the sculptor Hugo Lederer, the dramatist Gerhart Hauptmann, and the Göttinger mathematician Felix Klein (died 1925). Hilbert's award came in 1926. Did this mark of distinction—together with the other greatest honor bestowed by Germany, the shield of the German Eagle—afford artists and scientists some measure of protection against the racial laws? If it did not, does it at least give us a point of reference in assessing the cultural loss inflicted by the racial mania after 1933?

In reality, neither the Order of Merit nor the German Eagle protected "non-Aryans." Among the 1929 recipients were the glider pilot Robert Kronfeld and His Excellency, Theodor Lewald, the "non-Aryan" Reich commissioner for the Olympic Games. Kronfeld, who was Jewish, managed to emigrate to England. Theodor Lewald, who was only partly of Jewish origin, was permitted to keep his position until after the 1936 Games because his dismissal would have created a bad impression abroad; but afterwards he was speedily removed. Fortunately, he somehow survived the "Third Reich" in Germany and died at a ripe old age in Berlin in 1947.

We have already noted that the Prussian Order of Merit protected neither Albert Einstein nor Max Liebermann; they were fired and reviled all the same. Nor did it shield such "Aryans" as Max Planck, Nobel Prize laureate since 1918, member of the Order of Merit since 1915. In 1937 he was forced to resign from his post as president of the Kaiser Wilhelm Society for the Advancement of Science, as a consequence in large part of his courageous agitation on behalf of his Jewish colleagues. Another great German scientist, Richard Willstätter, a Nobel Prize laureate in chemistry since 1915 and member of the Order of Merit since 1924, moved to Switzerland in 1936 to escape the increasing anti-Semitic actions at the University of Munich.

This leaves the second part of the question concerning the "peacetime generation" of the Order. What points of reference does the list furnish regarding Jewish participation in the cultural life of Germany (or of Prussia)? What conclusions can be drawn that will aid us in estimating the cultural losses created by the persecution of the Jews?

The Order was established in 1842. That year a total of fifty-six German and foreign candidates were inducted into the order, including the composers Felix Mendelssohn-Bartholdy and Giacomo Meyerbeer, both of Jewish origin, and Karl Gustav Jacobi, who was, despite his comparative youth, the most distinguished mathematician after Karl Friedrich Gauss, who had recognized and supported Jacobi's work. Jacobi, the son of Jewish parents, was born in Potsdam in 1806. By 1860 a further fifty-three scientists and artists were granted the Order of Merit, and another forty by 1870; this last group included the German painter Eduard Bendemann, who was of Jewish origin. Thus the proportion of German Jews—4 out of 149—was not particularly large, even if considerably higher than was consonant with the proportion of Jews in the total population.

However, this impression is deceptive. A valid comparison requires omission of all those citations conferred on those whose connection with German culture is not evident, such as the poet Vasili Andreevish Zhukovski in St. Petersburg, the composer Gasparo Spontini in Italy, the zoologist and geologist, Louis Agassiz in Cambridge, Massachusetts, and the Parisian writer François René Vicomte de Chateaubriand.

This elimination changes the picture immediately, showing that in the years 1842–1870 there were 4 German Jews as against at most 100 German and Austrian non-Jews. Before recalculating, let us add the years from 1871 to 1918 to ascertain whether the imperial Germany of the Kaisers, with complete equality for German Jews, afforded a significant shift. During these forty-eight years a total of 186 orders were awarded in Germany and abroad. Focusing on contributions to German culture, we find that between 1871 and 1918 fewer than 120 scientists, artists, statesmen, writers, and engineers were thus honored; among that number only 3 can be counted as Jews: the violin virtuoso and composer Josef Joachim; the composer and incomparable pianist Anton Rubinstein, who, though born in the Ukraine, can be included in the German section, since he had been trained in Berlin by a German-Jewish teacher of composition, and always remained closely associated with German musical life for the rest of his days; and Adolf Mussafia, the Viennese scholar who had made a name for himself with his study of Romance languages.

It would seem, then, that the imperial period brought, not an increase in Jewish participation, but a slight decrease. Before jumping to premature conclusions, however, let us also make a brief survey of the years from 1918 to the present. Through 1933 the Order was awarded only thirty times and exclusively to Germans, who included the three men of Jewish origin already mentioned—Max Liebermann, Albert Einstein, and Richard Willstätter. With an interruption during the "Third Reich" the Order was not awarded again until 1952, when it was reconstituted "as a free and self-regenerating community of outstanding scientists and artists," as it was phrased in its preamble.

Since that time ninety-seven people have been inducted into the Order. By a generous estimate seventy-six can be linked to German culture. Four at most may be called German Jews by the same criteria used earlier. They are the famous nuclear physicist Lise Meitner; the art historian Erwin Panofsky; the Nobel Prize chemist Georg von Hevesy; and Otto Klemperer, the conductor and composer. It would seem, then, that there has been a steep rise in the proportion of Jewish recipients, perhaps occasioned by a desire for moral restitution.

However, we can safely ignore that aspect, since the reasons for the interruption in awarding the order during the Nazi terror results in a totally different picture. The numbers now reflect what Hitler and Goebbels would have called a list "entirely corrupted by Jewish poison."

The members of the Order inducted in the Hohenzollern period alone include a considerable number whom the "Third Reich" would have treated as "Jewish half-breeds." We need only name the architect Friedrich Hitzig; the meteorologist Heinrich Wilhelm Dove; the engraver Johann August Eberhard

Mandel; the Nobel Prize chemist Adolf von Baeyer; and the great astronomer Johann Friedrich Wilhelm Herschel. According to the findings of the Society for Jewish Family Research of Berlin of September 1931, Herschel was descended from Moravian Jews; he was the son of the Royal Hanoverian military musician Isaak Herschel and the grandson of the Royal Saxon court gardener Abraham Herschel. The same publication contains proof of the "non-Aryan" origins of another member of the Order, the founder of German agrarian chemistry, Justus von Liebig. His ancestors included a shoemaker, Samuel Abel, who married one Elisabeth, whose mother, Sophia Darmstädter, was a baptized Jew.

A considerable number of members of the Order were married to women of Jewish descent—from the sculptor Johann Gottfried Schadow to the judicial scholar Otto von Gierke, who was inducted as late as 1915. At least three of the scientists and artists honored with the Order married descendants of Moses Mendelssohn: the painter Ludwig Passini, the mathematician Peter Gustav Lejeune Dirichlet, and the writer Werner Bergengruen.

Still other members of the Order had "non-Aryan" daughters-in-law or sons-in-law, such as the physiologist Emile du Bois-Reymond, whose son, Alard, married Lili Hensel, also a descendant of Moses Mendelssohn. Reich Chancellor Bismarck's son, Herbert, was married to Marguerite Countess Hoyos, whose mother, Alice Whitehead, came from a wealthy Anglo-Jewish family. Its head at that time, Sir James Whitehead, sat on the board of the London Jewish Community.

These examples could go on to include several members of the Order whose Jewish origins cannot be accurately ascertained and are therefore considered "controversial." The composer Max Bruch, for example, was listed during his lifetime as a German Jew in the *Universal Jewish Encyclopedia* (New York 1939–1943) and in Dr. Adolph Kohut's two-volume *Berühmte israelitische Männer und Frauen in der Kulturgeschichte der Menschheit* [Famous Jewish Men and Women in the Cultural History of Mankind], published in 1901.

But shortly before the beginning of the Hitler regime, and nearly ten years after Bruch's death (he had never, by the way, objected to his inclusion among "famous Jewish men"), he was suddenly "Aryanized" in the strictly anti-Semitic encyclopedia compiled by P. Stauff. Never mind that he was the composer of probably the most popular Jewish religious music, particularly his arrangement for cello and orchestra of the "Kol Nidre." The "official" encyclopedia of Jews in music also omits Max Bruch. Even the title of "Kol Nidre" was missing from the index of musical works banned in the "Third Reich." Could the reason have been that Max Bruch had very influential "Aryan" relatives—the Krupp family in Essen?

The actual clarification of Bruch's status and that of eighteen or so other members of the Order is not important. For by now one thing should have become evident: the Order of Merit consists of an elite chosen by whoever is in power at the time. As such, it cannot help but reflect an accurate image, though on a greatly reduced scale, of the larger group from which its members were drawn. The Jewish middle class, then—and especially that of Berlin—would be represented just as heavily as it was on the playbill of the 1920s, which afforded such a revealing picture of the intimate fusion between Jews (and Huguenots) and segments of the nobility and the German-Christian bourgeoisie. It is therefore not surprising that the Jewish ratio was at least ten times that of the Jewish proportion of the total population.

Even a superficial glance at the list of distinguished members of the Order indicates that it could be conclusive only as regards some fields. There is a relatively large number of painters, engravers, musicians, archeologists, mathematicians, and natural scientists. Though membership is supposedly representative of the "nation of poets and thinkers," we find surprisingly few names of German philosophers and writers. Even some of the greatest names are missing altogether. It seems that the members were chosen, not only for individual achievement, but also and without fail by the criterion of the so-called higher interests of the state (which did not always coincide with the judgment of experts, or the general public, not to mention the opinion of posterity.)

German philosophy of the last 125 years is represented by only twelve members of the order. Conspicuous for their absence are Hegel, Marx, Nietzsche, and Max Weber. Nor are Friedrich Julius Stahl, Georg Simmel, Max Scheler, and Martin Buber on the list. The last four, together with Karl Marx, would have represented the strong Jewish strain in German philosophy, now completely absent from the membership of the Order. Not a single "non-Aryan" is among the elected philosophers, and only one—Albert Schweitzer—was married to a Jewish woman.

Even more surprising is the number of poets and writers who qualified for the Order. Not counting the purely military historians, there are exactly thirteen in as many decades during which the Order has been awarded. It could be concluded that only one German writer every ten years was worthy of the Order. Among those so honored there is not a single German Jew—naturally not Heinrich Heine. It is only among those chosen for the Order since 1952 that we find one Jewish "half-breed"—Carl Zuckmayer—and one "Aryan" married to a Jewish woman—Thomas Mann.

This underrepresentation in philosophy and literature—areas in which Jews were well represented otherwise—is no accident. First, these two areas are poorly represented altogether—indicating, perhaps, a marked uncertainty among the selection committees responsible for assessing philosophical and literary quality, or merely certain ideological and political considerations the committees felt compelled to honor. Second, the German writers, poets, and philosophers of Jewish origin, with few exceptions are much closer to what today would be termed "nonconformists" than are, for instance, the great "non-Aryan" scientists, jurists, and physicians.

Before addressing this question, however, and concluding our discussion of the Order of Merit, we will briefly deal with the German chemists among the membership. In the course of 125 years no fewer than nineteen of these were so recognized for their particular achievements.

Here the selection, viewed in retrospect, seems to have been a far happier one. At least many, if not all, of the great German chemists of the nineteenth and the first three decades of the twentieth centuries were inducted into the Order: Eilhard Mitscherlich, Justus von Liebig, Heinrich Rose, Robert Bunsen, Friedrich Wöhler, August Wilhelm Hofmann, Adolf von Baeyer, Richard Willstätter, and, in the later years, Otto Hahn, Otto Warburg, Heinrich Wieland, Georg von Hevesy, Adolf Windaus, Richard Kuhn, Adolf Butenandt, and the biochemist Kurt Mothes, of the University of Halle.

Almost exactly one-third of these "pour le mérite chemists"—six—were of Jewish origin. So we have a first fact to use in assessing the loss to this particular field by the Nazi racial mania. It is advisable, however, to check this finding, based only on the selection made for the Order of Merit. A comparison with the list of German Nobel Prize laureates in chemistry practically commands our attention.

Until 1933 Germany held the world's first place in chemistry, particularly in scientific research, as was clearly reflected in the Nobel Prizes. From 1901 to 1933 a total of thirty-one scientists* received the Nobel Prize for particularly distinguished achievements in the field of chemistry. Of these, fourteen were German nationals, five were British, four were French, three were Swedes, two were American, one was Dutch, one was Swiss, and one was Austrian.

The true extent of German preeminence in chemistry becomes clear when additional facts are considered. The Dutch laureate was selected while teaching and researching in Germany, where he was active for many years. Many others among the non-German laureates had studied at and graduated from German universities—such as the Scottish Sir William Ramsay, who had attended Tübingen University. The Imperial Chemical Industries (ICI)—the huge British chemical concern that gave British research scientists considerable backing was founded by a German, Ludwig Mond from Kassel, and developed by him into an industrial giant still headed by his descendants. Much additional proof exists of Germany's former greatness in chemistry. But nothing demonstrates it more clearly than the fact that up to 1933 more than half of all Nobel Prizes in chemistry were awarded to university professors and research scientists who were working in Germany.

Between 1934 and 1969 a total of forty-seven Prizes in chemistry were awarded. Of these, fourteen went to Americans, thirteen to the British; eight to Germans; two each to the Swiss, and the French nationals; and one each to Finland, Norway, Italy, Czechoslovakia, the Soviet Union, Sweden, Holland, and Hungary.

The extraordinary predominance of the Anglo-Saxon countries—3 to 1 as compared with Germany—and the emergence of the Scandinavians is clear. In actual fact, the situation looked even less favorable for the "Third Reich" and,

---

*Some laureates were awarded the Prize jointly with a colleague; all names are included in our count.

later, for West Germany. One of the nine German laureates, the Dutchman Petrus Debye, who received the award in 1936 while he was director of the Kaiser Wilhelm Institute in Berlin, emigrated soon thereafter to the United States, where he taught and where he died in 1966.

This special case leaves us with eight Germans from 1934 to 1969 as against thirty-one laureates resident in Anglo-Saxon or Scandinavian countries, or roughly two-thirds of all chemistry laureates during this period.

This leaves us with the question of the part Jews had in Nobel Prizes for chemistry in the years before and after 1933. We must also ask whether the strong increase in Anglo-Saxon and Scandinavian inclusion is related to the persecution of the Jews in Germany.

In fact, four of the fourteen German recipients in 1901–1933 were "non-Aryans." Besides Adolf von Baeyer and Richard Willstätter, who were also members of the peacetime generation of the Prussian Order of Merit, there were Otto Wallach, who received the Prize in 1910, and Fritz Haber, who was honored in 1918.

Haber's special achievements will be dealt with in a different connection. Otto Wallach, who came from Königsberg and died in Göttingen in 1931, was a student of Gustav Magnus and of Justus von Liebig. He became a university lecturer in 1873 and a professor in 1889. He was awarded the Nobel Prize "in recognition of his contribution to the development of organic chemistry and the chemical industry by his pioneering work."

Wallach, like Adolf von Baeyer, died before the Nazi seizure of power. Willstätter and Haber both died in exile. The latter voluntarily resigned all his posts in 1933 because he wished to be treated no better than his Jewish co-workers and colleagues who had been expelled.*

The decimation of the ranks of German chemists because of the persecution of the Jews soon affected the "Reich" most

---

*See Appendix for Haber's letter of resignation. Additional documents concerning the "Haber case," among others a report by Professor Hahn concerning the memorial service after his death, are also included. The memorial service was eventually allowed to be held in Berlin and served as a silent demonstration on the part of German scientists to protest Nazi racial policies.

unfavorably. The position of Germany before and after the Second World War on the worldwide "championship list" of Nobel Prizes in chemistry would have been far higher had it not been for the Nazis' reign of racial terror.

Max Ferdinand Perutz, for example, a professor at Cambridge University and British Nobel Prize laureate in chemistry in 1962, had emigrated to England in 1936, when he was a twenty-two year old chemistry student in Vienna. Two years later his Jewish parents were forced to flee and also found a refuge in England. In Vienna they had been major textile industrialists whose ancestors had introduced the first mechanized spinning mills and looms into Austria. England granted them asylum, possibly in recognition of what Great Britain owed other German Jews—the development of the textile industries of Bradford, Leeds, and Manchester had largely been their work. The founder of the Imperial Chemical Industries (ICI), Dr. Ludwig Mond from Kassel, previously mentioned, was also Jewish. Using his personal funds, he equipped the Davy-Faraday Laboratory, which became the Royal Institute. His son, Alfred, his successor in the chairmanship of ICI, was raised to the peerage, becoming the first Lord Melchett. Another German-Jewish immigrant (later Lord Hugo Hirst), founded the British General Electric Company, which he developed to its present-day importance.

Another Nobel Prize winner in chemistry, a Swede, Georg von Hevesy, was honored in 1943 "for his work concerning the use of isotopes as indicators for the exploration of chemical processes." The son of a privy councillor in imperial Austria, he studied first in Budapest, then at the Berlin technological institute, took his doctorate at the University of Freiburg, and worked in Zürich, and under Fritz Haber in Berlin. His training, his early research, and his teaching took him from Germany to Denmark and Sweden. In 1966 he died in Freiburg, a few years after returning to Germany, which he had left for the simple reason that he was also of Jewish origin. For him—as for numerous other Jews who were forced to flee beyond Hitler's orbit—Sweden became a second home. These scientists and artists made fundamental contributions to the scientific, artistic, and economic achievements of their adopted country.

The fact that the German-Jewish population had always contributed positively to the culture of this "Nordic-Germanic" country ought to have given the Nazi "racial" theorists some pause. The painter Isaak Grünewald, who studied with Henri Matisse, and worked in his native city of Stockholm, became one of the most vigorous shapers of modern European painting. The Josephson family gave Sweden a sizable number of artists and scientists—among them the painter Ernst Josephson, whose "Nöck" was particularly famous; the composer Jacob Josephson; the playwright Ludwig Josephson; the art historians Azel and Ragner Josephson; and finally, Erland Josephson, who succeeded Ingmar Bergman as manager of the Royal Theater in Stockholm. Early in the nineteenth century the Bonnier family emigrated from Dresden to Sweden and developed the publishing house founded by Albert Bonnier into the largest of its kind in Scandinavia; the same family produced such renowned artists as the painter Eva Bonnier. Oscar Levertin found his place among the outstanding men of Swedish literature as a poet and literary historian. Selma Lagerlöf's friend, the writer Sophie Elkan, translator of Pestalozzi, wrote a number of popular novels under the name Rust-Roest. Emil Schück, a professor for many decades, was at times president of the University of Uppsala; perhaps the greatest Swedish cultural historian, he wrote the history of the Swedish people, of Swedish literature (with Karl Warburg), and of the Swedish academy, to which he belonged from 1913 on. Karl Warburg belonged to the Scandinavian branch of this well-known German-Jewish family; he was deeply involved in establishing the famous Nobel Library.

These few examples, from the small "home team" of approximately 6,000 Swedish Jews before the onset of the German persecution of the Jews, demonstrate their immense cultural importance to this tolerant and helpful country in the north of Europe. During the Second World War, Sweden took in nearly all the Jews of Denmark and saved them from extinction; after the war the country also granted asylum to Jewish fugitives from Eastern Europe. A considerable number of the persecuted Jews of Germany found refuge in Sweden; among them were, along with Lise Meitner and the conductor Leo Blech, numerous German writers and poets of Jewish origin. Two prominent though strongly contrasting figures may serve as random examples: Nelly Sachs and Kurt Tucholsky.

However, before taking a closer look at these two and at the share of German Jews in German literature, we must return to Debye so as to come to a conclusion with regard to the situation of the chemists. As an "Aryan," Debye was not directly affected, and he would probably not have left Germany if he had not been so incensed by the persecution of his Jewish colleagues.

The three chemistry Nobel Prize members already mentioned—Perutz, von Hevesy, and Debye—would, under normal conditions, have added their strength not to the Anglo-Saxon and Scandinavian groups but to Germany. Such an eventuality would have redressed the balance, which unmistakably shifted to the disadvantage of German science entirely as the result of Hitler's maniacal racism. This loss to culture was also, of course, accompanied by disastrous consequences to the country's economy and therefore the general welfare.

Among the foreign Nobel Prize chemists, mainly the Americans, there are some scientists of German-Jewish origin who, without German anti-Semitism, might very possibly have joined German universities as students, teachers, and research scientists. A single example should suffice.

At the time of the "Third Reich," Melvin Calvin, now a professor at the University of California in Berkeley, was studying at the British University of Manchester. We can postulate that this native United States citizen may have preferred Germany, with its history of great scientists, for his studies, had it not been for the terror against the Jews. He might well have stayed on to teach in Berlin or Göttingen for a time. Two facts support this risky assumption. First, despite his Anglo-Saxon-sounding name, Melvin Calvin is of German-Jewish origin. Second, when he was awarded the Nobel Prize in chemistry in 1961, his acceptance lecture was dedicated almost entirely to German-Jewish scientists—Justus von Liebig, Adolf von Baeyer, Richard Willstätter, and Otto Warburg—whose great tradition he carries on in the United States.

With regard to chemistry, then, we can conclude that the signs of widespread loss, covering at least one-third of earlier research capability, are fully confirmed and that this deleterious outcome is the direct and indirect result of German anti-Semitism. Proof of this is found not only in the various membership lists of the Prussian Order of Merit, but also in an analysis of the distribution of Nobel Prizes in chemistry before and after 1933. This brings us to the question of whether the distribution of Nobel Prizes can also furnish useful information in an area in which the membership lists of the Order are almost silent—literature.

Between 1901 and 1933 a total of thirty-three writers of prose and verse received the Nobel Prize for literature. The distribution is: five Germans and five French; three Swedish, Norwegian, and British subjects; two Danes, Poles, Spaniards, and Italians; and one Belgian, one Swiss, one Irishman, one Indian, one United States citizen, and a stateless Russian living in France. The laureates' mother tongue, which is almost entirely immaterial in the exact sciences, is of the greatest importance in evaluating a literary work. This fact may explain in part why the literature of Scandinavia appears to be overrepresented and why, along with some world-renowned poets, some minor novelists who were practically unknown outside Scandinavia were singled out. The Stockholm juries seem to have been guided by criteria similar to those expressed by the novelist and playwright, Sholem Asch, who preferred Yiddish to every other language, claiming that the use of Yiddish allowed everyone to understand every word. Asch, was speaking half in jest; nevertheless, he pinpointed the dilemma that must be faced in judging literature one is unable to read at all in the original or only with difficulty.

We can, at least, attempt to appraise the works of the German recipients of the Prize. In the order in which they were selected between 1901 and 1933, the German recipients of the Prize are: Christian Theodor Mommsen, Rudolf Christoph Eucken, Paul Johann Heyse, Gerhart Hauptmann, and Thomas Mann.

Theodor Mommsen, born in Garding (at that time still Danish) in 1817, was a professor and historian at the University of Berlin. In 1902, at the age of eighty-five, he was awarded the Nobel Prize for literature with the citation that named him "the greatest living master of historical writing and in special recognition of his monumental history of Rome."

Rudolf Christoph Eucken, born in East Frisia in 1846, taught philosophy in Basel and Jena. His contemporaries saw him as a kindly and warmhearted man and an idealistic philosopher. In retrospect he appears somewhat naive and bombastic. Certainly he was not a gifted writer.

Paul Heyse, born in Berlin in 1830, was on his mother's

side a descendant of Moses Mendelssohn. The son of a Berlin university professor and noted linguist, Heyse studied classical philology, his dissertation dealing with Provençal poetry. At an annual salary of one thousand guilders, he became court poet to King Maximilian II of Bavaria. He developed a naturalistic style he referred to as the Falcon theory ("a strong German outline"), in which he wrote over a hundred novellas and several novels. He proved to be a truly brilliant translator of Italian poetry but had little success with his own verse dramas—though one of these, the patriotic *Kolberg* became the basis of a Nazi propaganda film urging "perseverance." He received the Nobel Prize for literature in 1910 as "Germany's greatest living poet," in the opinion of the secretary of the Swedish academy.

Gerhart Hauptmann was born in 1862 in Silesia and originally wished to become a sculptor. After discovering his true vocation, he rose to become the most significant German playwright of the turn of the century. The Nobel Prize for literature was awarded him in 1912. It is impossible to consider him in the framework of our examination without mentioning those men who made his work possible in various ways and helped him to gain recognition. The first of these was Max Heimann, a Jewish poet and essayist from Werder in the Mark. As a reader for S. Fischer Verlag, the publisher, he "discovered" Gerhart Hauptmann, promoted him in every possible way, became his close friend and eventually his brother-in-law. Heimann, a master of the German language and aphorisms, incidentally, coined the phrase, directed against the senselessness of the anti-Semitic assertion that practicing Jews could not be good Germans: "There is nothing unnatural in orbiting around two foci; some comets do it, as do all planets."

Max Pinkus played an even greater role in Gerhart Hauptmann's life. The Upper Silesian town of Neustadt was his home, and there he died at nearly eighty years of age in 1934. He belonged to a wealthy family of textile manufacturers and owned the famous linen- and damask-weaving mill of S. Fränkel. Max Pinkus, father-in-law of the Nobel Prize winner in medicine Paul Ehrlich, was a great friend of the arts, a selfless patron, particularly devoted to literature. Over a period of fifty years he cultivated his hobby into the famous Silesian Library containing 25,000 volumes. A close lifelong friendship tied him to Hauptmann, who after Pinkus' death, dedicated the requiem "Die Finsternisse" ["Darknesses"] to his great benefactor. Earlier he had erected a monument to his friend in the character of Privy Councillor Clausen in the play *Before Sunset*.

Finally, we must remember that Hauptmann's publisher, Samuel Fischer, was also a Jew; that the great German-Jewish theater manager Otto Brahm was the first to perform Hauptmann's plays; and that it was the pugnacious critic Alfred Kerr who helped to bring about the triumphal acclaim for Hauptmann's earlier works that had originally been rejected by conservative audiences.

In the period before 1933 Thomas Mann is the last German recipient of the Nobel Prize for literature. The son of a wealthy Hanseatic merchant family, he was born in Lübeck in 1875. At the age of twenty-five he achieved an extraordinary success with his novel *Buddenbrooks*. He was awarded the Prize in 1929 for this early novel and only secondarily for his subsequent essays, short stories, and novels, which dealt chiefly with the symptoms of decay within bourgeois society.

Always the great German novelist, Thomas Mann was forced to flee from Germany, was deprived of citizenship, and was robbed of all property. His works were banned from German libraries. He acquired, first Czech, then United States citizenship. But these changes did not stop him from being a German writer—as is obvious to anyone familiar with his *Doctor Faustus*, written in exile.

Mann used the considerable international prestige at his disposal to win homes for other refugees from the "Third Reich." He also became one of the great intellectual adversaries of Nazi tyranny, and after the war, he attempted, even if in vain, to bring about at least cultural and intellectual unification for Germany.

Thomas Mann's links with the German Jews were also many, going far beyond the fact that his wife was a daughter of the German-Jewish mathematician and art collector Alfred Pringsheim. Many artists, writers, and other celebrities of Jewish origin belonged to his intimate circle of friends. He sought the advice of Gustav Mahler, Arnold Schönberg, Bruno Walter, and Theodor W. Adorno for the difficult musical passages in *Doctor Faustus*. The characters of Rosenstiel and Breisacher in this novel—and even more so, all of the tetralogy *Joseph and His Brothers*—reveal how closely Thomas Mann felt connected to the German Jews.

Nevertheless, the fact remains that of the five Germans awarded the Nobel Prize for literature before 1933, only one—Paul Heyse—was of Jewish descent. If we take the Nobel Prizes as the only criterion, the participation of the German Jews in the literature of their culture would not have exceeded 20 per cent.

But before we discuss whether the Nobel Prize can really serve as a means for comparison, and what other possibilities there are for ascertaining the Jews' actual contribution to German literature, it may be worthwhile to look a little more closely at the other Nobel Prizes for literature.

From 1934 to 1969, thirty-two writers received the Nobel Prize. Six Prizes went to the French, five to the Americans, three to British, and two each to Italian, Soviet, and Swedish citizens and one to a Swiss. One prize each went to Ireland, Iceland, Finland, Denmark, Yugoslavia, Greece, Japan, Chile, Guatemala, Israel, and Switzerland.

After 1929, then, the German Reich and its successor states are not represented at all among the countries that could claim at least one Nobel Prize laureate for literature over three decades. The last award for Germany, in 1929, was when Thomas Mann was honored, shortly before he emigrated and took on American citizenship.

Of course the matter appears in a different light if we assume that nationality or residence do not determine one's culture, but that this is defined by origin, place of birth, allegiance to the home country, intellectual roots, and to a large degree, native language. In that view, even after 1933 German culture can, with more or less justification, claim a number of Nobel Prize winners, beginning with the laureate for 1966, Nelly Sachs. For thirty years a resident and naturalized citizen of Sweden, Sachs was born in Berlin into a well-to-do middle-class German-Jewish family. Before 1933 her writing was little known apart from a few expressionistic poems that appeared in magazines. These attracted the attention of Stefan Zweig—one of the "greats" of German literature of Jewish origin, who was never selected by the Nobel Prize committee. In 1921, Sachs also brought out a verse collection entitled *Legenden und Erzählungen* [Legends and Stories], dedicated to Selma Lagerlöf. The great Swedish writer then encouraged the young woman to develop her poetry; until that time Sachs' principal interests had been in music and interpretive dancing. It was mainly due to Selma Lagerlöf—and, after her death in 1940, to Prince Eugene of Sweden, whom she had asked for help—that Nelly Sachs was preserved for literature. At literally the last minute, Swedish intervention saved her and her mother from being transported to a Polish ghetto that was subsequently wiped out. She was thus able to find sanctuary and a new home in Stockholm, while all her friends and relations became victims of the "final solution." Her experience during the terrible years of suffering and her deep gratitude to the Swedish people brought Nelly Sachs' poetic gift to full maturity and to the climax, in 1966, when she was awarded the Nobel Prize, in recognition of "her outstanding poetic and dramatic works interpreting Israel's fate with powerful realism."

Nelly Sachs shared the prize with another poet who can readily be claimed as more than half belonging to German culture—Samuel Josef Agnon, Israel's outstanding poet. Agnon—whose real name was Czaczkes—was born in the little Galician town of Buczacz (then part of Austria) in 1888. At the age of fifteen he published his first poems in Yiddish. He lived in Berlin from 1913 to 1924, working as a writer and publisher. In Berlin he married a German Jew, Esther Marx. In 1919 he published his first longer work in German, entitled *Und das Krumme wird gerade* [And What Is Crooked Shall Become Straight]—which alone would be sufficient to assign a considerable part of his work to German literature, even at the risk of protests from Talpiot, the suburb of Jerusalem where Agnon spent his final years. He himself told an anecdote of being in a synagogue where the rabbi introduced him by saying, "Do you know who this man is? He is the world's greatest poet. No, what did I say? He is the greatest poet in Israel! No, what am I saying—he is the greatest poet in Talpiot!"

While Agnon would have accepted this modest identification, he would not tolerate a comparison between himself and Franz Kafka, who, though born and raised in Prague, must be included among the great Jewish names in German literature, worthy of, though not awarded, the Nobel Prize. Kafka once said of himself that he had "not caught hold of the last tip of the wind-borne Jewish prayer shawl, as the Zionists had done." Only a few of this gifted writer's stories appeared during his short lifetime. Kafka's principal works were not published until after his death in 1924. *The Trial*, *The Castle*, and *Amerika*, as well as letters and diaries, were edited by Max Brod, also a Jew born in Prague, another German literary great who was not awarded the Nobel Prize he deserved.

However, let us return to those recipients of the Prize who can—though only to a certain extent and with some reservations—be claimed for German culture. There was, for instance, Boris Pasternak, who was awarded the Nobel Prize for literature in 1958 and was forced to refuse it under strong pressure from his government. Though Pasternak was born in Moscow, his father, Leonid Pasternak, a painter and illustrator who painted portraits of Einstein and others, came from Odessa, a member of the remnant of the Eastern-Jewish middle class that had maintained cultural ties with Germany. This element is even more pronounced in Pasternak's mother, the musician Rose Kaufmann. As far as Boris Pasternak himself is concerned, it is interesting to note that he abandoned his study of law in Moscow at an early stage to go to Marburg in Germany a few years before the First World War. There he studied philosophy under the neo-Kantian, Hermann Cohen, founder of the so-called Marburg School. (Cohen, who was born in 1842 in Coswig and died in 1918 in Berlin, qualified with his major work, *Die Religion der Vernunft aus den Quellen des Judentums* [The Religion of Reason Arising out of the Sources of Judaism], as a Nobel Prize candidate for literature at least on a par with his more fortunate colleague in Jena, Eucken. Moreover, his *Deutschtum und Judentum* [Germanism and Judaism] should have made him eligible for the Order of Merit.)

As to Pasternak's connections with Germany, he translated into Russian not only Goethe's *Faust* and Kleist's *Prince von Homburg*, but also the poems of Rainer Maria Rilke whenever Stalin's government forbade publication of his own work. And while Pasternak's major work, the novel *Doctor Zhivago*, could not be published in the Soviet Union, it won great renown and many editions in Germany.

Another Nobel Prize laureate for literature whom West Germany could claim is Hermann Hesse, who was not Jewish.

Born in 1877 in southern Germany, he spent part of his youth in Basel, to which he returned frequently. His wife was from Basel, and since he became increasingly opposed to German nationalism after 1914, he gave up any idea of returning to Germany. He became a Swiss citizen and lived in the Ticino territory until his death in 1962. His strong antagonism to National Socialism formed a basis of mutual agreement with his numerous German-Jewish colleagues. He also maintained a close friendship with Romain Rolland. His *Glass Bead Game* was not allowed to be published in the "Third Reich." He claimed that one of his spiritual fathers was Baruch Spinoza, the Jewish philosopher who was expelled from the Jewish community by the rabbis of his day.

We might also attempt, at least up to a point, to claim the French philosopher Henri Bergson, literature prize laureate for 1927, for German culture. On both his father's and his mother's side he was of German-Jewish origin. But this exhausts our possibilities, at least as far as rescuing German literature, which was clearly neglected by the Nobel Prize committee for decades. Nevertheless, our study has shown that the proportion of Jewish poets, novelists, and philosophers among German writers of "Nobel Prize stature" is considerably larger than is revealed by the actual Nobel Prizes or by the membership lists of the Order of Merit. However, paraphrasing Kafka, we can say that we have got hold only of the tip of the iceberg of what was banned and burned and "obliterated" from public and private libraries in the "Third Reich" and subsequently killed by silence. After the catastrophic end of the Nazi nightmare only a small part of all these works experienced a sometimes surprising rebirth. The actual Jewish share of German literature is far larger than we can imagine. To do it adequate justice would require extending the scope of this chapter to encyclopedic size in order to encompass the innumerable mutual interrelations with the great non-Jewish figures of German literature. It would result in a complete history of nineteenth-and early-twentieth-century German literature, omitting only a very few important and some insignificant names.

However, this cannot and should not be our task. We will be content with an imaginary bookstore window in a large city shortly before the dawn of the "Third Reich." What would it have displayed?

A store window cannot feature everything—it must display a representative selection. Apart from the works of foreign and "Aryan" German authors—many of which would also soon be banned in the main—we would find the work of many German-Jewish authors.

Among the latest publications the window would include Döblin's *Berlin Alexander Platz*, Emil Ludwig's *Wilhelm II*, Vicki Baum's bestseller *Grand Hotel*, Wilhelm Speyer's slight but charming *Charlott etwas verrückt* [Charlotte Slightly Crazy], Lion Feuchtwanger's *Erfolg* [Success], Max Brod's novel *Eine Frau, nach der man sich sehnt* [A Woman One Desires], *Simson* by Felix Salten (creator of Bambi), and Franz Werfel's *Abiturieutentag* [Graduation Day]. Further we might find the sensational novel by Gabriele Tergit, *Käsebier erobert den Kurfürstendamm* [Käsebier Conquers the Kurfürstendamm], Arnold Zweig's *Sergeant Grischa*, and surely the latest printing of his *Claudia*. Still others would advertise *Der Fall Maurizius* [The Maurizius Case] by Jakob Wassermann, Ernst Toller's *Feuer unter den Kesseln* [Fire Under the Boilers], Walter Mehring's *Gedichte, Lieder und Chansons* [Poems, Songs, and Chansons], Joseph Roth's *The Radetsky March*, Anne Seghers' novel *Die Gefährten* [The Companions], Robert Neumann's amusing *Karrieren* [Careers], Stephan Zweig's fascinating biographies of Fouché and Marie Antoinette, Friedrich Torberg's novel . . . *Und Glauben, es wäre die Liebe* [In the Belief it was Love], Alfred Neumann's *Narrenspiegel* [Mirror of Fools], and Erich Mühsam's *Unpolitische Erinnerungen* [Apolitical Memoirs].

The adjacent window would display Kurt Tucholsky's *Lerne lachen, ohne zu weinen* [Learn to Laugh Without Crying]; a collection of essays, sketches, and poems from *Weltbühne* magazine, published by Rowohlt; Egon Erwin Kisch's *Der Rasende Reporter* [The Raging Reporter]; Franz Molnar's *The Play's the Thing;* and *Mord im Nebel* [Murder in the Fog] by Siegfried Trebitsch, a friend of George Bernard Shaw and a companion of Rainer Maria Rilke and Hugo von Hofmannsthal. Next to these we would find Rudolf Olden's *Justizmord an Jakubowsky* [The Execution of Jakubowsky], Arthur Schnitzler's *Fraülein Else, Die Katrin wird Soldat* [Katrin Has Gone for a Soldier] by Adrienne Thomas, Bruno Frank's

Politische Novelle [Political Novel], and *Sardinenfischer* [The Sardine Fishermen] by Elisabeth von Castonier. The display continues with the latest by Leo Perutz, Claire Goll, Richard Katz, Ludwig Wolff, Alfred Polgar, and Hermann Kesten. Ferdinand Bruckner's *Die Marquise von O* and *The Captain from Köpenick* by the half-Jewish Carl Zuckmayer might lie next to the plays of Carl Sternheim and Roda Roda's autobiographical novel.

The next window, reserved for sophisticated poetry, philosophy and political science, might feature Karl Wolfskehl's *Bild und Gesetz* [Image and Law], Else Lasker-Schüler's tale *Arthur Aronymus*, and a volume of poems by Elisabeth Langgässer (who was still very young and who, in 1936, was forbidden to write because of her Jewish origins on her father's side). There are also poems, aphorisms, and essays by Karl Kraus, Rudolf Borchardt, and Mascha Kaléko. This young woman, although only twenty, was already a literary celebrity in Berlin, where her poems were published in the *Vossische Zeitung* and the *Berliner Tageblatt*. She had been championed by Hermann Hesse and Thomas Mann as well as by Alfred Polgar and the man who actually discovered her, Monty Jacobs.

This window display would also include *I and Thou* by Martin Buber, Leo Baeck's *The Pharisees*, Max Scheler's *Die Stellung der Menschen im Kosmos* [Man's Position in the Cosmos], Maximilian Harden's last work *Von Versailles zu Versailles*, Ludwig Marcuse's biography, published in 1929, of Ludwig's Börne, Max Horkheimer's *Anfänge der bürgerlichen Geschichtephilosophie* [The Beginnings of Bourgeois Philosophy of History], Theodor W. Adorno's *Kierkegaard*, Herbert Marcuse's first work, *Hegels Ontologie und die theorie der Geschichtlichkeit* [Hegel's Ontology and the Theory of Historicity], and works by Kurt Hiller, Julius Bab, and Ernst Bloch, as well as Walter Benjamin's *Einbahnstrasse* [One-Way Street]. Benjamin had beaten the drum in Germany for Marcel Proust, the French novelist of German-Jewish ancestry on his mother's side. Besides books by Ernest Fränkel and Walter Fabian, we might find some surrealistic poems, perhaps Ivan Goll's *Die Siebente Rose* [The Seventh Rose], published in 1928, and most certainly the multi-volume history of modern culture by Egon Friedell, and an anthology of short stories compiled by Emanuel bin Gorion, whose real name was Berdyczewski and whose place of birth was Berlin. The latest biography of Theodor Herzl, widely read even among non-Jews, was written by Manfred George. (At the beginning of the "Third Reich" George succeeded in escaping to America by way of Prague, Paris, Spain, Prague again, Hungary, Yugoslavia, Italy, Switzerland, and France once more. In 1939 he began publishing the New York weekly *Aufbau* [Reconstruction] which speaks for the "other Germany" dispersed all over the world.)

Despite this lavish display of works all by German-Jewish writers, the hypothetical display windows can offer only a relatively small selection of all that "non-Aryan" poets, novelists, and thinkers contributed to German literature in the years just before Hitler's seizure of power. We did not mention earlier works except insofar as they were referred to in another connection. These writers would begin with Moses Mendelssohn and move through Dorothea Schlegel, Fanny Lewald, Ludwig Börne, Michael Beer, Berthold Auerbach, and Heinrich Heine, to end with Georg Hermann's and Alice Berend's novels depicting the Berlin middle classes, Paula Dehmel's children's books, Oskar A. H. Schmitz's essays, and Margarete Susmann's poems. Nor have we alluded to many who had begun to write and had been published, but who did not gain fame until later, such as Max Tau, Hilde Spiel, Balder Olden, Hannah Arendt, Hilde Domin, Marcel Reich-Ranicki, Wolfgang Hildesheimer, Hans Mayer, and Erich Fried (both members of Group 47), Ilse Aichinger, Ossip K. Flechtheim, Arthur Koestler, Manès Sperber (who grew up in Vienna and began to write and publish in Berlin), Salcia Landmann, Stephan Hermlin, Fritz Sternberg, Alfred Kantorowicz, Hans Steinitz, Peter Weiss, Hans Habe, Curt Riess, and Angelika Schrobsdorff. This group also includes Willy Haas (today "Caliban" in *Die Welt*), Wolfgang Ebert, Peter de Mendelssohn, and the painter of animals, book illustrator, and writer Erna Pinner (friend of Gottfried Benn and companion of Kasimir Edschmid on his world travels). Finally, besides Anne Frank, who was killed in Bergen-Belsen at sixteen and whose diary is one of the most widely read postwar publications in the German language, there is Edith Stein, student of Edmund Husserl and author of numerous works in philosophy and sociology. Born in Breslau, Stein converted to Catholicism in 1922 and, as a Carmelite, took the name Theresia Benedicta a Cruce. In 1942 she was deported to Auschwitz from the Dutch convent where she had found refuge and murdered along with millions of others.

The loss to German culture inflicted by the banishment, expulsion, and murder of a majority of German-speaking poets, novelists, and thinkers can only be estimated. It must also be taken into consideration that, together with those persecuted for their alleged "alien" origin, many "Aryan" proponents of German literature—some of the very best— were driven into exile, forbidden to write, arrested, even murdered for their refusal to bow to the dictatorship, to approve of the racial terror, and to assist through their work Hitler's preparations for war.

Certainly it is no misconception to assume that more than three-quarters of the German writers with worldwide reputations were forced by various means to stop working in 1933. Many were made mute forever.

The majority of these outcasts, of this elite of German intellectual life, who were driven into exile, into gas chambers, or into suicide—like Kurt Tucholsky, Stefan Zweig, Walter Hasenclever, Ernst Toller, Egon Friedell, and Walter Benjamin—were of Jewish origin. Unlike the scientists, artists, architects, and engineers, (whose work did not actually require use of the German language) few of these men and women, when they succeeded in fleeing, were able even in a limited way to continue their work. A great many—mainly those who found a new home in Israel—no longer wrote in German and have even changed their names. These include Moshe Ja'akov ben Gavriel, born in Vienna as Eugen Höflich; Schalom Ben-Chorin, descended from an old established Bavarian Jewish family; and Zvi Avneri, whose name used to be Hans Lichtenstein. Even the impressive number of contemporary poets, writers, and journalists of Jewish origin who are still or again writing in German mostly live abroad. After 1933 the places of those expelled, murdered, or otherwise lost to German culture were filled by others who were considered "true Germans," including crude opportunists and surely deluded idealists. Not a single one of them achieved the literary level, the variety and productivity of those who were treated as outlaws and outcasts. Thus a grievous chasm yawns between the last days of the Weimar Republic and the late 1940s. It was not until then that a German literature worthy of the name began to stir again.

Chapter 6

Crushed Laurels

In setting up a balance sheet intended to weigh the possible advantages against the possible disadvantages arising from Hitler's extermination of the Jews, we cannot avoid scrutinizing the course of the Second World War. In particular, we must ask whether Germany's prospects of winning this war improved or diminished because of the anti-Semitic measures.

Let us first examine a military question. Were there severe losses in fighting strength as a direct or indirect consequence of "racial" discrimination?

When, on September 1, 1939, Hitler used the Wehrmacht—the German army—to invade Poland without a previous declaration of war and thus unleashed the Second World War, the German Reich had roughly eighty million inhabitants, including those of the Saar, Austria, the Sudetenland, Memel, and Danzig.* To these must be added the Germans living in the "Reich Protectorate of Bohemia and Moravia."

The military forces recruited from this population and available in September 1939, comprised a field army of 1.4 million men and a reserve army of 1.2 million men, as well as

*Effective on September 1, 1939, the Free City of Danzig became part of the German Reich.

roughly 400,000 air-force troops, about 50,000 men in the navy, and 35,000 "Waffen-SS" (Weapons SS—as all special forces were called). About 500,000 civilians were also assigned to the armed forces, including women. Close to 4 million people—or a little under 5 per cent of the Reich's total population—were therefore inducted in the Wehrmacht when the war began.

As the war went on, the ranks of the three regular armed forces and the Waffen-SS swelled enormously. At the climax, in 1943, nearly 9.5 million men were in uniform, while at most 2.3 million civilians also served. If these maximum figures—nearly 12 million inductees altogether—are compared with the Reich population of 1939, mobilization approaches 15 per cent. However, if we base our calculation on the increased total population of one hundred million so-called Reich German and others of German stock during the later war years, then the highest degree of mobilization must have been approximately 12 per cent.

Using these figures, we will begin by asking what losses in personnel the German Wehrmacht suffered because those segments of the population affected by the anti-Jewish laws were not drafted or were speedily discharged if they had been inducted earlier. We must consult 1932 statistics, and assume that had there not been "racial" discrimination, the rate of Jewish emigration would have remained at its normal insignificant level.

Before 1933, there were 525,000 Jews living in the "old Reich." Four-fifths of them were German citizens. Practically without exception the remainder were eligible for naturalization on the spot. In Austria, there were somewhat over 300,000, and in the Saar region, Danzig, and Memel together, roughly 20,000 Jews. Somewhat fewer than 120,000 Jews, mainly of German nationality and German-speaking, lived in the areas of Czechoslovakia that were either annexed or declared a protectorate. Furthermore, there were at least 25,000 Jews in the Polish provinces that had been Prussian until 1920 and were reclaimed by Germany in September 1939. The total amounts to roughly 1 million people or nearly 1.2 per cent of the Reich's population. (We must remind ourselves, however, that we are dealing with a hypothetical figure. In reality it was really considerably reduced by emigration, flight, and expulsion.)

These Jews are clearly definable by their membership in religious congregations. In addition, there were those who were counted as Jews by the "racial" laws, although they themselves did not practice the Jewish religion. Then there were the "Jewish half-breeds" and those "Aryans" married to spouses who were Jewish or considered to be Jewish. We can only estimate the numbers in these categories, especially for those areas that were only gradually incorporated into the "Greater Reich."

In April 1935—that is, two years after the start of increased emigration—the Reich Ministry of the Interior gave the "non-Aryan" population of the current Reich as 2.3 per cent of the total population. The figure encompassed "Full Jews (Mosaic), 475,000; Full Jews (not Mosaic), 300,000; half-breeds 1st and 2nd grade 750,000; a total of 1,525,000." Although this compilation omitted "Aryan" spouses, it proved to be far too high, at least in the figures for "half-breeds."

In the 1939 census, the number of "Jewish half-breeds" was only one-third the number of "Full Jews."

But even these more accurate figures do not shed much more light on our investigation. First, they do not disclose to what extent the group of "half-breeds" in particular seized the opportunity to emigrate, as was possible until 1939. Second, certain other differentiations were introduced by the Wehrmacht, making it more difficult to estimate their actual personnel losses. For instance, all "Jewish half-breeds 1st grade" (half-Jews) had to be eliminated from active service, with only a few exceptions. "Half-breeds 2nd grade" (those with only one set of Jewish grandparents) could, as a rule, remain with their regiment, but only in exceptional cases would be given officer's rank; this last provision also applied to the husbands of "non-Aryan" women.

Despite these difficulties in arriving at precise numbers, we can venture a cautious estimate, using the fairly accurate data for the denominational classification of all the inhabitants of those areas which subsequently formed the "Greater German Reich" and proportions gathered from the 1939 census. The result reveals that *without the anti-Jewish measures* and the resultant emigration, in September 1939 roughly 2.8 million persons of German nationality and language would have been affected directly or, as spouses of "non-Aryans," indirectly by racial-discrimination laws.

Of this number, 12 per cent, or 336,000 men and women, would, had all of them been in the country and not subject to special treatment, have been drafted. This impressive figure would seem to furnish the required information about the total loss of personnel the German armed forces suffered because of the "Jewish" policy that took effect in 1933. Such a conclusion, however, would be quite mistaken.

The "non-Aryans" within the Reich were not only exempted from military service; they were held to be hostile. During the war, therefore, a considerable number of people, normally available to the armed forces, were declared "indispensable" and withdrawn from their normal military duties to be used against civilians who, seen objectively, were either fellow citizens or harmless noncombatants in conquered territory. We can only guess at the number of soldiers of every rank who were "relieved of their proper duties" in the pursuit of anti-Semitic measures. Numerous clues, however, support the conclusion that the decimation of personnel in the armed forces resulting from active persecution of the Jews can be placed at 40,000–50,000 men. Some of these were officials of the "Jewish Affairs Department," guards, ghetto sentries, or working in the administration, where they sorted and registered the booty taken from the Jews. Some belonged to the SS Deathheads units and the special task forces that prepared for and carried out the mass killings.

Along with their victims, who were nationals of the German Reich, and those who escaped the "final solution" but were deemed unworthy of military service, the controllers, guards, and members of the execution squads together comprised a noncombatant army of nearly 400,000 men—a group larger than the totality of the Weapons SS in 1943, and nearly as large as the entire armed forces of today's West Germany.

Before we look further into other and more important disadvantages to wartime Germany as a result of the persecution of the Jews, we must first give some thought to the soldiering abilities of those disqualified in 1939 as unfit for military service. Today, when Jewish militancy and the courage of Jewish men and women are being tested daily and not found wanting, and at a time when the combat effectiveness of the Israeli army has become a long-standing historical fact, doubts about the military aptitude of the Jews must appear absurd. Nevertheless, it is just possible to object that it is quite a different matter to fight for one's own country and to take up arms for some nation in which one's people are a tiny minority. This possible objection is easy to counter. The military statistics of the First World War leave no doubt that the German Jews made exactly the same sacrifices as all the other German groups.

From 1914–1918 roughly 100,000 soldiers of the Jewish faith, including a great number of volunteers, served in the German army, the navy, or the colonial troops. The extent of mobilization, which was almost exactly 17 per cent of the total population, was slightly higher for Jews—17.7 per cent—because of the greater number of young Jewish volunteers.

The proportion of Jewish combatants on active duty and of Jewish war dead was exactly the same as the percentage for comparable groups—for example, the total population of such major cities as Munich. But even a hundred years earlier the German Jews had already demonstrated a patriotism completely in line with their military capabilities. In the Wars of Liberation of 1812–1813 the percentage of Jewish volunteers was more than three times the proportion of Jews in the total population. Jews fought with Lützow's volunteers—for instance, the painter Philipp Veit. Even in the most exclusive regiments they were promoted to officer rank "for outstanding bravery"; one lieutenant of the guards, Meyer Hilsbach from Breslau, who fell at Grossgörschen, serves as an example. There are at least seventy-one known cases of Jews who were awarded the Iron Cross, including Meno Burg, who became known as the Jewish Major. Even the Prussian Order of Merit, the highest Prussian distinction for bravery was awarded to such Jews as Simon Kremser, who, when he was war commissioner on General Blücher's staff in 1806, had displayed the greatest sangfroid in rescuing the Prussian war treasure from capture by the French. Esther Manuel, called Grafemus, the young woman volunteer who was glorified in the "Third Reich" as "Black Hunter Johanna," was also Jewish. After she was wounded twice, she was promoted to the rank of sergeant major and given the Iron Cross.

Jewish patriotism during the First World War was therefore taken for granted as merely the continuation of a tradition that was over a century old. In the period 1914–1918 more than 50,000 "full blooded" Jews, including roughly 35,000 members of communal Jewish congregations, were decorated for bravery. Among them were two of the youngest war volunteers, Josef Steinhardt, born in 1899 in Mannheim, a sergeant who died at the front in 1917, and Richard Bing, born on February 12, 1899 in Beuthen. The very youngest German volunteer was Eugen Scheyer, a young Jew who was only fourteen years old at the time he enlisted. The first member of the imperial diet to die in battle was the volunteer Ludwig Frank, whose death occurred as early as September 3, 1914 at Lunéville; he was a Social Democrat of Jewish origin. Jewish student fraternities joined the colors in a group, and we know of Jewish families where as many as ten sons joined up at the beginning of the war.

Flight lieutenant Wilhelm Frankl, who died in battle in 1917, was awarded the Prussian Order of Merit. Flight lieutenant Max Pappenheimer, who was killed in 1918, received the Golden Cross for Military Merit "for a feat of outstanding heroism in the face of the enemy." At least four other Jewish soldiers were awarded this distinction during the First World War. As chance would have it, the last Prussian general to receive the Order of the Black Eagle, the highest distinction to be conferred by the disintegrating monarchy, was Walter von Mossner, who was given the medal in the autumn of 1918. Mossner was born in Berlin in 1846. It was only against the violent opposition of the officers' corps and after the king had asserted himself on his behalf that he was able to become an ensign in a feudal regiment of hussars. He achieved the rank of commander, first in the hussars guards, then in the guards' cavalry division, and before he was pensioned, he was Governor of Strasbourg. In 1914 he chose to be reinstated as a commanding general.

These few examples deal exclusively with the military achievements and careers of "full blooded Jews" by the definition of the Nazi "racial" laws. Let us also mention a few of the countless thousand "Jewish half-breeds" who took part in the First World War and distinguished themselves then or later in one manner or another. The Prussian cavalry general (and Turkish marshal) Otto Liman von Sanders, for instance, was born in 1855 in Pomerania, the son of the Jewish estate owner. Shortly before the outbreak of the war, he became head of the German military mission in Constantinople and, as Turkish commander in chief, the victorious defender of the Dardanelles and the "Lion of Gallipoli." Admiral Felix von

Bendemann, head of the naval station on the North Sea, was
the son of the Jewish painter, Eduard Bendemann. Lieutenant-
general Johannes von Hahn, the grandson of Elkan Markus
Hahn, led the Thirty-fifth Infantry Division in 1914 and in
1918 took over the command of the Posen fortress; after the
war he joined the right-wing German Nationalist Party. Theodor
Duesterberg, grandson of the head of the Jewish community
in Paderborn, Selig Abraham Duesterberg, was a brilliant
general staff officer; after being heavily wounded at Ypres he
was transferred to the supreme command of the army, where
in November 1918 he spoke out passionately against acceptance of the armistice conditions. Soon after the war, he took
over as "deputy leader of the league" of the Nationalist Party's
veterans', the "Stahlhelm" [Steel helmet], association, and in
1932 he was the right-wing candidate opposing Paul von
Hindenburg in the presidential election. Because he was of
Jewish descent, Duesterberg was relieved of all his posts in
April 1933 and expelled from the "Stahlhelm." Franz von
Stephani was the last commander of the guard battalion of the
First Prussian Infantry regiment in 1918. From 1933 on,
despite his Jewish descent, he was "league captain" of the
"Stahlhelm." He also served as a member of the Reichstag
and held the rank of Obergruppenführer in the Storm Troopers.
Finally there is Erhard Milch. In the First World War he
achieved the rank of captain in the air force. After 1933 he
was declared to be "Aryan" by his war comrade Hermann
Göring (who declared, "I'll decide who is a Jew"). At the
beginning of the Second World War in 1939 Milch was a
general in the air force and denied his true origin by disown-
ing his Jewish father, a senior apothecary in the navy. Eventually Hitler promoted Milch to the rank of Field Marshal.

According to official records, in 1934 only five officers and
thirty-four men of "non-Aryan" descent were discharged from
the Reichswehr, as the hundred-thousand-man army of the
Weimar Republic was called. Only two officers and nine men
were dismissed from the navy. However, a number of officers
had retired much earlier.

One young naval officer in particular was forced to take off
his uniform as early as 1930, not because of his Jewish
descent, but for "improper conduct in a love affair." This was
Reinhard Tristan Eugen Heydrich, son of a musician who
founded the First Conservatory in Halle for Music, Theater,

and Education. The father is listed in Riemann's 1916 encyclopedia of music as "Heydrich, Bruno, actually Süss."

Reinhard Heydrich was born in Halle in 1904, joined the Nazi Party after his dismissal from the navy, and in 1931 became Himmler's deputy for secret service and security.

After 1933 Heydrich headed the political police in Bavaria, in 1934 also took over the Prussian secret police (Gestapo), and in 1936 became "Chief of the Security Police," which oversaw all political and criminal police organizations of the Reich. In addition, he himself established and built up the Party "Security Service" (SD) within Himmler's jurisdiction. It was this extraordinary instrument of power that brought him his speedy advancement.

In September 1939, shortly after the outbreak of war, his Party and state functions were amalgamated. As head of the "security police and SD" with the ranks of SS Obergruppenführer and general of police, he became controller of the "Reich Security Central Administration" (RSHA), which embraced all the security and criminal police departments, the Gestapo, the SD with its own foreign secret service, and, during the war, the notorious "special units," which were in charge of concentration camps, gas chambers, and other murderous activities.

Heydrich clearly had one of the strongest positions of power as well as command over the total apparatus of the terror wielded by the "Third Reich." His only superiors were Heinrich Himmler, "Reichsführer SS" (Reich Leader SS) and the Führer (Hitler) himself. And since Heydrich surpassed Himmler in energy, intelligence, and organizing talent—and most certainly in brutality, unscrupulousness, and cunning—he felt destined to be Hitler's successor—even before he was named "Reich Protector" in Bohemia and Moravia" and ruled in Prague.

Hitler himself was quite aware of Heydrich's Jewish descent, and Himmler also knew. Robert M. W. Kempner, United States prosecutor at the Nuremberg War Crimes Trials, reports in *Eichmann and Accomplices* that when the conjecture was first raised during preliminary questioning, he had spoken to the defendants and witnesses about it on various occasions.

The testimony established the fact that, within the terms of the racial laws of the Third Reich, Reinhard Heydrich had not been by any means "racially pure." The official of the Third Reich responsible for such racial questions, the former state secretary within the Ministry of the Interior, Wilhelm Stuckart* "responsible" for racial and half-breed problems, declared to me on May 25, 1946, "Through my departmental manager, ministerial adviser Hering, responsible for this subject, I was informed that Heydrich, whose father had headed a music school in Halle, had been considered Jewish or partly Jewish. I therefore had the matter investigated by the chief of counter-intelligence, Admiral Canaris. He succeeded in obtaining photocopies of the certificate of origin. They proved the non-Aryan descent of Heydrich. Canaris deposited the photocopies outside Germany and informed Heydrich accordingly. He himself was thus able to protect himself against any attack by Heydrich."

This statement was later confirmed in various ways. According to Joachim C. Fest, in *The Face of the Third Reich*, there is the testimony of a pianist, Helmut Maurer, who worked with Canaris, one of Heydrich's strongest opponents. As late as 1940 Maurer was able to obtain copies testifying to Heydrich's "non-Aryan" descent from the Halle records office. As Maurer recalled, Heydrich's ancestors on his father's side were of Jewish origin. This assumption seems to be contradicted by a document available in a photostatic copy at the Institute for Contemporary History in Munich, a certificate issued by the Nazi Party in 1932–1933 at the request of the gauleiter of Halle-Merseburg, one Jordan. The document examines Heydrich's paternal lineage and declares it to be without blemish. Martin Bormann's personal file on Heydrich contains a list of ancestors which omits the names, parents, and origin of the maternal grandmother. It can no longer be definitely determined whether on his father's side or his mother's side or even on both Heydrich was fully or partly of "non-Aryan" descent. The fact that he was at least partly of Jewish descent, however, is no longer in doubt, since we have numerous remarks by both Himmler and Hitler that have been preserved

---

*Jointly with Hans Marie Globke (later Secretary of State in the Adenauer government), Stuckart drafted the commentary covering the so-called "Blood Protection Laws."

by several reliable witnesses, sometimes in their diaries. Unquestionably both Hitler and Himmler knew that Heydrich was "non-Aryan." The bureaucratic "Reichsführer SS" (Himmler) therefore thought he would have to part with the head of his secret service. But after a lengthy conversation with Heydrich, Hitler found the "blond beast"* to be a highly gifted but equally dangerous man, whose gifts should be retained for the Nazi movement. Such people could be employed if one had a hold over them. For this purpose, his non-Aryan descent was eminently suitable, as already demonstrated by Canaris.**

Subsequently Hitler charged Heydrich with what Hitler considered "the most important task of all"—the "final solution of the Jewish problem." Heydrich prepared for and commenced the execution of this ghastly command. That continuation of the organized mass murders had to be left to his associate, Adolf Eichmann, was due entirely to the fact that on June 4, 1942, Heydrich, the "Reich Protector," was assassinated. According to Himmler's confidant, Felix Kersten, in his diary, Hitler bitterly compared Heydrich's death to a "battle lost."

With these words by the "Führer," let us move our examination from the quantitative and qualitative inroads made on the military potential of the Nazi Reich because of its anti-Jewish policy, to a source of losses far greater than those of a battle. We are referring to the "non-Aryan" human potential that the Nazis tried to exterminate, while including in its ranks only the sum, represented by scoundrels such as Heydrich.

There is a macabre irony in the fact that the cause of those immensely greater military (and political) disadvantages to the Third Reich lies in the special mandate Hitler gave his latter-day Torquemada, of whom Himmler said to Kersten, "He had conquered the Jew within himself purely intellectually and had swung over to the other side. . . . In his fight against the Jews, the Führer really could not have picked a better man than Heydrich. He knew no mercy toward the Jew."

The mandate given by Hitler to Reinhard Heydrich, con-

*This is what Heydrich's coworkers in the SD called him. See Willy Frischauer, *Himmler, The Evil Genius of the Third Reich* (London, 1953), p. 35.

**Information taken from Felix Kersten, *The Kersten Memoirs* (New York, 1957).

cerning the "final solution of the Jewish problem" on January 24, 1939, and the extension of the "German sphere of influence in Europe" on July 31, 1941, sealed the fate of most of the Jewish communities in Europe. But it also determined the end of the Third Reich and of Hitler as well. Why this should be so requires some amplification.

In the autumn of 1939 Hitler unleashed the war he had intensively prepared for over the years and had wanted from the very start. Despite the pact just concluded with Soviet Russia for friendship and nonaggression, his principal aim was the conquest of all of Eastern Eurpoe, penetrating deep into Russia. From the West he really wanted nothing except to be left unhampered during his eastern campaign. The declarations of war by France, Great Britain, and the Commonwealth nations following his attack on Poland he considered a regrettable misconception of his true intentions and a minor interference without serious consequences to his ultimate objective. As far as France went, he could easily remedy the situation by speedy conquest before he undertook the actual eastern campaign, to which the conquest of western Poland was merely a prelude. As for England, negotiations would do the trick, and he hoped to make it clear to the British that in reality there were no differences of interests between Berlin and London, but rather far-reaching mutual agreement, at least concerning the assessment of the "Bolshevik world danger." It was precisely in London that Hitler hoped to find understanding for his intention to concentrate all German energies on conquering space in the East, destroying the Soviet power, and gradually establishing a Germanic Reich of "the plow and the sword" from the Rhine to the Volga. This project was to proceed hand in hand with the abandonment of any claims to overseas colonies, maritime supremacy, and hegemony in world trade.

Hitler's premise—that Germany, "the nation without living space," was not viable without considerable expansion of territory—was fundamentally mistaken, of course. This assumption, once widely held, has long since reached the point of absurdity, especially in West Germany. Never before have so many Germans lived so closely together and enjoyed such material prosperity. Nevertheless, Hitler's actual objective, and that of his followers, was the violent acquisition of space in the East at the expense of Russia, Poland, and the border states. Only the conquest of such "living space," they argued, could guarantee the existence of the German people and insure the Reich's development into a world power. However, the noble aim required war, initially against Poland, then against Soviet Russia.

The basic features of this plan can already be found in the chapters setting out this program in Hitler's *Mein Kampf:*

> The right to claim soil and territory can become a duty if, without extension of their area, a great people appear doomed to extinction. . . . Germany will either be a world power or cease to exist. To be a world power requires the size which in modern times confers the necessary standing as well as life for its citizens. . . . With this, we National Socialists consciously draw a line under the foreign-policy guidelines of our prewar days. We start where they left off six hundred years ago. We stop the eternal Germanic drive to the South and the West and cast our sights on the land in the East. At long last we put an end to the colonial and commercial policies of the prewar era [which, as he explained elsewhere brings Germany into conflict with England, and this should be avoided at all costs] and we convert to the territorial policy of the future. If, however, today in Europe we speak about new territory and soil, we can think primarily, *only of Russia* and its subject border states. Destiny itself seems to point a finger in this direction. . . . The huge nation in the East is ready to collapse. We have been chosen by fate. . . . Our task, the mission of the National Socialistic movement is to arouse our own people to the political insight that its future will be achieved, not by the intoxicating effect of a campaign like Alexander's, but rather in the industrious labor of the German plow for which the sword has only supplied the land.

Like most of the Führer's ideas, this plan for colonizing the East at the expense of a Russia ripe for disintegration was not new. As early as 1914 something of the kind was already in the minds of many, politicians, officials, and military men— some of them quite influential—not to mention all kinds of visionaries.

At that earlier time it was, of course, the czar's Russia that was considered ripe for assault. In hindsight it can be said that the German planners of 1914 were a little more realistic than those of 1939. After its humiliating defeat in the Russo-Japanese war of 1904–1905 and the numerous workers' and peasants' revolts, suppressed only with difficulty, it was true that Russia was quite vulnerable. And whoever chose to take the field against Russia in 1914 with the aim of abolishing the despotism of the czar's regime could be assured of the applause, not only of the middle class, but also of the workers in every Western nation.

The latter argument, however, does not apply to Britain and France. The usefulness of the alliance, however unnatural, between the Western democracies and the czarist empire was clearly too important, at least for as long as the attacking Germans had superior strength. It was, however, persuasive in Germany itself, where resistance to the war by the socialist-leaning working classes had to be overcome. The same was true in the neutral nations, most of all in the United States, where strong sympathies with Germany were intensified by the onset of hostilities with the hated czarist empire.

But who were Germany's friends in the United States at the beginning of the First World War? This question is of great importance, not only because America's subsequent entry into the war against Germany was crucial to its outcome, but also because the answer allows us to arrive at significant conclusions that throw quite a bit of light on the disadvantages to Germany during the Second World War of its anti-Semitic policy.

At the start of the war in 1914, it was natural for the emigrants from Germany, including many Jews, to be in sympathy with their old home. Furthermore, the strong Irish element in the United States was pro-German because it saw Germany as a powerful ally in the Irish struggle for liberation. The third important force in the United States that sided unequivocally with Germany was the mass of Jewish emigrants from Eastern Europe, which formed the largest population group—roughly 1.3 million people—in New York alone.

How strong the pro-German feelings among Americans of Eastern Jewish origin were—not only at the start of the war, but as late as the beginning of 1916—is documented in an article by Dr. S. M. Melamed that appeared in *Süddeutsche Monatshefte* in February 1916. It mentions among other things that the friends of the Entente were "highly incensed by the openly pro-German attitude of the American-Jewish masses, expressed daily in the Yiddish press." To explain this attitude, the article continues, "The [Jewish] masses do not wish to suppress these sentiments and relinquish their vital interests. Today they preach a very practical policy: 'We go along with the Germans because we expect them to liberate our suppressed brothers in the East [of Europe], because they are the enemies of our enemies, and—the main motive—because we are linked to Germany by cultural bonds of over five hundred years' duration.'" What is more, Germany had remained a source of inspiration: "All the great cultural movements of the Jewish masses in East Europe, from the Enlightenment . . . to Zionism have taken fire from German culture, and despite the thirty years of anti-Semitism* in Germany, the cultural ties between Germans and Jews have not been broken. This cultural association with the Germans and the anticipated political deliverance of the Eastern European Jews with German aid determines the outspoken pro-German attitude of the American Jewish masses."**

The Eastern Jews of America felt very strongly pro-German and had high hopes for a victory of the Central Powers over Russia even though only memories linked them with the Old World. How much greater, then, were the sympathies and hopes for Germany and its war efforts on the part of those Jews who still lived in Eastern Europe?

This topic, too, is discussed in the February 1916 issue of *Süddeutsche Monatshefte*, which deals entirely with this question. Various contributions by reputable experts illuminate the subject.

There is, for instance, a report by Silvio Broedrich. According to Broedrich, who was familiar with conditions in Kurland (later Latvia), the roughly 40,000 Jews resident in the area

---

*This reference is to the new anti-Semitism of the second half of the nineteenth century, which was no longer based only on religious grounds but was "racial" and political. Begun in Austria, it gained a foothold in Germany.

**See Appendix for the Yiddish poem by Morris Rosenfeld, living in New York, "Hoch der Kejser".

before 1914 formed a "community of consciously pro-German sentiment." German-speaking, they worked closely with the Germans of Kurland in political matters. As a consequence, even in peacetime, the Kurland Jews were subject to a lot of trouble from the Russians. This did not deter them from retaining their loyalty to the Germans even after the war had started. "Their highest hopes for a union with the German Reich depend on a victory by the Germans, just as much as ours do. All of those who have lived with them in Kurland from the beginning of the war until their dispersion* will bear witness to this."

A former Russian university professor, who wished to remain anonymous for the sake of relatives left behind, reports that the Jews of Lithuania "spoke a special dialect with some affinity to High German." They "wear modern clothing, and beards trimmed in European style are not uncommon."

The "Litvaks"—as the Jews living in Lithuania (in Vilna, Kovno, and Grodno) were called—accounted for approximately 15 per cent of the total population of 4.7 million people. With the Germans they formed the "essential section of the urban population." The "Litvaks," too, looked forward to a German victory over the Czar as a means of substantially improving their position, and the great majority of them sympathized with the Germans. The feelings of the roughly two million Jews of Russian Poland are made clear in extracts from the wartime diary of an anonymous "well-known and respected figure in the public life of the Polish Jews, totally reliable."

November 23, 1914. A short summary of the most frequent denunciations . . . against the Jews, which the Russian officers believe and which have led to many unjustified punishments and executions:

1. The Jews had taken a coffin for burial, but the coffin had contained not a corpse, but gold for the Germans. . . .

2. The Jews stuff geese with gold coins and then take them to Germany.

3. A Jew had suddenly thrown himself to the ground

---

*Roughly 30,000 Kurland Jews were deported along with the leading Germans during the first fifteen months of the war. The Russian military authorities sent most of them to Siberia.

in an epileptic fit, while in reality he had been speaking to the Germans through a secret telephone. . . .

4. The air-force officers throwing bombs on Russian positions and towns were . . . Jews.

A witness, the diary went on, testified that through field glasses she had seen the officers' *tallis* (prayer shawl) and *peies* (ritual curls).

This and similar documents are supplemented with reports that make harrowing reading and reveal the excessive hopes placed in a final German victory. The Eastern Jews not only in Kurland, Lithuania, and Poland, but also in the White Russian, Ruthenian, and Ukranian territories come to life in their overwhelming desire for deliverance from an oppression that had grown intolerable. It becomes evident how much confidence they placed in the promise contained in a proclamation published at the beginning of the war by the high command of the joint German and Austro-Hungarian forces. Written in Yiddish, it appealed *"Zu die Jiden in Paulen"* to support the fight against the Czar with all available means, to close the ranks, to blaze the trail for freedom and justice.*

At the same time it was remembered in Germany that most of the Jews of Russia, roughly six million, had come from the German area and that 97.64 per cent of them spoke Yiddish, a German dialect. Derived from Middle High German, Yiddish resembled High German in vocabulary, construction, and sound far more than any Low German dialect or a Bavarian or Suabian vernacular. In fact, it contained "hardly more than five out of one hundred words . . . of non-German origin." It was also noted that "the hard *cȟ*, always pronounced like *Nacht*, certainly is not derived from the Hebrew, but used to be quite common in German and has been retained in such border dialects such as Alemannic and Dutch." Even the caftan, the long overcoat worn by Eastern Jews, was at long last recognized for what it really was: the particular

---

*This is the only known utterance in Yiddish by the man responsible for this appeal, General Erich Ludendorff. In reality a staunch anti-Semite, Ludendorff ws one of Hitler's companions and a co-conspirator, in the putsch. On this occasion, however, he declared, "We come to you as friends and saviors! Our flags herald justice and freedom for you: Equal and full civil rights, genuine freedom of religion . . ." See also Appendix.

garb worn by citizens of German towns during the Middle Ages.

To cut a long story short, Berlin and the high command for the East were fully aware of the splendid opportunity to add another 6 million faithful Jewish allies inside the enemy country to the roughly 1.8 million Germans living in the Russian empire, whose loyalty to Germany was not always steadfast. It was also anticipated that valuable aid in spreading German culture in occupied zones and the territories still to be conquered would result from mobilizing Eastern-Jewish sympathies, which were fervent in any case. These sympathies, it was further thought, would help to promote German trade with the Near and Far East by the overland route (which was vital because the British had blockaded all sea approaches). And last, they would provide highly welcome assistance in counteracting all endeavors by the Entente to enlist the United States and other neutral countries on its side.

Today we know that none of these hopes materialized—swift victory in the East, immediate dissolution of the czarist empire, or United States refusal to join the Entente. The military reverses suffered by the Germans—and especially by the Austrians—on the Russian front led to pogroms that massacred the Jews in the evacuated territories, who had again fallen into the hands of the Russians; others were subjected to mass deportations to Siberia. The transfer of power in Germany from the normally more flexible politicians into the hands of the narrow-minded military—more often than not with a "nationalist" anti-Semitic bias, headed by the anti-Semite Ludendorff—put an end to any chances of a solid alliance between Germany and the suppressed Jews of Russia. Wild plans for annexations and Germanization, providing even for deportation of "undesirable" population groups,* in particular

---

*See Fritz Fischer, *Griff nach der Weltmacht: Die Kriegszielpolitik des kaiserlichen Deutschland 1914–1918*. See concerning this: [Grasping for World Power: War-Aims Policy of Germany under the Kaiser 1914–1918] (Düsseldorf, 1964), p. 130: "The Polish frontier strip possibly along the Warthe-Narew line as far as and including Suwalki . . . was to be 'cleared of all humanity' by partial evacuation of the Polish peasantry and of all the Jews." See also: Immanuel Geiss, *Der Polnische Grenzstreifen 1914–1918* [The Polish Frontier Strip 1914–1918] (Hamburg and Lübeck, 1960).

the Jews, into the "remainder of Russia" led to a strong decline of confidence. The initial enthusiasm of the Eastern European Jews for the German cause turned to skepticism and resignation, which was bound to have a negative effect on the Jewish masses in North America. Finally, the revolution by which the Russians liberated themselves from the yoke of the czars made any German-Jewish alliance for the same purpose irrelevant.*

As early as April 2, 1917, while the Kerenski government was still in power, all regulations discriminating against the Jews of Russia were dropped. The opponents of the revolution in those border areas of Russia that were still partly under German influence were busy turning the Jews into scapegoats for their defeat and "punished" the Jews with bloody pogroms for the overthrow of the czar. This time it was not the Germans, but other Russians who became the Jews' saviors and deliverers. The devastating blows the Red Army administered to the last supporters of the czar and the troops sent for intervention and assistance by the Entente brought an end to the Jewish persecutions principally in White Russia and the Ukraine. The ingenious originator, organizer, and first commander in chief of the Red Army was the Jewish son of a simple farmer from a small village near Elisavetgrad. His name was Leib Bronstein, and he was known as Leon Trotsky.

By the time, twenty-five years after the start of the First World War, the German armies again marched toward the East and, without a declaration of war, first invaded Poland and, not quite two years later, tried to conquer the Soviet Union, completely disregarding the existing pact of friendship and nonaggression, a number of things had changed.

---

*Egmont Zechlin has described in detail the complete transformation of the relationship between Germany and the Eastern Jews in his excellent and thorough study, *Die deutsche Politik und die Juden im ersten Weltkrieg* [German Policy and the Jews in the First World War] (Göttingen, 1969). The work also deals with the various consequences. Two of Zechlin's findings are of particular interest; the attitude of many prominent German Jews to the question of barricading the eastern borders of Germany against immigrating Eastern Jews; and the tactic adopted by German anti-Semites in the autumn of 1918 holding "the Jews" responsible for the impending military collapse.

When Stalin took over, roughly three million Jews were living in the Soviet Union. Though no longer threatened by pogroms, they were subjected to persecutions of another kind. Like all other religious groups, the Jewish communities with all their institutions had been abolished. The encouragement of Yiddish cultural life had already ceased by about 1930, while Zionism (and later so-called cosmopolitism) were ruthlessly opposed. The strong middle-class element among Russian Jews had, in any case, been destroyed by the revolution and most of its members forced into Western emigration, not to mention the minute upper class of wealthy industrialists, bankers, and merchants. The bulk of independent artisans had been forced to join the gray army of factory workers and felt debased. In addition, there was increasing anti-Semitism, though it was frowned upon by state and Party because it was considered to be irreconcilable with the principles of Communism. Still somewhat latent, the sentiment was predominant among the lower middle classes and the administrative bureaucracy, where the emancipated Jews were felt to be a worrisome competition.

Under these circumstances the relationship between the Jewish population of Russia and the new state was by no means free of friction. The new features felt to be most painful were the suppression of religion and the strong measures used to combat Zionism. There could be no thought of any alliance between Judaism and the Communist Party, let alone of "Jewish rule," despite the fact that, during and shortly after the October Revolution, veteran Communists of Jewish origin formed a considerable percentage of the top leadership. However, out of a population of more than 3 million Jews living in the Soviet Union, hardly more than 0.6 per cent (1922: 19,562) and subsequently a maximum of 1.2 per cent were Party members. Their share in the total membership of the Communist Party of the Soviet Union, originally 5.2 per cent, declined from year to year. Furthermore, the number of prominent Communists of Jewish origin rapidly decreased. Many of them were either Trotskyites or were thought to be Trotskyites—which came down to the same thing.

There is, in addition, another quite nonpolitical indication, that proves the alleged control of Soviet Russia by the Jews of that country to be mendacious propaganda: the misery in which most Soviet Jews still lived long after Communism was firmly consolidated. According to the last prewar statistics,* in the Ukraine and in White Russia, where four-fifths of all the Soviet Jews were concentrated, the unemployment rate was considerably higher than in the rest of Russia. It was fivefold among Ukranian Jews, and as much as nine times higher than the average for those in White Russia.

This circumstance, as well as the whole social structure of the Jews in the Western part of the Soviet Union, contradicts the assertion that the Jews ruled Russia. For instance, 16.7 per cent were laborers and only 0.7 per cent practiced a profession. In reality, roughly 98 per cent of the 3 million Jews in the Soviet Union were poor and without influence. They held neither membership in the Communist Party nor any function or office; furthermore, they had to resign themselves to the suppression of their religion, of their culture, and of their longing for Israel.

It seems clear, then, that the situation of the Jews in White Russia and the Ukraine that the advancing German armies found during the Second World War differed hardly at all from the one that prompted the German and Austrian forces in the autumn of 1914 to address their appeal *"Zu die Jiden in Paulen."*

The factor that altered the whole situation and changed the probable sympathy of the Eastern Jews for the Germans to abhorrence and mortal fear was the completely different attitude of the political and military leaders of Germany toward the Jews, not only in Russia, but everywhere. By 1939 the German views could no longer be ignored or misunderstood, even if the organized mass murder of nearly every Jewish man, woman, and child within the grasp of German power became apparent only as the war progressed.

There can be no doubt whatever that the "Jewish policy" of the German leaders turned a strong element of the population of the very area they wished to win for Germany into adversaries filled with fear and hatred. The Germans completely disregarded the fact that the overwhelming majority of these people could have been potential allies, who were also closely linked with Germany in language, culture, and economy.

---

*Bulletin of "Ort," number 1–2 (Moscow 1928).

Moreover, what was true for European Russia also applied with a few qualifications to the other countries of Eastern Europe. This gives us scope for a careful calculation permitting certain conclusions after necessary corrections. Before 1939 some 270,000 Jews lived in Lithuania, Latvia, and Estonia, accounting for 7.3 per cent of the total population of, for instance, Lithuania. In Poland there were 3.3 million, constituting nearly 10 per cent of the population. In the Eastern areas of Czechoslovakia not yet under German domination, roughly 280,000 Jews were resident, and in White Russia, the Ukraine, and the rest of Western Russia there were at least 2.8 million Jews.

To this figure, totaling 6.65 million Jews of Eastern Europe, must be added the 1.35 million Jews of Hungary and Romania, resulting in a sum total of 8 million to serve us as a basis for further examination. In order to understand what a reservoir of roughly 8 million people—of whom surely 95 per cent were well disposed—would have meant to the German armed forces in an area still to be conquered and administered, it is not sufficient merely to imagine the added military reinforcements—the 50 or 60 divisions that would have become available, even at only half the rate of mobilization used in the Reich. The actual reinforcement to the German armed forces during the Second World War from the acquisition of so-called Volksdeutsche (ethnic Germans—that is, Germans living abroad, often for generations)* can serve as an indicator.

It is also not enough merely to include the enormous relief to administrations, supply lines, transportation, the overall economy, and general health that would have resulted. And, it would have meant the availability of local guides familiar with the territory and fluent interpreters.

We must also take into account the military weakening of the armed forces that resulted from having to deal with nearly eight million potential sympathizers and potential allies, now deadly enemies marked for extermination. These people had to be tracked down, herded together, carefully guarded, and "administered" with the usual pettiness, until the final act of murder. And we have not mentioned the diversion of several

---

*The same territories that in 1939 sheltered roughly eight million Jews at the same time held, at a fairly accurate estimate, half as many ethnic Germans.

frontline operational divisions to act as executioners, and the allocation of immense quantities of rolling stock for transportation.

Even if we allow for the fact that those doomed for extinction had been crammed together in a manner that no army, however hard-pressed, would have tolerated, many hundreds of locomotives and umpteen thousands of freight cars were required to take all the millions of caught victims over hundreds—and sometimes over stretches of thousands—of kilometers to the gates of the extermination camps. One does not have to be a specialist in logistics to visualize the immense transportation problem exacted by the "final solution," or to understand how gravely this procedure hampered the supply lines and mobility of the German armies engaged in a war on several fronts.

And yet all this falls far short of allowing us to arrive at a conclusive understanding of the military drawbacks incurred by the Nazi "Jewish policy" as they affected the German armed forces out to conquer the "Eastern sphere." We must also take into consideration the fact that the ranks of potential allies furnished not only passive adversaries and victims of the "final solution," but also active resistance fighters, partisans, and regular soldiers in the enemy forces.

If we disregard the ghetto uprisings in Warsaw and Bialystok, then the various acts of resistance may appear as insignificant from a military point of view. But altogether they certainly tied down several divisions which could otherwise have been usefully employed elsewhere. The same is even more true for the activities of the partisans, who were joined by all those able-bodied fugitives who had managed to escape the German death squads.

And of course the mass murders in the German-occupied areas affected the fighting spirit of the Jewish population in the unoccupied part of the Soviet Union. The high morale of the Jewish soldiers in the Red Army was further boosted by the certainty that they would be murdered should they fall into German hands.

Official Soviet statistics list 425,000 Jewish Red Army members during the Second World War. Of these—almost half—212,000 were killed in action—a great many more than the 100,000—or 15 percent—of the Jewish contingent of the Russian armies who were killed in the First World War.

Of these, 121 Jewish Red Army soldiers received the highest award for bravery, the golden medal "Hero of the Soviet Union." Among them were such outstanding air-force officers as Rudolf Korabelnik, Jakob Smushkewitsch (who commanded first the Soviet Air Force and then the Red Fleet), and Colonel General Lew Dovator from Witebsk, who in December 1942 died outside Moscow, after he and his corps of Cossacks had halted the German advance on the Russian capital. Generals Moshe Weinryb and Jakob Kreyzer distinguished themselves at Stalingrad. Weinryb fell during the liberation of the Ukraine. Among the Jewish war dead, the highest-ranking officer was the tank commander and Marshal of the Soviet Union, Iwan Tschernijakovsky from Kiev. His growing fame finally led to the nickname "The Invincible." He was killed in April 1945, at the age of thirty-eight, during the conquest of Königsberg.

Finally the "Lithuanian Division" merits special comment. This elite unit, known for its aggressive spirit and death-defying courage in assault, was feared by the enemy. It was made up primarily of "Litvaks," whose songs, colloquialisms, and command language were Yiddish.

These few facts are enough to indicate that, even though they were religiously and culturally suppressed before 1939, and even though 98 per cent of them were not Communists, the Jews of Russia unreservedly joined in the defense of their country and their own cause after Hitler's attack on the Soviet Union, that they endured immense sacrifices, and that they contributed in considerable measure to the final victory over the aggressor.

In summary we can say that Germany's chances of winning the war of conquest of the allegedly vital "living space in the East" (for which preparations had been made for some time), were considerably diminished by the concurrent persecution of the Jews. Some of the detrimental effect was due to the political considerations that compelled the German military command to forego the induction of "non-Aryan" contingents—as many men as serve in today's West German army; another factor was the misuse of frontline troops and immense quantities of rolling stock for the "final solution." The main circumstance operating to Germany's detriment, however, was the fact that many millions of people who traditionally were pro-German and felt linked to Germany by language, culture, economics, and other aspects had been proclaimed enemies and either murdered or forced into the opposite camp and roused to the highest pitch of resistance.

Numerous political side effects disadvantageous to Germany followed in the wake of these purely military impacts, and these again worsened the military position. It need hardly be stressed that the persecution of the Jews had a negative influence on the prospects for an arrangement with Great Britain such as Hitler had hoped and striven for (or at least silent acquiescence by the Western powers to Germany's expansion eastward), and on United States sentiments.

Unlike the situation during the First World War, in 1939 Germany could not count on the sympathy of the American Jews. It is understandable that the Jews of the United States gave their fullest support to the arms aid given by the United States—long before the country entered the war—to a Britain unprepared for a clash with Germany. It was Bernard Mannes Baruch, the son of German-Jewish immigrants from Schwersenz in Posen, in those days a Prussian province, an adviser to President Franklin Delano Roosevelt and friend of Winston S. Churchill, who as early as 1939 was entrusted with organizing and overseeing the American war economy. In the spring of 1941 Baruch helped to introduce the lend-lease system, which became the basis for intensified support for the nations fighting Hitler, in particular Great Britain.

Many of Roosevelt's other principal advisers were Jews from Germany or Austria. One such was Charles Michelson, a leading Democratic politician and New Deal expert. He was a brother of the great American physicist and Nobel Prize laureate of 1907, Albert Michelson, who came from Strelno in Posen. Others were Felix Frankfurter, born in Vienna, an eminent lawyer, Harvard professor, and later a Justice of the Supreme Court; and the banker and longtime Governor of New York, Herbert H. Lehmann, a close friend of Roosevelt and the descendant of a Jewish family from Bavaria, whose son Peter volunteered for the American Air Force and crashed over England in 1944, a highly decorated fighter pilot.

The fact that in the Second World War the United States soon gave up its neutrality and came to the assistance of England and subsequently of Russia completely nullified any chances of a German victory, if there had ever been any. Military considerations apart, Germany could not win a war against the combined resources of the British Commonwealth and the United States. Furthermore, Berlin had completely underestimated the strength of the Soviet Union and had intentionally refrained from exploiting the possibilities of winning important allies against the Soviet Union. (And by this we mean not only the German policy against the Jews, but also the disgraceful treatment of other subjected Eastern people considered "racially inferior.")

Besides the enormous deterioration of the military and political preconditions for a German victory, brought about directly or indirectly by the "Jewish policy" of the "Third Reich," a further important factor had a negative influence on Germany's position. In all essential sectors of the Reich the specialists were missing. This was true not only in the different branches of the armaments industry and in the scientific research crucial to the war effort, but also in the organization of the war economy, in the health services, and in those departments whose job it was to develop effective propaganda for abroad.

The direct link between the bottlenecks in personnel and the elimination of the "non-Aryans" from all fields may seem surprising, but it can easily be proved. By 1937 nearly 40 per cent of all university instructors from the "Old Reich" had been dismissed, mainly on the basis of the "racial laws." Many more professors, assistants, and other scientists—including many "Aryans" who sympathized with their dismissed colleagues—had also left. Germany as a whole, and after 1938 Austria and Czechoslovakia as well, lost roughly half of their scientists and their highly specialized technicians.*

In other fields important to the war effort, the situation was similar. Not until the middle of 1942 did the Nazi leaders realize their fatal mistake:

> In a remarkable address at a secret conference concerning the future of the Reich Research Council, in the presence of most of the members of the council [which

---

*According to Pross, *op. cit.*, by 1938 roughly one-third of the entire faculties of German universities had been dismissed, forcibly pensioned off, or transferred, chiefly for "racial" and political reasons. By 1939 presumably 45 per cent of all university posts had been newly filled.

included Göring, Milch, Speer, Funk, Ohnesorge, and Rosenberg] Göring described the annoyance that the persecution of Jewish scientists was causing the Führer as well as himself: "What the Führer objects to is the regimentation of science as such, somewhat along the following basic principles: Yes, this product is very valuable, extremely valuable, and would advance us quite considerably. We cannot use it, however, because the man happens to be married to a Jewess; or because he is a half-Jew. . . . I myself have now related this to the Führer. In Vienna we have now put a Jew to work for two years, another one in the area of photography, because they have certain things we need and that would at this moment absolutely advance our cause. It would be madness now to say here: That one has to go! It's true he was a very great researcher, a fantastic brain, but he has a Jewish wife and cannot be at the University, etc. In the realm of art, including the operetta, the Führer has granted exceptions for the sake of continuity. All the more will he grant and approve exceptions that deal with really great research projects or the researchers involved.*

In the light of what had gone before, Göring's admonitions cannot help but appear paradoxical; with the exception of the two anonymous examples cited, his remarks refer only to people married to Jews and to "half-Jews." Measured against the total loss, they could only effect minute corrections.

In order to gain some insights into the contribution by German Jews to their homeland's war effort, it may be useful to make a comparison with conditions prevailing during the First World War. A few typical examples, taken at random from the profusion of cases available, will give us an approximate, though incomplete picture.

Germany's supply and distribution of raw material in the First World War—a difficult but vital problem for the blockaded country—was organized and controlled by Walter

---

*From the minutes of the meeting of July 6, 1942, in the Aviation Ministry, contained in the "Milch Documents" (Vol. 58, pp. 3640–3714) found by the Americans in 1945; in David Irving, *Virus House* (London, 1967).

Rathenau, head of the AEG concern founded by his father, Emil Rathenau.*

To overcome the British blockade, Albert Ballin, head of the HAPAG shipping line, adviser and friend of Kaiser Wilhelm II, immediately after the outbreak of the war placed the total apparatus of his international company and, most important, its network of agents in neutral countries at the country's disposal. In despair over Germany's losing the war, he committed suicide on November 9, 1918.

The former Secretary of State, Bernhard Dernburg, until 1909 head of the Reich Colonial Office, assumed control of the German propaganda service in the United States in 1914. It was very successful for a time. Dr. Kurt Hahn, principal aide to Prince Max of Baden, German chancellor near the end of the war, served as an expert on Britain within the foreign division of the supreme army command because of his extensive knowledge of British conditions. After the war he and the Prince founded a boarding school in Salem that was to gain wide recognition.**

The feminist Josefine Levy-Rathenau distinguished herself

---

*Translator's note: Walter Rathenau was also a popular though controversial writer on various topics, blending philosophy with economics. Today, fifty-six years after his assassination during his tenure as Foreign Minister, discussions concerning his personality and theories are still being published, while his correspondence with political figures of his day and with others was published with great public interest soon after his death. A sample from one of these may afford readers a glimpse of the unusual inspiration he was to thousands of fair-minded moderates and to the German intelligentsia, which was not yet completely disillusioned about the future of human progress. In a letter to President Wilson, Colonel Edward M. House called Rathenau a "capable and down-to-earth man" with "a clear conception of the situation and such a prophetic anticipation of the future. . . ."

**Translator's note: "On the evening of April 28 (1932) I met Kurt Hahn. Soon after he left Germany and his school at Salem and came to England. He founded Gordonstoun on the East Scottish coast, an admirable school which counts the Duke of Edinburgh among its old boys. Hahn encouraged resourcefulness and physical fitness more imaginatively than most pedagogues. He taught boys to build and navigate boats, and he claimed to cure stammering by high jumping . . . Hahn was a brave man with great personality and driving power and a sense of humor. . . ." From *Hugh Dalton's Memoirs 1931–1945, The Fateful Years* (London, 1957), p. 40.

in 1914 as a cofounder and organizer of the women's national service.

German and Austrian Jews also contributed considerably to the war effort in technology and science. Hans Goldschmidt, for instance, son of the founder of the chemical factory, Theodor Goldschmidt, was indispensable as an expert metallurgist; during the First World War he developed procedures for the manufacture of bombs and tracer ammunition. Professor Reinhold Rüdenberg was chief electroengineer of the Siemens concern and instrumental in providing significant improvements in the equipment of the communication troops. Karl Redlich, designer of the Tauern tunnel, was a specialist for the most complicated railway constructions. Max Kurrein, subsequently professor at the technical college in Berlin and thereafter at the technical college in Haifa, was the head designer and technical manager of the armaments factories for the Viennese arsenal. Robert von Lieben, a Jewish scientist who invented the amplifier tube and founded modern radio technology, had died as early as 1913; his assistant, Siegmund Strauss, was the manager of the aviation experimental division and did outstanding work in further developing radio technology. Siegfried Popper, chief designer for the Austrian navy with the rank of admiral, introduced numerous innovations in battleship design and in the construction of special vehicles. Benno Strauss, the developer of stainless steel and carbide metal, was responsible for the worldwide reputation of Krupp's research division during his thirty-eight years with the firm; he developed the metallurgy necessary for the construction of modern submarines. In 1934 Professor Strauss retired from Krupp with a handsome parting gift; later on, obviously forgotten by the powerful Essen firm, he became a victim of the "final solution."

Important contributions to the war effort in airplane construction and related fields were made by Edmund Rumpler, who gave Germany his brainchild, a plane known as the Rumpler Taube (pigeon). He also designed the twin-engine plane. His Jewish colleague, Wiener, of the Albatross Works developed a new observation plane and flew the test runs himself. The Jewish proprietors of the Raab-Katzenstein aviation works helped to build up the air force. And the instructor who taught the first German air-force officers was a Jew, Willy Rosenstein.

The renowned mathematician Richard von Mises was the founder of aviation mathematics and a fighter pilot during the First World War; he was also considered the most significant theoretician in flight mechanics. Karl Arnstein, head designer of the Zeppelin Works, stayed on after the war to build the transatlantic airship *Z.R. III*. Captain Leo Löwenstein, subsequently chairman of the German association of Jewish veterans, during the war invented phonometry (the use of sound waves) crucial to anti-aircraft defense.

In chemistry the achievements of German Jews were also outstanding. Privy Councillor Adolf Frank—in teamwork with his son Albert and another Jewish scientist, Nikodem Caro—developed the so-called Frank-Caro procedure for deriving calcium cyanamide from the atmosphere; as such he may be considered the father of the German potassium industry, which was to assume great importance for the German economy, both in wartime and in peacetime. Another procedure developed by this research team made possible the extraction of hydrogen from water, used during the First World War to supply hydrogen for airships, for the fat-hardening industry, and the ammonia-synthesizing procedure developed by Professor Haber.

Fritz Haber, also a German Jew, made what may be the greatest single contribution to the German war effort. As director of the Kaiser Wilhelm Institute for Physical Chemistry, founded by Leopold Koppel, he laid the scientific foundations for ammonia synthesis, for which he was awarded the Nobel Prize in 1919. His procedure made Germany independent of Chile saltpeter. This move was of crucial importance for the German economy and consequently for the feeding of the population during the war years, since the British blockade put an end to all imports. Haber's invention also made it possible for the German explosives industry to function without imported saltpeter, guaranteeing the continued supply of German ammunitions during the First World War.*

This process also formed the basis for the poison gases

---

*The conservative deputy Vorster, a man by no means pro-Jewish, declared in parliament during a discussion of ammunition supplies, "Without Professor Haber's new nitrogen procedure, the war would have been lost in three months." Other experts believed that Germany could have held out until 1915–1916.

produced in the First World War, to Professor Haber's subsequent regret. Haber himself directed the chemical warfare as well as the anti-gas defenses of the German forces.

These roughly two dozen names represent a modest selection and do not touch on such important fields as medicine. They do, however, give us a rough idea of the achievements of the German-Jewish researchers and technicians during the First World War, and they do allow a guess as to the deficiencies during the Second World War that followed from the "racial" policy of the "Third Reich."

In the years 1933–1939 the German leaders not only deprived the country of many outstanding experts who would have been available to military research and development, but furthermore, they drove them into the enemy camp.

Reinhold Rüdenberg, for instance, was one of the greatest electromechanical scientists of our day. He invented the self-starting eddy-current induction motor and the electron microscope. In 1933 he was forced to relinquish his chair at the technical college in Berlin; he was also fired from his job as chief electrical engineer at Siemens; in 1936 he fled to London. Soon thereafter he was appointed to the Harvard faculty and enriched the electrical industry of the United States with numerous important inventions, for which he successfully registered a total of over 300 patents. After the war he succeeded in the direct conversion of atomic power into alternating current.

Georg Schlesinger, Germany's leading machinery designer, was until 1933 professor at the technical college in Berlin; soon after his dismissal he went into exile. During the Second World War he became a director of the research department of the British Institute for Production Engineers.

Finally, Paul Schwarzkopf, born in Prague, by profession a metallurgist, directed Berlin's Wolfram Laboratory during the First World War, then managed the German incandescent-filament factory, and finally headed the Plansee metal works. In 1936 he was forced to emigrate, and he rendered important service to the Allied war effort from the United States, where he invented powder metallurgy and worked as chief metallurgist at the American Electro Metal Corporation.

In his study *The Rescue and Achievement of Refugee Scholars* Norman Bentwich reports:

The research work undertaken by other scientists who had fled to England and had been drafted to support the war effort was less sensational but no less important. Three of them—Dr. H. R. Fehling, Dr. J. Mazur, and Dr. P. O. Rosin—belonged to the team that developed a process for the dispersion of fog, which considerably increased the security of the air force squadrons. Two of them received the award offered by the British government. . . . Many other refugees from Germany participated in the "Pluto" project. This "pipeline under the ocean," incorporating an underwater pipeline system along the bed of the English channel, crucially improved the fuel supply of the invasion forces in the summer of 1944. Then there was a specialist in glacier exploration, Dr. M. F. Perutz from Vienna. In 1962 he received the Nobel Prize for chemistry in consideration of his pioneering achievements concerning proteins and nucleate acids. During the Second World War, he was a member of the team working on the project "Operation Habakkuk" with the object of establishing large artificial ice floes as air bases on the high seas of the Atlantic. . . ."

These few examples chosen at random from the many hundreds available should suffice. In any case, an exact calculation of the losses inflicted on the German war economy by the "elimination" of Jewish research scientists and technicians is not possible, any more than it is possible to calculate the gain to the Allied war effort from the additional knowledge and capabilities brought by the emigrants who had fled from Hitler.

Nevertheless, it is more than obvious that Germany's losses and the corresponding gains of its enemies must have been considerable. How far the balance swung in favor of the Allies may be illustrated by means of a last example of special significance. The specific technology involved contributed decisively and to a larger degree to the great turning point in the fortunes of war that took place in 1942–1943.

This is the direction-finding technique known as radar, which not only increased the effectiveness of the air raids over Germany, but also made possible the victorious Allied advance through the North African desert, the successful landing in Normandy, and the elimination of U-boats (German submarines) from the Atlantic.

Radar was not an American and British monopoly; the Germans had also developed a similar apparatus. The German radar systems, however, were based on longer wavelengths and did not reach as far as the Allies'. According to the experts on both sides, this minor but crucial drawback contributed more than any other technical factor to the Allied victory over Germany.

For the purposes of our study, it would be of great interest if we could be certain of the extent to which Jewish physicists and technicians driven out of Hitler's Germany contributed to the improvement of the Allied radar systems and, conversely, how their absence affected German development. But of course no such calculation can be made. Qualitative measurements in the area of scientific-technical achievements are always questionable, especially when large teams do the work. However, another point of reference permits us to form some conclusions. According to official statements, "only" about 10 per cent of the scientists who developed radar in the United States were Europeans who had fled to America to escape anti-Semitism. They include two subsequent Nobel Prize winners—Hans Bethe, physicist laureate in 1967, and Felix Bloch, who was honored in 1952; both had left Germany in 1933 to escape "racial" persecution. The greatest contribution to the United States development of radar may be attributed to the Dutch Jewish physicist, Samuel Goudsmit, of whom we will have more to say in the next chapter.

These items, which can be supplemented with many more case histories, give us food for thought. At the very least, we must ask whether the migration of such reputable physicists is related to the inferiority of Germany and the superiority of the Allies—a difference which, though minimal, was crucial—in the particular field in which these scientists were expert.

Summarizing the results of our examination of the possible effect of German anti-Semitism on the final outcome of the Second World War, we cannot fail to note certain consequences of the anti-Jewish policy of the "Third Reich." They point to military, political, economic, and scientific disadvantages, each of which alone was already powerful and possibly decisive. Taking them all together, we can only speculate whether they made the difference between victory and defeat. Even so, as Winston Churchill declared in 1940: "Since the Germans drove the Jews out of Germany and lowered their own technological standard, we are ahead of them." And in 1943 Admiral Dönitz, writing to the Research Council, complained that "the enemy has nullified U-boat warfare by his scientific superiority." These and similar judgments seem to confirm the validity of the assumption that the expulsion of the "non-Aryan" scientists did not fail to have its effects on the conduct of the war and that these effects were highly detrimental to Hitler's Germany.

One factor, however, makes idle any speculation about whether Germany could have won the war if it had not been hampered by its vicious policy toward the Jews. The atomic bomb destroyed the Japanese city of Hiroshima on August 6, 1945 and significantly altered the balance of power in favor of those who possessed it.

And it is precisely the existence of the atom bomb and the history of its development that must dispel any lingering doubts about whether Germany deprived itself of a chance to win the Second World War by its post-1933 treatment of the Jews.

Chapter 7

The Bomb That Went into Exile

What connection is there between the atom bomb and the persecution of the Jews in Europe? This weapon, developed in the state of New Mexico, was first used against the Japanese city of Hiroshima on August 6, 1945, three months after the unconditional surrender of Hitler's Reich. How, then, can it have anything to do with the persecution of the Jews in distant Europe, let alone with the question of whether Germany could have won the Second World War had it not been for its anti-Semitic policy?

The war in Europe had, it is true, been decided long before the use of the bomb. The Jewish people of Germany and its neighboring countries had already been "eliminated," driven out, and largely annihilated before the so-called Manhattan Project became crucial to the conduct of the war.

Despite such objections, in themselves perfectly justified, we will state unequivocally—and prove as far as proof is possible—that there would have been no Manhattan Project, and consequently no atom bomb, had it not been for the anti-Semitic policy of Hitler's government. Indeed, there would have been no United States atom bomb until at least 1946 if the Jews of Europe had not been persecuted.

* * *

It is by now a well-known story how the United States was induced to consider the military possibilities of nuclear fission before it would have been too late to develop the atom bomb for use in the Second World War.

On October 11, 1939, a few weeks after the German invasion of Poland, President Roosevelt met with an old friend and adviser, Alexander Sachs, who handed the President a memorandum after reading it aloud. The memorandum mentioned recent noticeable interest on the part of Germany in uranium. It recommended immediate intervention by the United States government with Belgium, in order to safeguard the uranium reserves of the Congo. It further suggested financial assistance for and acceleration of American atomic research.

At first the document did not have the desired effect. Roosevelt merely acknowledged that he found the subject raised by Sachs "rather interesting." However, he clearly considered any intervention to protect the uranium deposits in the Belgian Congo to be premature. Nor did he address the matter of encouraging American atomic research.

Sachs was extremely disappointed. But he did not give up the hope of gaining the President's assent to these propositions. He was all the more hopeful as he had succeeded in obtaining an invitation for breakfast with Roosevelt on the following morning. Sachs recalled:

> That night I got no sleep at all. I was staying at the Carlton. I paced my room restlessly and tried to sleep sitting on a chair. Quite close to the hotel there was a small park. To the surprise of the porter, I left the hotel three or four times between eleven o'clock and seven in the morning and went over to the park. There I sat on a bench and meditated. What could I say to win the President over to this cause, which was already nearly lost? Suddenly and intuitively I had a brainstorm. I went back to the hotel, showered, and was at the White House soon afterward.

Roosevelt was seated at the breakfast table in his wheelchair, all alone, when Sachs joined him. The President asked playfully what brilliant new idea his friend had prepared for him today and how long the explanation would take this time.

Sachs replied that he would merely tell a story. He then told of the time in 1806 when Robert Fulton had approached Napoleon with an offer to build a fleet of steamships for use in the French war against England. Fulton had been laughed at; in those days not even a Bonaparte could imagine ships without sails. "According to the English historian, Lord Acton, this is an example of how England was saved through the short-sightedness of the enemy," Sachs ended his story. Then he added, "Had Napoleon had greater imagination and humility, the history of the nineteenth century would have been quite different."

President Roosevelt seemed much impressed. He was silent for several minutes. Then he called the butler who had served the breakfast and asked him to bring and open a bottle of vintage brandy. After the glasses had been filled and emptied with a toast to the health of Alexander Sachs, the President summoned his closest aide, General "Pa" Watson. Pointing to the memorandum, the importance of which he had misjudged the previous day, he uttered the famous sentence, "Pa, this means that we must act."

Such was the starting point of an effort that was to develop into the greatest scientific and technical enterprise in history, the Manhattan Project. There is, however, a curtain raiser to the memorandum handed to the President by Sachs. And two years would have to pass from the time Roosevelt requested action to the first real financial and technical beginning of the American atom bomb. During this period, there was no certainty whether the supporters of the project would be able to implement it, let alone carry it to its goal. There was opposition of every kind on one side, errors and mistakes on the other.

But we will begin by studying the background of the memorandum that was to trigger President Roosevelt's decision. In the summer of 1939, when the clouds of war were gathering over Europe, unnoticed by the people, who had been lulled into a false sense of security by the Munich agreements, extremely alarming reports from Germany reached some of the physicists living in the United States: The first conference on nuclear physics had been convened in Berlin by the head of the research department of the Army Ordinance Office. This event seemed to indicate that, at the very least, the possible military applications of nuclear physics were being investigated. Another message from Berlin reported that a few weeks earlier Paul Harteck, the Hamburg physicist, had pointed to the "possibility in principle of starting a chain reaction in uranium." Subsequently it became known that Marteck had "recommended that the Reich War Ministry follow this up." A third report from Germany was particularly disturbing. The Reich government had abruptly blocked the export of uranium ore from the Sudeten territory Germany had occupied the previous year.

All these reports (which reached the United States by routes to be discussed below) seemed to indicate clearly that the political and military leadership in Berlin was already thinking about something that, in the rest of the world, was occupying the minds of only a few scientists—the truly incredible possibilities presented by the enormous volume of energy that would be released during a nuclear chain reaction in uranium.

One of these scientists in the United States who was unable to sleep at night in light of the reports from Germany was Leo Szilard. Born in 1898 in Budapest, the son of Jewish parents, he had worked in Berlin until 1933, where he had held a position as a university lecturer. By way of Vienna, where he remained for only a few weeks, he escaped to England. After several years of teaching and research at Oxford, he went to the United States. In the summer of 1939 when the disturbing reports from Berlin reached him, Szilard still had no permanent position. He was merely a special student in the physics department of New York's Columbia University, with laboratory privileges. He had arranged for the equipment he had left behind in Oxford to be sent on to him, and he borrowed one gram of radium—against a security deposit of $2000—loaned him by the Jewish manufacturer Liebowitz in New York. This arrangement allowed him in March 1939 to conduct a crucial and successful experiment, which he later described himself.

> Everything was ready. We had only to press the button and watch the surface of the television screen. If signs of light appeared, it meant that during the splitting of uranium, neutrons were being expelled. This would indicate the possibility of releasing atomic energy in our lifetime. We pressed the button. We saw signs of light.

We watched them, awestruck, for a few minutes. Then we turned it off. That night I realized that the world had entered a path strewn with worrying hazards.

Szilard, however, did not resign himself to the contemplation of pessimistic thoughts. Instead, he took action. One of the first men he approached was the Italian nuclear scientist and Nobel Prize winner of 1938, Enrico Fermi. Fermi left Italy because he was worried for his Jewish wife, Laura, and was fearful of events in Europe; he was now working at Columbia University in the same building as Szilard. At first he listened with some skepticism to Szilard's proposition that they stop publishing the results of their research so as to avoid making it easier for the European dictatorships—especially Hitler's "Third Reich"—to gain important new knowledge in the field of nuclear physics. It was only a few weeks later that Fermi was persuaded; thereafter he vigorously supported Szilard's proposals.

As far as other nuclear scientists were concerned—especially those who had not just recently arrived from Europe—Szilard met with incomprehension and rejection. It seemed to these scientists too strange to abandon, for purely political reasons, an international cooperation practiced for centuries, and with it possibly their claim to being first—which, according to custom, could be established only by publication. They would be giving up fame merely for the sake of annoying self-censorship.

Of all the outstanding nuclear scientists in the United States, only three understood Szilard immediately and supported his proposition energetically: Eugen Wigner, Victor Weisskopf, and Edward Teller.

Wigner was born in 1902 in Budapest, the son of German-speaking parents. He had studied in Berlin and emigrated early to the United States, where he taught at Princeton University from 1938 on.

Weisskopf, born in Vienna in 1908, had received his first scientific training in Göttingen and had soon moved to Copenhagen, where he worked under Niels Bohr, the famous Danish researcher. Eventually he accepted an appointment to the faculty of the University of Rochester.

Teller, born in 1908 in Budapest, left Germany in 1933 after having studied in Karlsruhe, Munich, and Leipzig, as well as Göttingen, where he had written a treatise on optics with Max Born. He also went to Copenhagen, where he had been one of Bohr's most brilliant students. In Copenhagen he struck up a close friendship with another one of Bohr's students, whom he had first met in Heisenberg's classes in Leipzig— Carl Friedrich von Weizsäcker. Finally, in 1935, Teller was invited to teach at Washington's George Washington University.

These three young nuclear scientists all had their roots in the old imperial Austrian monarchy and had been trained at German universities. In the summer of 1939 they allied themselves with Szilard and finally also brought Enrico Fermi over to their side. All were of Jewish descent, and all five had fled from the country they considered their spiritual home only because of the anti-Semitism that began to rule the German universities in 1933. The joint efforts of these scientists brought about, if not a complete and permanent ban on publication in their special field, at least an awareness of the dangers and a growing realization of the disastrous consequences that could follow unless a painstaking watch was kept over the Axis powers and any possible lead of theirs in the field of nuclear fission.

The Szilard Group, as it was called, had even more difficulty in approaching nuclear physicists in the other Western nations with their proposal to stop all publication in the field. As early as February 1939 Szilard had approached the famous French scientist, Frédéric Joliot-Curie and had called his attention to the possibility of a chain reaction. Szilard had added, "Under certain conditions, this could lead to the construction of bombs that would be most dangerous in general, but especially in the hands of certain governments."

At first there was no reaction from Joliot-Curie. When he finally cabled the United States to the effect that he considered Szilard's proposal "very sensible," he qualified his opinion with, "But it comes too late" and referred to the latest press reports dealing with advances in the field of atomic research.

In actual fact, it was not too late. The newspaper articles cited by the French scientist were worded far too generally to have done any damage of the kind Szilard foresaw. The truth of the matter was that at the time Joliot-Curie did not take these matters very seriously and mainly did not wish to be prevented from bringing out an important work he had just completed.

Joliot-Curie's publication, which dealt with an experimental realization of precisely the chain reaction Szilard and his friends hoped to keep from the Axis scientists, again nullified all their efforts to effect a British-American-French publication ban—and just after the British and Americans had agreed to cease publishing!

Szilard was even unable to prevent publication of his own pioneer work on a chain reaction in uranium, and was given a hint that he might lose his place at Columbia if he continued to be "uncooperative."

The disputes concerning the pros and cons of a publication ban, initially ending in a reverse of the Szilard Group, did have the effect of prompting Szilard and his friends to make every effort to develop suitable substitute measures. Wigner suggested starting a drive to arouse the interest of the highest authorities in Washington and to draw their attention to the latest results of nuclear research especially to the "possible sudden menace" implied by the forward strides they believed Germany had made.

The group was in full agreement with Wigner's proposal. At the same time they realized clearly how extraordinarily difficult it would be to capture the interest of Washington. This may sound strange in the light of further developments, but at the time no one beyond the small circle of highly special-ized scientists had an inkling of the opportunities for military technology that were inherent in the most recent discoveries of nuclear research.

It was not even understood that within a short period uranium ore could achieve strategic importance. Until this time only insignificant amounts of the rare metal had been utilized—for instance, in the watch-making industry, where it was used to make dials that glowed in the dark. The mere suggestion that the uranium deposits of the Belgian Congo be protected against seizure by the Axis powers would therefore have evoked at best a patronizing smile on the part of Washington.

Even Enrico Fermi had preached to deaf ears when, in March 1939, he had endeavored to make it clear to American military heads what revolutionary military opportunities were present in the "chain reaction of uranium." Niels Bohr also went unheeded when he expressed a similar warning at a meeting of the American Society for Physics.

If, however, such international celebrities as the Nobel Prize laureates Fermi and Bohr had been unable to make any impression with their warnings, how much chance was there for the unknown scientists from Central Europe? Of all of them, only Wigner was already a naturalized United States citizen, while Szilard, Teller, and Weisskopf still had the official status of foreign refugees.

In this rather hopeless situation, Szilard had a brainstorm: an even more famous scientist might be able to help—Albert Einstein, who had been teaching at Princeton (where Wigner also taught) since 1933. It should be possible for Wigner to get in touch with the "father of the theory of relativity" and to gain his support for the plans of the Szilard group.

At first they were only thinking of using Einstein's excellent relationship with the Royal Court in Belgium to draw the attention of the Brussels government to the importance of the uranium deposits in the Congo and to gain Belgian protection against a seizure by the Axis powers. However, Szilard's first contact with his famous colleague immediately introduced a different and crucial trend. Robert Jungk has described it both amusingly and impressively in his brilliant study, *Brighter than a Thousand Suns*:

> As a matter of fact, Einstein was just about to proceed on holiday to Long Island, outside New York. Even so, he did not object to the two colleagues' looking him up with their important problems. So it was that on a hot July day in 1939 Wigner and Szilard started on a trip to the beach resort of Patchogue. Arriving after a two-hour car journey, they soon realized that the address did not seem correct.
>
> "Perhaps I misunderstood the name of the place over the telephone," Wigner suggested. "Let's look on the map for a similar name."
>
> "Peconic—how does that sound?" Szilard asked.
>
> "That's it!" Wigner said at once. "I remember it clearly."
>
> Arriving in Peconic, the two motorists asked all over for the bungalow of Doctor Moore, the owner of the cottage rented by Einstein. A group of summer guests in shorts and colorful bathing suits came strolling by. "Doctor

Moore's bungalow? Never heard of it." They did not seem to fare any better with the local inhabitants. They continued driving around, but it became more and more hopeless. Eventually Szilard said to his companion, "Let's give up and go home. Perhaps it is not meant to be. We should probably make a terrible mistake if, with Einstein's assistance, we approached the authorities. Once the state has got hold of something, it won't give it up again."

"We have an obligation to go through with it," Wigner replied. "It's our contribution to preventing a terrible calamity."

And so the search went on.

"What about just asking where Einstein lives? Every child knows him," Szilard suggested. Immediately this was put to the test. A sunburned youngster stood on the streetcorner, tinkering with a fishing rod.

"Do you know where Einstein lives?" Szilard asked, more in a joking vein than seriously.

"Sure! I can take you there."

Thus fate, led by innocence, continued on its course.

The visitors were kept waiting briefly on the open porch of the cottage. Then Einstein emerged in slippers and led them to his study.

Szilard reported on this important first discussion.

Einstein had not perceived the possibility of a chain reaction in uranium. No sooner had he listened to me, however, than he grasped the implications and was immediately prepared to help us and to stick his neck out. In the meantime it seemed desirable to inform the State Department in Washington of what we planned before we got in touch with the Belgian government. Wigner offered to draft a letter to the Belgian government, to send a copy to the State Department, and to allow two weeks for objections if they believed that Einstein should abandon the idea of mailing such a letter to Belgium. This was the situation when Wigner and I left Einstein's house on Long Island.

Having Einstein as an ally was indeed an important step forward. Szilard realized, however, that even a letter from this scholar might fall into the wrong hands at the State Department or might not receive sufficient attention. He discussed the problem with a few close friends, including some who were not nuclear physicists. One of them, Gustav Stolper, thought of a solution.

Stolper was born in 1888 in Vienna, where, as a young man, he was a professor of economics and a highly respected publisher. Moving to Berlin he published first the journal *Börsencourier* and then the highly reputable weekly that he founded, *Der deutsche Volkswirt*. He also acted as Berlin's correspondent for the London *Economist* and was a member of the German Reichstag, representing the German State Party, a forerunner of the present Free German Party. He had considerable influence on the Party's economic policies before 1933, when he emigrated and settled in New York. Stolper had influential friends in New York, one of whom was the banker and scholar Alexander Sachs.

Sachs had won Roosevelt's special esteem for his precise predictions of market trends. As one of the renowned Brain Trust, whose members had free access to the White House at any time, he was among the closest advisers to the President.

Stolper therefore arranged for a dialogue between Szilard and Sachs. And since the banker was immediately agreeable to passing on to Roosevelt the letter which Einstein was planning to write, a start was made to draft this document. The final texts—a long and a short version—went far beyond what Einstein had originally approved. With a direct line to the President of the United States, the scientists would not limit themselves to the proposal, discussed with Einstein, that the United States intervene with Belgium to safeguard the uranium ore of the Congo. In addition, they called attention to the increasing indications of German activity in this field, advising an intensification of American nuclear research. They stressed their belief that this research should be facilitated, not by government agencies and public funds, but by private individuals and firms, since such research would have to be carried out in absolute secrecy. Such supporters should be enlisted by a confidential agent of the White House. The scientists were still careful not to expose nuclear research to government interference, or to acquaint the military with the potential of a new nuclear-arms technique, or to call for the construction of an atom bomb. They merely wished to prevent the Axis powers from gaining an advantage and one day pressuring a wholly unprepared world into every conceivable concession with the threat of a terrible weapon of destruction.

On August 2, 1939 Szilard drove to Long Island for the second time, bringing the finished drafts. This time Teller accompanied him, because Wigner had gone to California. Einstein chose to append his signature to the more detailed version. A file containing a memorandum drafted by Szilard and the letter signed by Einstein was handed to President Franklin D. Roosevelt in the White House on October 6, 1939, five weeks after war had broken out in Europe.

The following morning, Roosevelt, at last convinced by Sachs, spoke those fateful words, "We must act."

Let us pause for a moment to consider this dramatic development from the point of view of our study. There is no doubt that the efforts of the Szilard Group and their friends were responsible for the United States' political leaders' taking serious note of the strategic importance of nuclear-research findings. This attention led to the conclusions that finally resulted in the Manhattan Project. The warnings and promptings of the Szilard group had made a powerful impression on Roosevelt at an early stage. Had this not been the case, the Americans would certainly not have succeeded in creating the crucial nuclear weapons in time to affect the outcome of the Second World War.

The connection between the impulse leading to America's decision to develop nuclear arms and the persecution of the Jews in Europe can be amply proven. Without exception, all the warnings and promptings leading to Roosevelt's decision originated with or were channeled to the President by persons directly or indirectly affected by that persecution. Had it not been for anti-Semitism in the Third Reich, most of them would not have fled to America but would have stayed in Europe, principally in Germany.

We are already aware that all the scientists in the Szilard Group were of Jewish origin and had been forced to give up their work in Germany by an institutionalized and growing anti-Semitism. It has been mentioned elsewhere that the Italian Nobel Prize winner Enrico Fermi had emigrated to America out of concern for his Jewish wife once Mussolini, under pressure from Hitler, initiated anti-Semitic measures in 1938. Along with Fermi we must also mention the name of Niels Bohr, the Danish nuclear physicist and recipient of the Nobel Prize, whose warning in the spring of 1939 had initially made no impression in New York. The son of a German-Jewish mother, he himself was married to a Jewish woman. Gustav Stolper, the liaison man between Szilard and Sachs, was also Jewish, as was Alexander Sachs, born in 1893 at Rossigen in what was then Russian Lithuania, and who had left Europe at the age of eleven.

Of course Albert Einstein was also a German Jew, born in Ulm. It was his signature that lent the necessary weight to the letter addressed to the President of the United States. From 1914 to 1933, he had headed the Kaiser Wilhelm Institute for Physics in Berlin. Einstein had also taught at the University, had received the Nobel Prize in 1921, and had emigrated to the United States only after Hitler had come to power and he had been dismissed. A chair had been created for him at Princeton University.

It is a bitter irony of history that it was Albert Einstein, a man of peace and goodwill and one who abhorred violence, who lent his high scientific reputation and his moral authority to the cause that led to the production of such terrible weapons of destruction.

Einstein in those days was convinced of two things. One was that, having been alerted to the terrifying possibilities of a chain reaction in uranium, the American President should be left in no doubt as to what appeared to be already taking on the form of a concrete danger within Hitler's sphere of power. Secondly, he believed that the American President would never agree to the release of such frightful forces of destruction except in retaliation to similar weapons and the extreme danger of succumbing to an unscrupulous enemy.

Subsequently Einstein was to remark that he and the other scientists who had assisted in the successful completion of the Manhattan Project had been cruelly deceived. This was after he had been given the full details regarding the use of atom bombs against the poorly defended cities of Japan, a country that was already collapsing and on the brink of capitulation.

Indeed, this deception, practiced from the outset, was unintentional and was therefore all the more tragic. It affected all those who had counseled the authorities to be alert to the

possibilities of nuclear research and who later contributed to
the Manhattan Project. They were motivated by the greatest
concern about the threat of a German atom bomb, which
subsequently proved to be no more than an imaginary specter.
This was equally true not only of Einstein, but also of Fermi,
Bohr, Szilard, Wigner, Teller, and Weisskopf and, to the same
degree, of all the others who became involved subsequently.

In order to understand how this mistaken assessment, so
fatal in its consequences, could have been made, we must
look into some important events in Europe before returning
to further developments in the United States after Roosevelt's
historic decision of 1939 and to the actual Manhattan Project.
They not only explain why the danger of a German atom
bomb was considered genuine, but also give some important
pointers to our study on the question of whether all of the
political and military developments resulting from the creation of the terrible new weapon have a direct link to the
persecution of the Jews waged by the German government
throughout its total sphere of power in Europe.

To examine systematically this subquestion of the grounds
for the misconception concerning the threat of a German
atom bomb, we must first of all ask, where, just before the
outbreak of the Second World War and during it, it was
possible to consider turning available nuclear research to
military use.

Outside Europe and North America, there was only one
nation with the industrial capability and scientific skills to be
able to attempt construction of an atom bomb—Japan. But
when, only a few hours after the bomb had been dropped on
Hiroshima, the highest Japanese military leaders asked the
greatest nuclear scientist in their country, Bohr's former student Professor Yoshio Nishina, "Would you be able to construct an atom bomb?" He had to admit to being unable to do
so.

And since no one outside the borders of Japan had ever
seriously considered a possible threat of nuclear weapons
from this quarter, our further reflections can be concentrated
on the position in Europe. Taking into consideration the
scientific capability of prewar times, several countries merited,
at least theoretically, some consideration as possible contend-
ers for the development of nuclear weapons. However, the

policy of the Axis countries, principally the anti-Semitism propagated even beyond Germany at Hitler's instigation, had led to a number of changes.

For a time, Italy's physicists had been in the forefront of international nuclear research. However, the anti-Semitic laws and regulations demanded by Hitler and reluctantly initiated by Mussolini had driven into exile the very scientists who would have been indispensable to a possible Italian contribution to the development of an Axis atom bomb.

Along with Enrico Fermi, we must mention his most important student—Emilio Gino Segrè. Also of Jewish origin, he emigrated to the United States in 1938 and became a professor at Berkeley. Later, as head of an important working group in Los Alamos, he was counted as one of the fathers of the American atom bomb. In 1959 he received the Nobel Prize for physics. Remarkably enough, from Marconi to the present day, only two Italian physicists have been awarded this highest honor in science—Fermi and Segrè.

In the field of nuclear research, two other important scientists who were forced to interrupt their work in Italy in 1938 and go into exile because of their Jewish origin were Bruno Rossi and Bruno Pontecorvo. Rossi played a prominent part in the Manhattan Project. Pontecorvo, after emigrating to England, became a member of the Anglo-Canadian Atomic Energy Team and subsequently head of the nuclear physics department of the British nuclear research center at Harwell. This was, of course, before his disappearance in 1950 under mysterious circumstances and his final reappearance in the Soviet Union.

The total result of the anti-Semitic persecution in Italy was the demise within the shortest possible time of the Italian nuclear research project, up to then quite a promising effort.

France, overrun by German military power in the summer of 1940, forced to capitulate, and almost entirely occupied, was in a different position. As we already know, the country had an important nuclear research center under the direction of Frédéric Joliot-Curie. At about the same time Szilard and his friends tried from the United States to bring about a ban on publications intended to thwart the Axis powers, Joliot-Curie and his closest collaborators, Hans von Halban and Leo Kowarski, succeeded in causing a chain reaction in uranium. Within the laboratory, this crucial experiment was of the greatest importance for the development of nuclear weapons. Despite all exhortations, the French team published the results immediately. Probably at this time their scientific ambition was greater than their understanding that they were making dangerous secrets accessible to France's potential enemies.

As soon as war broke out, Joliot-Curie was vehement in his demands for the strictest secrecy in the field of nuclear research. He contacted the French Minister of War and advocated the speedy acquisition of large uranium reserves and of heavy water. He was even prepared to inform the military in detail concerning the most recent stages of research and the resulting technological possibilities for armaments.

This patriotic ardor might have had disastrous consequences for France's allies when, in mid-May, the French front crumbled at Sedan and the German armed forces started their drive toward Paris. It was there that Joliot-Curie had established not only a highly qualified team of nuclear scientists, but had also acquired the most modern equipment. He had also developed further his plans to build nuclear weapons. Furthermore, he was the sole owner of all the available stocks of heavy water (a source of deuterium) in Europe. Because of pressure exerted by Joliot-Curie, this precious raw material—in all 183 kilograms—had been bought and brought by special plane from Norway before German troops landed there in April 1940.

Plans, raw material, equipment, and last but not least, scientific personnel for the development of an atom bomb, all were precariously protected against seizure by the Germans by a crumbling frontline, and that for only a foreseeably short time.

Given this situation, Hans von Halban and Leo Kowarski undertook to remove the deuterium stock to safety. Traveling along hazardous routes, they first moved the heavy water containers to Clermont-Ferrand, then to Bordeaux, and finally, on board a coal steamer, to England. They also rescued other raw materials important to the war effort, such as most of the French stocks of industrial diamonds. However, by far the most significant item they took to England was their own scientific knowledge.

With his consent, more of Joliot-Curie's collaborators

landed in England before the Germans marched into Paris, among them Bertrand Leopold Goldschmidt, subsequently a group leader at the Anglo-Canadian nuclear project, and Jules Gueron, who worked on in Cambridge, and then in Montreal as a group director of the same project. While Goldschmidt and Gueron were Jews born in France, Hans von Halban, born in Leipzig, had been forced to abandon his scientific work in Germany for no reason other than his Jewish origins. He first emigrated to Copenhagen and found employment under Niels Bohr before moving on to Joliot-Curie in Paris. Leo Kowarski was also a Jew; he fled to France from the German-Lithuanian frontier area. Had working conditions even before 1933 not been so poor for an Eastern-Jewish scientist in Germany, he would have preferred finishing his studies in Berlin rather than in Paris.

These circumstances that led to the exodus of Joliot-Curie's principal associates, combined with his personal loyalty although he remained in Paris, had some effect. Not wishing to desert his valuable equipment, he destroyed all his notes on his most recent research before the entry of the Germans. He also made sure that his laboratory stopped all work of interest to the military.* All these measures eliminated France from the nations where development of an atom bomb would have been possible during the war.

The next country in question is Denmark, which was occupied by the Germans in April 1940. Though this nation had never undertaken military nuclear research, there was an availability of important results of theoretical and experimental research, numerous items of information about the achievements and aims of work carried on in other countries, and a team of highly qualified scientists under the leadership of Niels Bohr. This world-renowned scholar stayed in Copenhagen after its occupation by the Germans in spite of the danger to him. He was aware of the fact that his presence formed an effective protective screen for the numerous Jewish associates in his institute. In the early days his great

---

*The agent acting for the German military to supervise the Joliot-Curie Institute was his former student Wolfgang Gentner. Joliot-Curie made a "gentleman's agreement" with Gentner that forbade the use of the institute for war research.

popularity and international reputation was a sufficient deterrent to keep the Gestapo from moving against him.

In the autumn of 1943 the shipping expert at the German embassy in Copenhagen, Georg Duckwitz, learned that all the Jews in Denmark were to be arrested and deported in one concerted action on the night of October 1st. Bohr and his wife were also slated for the "final solution." Duckwitz (who after the war became West German ambassador to Denmark and, in 1967, Willy Brandt's first Secretary of State) managed to warn the Danish court, which led to the failure of the planned Gestapo action. It was only after nearly all the Jews of Denmark had been saved from deportation by clandestine evacuation to Sweden in an action directed by King Christian X, with the active help of the Christian population, that Niels Bohr himself left for Sweden in a fishing boat. (Just afterwards the Gestapo came to occupy his institute and take him into "protective custody.") From Sweden the British ferried him in a small fighter-plane to Scotland. Before the end of 1943, using the cover name Nicholas Baker, Niels Bohr arrived in the United States. He soon became involved in the Manhattan Project and the development of the first atom bomb.

It was the reports brought to America by this most recently arrived fugitive from German despotism, Mr. Baker, about the progress of atomic research in Berlin that strengthened the assumption among scientists and military men alike that the Germans might already have achieved a considerable forward leap in the development of nuclear weapons. Spurred on by this fear—unfounded as it was later proved to be— they intensified their endeavors to overtake Hitler.

The next country to be examined will be Great Britain. In point of fact, except for the United States, it was only in the British sphere of influence that progress in the development of nuclear weapons in time to affect the outcome of World War Two was possible and actually under way.*

British nuclear scientists, under the leadership of Ernest Rutherford from New Zealand, had devoted special attention to the problem of nuclear fission and had done pioneer scientific work during the First World War. After Rutherford's death

---

*For various reasons Soviet researchers were still far from considering the construction of nuclear weapons.

it was primarily James Chadwick, Nobel Prize laureate in physics for 1935, who continued his work, though there was no objective such as harnessing atomic energy or producing nuclear weapons. The work concerned theoretical physics.

This situation did not change until the spring of 1939, when signs of military conflict with Germany increased. At that time a British physicist, George P. Thompson, having read the newly published work of Joliot-Curie and his collaborators, drew the attention of the Royal Air Force to the extraordinary importance of this latest nuclear discovery.

Astonishingly, Thompson's messages were at least taken seriously enough for him to be granted modest financial backing and assistance in the procurement of certain raw materials. A few months later, however, when war broke out, the military declared that nuclear research could not be given priority, since it was of insufficient importance to the war effort and must consequently step aside for other truly important military tasks, concerned with armaments, supply, and research.

This extraordinary decision had an even more remarkable result. Once it was established that nuclear research was looked upon by the British leadership as fairly unimportant to the war effort, it was left by and large to the "refugees," those predominantly German-Jewish Continental Europeans who had fled from England's enemies. With the significance of atomic research rapidly increasing, the influence and standing of the scientists from the Continent was considerably enhanced, chiefly because of the recognition given them by the military.

Some of the scientists who emigrated to the United States noted with discreet envy how much better their colleagues in England were treated by both the civil service and the military. According to Robert Jungk, Weisskopf recalled "that as a former Austrian he was once grudgingly granted permission by the American authorities to participate in a special conference with 'three English gentlemen' who were expected from London for a discussion concerning the Manhattan Project. Upon the arrival of the three Britishers, it came to light that they were none other than . . . Halban, Peierls, and Simon."

Hans von Halban has already been discussed. Rudolf Ernst Peierls, born in Berlin in 1907, had studied in Berlin, Munich, and Leipzig, and had joined the research group of the AEG. As a Jew, had left Germany in 1935. Since 1937 he had held a chair in mathematical physics at the University of Birmingham, where he concentrated on problems of atomic energy, and from 1943 on, he worked with others in New York and Los Alamos on the Manhattan Project. Franz Eugen Simon, also Jewish, was born in Berlin in 1893; he was a professor in Breslau and Berlin before fleeing from Germany. Exiled in England, he soon became a professor at Oxford. As a result of his work, particularly at low temperatures, which was basic to nuclear physics, he became one of the founders and leaders of the British atomic energy project. He died in 1956 in Oxford as Sir Francis Simon.

The true situation emerges clearly from this short survey of the research progress in nations other than the United States. The fact is, that during the Second World War, the capacity even to consider building an atom bomb was, except for Germany, present only in the Anglo-Saxon countries. Those countries soon combined their efforts in this field, giving priority to the Manhattan Project. Elsewhere there was a lack of will, of available material and personnel, or perhaps even an understanding of the military application of previous nuclear research. The realization of the enormous danger of an enemy lead in the development of nuclear weapons was fully grasped in the Anglo-Saxon countries, whose highly industrialized areas and concomitant population density made them most vulnerable to possible atomic attack. Under the mistaken belief that the Axis powers had technical superiority, supreme efforts were made either to overtake them or at least to gain equality.

At a cost of several billions of dollars, and with the employment of more than 300,000 people of the most diverse skills, the Manhattan Project grew, at a rate never equalled in the history of science or technology, to be the greatest single war effort of all time. It was not possible to test a small model of the bomb, so the necessary theoretical calculations alone preceded production of the first bomb. This required years of work by large teams of scientists in widely diverse fields and with varying degrees of skill. Strictest secrecy demanded that the entire project be broken up into hundreds of individual units, which in turn required precise coordination and a vast administrative apparatus. Most of all, however, the project could not move forward without the aid of a major portion of the world's top scientists in every field, especially physics, mathematics, and chemistry, in addition to as many nuclear physicists as possible.

After the Manhattan Project was started, when it became even more evident what tremendous difficulties would have to be overcome, the British and Americans should have realized that there was no need to fear a German atom bomb. Hitler's Reich was in retrospect clearly no longer capable of efforts on the scale undertaken by the United States. The belief nevertheless persisted that Germans had gained a head start, and the Manhattan Project workers continued to believe that it was necessary to catch up.

How could such a mistaken assumption arise? What was it that held even the recent emigrants to the belief that there was danger from a German atom bomb? And if there really was such a possibility, what prevented the construction of a German atom bomb?

One of the most important, if not the most crucial, preconditions for Germany's building an atom bomb that could still have been decisive for the outcome of the war, would have been the availability of a team of dedicated, highly qualified nuclear physicists prepared for close cooperation and convinced of the necessity for the utmost effort. Today we are in a position to make this judgment, based on what the Americans experienced with the Manhattan Project. First, let us examine whether this criterion could be met in any way.

Before 1933 Germany was the leader in the natural sciences. In the international "atom club," as it was known, the world's top nuclear physicists had gathered in a group founded on the basis of relationships between students and teachers and on personal friendships. The Germans were far more strongly represented than any other nation. Furthermore, among the forty-six Nobel Prize laureates in physics between 1901 and 1939, fourteen members—that is, more than 30 per cent—had their roots in German culture.

Of these fourteen German or German-Austrian Nobel Prize laureates in physics (including those who would win the Prize by 1939), four had died by 1933. The other ten lived and worked in their home country without any thought of emigrating.

In order to round off this picture, we must add those who before 1933 also lived and worked in Germany, and were among the coming scientific stars who received the Nobel Prize in later years. This raises the number of active leading physicists in Germany and Austria in 1933 who would eventually win the Nobel Prize for physics to eighteen. In the order in which they won the Prize, they are Philipp von Lenard, Max von Laue, Max Planck, Johannes Stark, Albert Einstein, James Franck, Gustav Hertz, Werner Heisenberg, Erwin Schrödinger, Victor Franz Hess, Otto Stern, Wolfgang Pauli, Felix Bloch, Max Born, Walther Bothe, Eugen Wigner, Hans D. Jensen, and Hans Bethe.

Nine of these eighteen were directly affected by the persecution of Jews initiated in 1933 and were forced to emigrate. These were Einstein, Franck, Hertz, Stern, Pauli, Bloch, Born, Wigner, and Bethe. One man, Victor Franz Hess, chose emigration because of his Jewish wife. Another one, Schrödinger, renounced his teaching post at Berlin University because of his dislike of National Socialism, in particular its "racial" policies. He first went to Graz, then to the United States, and finally to Ireland.

It is unquestionable, therefore, that among those who sooner or later won the Nobel Prize for physics, more than 60 per cent were lost to Germany, mostly as a direct consequence of the "Jewish policy" of the "Third Reich."

With regard to the special area of nuclear research, the calculation based only on one indication, the Nobel Prize for physics, cannot precisely document the total loss suffered by Germany's scientific capability. On the one hand, several of the Nobel Prize physicists mentioned played only a small part or did not participate at all in nuclear research. Furthermore, one looks in vain among the scientists who were later awarded the Nobel Prize for some of the most important researchers and teachers in nuclear physics—Otto Hahn, for instance, (who received the Nobel Prize in 1944 for chemistry), or his kindred spirit and close collaborator of many years standing, Lise Meitner, who was later awarded the Enrico Fermi prize; or her nephew, Otto Frisch, together with whom she was able to furnish scientific proof that uranium atoms exposed to slow neutron bombardment split into two large fragments, or Carl Friedrich von Weizsäcker, the outstanding nuclear physicist and philosopher, or even Arnold Sommerfeld, pioneer in

The Bomb That Went into Exile   181

nuclear research and teacher of genius to a number of younger Nobel Prize laureates.

The list could go on, but whatever its length, it would not change the outcome of our original calculation; since both Lise Meitner and Otto Frisch were forced out of Germany because they were Jewish, while in 1938 Arnold Sommerfeld was thrown out of the teaching profession in Munich for "racial" reasons.

This loss—estimated at roughly 60 per cent of the highly qualified nuclear researchers—was caused by the Jewish persecution in Germany. However, many factors combined to bring about the final outcome that nuclear arms were not built in Germany during the Second World War. The contrary assumption in the minds of the emigrant scientists played a crucial part in setting into motion and accelerating the Manhattan Project.

The persecution of Jews in Germany led to the dismissal of several Jewish professors of science in the first weeks after January 30, 1933. This action sparked another that has attracted hardly any attention. Numerous "Aryan" scientists, who until that time had bothered little with politics, and had certainly not allowed politics to influence their own attitudes as researchers, now recognized—some instantly, others gradually—that such a way of life was no longer possible.

First some very reputable scientists courageously (but of course in vain) objected to the expulsion of their Jewish friends and colleagues. For instance, twenty-two professors— among them Heisenberg, von Laue, Planck, Hilbert, and Prandtl—protested the dismissal of the Jewish professor of mathematics Courant, who had been seriously wounded in the First World War. Even in 1938, when Lise Meitner was to be dismissed, not only Otto Hahn, whose shadow Meitner had been for a quarter-century, but also Max Planck*

---

*Max Planck (1858–1947) was forced to resign the directorship (which he had held since 1930) of the Kaiser Wilhelm Society for the Advancement of Science in 1937. He had made himself most unpopular in the eyes of Hitler on two counts: his courageous intervention on behalf of dismissed and persecuted Jewish colleagues, and his strictly scientific attitude toward Einstein's theory of relativity and supplementary work in connection with it. His son Erwin, born in 1893, was sentenced to death and murdered by the Nazis as late as 1945 for active resistance to the Nazis.

intervened. Until that time, Meitner, an Austrian national, had been able to work unhampered by the "racial" laws. Both Hahn and Planck tried—going directly to Hitler—to gain at least a delay for Meitner and their other Jewish coworkers at the Kaiser Wilhelm Institute. Of course their efforts were as fruitless as the other protests and pleas made by reputable scientists in previous years had been.

However, even if the aim of achieving an amelioration of the Jewish policy failed completely, the preoccupation with this problem and the depressing futility of protesting it had another effect. It awakened some to consciousness of being national and world citizens, particularly among those who could be considered indispensable. They recognized that Hitler's government was different from any earlier governments: without scruples, without morals—even criminal! And this understanding led some of the most important German nuclear scientists to the decision—of great significance to this study—that the Hitler regime must not be allowed any opportunity to utilize the latest results of nuclear research for military purposes.

These scientists in the area of German nuclear research were exposed to unbelievable mental stress. Otto Hahn furnishes a classical example.

Special circumstances, unrecorded in any scientific journal, attended Hahn's famous Nobel Prize-winning experiment, which he conducted with Fritz Strassmann. This was the first successful split of a uranium atom by bombardment with neutrons. But these scientists had more than scientific difficulties to overcome.

There was, first of all, the general mood in Berlin during those weeks when the city had not yet recovered from the pogroms of November 9, 1938, even today still euphemistically termed the "crystal night."* Several people close to those

---

*Translator's note: In retaliation for the assassination in Paris of a German embassy official, the SS unleashed its rowdies all over Germany. In one night almost all synagogues were torched, the shop windows of Jewish stores were smashed, Jewish homes were robbed and vandalized, and Jews were beaten and dragged off to camps in great numbers. Later, Goering was furious because most of the buildings actually belonged to Aryans. Just replacing the glass (which had to be imported from Czechoslovakia) would have consumed too much of Germany's foreign reserves. They finally arrived at a solution—the Jews would have to pay all liability insurance! But of course the synagogues were never repaired.

involved in the experiment—Hahn, Strassmann, and two women assistants, Lieber and Bohne—had been reviled, ill-treated, robbed of all their possessions, thrown into concentration camps, or driven to suicide.

It was at that point that Meitner's forced departure rent the fabric of scientific and human relations. These shocking circumstances further laid on Hahn obligations of friendship that were not conducive to intensive work. For instance, his diary has two entries for December 17, 1939. One reads, "Exciting ra[dium]-ba[rium]-me[sothorium] fractionation." The other notes, "Department of Finance on behalf of Lise Meitner." The second entry relates to the fact that the government demanded from all Jews that they make a payment to their tormentors, the organizers of the pogrom, to repair the damage inflicted when their homes and businesses had been smashed. At the same time that he successfully demonstrated uranium fission, Otto Hahn also had to find a new tenant for the apartment Lise Meitner had just vacated; after all, the money for the "Jewish tax" had to be scraped together.

Personal worries were also connected with the persecution of the Jews. At that time an anti-Semitic exhibit under the title "The eternal Jew" had just opened in Berlin. Evidently in order to incite passionate hatred among the populace against the Jews, portraits—many of them strongly retouched—of those who were outcasts were shown. They included, along with one of Lise Meitner, a picture of Hahn himself!

The "error" was corrected by the exhibition organizers only after a hasty conversation Hahn had with the president of the Kaiser Wilhelm Society, Carl Bosch, who intervened immediately.*

On the evening of this exciting day—December 19, 1938—Otto Hahn wrote his Christmas letter to Lise Meitner from his laboratory. "In between, when I can get to it, I am working, and Strassmann is working indefatigably on the

---

*Because of his "Jewish-sounding" surname, Otto Hahn was frequently thought to be Jewish. In fact, he did have Jewish ancestors on his *mother's* side, a closely guarded secret that was hushed up because German science could not afford the loss of this scientist of the highest international repute.

uranium extracts assisted by Lieber* and Bohne. Soon it will be 11 P.M. At a quarter to twelve Strassmann will return so that I can gradually wend my way homeward. There is something so remarkable about these radium isotopes that for now we are telling no one but you."

It was a letter fraught with weighty consequences. It reached Lise Meitner right after she had had a Christmas visit from her nephew, the physicist Otto Frisch, who had fled to Copenhagen. In a small seaside resort deserted during the winter, aunt and nephew discussed what the two nuclear chemists were finding out in Berlin.

David Irving describes what happened next.

> No sooner were the Christmas holidays over than Lise Meitner returned to Stockholm, while Dr. Otto Frisch travelled back to Copenhagen, where he informed Niels Bohr of Hahn's discovery, as yet unpublished in Berlin. He also explained to Bohr what conclusions he and his aunt had reached with regard to the amounts of energy released. Shortly thereafter Bohr went to the United States, where he remained for several months. The secret crossed the Atlantic with him.**

In the meantime, Otto Hahn, whom Meitner had fully informed about the outcome of her calculations, completely understood the possible consequences of his successful experiment. In February 1939 he expressed his thoughts openly to a young colleague, Carl Friedrich von Weizsäcker. "If my discovery were to lead to Hitler's getting an atom bomb, I would commit suicide!"

The thoughts of the few remaining members of the international "atom club" who were still in Germany were similar to Hahn's.

Petrus Debye, the Dutch scientist who had been living in Germany for over thirty years, 1936 Nobel Prize winner in chemistry and eventually director of the Kaiser Wilhelm Institute for Physics, steadfastly refused to accept German citizenship or even to make a declaration of unmistakable

---

*Clara Lieber, also of Jewish descent, soon emigrated to America.
**David Irving, *The Virus House* (London, 1967).

sympathy with Hitler, the Reich, and "German" physics; he preferred to leave Berlin and to accept a professorship in the United States.

According to Robert Jungk, the most important element that prevented the building of a German atomic bomb was "the personal attitude of the most important German atomic researchers who, fortunately, did nothing to advance the construction of such a bomb in the face of a bureaucratic lack of comprehension and technical deficiencies. They successfully diverted the National Socialist authorities from thinking of such an inhuman weapon."

The contrary opinions voiced after the war by some Americans were taken up by Carl Friedrich von Weizsäcker, Heisenberg's closest collaborator. In a private letter addressed only to Max Himmelhuber, Weizsäcker gave the reasons for this reluctance.

> One must understand that it would be too much to expect from the American physicists, frequently conscience-stricken because of the atom bomb, that they admit publicly or privately that the German physicists gave some careful thought to the moral aspect of the matter even earlier than they themselves did. Furthermore, I do not find that we Germans are in a position that gives us the right to advance such a claim in public. While I do believe that we gave considerable thought to the moral problem of the atom bomb at a very early stage and that during the war we did nothing in this respect with which we should reproach ourselves today, I believe that both as a nation and generally as individuals we have not overcome the moral problem of National Socialism sufficiently to permit us to feel superior. For this reason Heisenberg and I have always chosen the formula of saying publicly merely that we could not make the bombs and were happy not to.

Another famous nuclear scientist who remained in Germany, the Nobel Prize laureate Max von Laue, expressed in the spring of 1940 why one could "not make the bombs." He was speaking to his colleague, the physicist Fritz Houtermans, who had been handed over to the Gestapo by Soviet Russia and who was later conditionally released. Like von Laue,

Houtermans was anti-Nazi and extremely worried. "My dear colleague," von Laue said bluntly, "an invention one does not wish to make, one does not make!"

If the persecution of the Jews in Hitler's Reich caused the departure of a number of scientists who were indispensable or nearly indispensable to the successful continuation of German nuclear research, it also awakened the conscience of the most important of the remaining nuclear physicists. It drove them to passive resistance, certainly with regard to the military utilization of nuclear discoveries. These two factors should not blind us to the fact that the Nazi regime retained a remnant of older and younger scientists who were technically qualified and who might have been capable of executing a possible command of Hitler's to build a German atom bomb. If they had started early and done the job in a few years, they might just have been in time to influence decisively the outcome of the war. Furthermore, these men had no scruples worth mentioning that might have prevented them from handing the "Führer" such a weapon. Among the German atomic physicists, as among intellectuals in other fields, there were a few dedicated Nazis and a few ambitious opportunists, along with quite a few weaklings who would do anything asked of them even against their own better judgment.

However—and perhaps this is the most remarkable consequence of Hitler's fanatical hatred of the Jews—the "Führer," who liked to think of himself as "the greatest field marshal of all time," did not recognize the military possibilities of nuclear research at all. He laughed at the mere idea that theoretical physicists should be able to think up anything useful, let alone something crucial to the outcome of the war.

Such capabilities Hitler granted at most to the practitioners of a "German physics," who had agreed with him completely in denouncing Einstein's theory of relativity, calling it a "Jewish bluff." Further results based on Einstein's and Bohr's theories were summarily dismissed as "Jewish speculations." In addition, since modern physics is primarily based on the theoretical insights gained by Jewish scientists, all "Aryans" who used them as a basis for their work were declared to be "spiritual Jews." Hitler was confirmed in such nonsense by two Nobel Prize winners in physics. One was Professor Philipp von

Lenard,* born in Pressburg, who was just over seventy in
1931 when he became emeritus, and who was a maniacally
obsessed anti-Semite. The other physicist, Johannes Stark,
received the Nobel Prize in 1919. While his authorship has been
disputed by his heirs, Stark is associated with an article that
appeared in the official organ of the SS, the *Schwarzes Korps*,
in 1937. Under the title "White Jews in Science," the article
seemed to confer scientific authority on Hitler's anti-Semitism.**
"The political influence of the Jewish mentality at the
universities was obvious," the article notes.

> The political influence of the Jewish mentality at the
> universities was obvious. The influence was less obvious
> but just as damaging in scientific respects. It hampered
> Germanic research focused on reality by imposing Jew-
> ish intellectualism, dogmatic formalism, and propagandis-
> tic methods. It sought to train the student body, and
> especially the younger generation of teachers, in Jewish
> ways of thinking.
>
> Indeed, in 1933 teachers and assistants of the Jewish
> race had to relinquish their jobs. Futhermore, at the
> moment, Aryan professors with Jewish wives are being
> dismissed. However, the great number of Aryan Jewish
> sympathizers and disciples of Jews, who used to support
> the Jewish dominance at German universities, either
> openly or covertly, have kept their positions. They
> retain the influence of the Jewish mentality at German
> universities.

This article was remarkable from many points of view. It
claimed that the Nobel Prize winners Heisenberg, Schrödinger,
and Dirac were "Einstein's disciples"; it called Heisenberg
himself the "representative of Judaism"; and it demanded all
their "disappearance." None of these statements could have

*Philipp von Lenard joined the Nazi Party in 1924. According to
reliable sources, he himself was of "non-Aryan" descent, being the son of
a Jewish merchant in Pressburg, David Lenard. Whatever the truth of
that claim, he received his scientific training at the hands of a "non-
Aryan," the physicist Heinrich Hertz.
**See Appendix for the full wording of this very enlightening article.

been printed had not the Nazi leadership, chiefly Hitler himself, held at least similar opinions.

Today we know that Hitler actually viewed as dangerous enemies those leading scientists who disregarded as nonsense the distinction between "German" and "Jewish" physics and only recognized correct or incorrect physics. He met them partly with suspicion and partly with derision. By this attitude the "Führer" of the Reich gave up his last chance of maintaining a functioning scientific community in the area of nuclear physics. In a blind overestimation of their own strength, Hitler and his henchmen renounced any serious attempt to examine what atomic research might have been able to furnish to the technology of weaponry and energy.

In his gripping account of the supposed race to build the atom bomb between the Americans and the Germans, David Irving stated that "in 1942, four years after Otto Hahn's discovery of nuclear fission, German atomic research was on a level with that of the British and Americans." He added with noticeable surprise, "By the end of the war in 1945, the German scientists had hardly improved on the results of 1942, while the United States had established the unwieldly industrial apparatus, had successfully ignited the first plutonium bomb, and shortly afterward had dropped operational bombs on Hiroshima and Nagasaki."

Irving concluded, "The greatest obstacle to the speed of German research was the government's attitude toward pure science."

The almost complete lack of interest in nuclear physics on the part of the German supreme leadership does not mean that no one in Germany was any longer occupied with atomic research. In actual fact, three research groups emerged, which enjoyed completely different sympathies and support. Irving describes their activity in detail. With an understanding of the subject matter and with much intuition, he was aided by hitherto undiscovered documents that were stored in a warehouse of the United States Atomic Energy Commission in Oak Ridge, Tennessee. He remarks on the lack of coordination, of central guidance, of urgency, and of the necessary priorities.

What his investigation overlooked in part—what it could not help but overlook—were certain nuances and imponderables that hardly ever find expression in documents. These include the reluctance of the most important scientists to divulge findings of military value, or even to bring them to the notice of a hated government.

These are the facts. On June 4 (or June 6, according to another version), 1942, the minister for armaments, Albert Speer, had Heisenberg report to him concerning the stage reached by German atomic research. Heisenberg remembers that at the time "definitive proof was available showing that the technical exploitation of atomic energy in a reactor was possible. It is also probable that explosives for atomic bombs could be produced in a uranium reactor. However, no studies concerning the technical aspect of the atomic bomb had yet been undertaken, such as the minimum size required for the bomb. Greater interest was expressed in the determination that the energy developed in the uranium reactor could be used for driving machinery. This seemed an easier goal, to be achieved by simpler methods."

To the great relief of those who did not wish to build an atom bomb for Hitler, the final result was Speer's decision that the modest working style followed so far was to be continued. With this decision, the improbable prospect of the Reich's arming itself with nuclear weapons during the war faded for good.

As a further curious fact we might mention that even in the spring of 1945, shortly before collapsing, the mighty Hitler realm was technically not as advanced as the United States had been several years earlier, at a time when the whole world feared Germany might possess a hidden trump card in the form of operational "secret weapons." Neither assembly plants for producing U_{235} or U_{239}—the elements for chain reactions in atomic bombs—were available, nor even a uranium reactor remotely comparable to the American and British "piles." It was only in February 1945 that they started on the construction of a larger reactor in a rocky cave owned by a country innkeeper. Near the end of the war this device, still unfinished, fell into the hands of the Americans.

The German scientists really had not been in a hurry, nor had they been given any incentive to hurry. The extent of the leaders' preoccupation with atomic research is typified by a memorandum found in the files of Reich Marshal Hermann

Göring. In it he names Heisenberg as "the boss of this theorizing group" and notes that "to this day, in 1942, in one of his papers he eulogizes the Danish half-Jew, Niels Bohr, as an absolute genius!"

Clearly the persecution of the Jews drove nearly all German atomic scientists of any standing into emigration if they were immediately affected or were sympathizers of victims; into isolation; or into passive resistance. The question remains whether other causes could have decisively contributed to Germany's losing its original early lead in atomic research and in the presumed race for the bomb.

Was it perhaps his self-delusion and megalomania that led Hitler to believe that he would be able to achieve a speedy final victory with only the weapons available at the outbreak of the war? This seems to be indicated by the fact that several attempts were actually made to interest the "Führer" in the construction of atomic bombs. When it was already too late, in 1944, Paul Harteck tried to persuade Colonel Schumann, director of the research division at the army ordnance department, to do some prodding at the "highest level." But the colonel declined. Carl Friedrich von Weizsäcker, who was present, has a plausible explanation. "I remember that Schumann, who was an inferior physicist but a very able tactician, once urgently advised against saying anything about atom bombs in the highest quarters. He suggested, 'If the Führer hears about it, he will ask, How long will it take you? Six months? Then, if we don't have the atom bomb within six months, there will be hell to pay.' "

Then there was the attempt by Dr. Wilhelm Ohnesorge, for many years Reich postmaster general, to draw Hitler's attention to the possibility of building an atom bomb. It was his ambition to surprise the "Führer" one fine day with a "wonder weapon" or at least a brand-new procedure for energy gain. Ohnesorge persuaded Hitler to promote a private institute, independent of official bodies, under the direction of the inventor Manfred von Ardenne, and which employed the atomic physicist Fritz Houtermans, the one-time fugitive from Nazi Germany who had been handed over to the Gestapo by the Russians. As early as the summer of 1941, Houtermans had developed ideas similar to Harteck's, but he took good care not to publicize his thinking or to let any written materials get out.* Only after Harteck's proposal became known to the circle of atomic physicists, did Houtermans reluctantly disclose his secret, since it could no longer influence the outcome of the war. His paper, only slightly revised in August 1944, was entitled, "Zur Frage der Auslösung von Kern-Kettenreaktionen" [On the Question of the Release of Nuclear Chain Reactions].

Near the end of 1940 Hitler had already been informed by his postmaster general about the "uranium bomb research" on the part of his otherwise so peaceful department. However, when Dr. Ohnesorge, bursting with pride, wished to report in detail to the "Führer" what Manfred von Ardenne believed he had discovered in the way of opportunities for armament technology, Hitler rebuffed him scornfully. No, the "Führer," spoiled by "lightning" victories, did not wish to hear any more about secret weapons with the "post-office trademark," all the more since they appeared still to be in the theoretical stage. He had never believed in the usefulness of "purely speculative" research, had always considered it to be the futile "bragging" of Jewish intellectuals that was sometimes unfortunately adopted by "Aryan" scientists and typical "spiritual Jews" and "Einstein disciples."

To some, this explanation might appear too fantastic. It seems inconceivable that the man entrusted with the leadership of a nation should have been so obstinately stupid and self-deluded. However, the story is confirmed by Hitler's closest collaborator in the field of armaments, Reich Minister for War Production, Albert Speer. "On the suggestion of the nuclear physicists we scuttled the project to develop an atom bomb by the autumn of 1942." He adds in his memoirs that he asked the physicists again "about deadlines" and was told "that we could not count on anything for four years," and that Professor Heisenberg had previously given a reason for the delay: "We lacked the technical experience."

Speer continues:

> Perhaps it would have proved possible to have the atom bomb ready for employment in 1945. But it would have meant mobilizing all our technical and financial

---

*Contradicting Jungk, Irving insists that Houtermans had let at least Heisenberg and some other physicists into the secret.

resources to that end, as well as our scientific talent. It would have meant giving up all other projects, such as the development of the rocket weapons. From this point of view, too, Peenemünde was not only our biggest but our most misguided project.

Our failure to pursue the possibilities of atomic warfare can be partly traced to ideological reasons. Hitler had great respect for Philipp Lenard, the physicist who had received the Nobel Prize in 1920 and was one of the few early adherents of Nazism among the ranks of the scientists. Lenard had instilled the idea in Hitler *that the Jews were exerting a seditious influence through their concern with nuclear physics and the theory of relativity.**

In his table talk Hitler occasionally referred to nuclear physics as "Jewish physics"—with a bow to his illustrious Party comrade. This epithet was adopted not only by Rosenberg but clearly also by Hitler's Minister for Education, Rust, who had authority over the universities and the Kaiser Wilhelm and other institutes, which made him reluctant to support nuclear research.

There is further impressive testimony for Hitler's narrow-minded obstinacy as well as for the fact that hatred of the Jews took precedence with him over everything else, even at the cost of Germany's destruction. It comes from Richard Will-stätter's memoirs. In *Aus meinen Leben* [Out of my Life] he recalls that Privy Councillor Carl Bosch requested an audience with the Führer at a time when the cleansing of the Kaiser Wilhelm Institute and the universities was already far advanced and he wished to warn against the widespread dismissals of "non-Aryan" scientists. However, the Führer insisted on the strictest implementation of the measures.

---

*In a footnote Speer explains: "According to L. W. Helwig, *Persönlichkeiten der Gegenwart* (1940), Lenard inveighed against 'relativity theories produced by alien minds.' In his four-volume work, *Die Deutsche Physik* (1935), Helwig considers physics 'cleansed of the outgrowths which the by-now well-known findings of race research have shown to be the exclusive product of the Jewish mind and which the German *Volk* must shun as racially incompatible with itself.'"
Albert Speer, *Erinnerungen* (Frankfurt, 1969); trans. by Richard and Clara Winston as *Inside the Third Reich* (New York, 1970). Italics added.

Thereupon Bosch drew attention to the considerable damage threatening the application and development of chemistry and physics in Germany. "Well then, we'll get along without physics for a century!" Such was the Führer's reply, according to Bosch.

The question still remains whether, apart from the emigrants and those scientists who either sympathized with them or were themselves decisively opposed to Germany's building an atom bomb, no capable nuclear physicists could be found in the Greater German Reich of the early 1940s who might have been able and willing to produce a nuclear weapon.

Beyond a doubt there were a few who were prepared to do this work, and David Irving has amassed a great deal of material on the subject. The conclusion is clear enough. Those who could have, did not wish to; and those who wished to, could not. They lacked the intelligence, the experience, or the exchange of ideas with colleagues so necessary to stimulate important impulses. It may be that they were insufficiently prompted and encouraged.

As Irving attests, "many physicists" had reservations on moral-political grounds, and he leaves the question of their capability open. He mentions by name Heisenberg, von Weizsäcker, and Fritz Houtermans, all of whom felt pressing concern about whether work on the uranium project could be ethically justified.

Another expert of considerable competence went so far as to say that only one of the nuclear scientists left in Germany could be considered sufficiently competent to have been "the head of a German atom bomb project." This expert, Professor Samuel Goudsmit, himself a high-ranking member of the international "atom club," was scientific director of the so-called Alsos Mission in 1944–1945. This was a special team that was charged by Washington to explore a possible lead by Hitler's Germany in the field of atomic weapons and, if necessary, take "appropriate measures" to remove the threat.

Almost immediately—in November 1944—Goudsmit learned that a German lead in atomic weaponry was out of the question when the records of the German atomic project left by Professor Weizsäcker in conquered Strasbourg fell into his hands. Instead they proved that Germany's development lagged by at least two years behind that of the United States. But, Jungk reports,

> The Alsos Mission could not close the books on its inquiry once it had Weizsäcker's papers, since Washington feared that the records might be a German war ruse. Speculation that work on the construction of an atomic bomb was continuing somewhere in Germany must continue until all important physicists had been arrested and all laboratories taken over.
>
> Goudsmit always insisted that *only Heisenberg could be the "brains" behind a German uranium project*. He scornfully rejected the skepticism of the American military authorities, who believed that perhaps, after all, other German physicists, of whom Goudsmit had never heard, might be secretly working on such a weapon. "Perhaps a paperhanger could imagine himself to have become a military genius overnight, and a champagne salesman"—this was a reference to Ribbentrop—"can dress himself up as a diplomat; but such outsiders could never acquire scientific knowledge fast enough to build an atomic bomb."

Ironically, when Sam Goudsmit—whose elderly Jewish parents in Holland had been seized by the SS, deported, and gassed—finally came upon the hiding place of the German uranium project, he did not find Heisenberg, who had fled to his family in Bavaria. But on Heisenberg's desk he found a framed photograph showing two men exchanging a cordial handshake, clearly on the best of terms. They were Professor Werner Heisenberg and his host during a visit to the United States in 1939—Sam Goudsmit.

In sum, the results of our secondary investigation into the chances for the successful construction of a German atom bomb during the war reveal that this possibility had already been greatly reduced by the exodus of many outstanding nuclear physicists; that they were further diminished by the resistance of the remaining leading "Aryan" scientists; and that the anti-intellectualism of Hitler and his clique, rooted in anti-Semitism, prevented an awareness of potential last chances. But how did the fatally mistaken assessment of Germany's position come to be so firmly held by the very people whose expulsion had so severely reduced Hitler's chances of obtaining a nuclear weapon? How was it that the experts who had emigrated could seriously believe that the Germans had made headway in atomic research?

First there was the bitter recognition of the emigrants, gained between 1933 and 1938, that all the prognostications concerning a weakening of Germany as a result of the elimination of the Jews were quite obviously wrong. The Hitler regime had survived all crises superbly, and in the summer of 1939 it gave the impression of being stronger and more secure than ever before. The actual shortcomings—especially in scientific research and in the leading scientists' willingness to cooperate with the state apparatus—were hidden behind a most impressive facade and were veiled by all kinds of declarations, made for a variety of motives, that appeared to prove the reverse.

The speed, the volume, and the precision of the German war preparations, along with the brazen and challenging speeches accompanying them, gave rise to the fear that Hitler had a card up his sleeve—all the more so as he asserted that he had "included every risk in his calculation." The nuclear scientists who had fled Germany were forced to assume that the secret weapon could only be an atom bomb. They realized that in the field of nuclear fission Germany was theoretically as far advanced as they were and that Germany certainly had the technology to extract all practical benefits from the latest theoretical findings. After all that had happened, the Reich leadership was the least likely of all governments to have moral scruples about using the newly discovered energies as tools of destruction.

The messages that arrived from Germany—frequently at first, more sparingly later on—some by way of Niels Bohr in Copenhagen or Lise Meitner in Stockholm, others by diplomatic or secret-service channels—confirmed the emigrated nuclear physicists in their fears because they misinterpreted them on the basis of their all too understandable suspicion. The fact that, shortly before the outbreak of the war, scientific papers were published in Germany on uranium chain reactions, such as an article by Siegfried Flügge, one of Hahn's closest collaborators, led to the mistaken belief that Berlin had moved on to a much more advanced stage. At conferences abroad, German nuclear physicists occasionally hinted that they were conscious of the dangers inherent in an atom bomb, and that they themselves would do nothing further to instigate such a development; these veiled statements were misunderstood either as well-intentioned warnings or as cunning camouflage. These covert allusions could not deflect the German emigrants from their assumption of a German lead in this field; they only strengthened their misgivings. For example, in 1939 the Reich's government introduced a ban on the export of Bohemian pitchblende. Outsiders speculated that this was the result of a recommendation made by Heisenberg's student von Weizsäcker and passed by his father, Secretary of State in the foreign office, to Hitler. From this they mistakenly concluded that the pitchblende was being used to build an atom bomb. In reality one of the army's research departments, in complete ignorance of the possibilities of atom bombs, had bought up all available uranium oxide to use in the production and testing of metal alloys for armor-piercing shells.

A number of other misleading signals brought the refugee scientists from Germany to the conclusion that within a short period Hitler would be able to deploy nuclear weapons. The principal fact that confirmed their mistaken view was that atom bomb projects did exist in Germany, as they learned from the physicists who fled after the outbreak of the war. They found these details sufficiently disquieting to dispel their last doubts about the reality of the danger. No one could imagine that the apparently perfect German state apparatus would not, with legendary thoroughness, follow through immediately once such a promising possibility had been discovered.

However, in a remarkable example of reality being stranger than fiction, the highest German leadership indulged in scorn for nuclear physics only because it was largely based on "Jewish speculation." They never even considered the possibility that the much-maligned emigrants might be able to construct an atom bomb themselves.

The only question that remains is whether the scientists who fled from Europe were really so competent that under other circumstances they could have built an atom bomb in their home countries. This question is closely linked to the one first stated but as yet unanswered: Would there have been no Manhattan Project without Hitler's anti-Semitic policy, and therefore also no American atom bomb, so significant in the outcome of the Second World War?

We already know that the impetus for what was to become the Manhattan Project was supplied to President Roosevelt by a group whom Hitler's Jewish policy had deprived of their home or who had had their eyes opened as a result of it. It is still necessary to examine the participation in the actual Manhattan Project of those who were directly or indirectly affected by the "racial" policy of the "Third Reich." This inquiry will also give a straightforward answer to the question of the emigrants' competence to construct an atom bomb.

Roosevelt made his decision on October 12, 1939, on the strength of Einstein's letter, the memorandum by the Szilard group, and Alexander Sachs' eloquent description of the inherent dangers. But nearly twenty-six months passed, during which the project lay dormant, before the atom bomb construction project actually began, on December 6, 1941. This turned out to be the day before the Japanese surprise attack on Pearl Harbor.

Although even a man as powerful as the President of the United States could not work miracles, a delay of more than two years was unusual. Obviously the various departments and congressional committees that had to clear the project were far from being as convinced of the necessity for speed and the importance of the whole matter as were its initiators or even Roosevelt himself. After the war Szilard expressed the opinion that official red tape and military shortsightedness had delayed the Manhattan Project by at least a year. But it is equally remarkable that even before Pearl Harbor and America's subsequent entry into the war, the initial move had been made to build an atom bomb.

Three main factors were instrumental in arriving at the final decision, made only a few days before the unexpected declaration of war on Germany, seriously to go ahead with the construction of atom bombs in spite of the tremendous financial and technical effort such a project required.

The first was the intensified activity of the Szilard group and its growing number of friends, as well as a second letter from Albert Einstein of March 7, 1940, addressed to President Roosevelt. Einstein once more emphatically called attention to the "increasingly intensive interest in uranium in

Germany since the beginning of the war," and urgently advised that the terrible menace this fact foreshadowed be countered speedily.

Second was America's growing sympathy with and concern for Great Britain, from where the surprising message arrived in the summer of 1941 that it was now "fairly probable that the atomic bomb could be produced before the end of the war." This state of affairs again was directly linked with the outcome of research by Simon, Peierls, Halban, Frisch, and other "refugee scientists" and to the warnings, made mainly by Peierls and Frisch, to the highest British authorities. These warnings, similar to the endeavors of the Szilard group in the United States, called attention to the dangers inherent in presumed German superiority in the development of nuclear weapons.

Third was the notable decrease in American isolationism along with an increasing willingness to join the war against the Axis powers in order to end Hitler's despotism. Contributing to this change of sentiment was, in particular, the arrival in America of horrifying, almost incredible, reports concerning the pattern and volume of atrocities committed against the civilian population, mainly Jews, under Hitler's control.

We have already called attention to the strength of the cultural and sentimental ties between the most influential Jewish circles in the United States and the old Germany, from where these people or their parents had come. News of the first anti-Semitic measures in 1933 had been received with shock and had transformed the original sympathies into increasing loathing. Now, after the first reliable accounts of mass deportations and the extermination of whole communities, the resentment grew so great that even those White House advisers who until then had had severe reservations turned into zealous supporters of any methods required to terminate such barbarism. This included coming to grips at long last with the atom bomb project the predictable immense financial and technical drain which had caused many to hesitate initially.

So there can be no doubt that the Nazi persecution of the Jews crucially contributed in various ways—some directly, some indirectly—to create the situation where the necessary means were provided to make a substantial start on the Manhattan Project even before America entered the war.

Brigadier General Leslie R. Groves took charge of the military management of the project for nuclear weapon construction, which was given the code name "Manhattan Project." On September 17, 1942, he was given his new and highly responsible assignment; he was eminently qualified for it, having supervised other complex institutions, including the Pentagon. At the time he told his liaison and security officers, "Your job here will not be easy, for you will have to watch the greatest collection of unpredictable crackpots ever assembled."

Who were these "crackpots"? Of course, the project's pioneers were included—Wigner, Teller, Weisskopf, and of course Szilard, who was singled out at once for "re-education" by Groves. Szilard, who had been the first to advocate the strictest secrecy concerning all the findings of nuclear research, was the one who, in conversations with his closest colleagues, disregarded the military censorship regulations, which were far in excess of any reasonable measure. Subsequently Groves was to say, "Well, certainly without the stubbornness of Szilard during the early years of the war, we would never have had an atom bomb. But once the project got going, I would have been glad to see him drop out of sight."

Szilard did not oblige the general. Furthermore, he and the other "crackpots" were indispensable. They continued to puzzle and outrage the professional soldiers with their disregard for military conventions, their sophisticated jokes, and their boundless intelligence. One very young man stood out in these respects—Professor Richard Feynman. He was born in New York in 1918, the son of Jewish immigrants from Eastern Europe. After the war he was awarded the Einstein Prize and, in 1965, the Nobel Prize. But even at the time of the Manhattan Project he was already considered a brilliant theoretician. He once managed to open General Groves' heavily guarded safe, which was further secured with the most sophisticated combination locks, and in which the top-secret research results were kept. Feynman left a note reading, "Guess who."

But this brazen and seemingly frivolous prank had a deeper meaning. Feynman wished to prove that the exaggerated security measures were detrimental to cooperation and to the work "atmosphere." According to Robert Jungk,

> The innumerable administrative and technical hurdles placed in the path leading to unleashing atomic energy were overcome eventually solely and alone by the determination and endurance of the scientists. . . . Time and again they took the initiative to give the world this terrible weapon. What chiefly drove many of them was the honest conviction that this was the best and the only way to prevent the use of atomic weapons in this war. They said, 'In the case of a German atomic threat, we have to have a counterweapon. Once this balance of power has been achieved, Hitler, like ourselves, will desist from using such a monstrosity.' The idea, however, that the Germans held a dangerous lead was so firmly rooted that it was treated as a certainty. . . . This presumption, which was used to allay any doubts that might arise, was never questioned. In 1941 the chemist Reiche, who had fled from Germany only a few weeks previously, arrived in Princeton and reported that to date the German physicists had not worked on a bomb and would try as long as possible to distract the German military authorities from considering this possibility. This message was forwarded to Washington by another scientist who had emigrated to the United States, the physicist Rudolf Ladenburg. But it does not seem to have reached the scientists engaged in the atomic project.

This is not surprising, since the nuclear scientists based in Los Alamos—as well as those in Oakridge and Hanford, the two other secret research centers—were working in practically total isolation from the outside world. They fully understood that their mail had to be censored and that they were bound to the strictest nondisclosure to any outsider concerning the nature and objective of their work. They also accepted as a matter of course that they could not publish their research results before the end of the war; after all, it was some of them who had suggested such a procedure, even years before the United States entered the war.

However, the military demanded that they observe the strictest secrecy even within the project; no department should know what another was doing, and only a small, select team of the leading scientists—unlike the mass of their scientific and technical associates—was to be told the final objective of the total. The scientists felt that these regulations went too far, hampered smooth cooperation, and prevented the indispensable free exchange of ideas between researchers in various fields. Besides, there was bound to be a detrimental effect on morale if the excessive secrecy kept long-term routine work from having any clear meaning.

For instance, the army of mathematicians and technicians at the mathematical center in Los Alamos were for a long time left completely in the dark about the purpose of their complicated daily calculations. They therefore did their work listlessly and without interest. Laura Fermi recalled, "Finally Ernst Feynman won permission to tell these people what they were trying to produce in Los Alamos. Thereupon the output of the department increased considerably, and some of its members even volunteered to work overtime."

Barely a dozen of the most highly qualified scientists made up the small "inner circle" of those who were fully informed. Their closest coworkers, as well as the team supervisors and their assistants in the most important subsections at least knew the objective and purpose of the larger project. They were also given the broad outlines of progress and the approximate stage of development reached by other departments.

These two top groups—including the initiates and those who knew most of what was going on—along with those who were responsible for the most important administrative, research, advisory, coordinating, and supervising tasks formed the brains and spine of the whole project; it could never have been implemented without them. Only their high intelligence, their scientific skills, their hard work, their enthusiasm, and their exemplary cooperation could have brought about the final success of the endeavors of a whole army of scientific, technical, administrative, and other assistants. They were directed by a man they respected, even though in their respective fields many of them were equal in experience and scientific reputation and in some cases even superior to him. There was hardly anyone in these two leading groups who could have been spared.

This last fact is of decisive importance for the outcome of our investigation into the members of the leading group who were directly or indirectly affected by the persecution of the Jews in Europe. Some of them are already known to us— Eduard Teller, who would later be known as "the father of the hydrogen bomb"; the future Nobel Prize laureate, Eugen Wigner; Victor Weisskopf; and Leo Szilard. We already know that Otto Frisch, Rudolf Peierls, and Hans von Halban came from England to assume positions of responsibility in the Manhattan Project, as did Niels Bohr at a later stage. We have already mentioned the Jewish scientists driven out of Italy—Emilio Gino Segré (later awarded the Nobel Prize) and Professor Bruno Rossi, both of whom went to Los Alamos, and of course, Enrico Fermi.

Other scientists of international repute who were forced to leave Germany and became deeply involved in the Manhattan Project were James Franck, Nobel Prize laureate of 1925 and a professor in Göttingen until 1933; Felix Bloch, a student of Heisenberg and Niels Bohr, who at the age of twenty-seven taught theoretical physics at the University of Leipzig and who received the Nobel Prize for physics in 1952; Hans Bethe, star pupil of Arnold Sommerfeld and, before his emigration to the United States, lecturer in theoretical physics at the University of Munich and who would also become a Nobel Prize laureate; and the expert in low-temperature physics, Immanuel Estermann, born in Berlin and employed by the Carnegie Institute since 1933.

These fifteen names are only listed as examples, since many others could be added. They clearly indicate that, except for the persecution of the Jews in Europe and the resulting flight of leading nuclear physicists to the United States, the Manhattan Project could never have been realized. Among the other scientists in the top group there was an uncommonly high percentage of Jews of Middle or Eastern European origin. Though they had been living in the United States long before 1933, they were understandably more strongly affected by the events in Hitler's sphere of influence than were people who had no relatives, teachers, students, or colleagues who became victims of the gas chambers. For the scientists who were thus affected, it cannot be estimated to what extent these circumstances acted as a spur to accelerate their work. However, it can be safely assumed that this aspect did speed up the entire Manhattan Project.

For instance, Isidor Isaac Rabi, one of the scientific advisers who contributed considerably to the success of the endeavor, was born in Rymanów in what was formerly Austrian Galicia) and as a child had come with his parents to New York, where his father owned a small grocery store. After studying chemistry and physics at Cornell University and taking honors, the highly talented young man was able to continue his studies in Europe thanks to two scholarships. He attended Bohr's lectures and seminars in Copenhagen and studied with Arnold Sommerfeld in Munich, as well as enrolling in Hamburg and Leipzig. Shortly before the Nazi Party could capture the first positions of power in Germany, he was appointed a lecturer at Columbia University, was soon named professor of physics, and became prominent through his research on the magnetic conditions in the atom nucleus. In 1944 he was rewarded with the Nobel Prize for physics, and later he headed the committee of national science advisers to the President.

In the spring of 1945, out of the six heads of the principal science sections in the Manhattan Project who provided the top leadership together with the science director, two had fled from Europe to escape the persecution of the Jews: Enrico Fermi, in charge of "advanced development," and the principal departmental head for theoretical physics, Hans Bethe. Of the remaining four, only two were native-born Americans of non-Jewish origin—the co-chairmen of the "experimental physics" section were the scientists J. W. Kennedy and C. S. Smith. The other two—C. B. Kistiakowsky and R. F. Bacher—were Jews of European origin. Professor George B. Kistiakowsky, head of the department charged with developing the bomb's detonator system, was born in Kiev in 1900. After the October Revolution he volunteered to fight on the side of the White Russians, found refuge in Germany after the victory of the Red Army, and studied in Berlin, where he received his doctorate. He was then called to Harvard University and accepted the chair in physical chemistry.* Dr. Robert Bacher, head of the department responsible for the "physics of the bomb" was born in 1905 in

---

*After the war, Professor Kistiakowsky became one of the closest advisers and special assistant for science and technology to President Dwight D. Eisenhower.

Londonville, Ohio, of a Jewish family which had emigrated from Austria, leaving many relatives and friends behind.

We must mention at least three other scientists of particular importance to the Manhattan Project who had fled from Europe because they were Jewish. The first is Eugen Rabinowitch. Born in St. Petersburg in 1905, he worked in Germany until 1933. On the project, he was responsible for the "chemistry of the bomb." Hans von Neumann, born in Budapest, taught at the University of Berlin until 1933. He was "chief mathematician" and the "computer father of Los Alamos." Finally there is Georg Placzek, a renowned nuclear physicist from Prague, a follower of Niels Bohr, and a close friend of Bethe and Weisskopf. He had studied and was highly respected in Vienna, Berlin, and Göttingen. A linguist and versatile man of many talents, he played an important part in Los Alamos as the connecting link of the scientific and human relationships of the international research team.

Last but not least there is Robert Oppenheimer. The man who acted as overall director of the Manhattan Project, he coordinated the work of the principal departments, became the driving force behind the whole enterprise, and thus is regarded as the "father of the atom bomb."

Oppenheimer was born in New York in 1904, the son of Jewish immigrants. He studied in Göttingen and earned his degree *cum laude* under Max Born. After a further two years in Europe, he eventually joined the faculty of the University of California at Berkeley and lectured at the California Institute of Technology in Pasadena.

This brilliant young physicist, who was already considered a candidate for the international "atom club," was a highly educated, scholarly man of many interests. He had never bothered much with politics until the events in Germany in the spring of 1933 frightened and shocked him out of his placid existence as simply a man of science. When close relations and colleagues of his became victims of "racial" persecution in the land of his spiritual growth, Robert Oppenheimer began to take a passionate interest in the events he found almost incomprehensible. After Bohr's 1939 lecture to an audience of leading American physicists in which he pointed out the possibility of atomic fission and the tremendous volume of energy that could be released, Oppenheimer began to think with the same consternation of a probable German lead in the development of nuclear weapons—and the danger it brought with it of dominance by Hitler. This was also felt by his colleagues Szilard, Wigner, Teller, Weisskopf, Fermi, Bethe, Franck, Segré, von Halban, Rossi, Peierls, Frisch, von Neumann, Rabinowitch, Placzek, and all the other renowned scientists who had fled from Germany and who later would contribute so much to the Manhattan Project under Oppenheimer's direction.

Robert Oppenheimer never received the Nobel Prize. But as Laura Fermi, Enrico Fermi's widow, correctly remarks in her book, *Illustrious Immigrants* (Chicago, 1968), the glamor attached to the Nobel Prize award occasionally causes other high scientific awards of similar distinction to be overlooked. Referring to the Enrico Fermi Award donated by the American Atomic Energy Commission and named after its first recipient, Laura Fermi continues:

> Before 1963—that is, as long as the commission was only concerned with honoring scientific achievements in the field of nuclear research, without considering technical or administrative merit—eight men received the Enrico Fermi prize: Fermi, Hans von Neumann, Eugen Wigner, Hans Bethe, Eduard Teller, Ernest Lawrence, Glenn Seaborg, and Robert Oppenheimer.

The official history of the American atomic project, *The New World 1939–1946*, contains a set of photographs with the simple caption, "Four scientists of Los Alamos." The four, surely not chosen at random, are all emigrants from Europe who were affected by the persecution of the Jews—Hans Bethe, Enrico Fermi, Hans von Neumann, and Georg Kistiakowsky.

In summary, then, we can state that both the United States' possession of atom bombs before the end of the Second World War and the failure to develop nuclear weapons in Hitler's Germany were an inevitable consequence, directly and indirectly, of Nazi "racial" persecution.

If one more argument were needed to persuade everyone that Germany could never have won the war, if only as a result of its Jewish policy, this proof was delivered by the Los Alamos laboratories in the form of this terrible weapon of destruction. As we have seen, its construction was mainly due to the speedy initiative, untiring exertions, and extraordinary capabilities of those men who had looked upon Germany as being at least their spiritual home and who had been ruthlessly expelled.

Chapter 8

Politics and Morality

There is no doubt that it was chiefly Jews—specifically, Jewish scientists from Germany—who handed the most terrible weapon in the history of modern warfare, the atom bomb, to the United States. Without the Jewish refugees from Hitler's Europe, the United States would not have become the only atomic power in the world as early as 1945.

Diehard German anti-Semites may take some comfort from this fact, may even see it as retrospective justification of their Führer's satanic hatred of the Jews and of his strong, instinctive aversion to "Jewish physics." But clearly such people confuse cause and effect. None of the nuclear physicists and none of the other scientists involved—from Germany or from any of the other countries subjected to Hitler's anti-Semitic policy—would have fled from Hitler, nor would they have felt compelled to urge the President of the United States or any other government to construct an atom bomb or would have been driven to support and further its construction with all their skills; none of this would have happened if terror on an unprecedented scale, wholly unimaginable, had not thrown the highly civilized German Reich back into the darkest Middle Ages. The whole world learned to live in fear as it witnessed the vehemence and brutality with which one neighboring state after another was ruthlessly invaded and then "incorporated" into a tyranny of horror. These circumstances, arousing concern among only a few experts at first, brought about the fear that, using nuclear arms, Hitler might subjugate the rest of the world as well. This ironically steered a few peaceloving scientists to the construction of an annihilation device and led them to its ultimate assembly with all the energy they could muster.

But no sooner was the danger of Nazi world supremacy over than many of the same scientists strongly endeavored to prevent use of the new weapon, for which there was no longer a necessity. A particularly impressive document of this movement, signed by Leo Szilard among others, is the so-called Franck Report, named for the man who instigated it— James Franck, formerly professor at Göttingen and Nobel Prize laureate for 1925.*

Franck had won the Prize jointly with Gustav Hertz, another famous German Jewish physicist and the nephew of the discoverer of electromagnetic waves, Heinrich Hertz, after whom the measuring unit of the phenomenon was named. The 1925 Prize was awarded for "the discovery of the laws applying during a collision of an electron with an atom."

Because of his scientific worldwide reputation—possibly also because he was a Hanseatic gentleman, half liberal, half conservative, and certainly not a leftist—James Franck had not been fired like other Jewish university teachers as soon as the Nazis seized power. He was too high-minded, however, to accept such a token of clemency; on April 17, 1933 he offered his resignation. Two days later he went a step further by sending a statement to the few newspapers that had not yet been "coordinated" by the regime, explicitly noting that his resignation was an act of solidarity with his Jewish colleagues who had been fired. "We Germans of Jewish descent are treated as aliens and enemies of the fatherland," Franck declared bitterly, and he added that under these circumstances he did not wish to enjoy a privileged position.

A number of "Aryan" colleagues took this dignified attitude of Franck's very much amiss. Full of indignation, they turned against what they considered the "grossly ungrateful" Jew, Franck. This situation indicates that the luminaries of science

---

*See Appendix for the complete text of this report.

do not always behave as they might be expected to. Forty-two professors and lecturers at the University of Göttingen signed a statement addressed to the local Nazi Party condemning Franck's actions "in the strongest terms," because they played into the hands of "foreign atrocity propaganda." Only one scientist had the courage to join Franck immediately and to protest openly against the dismissal of his Jewish colleagues. Otto H. Krayer, the physiologist and pharmacologist, did not allow himself to be intimidated; he was promptly dismissed and emigrated soon thereafter.

This retrospective glimpse into 1933 should illustrate that it has always demanded courage for a scientist to protest against an action of the state that appears to him to be immoral. Those emigrants among the atomic researchers of Los Alamos who turned against the operational use of the bomb they had themselves constructed—and that had been produced by their host country at enormous financial sacrifice—were not threatened with concentration camps; but even so, they faced ostracism and reproach for being ungrateful.

It is therefore worth emphasizing that the Franck Report, which aimed to prevent the use of the atomic bomb, had two principal coauthors along with James Franck. These were scientists who, until 1933, lived in Germany and had come to the United States as refugees: Eugen Rabinovitch and Leo Szilard. It was Leo Szilard, the actual initiator of the Manhattan Project, who in the spring of 1945 made an almost desperate attempt "to recapture and imprison the sinister genie which, like the fisherman in the Arabian Nights, we let out of the bottle, before it can wreak havoc."

Later, with amazing frankness, Leo Szilard related, "During all of 1943 and part of 1944, our greatest fear was that the Germans might be able to produce an atom bomb prior to the [Allied] landing in Europe. . . . However, in 1945, when we stopped worrying what the Germans might do to us, we started asking ourselves with some concern what the government of the United States might do to other countries."

Once more, Albert Einstein was approached by Leo Szilard, hoping that Einstein would again lend his immense prestige to an appeal to the President of the United States not to drop the bomb. Einstein signed a prepared letter, which was sent to President Roosevelt from Los Alamos together with a memorandum from the scientists. Roosevelt died on April 12, 1945, before he had time to read the document. Einstein's letter, together with the enclosures, was found among the papers waiting for his successor, Harry S. Truman. Truman was not the sort of man to attach importance to the urgent appeal of a few "eggheads" who had arrived in the country as refugees. He consented to dropping the first atom bomb on a Japan that was seemingly already defeated.

We can imagine how those scientists, who had fled the barbarism of the Third Reich to the United States, felt about this extremely brutal use of atomic weaponry by the country whose high ethical standards they had trusted. We know how some of these scientists were affected by a military action that was completely unnecessary, as we know today.

Norbert Wiener, the famous mathematician, philosopher, and founder of cybernetics, the son of an Eastern-Jewish immigrant, had risen to the rank of a Harvard professor. At the age of eighteen he was already a university lecturer, and during the war he contributed considerably to the United States war effort. Under the impact of Hiroshima, Wiener refused the request of an armaments firm for a copy of a report Wiener had compiled for the Pentagon. He added an explanation.

> The experience of the scientists involved in the construction of the atomic bomb has shown that with every study of this nature, they finally place unlimited power into the hands of just those whom least of all they should trust with its implementation. . . . I do not wish to participate in the bombardment and poisoning of defenseless people. For this reason I have no intention of publishing any future work of mine that might be harmful if placed in the hands of irresponsible militarists.

Leo Szilard also remembers.

> It was not long after Hiroshima that I visited Einstein. When I entered his study, he looked at me sorrowfully and said, 'There you have it. The old Chinese were quite right. It is really best not to do anything at all.'

Einstein also learned, to his deep disappointment, of the abuse of a defensive weapon, intended for a specific emergency, on the part of a government he had thought he could trust. His nephew, Dr. Josef Spier, reported years later in an interview on West German radio that the news of the American nuclear attacks on practically defenseless Japanese cities had hit Einstein very hard indeed. Dr. Spier declared, "Toward the end of his life he was a very unhappy man. I will now reveal a secret that Einstein told me in 1954. He made me promise never to mention it in his lifetime, and I have kept my promise. On this day, which was to be the last time I saw him alive, Einstein said to me, 'Do you know, my son, I have found something else on the border area of mathematics and astronomy. And recently I destroyed it. To have committed one crime against humanity is quite enough for me. It will not happen a second time.'"

Other high-ranking physicists—such as Victor Weisskopf, Hans Bethe, and Georg Placzek—also decided to refuse all further cooperation in the development of nuclear weapons. They took their stand in spite of the very tempting offers made to scientists to carry on research in their special field with the most modern equipment and almost regardless of cost. They agreed that—as it was later phrased—"after such a war (with even more sophisticated nuclear weapons), even if we should win it, the world would no longer resemble the world we hoped to preserve. We would just lose the very things for which we fought."

The physicist, Nobel Prize laureate, and philosopher Max Born, who had emigrated from Göttingen to England, refused from the outset to cooperate in the development of nuclear arms. Like Sigmund Freud earlier on, Born searched for ways to prevent the abuse of scientific discoveries and for the complete prevention of war. This endeavor was discussed in an extensive correspondence with Einstein. Born's attitude was summed up by his English colleague, Kathleen Lonsdale. "The risk has always got to be taken that a person's work and achievement, good in itself, might later be abused. However, once it is known that the purpose of the work is criminal and evil, then personal responsibility cannot be evaded."

Such considerations led Klaus Fuchs, a pupil of Max Born, to become a traitor by divulging American atomic secrets to the Soviet Union. Fuchs, the son of an evangelical theologian,

an acknowledged follower of the beliefs of the Quakers and
the religious socialists, had turned his back voluntarily on the
Third Reich. He had attended Max Born's lectures in
Birmingham, had then assisted Peierls, and had finally arrived in the United States as one of the most important
members of the British nuclear-research team. From November 1944 on, Fuchs worked at Los Alamos, where he was
considered to be not only a very competent scientist, but also
an unusually helpful colleague, who took the commandment
to love his neighbor very seriously.

After Klaus's conviction by a British court, his father, professor Emil Fuchs, was able to talk to his son alone. Following this conversation, he gave his own version of the motives
that had induced the brilliant young scientist to commit treason.

As his father, I detect a great inner distress starting from
the moment when he discovered that he was working for
the bomb. He said to himself: If I don't, it will continue
anyway, with all its danger for mankind. Then he found
the escape out of this hopeless dilemma. Neither he nor
I have ever blamed the British people for his conviction.
He endures his fate bravely, with clear determination.
He has been justly sentenced according to the English
law. However, there must always be individuals who are
willing to take on themselves the burden of such guilt and
who bear the consequences of a strong will. They believe
themselves to be endowed with clearer insight than the
powers that be, who are the ones who make the decisions at the crucial moment. . . . Even so, my son risked
an outstanding and highly paid position and an even
more glamorous future. I can only respect his decision.

Klaus Fuchs was one of the very few non-Jewish German
emigrants among the atomic research men. Had he been
Jewish, as his teachers and most of his colleagues were, that
fact would have provided fresh ammunition to the anti-Semites.
As it was, he was just a refugee, a fellow without a country
who had betrayed Germany—both the "Third Reich" during
the war and West Germany after the war (because it was a
member of the cold-war coalition against Russia at the time of
his conviction)—not to mention England and the United States,
to both of which he owed a debt of gratitude. When it comes

to gratitude, however, hardly anyone ever mentions the indebtedness of Germany and the Western Allies to the German emigrants who contributed so much to terminating Hitler's reign of terror and who certainly salvaged some of the honorable reputation lost by their fatherland. Of course Klaus Fuchs, the Soviet spy, was a Communist, and worse, an armchair Bolshevik, who was under no material pressure to subscribe to socialist ideas—a typical "leftist intellectual," a title favored by pseudo-intellectuals as a term of abuse. Moreover, every anti-Semite knows that this admirer of Einstein and student of Oppenheimer was a "White" or "spiritual" Jew.

Fuchs, the obsessed traitor, acted out of conviction, and believed that, if he could not rid the world of nuclear arms, he must at least bring about an atomic stalemate between the superpowers. Let us leave him to the judgment of coming generations. However, we should remind ourselves that "Communists" and traitors were not the only ones to be publicly branded as "Einstein disciples" and "White Jews," but that even nuclear physicists who were far above such reproach or political stigma—including Max Planck, Werner Heisenberg, Paul Dirac, and Erwin Schrödinger—were reviled with these phrases, intended as abusive epithets.

In actual fact, the "wholesome feelings of the people" that the Nazis had hoped to arouse with their invective had been unable to distinguish between Aryan and non-Aryan scientists and artists either in the field of theoretical physics or that of modern art. And there was an area, which we will now examine, where Germans with Jewish and with Christian ancestors were lumped together without the usual "racial" reservations.

We are referring to the group of politicians and intellectuals of the German left, who in Nazi terminology were called "November criminals." Before taking a closer look at this group and examining why the socialist and pacifist leaders also included a greater number of German Jews than their percentage in the total population would have warranted, we must once again be reminded of what the German Jews actually were: German citizens who had not converted to Christianity and had therefore endured centuries of cruel suppression and persecution.

This group destiny, in particular after their emancipation,

predetermined the Jews' role as the saviors of other persecuted, oppressed, and exploited people. It drove them to
work for human rights more vigorously than some others who
had benefited less from the exercise of these rights, and to
engage their faculties precisely in the cause of those who had
been deprived of education and knowledge as well as all the
other prerequisites of a life worth living.

Of course not all German Jews sympathized so strongly
with the fate of the exploited and powerless masses. Only a
relatively small elite engaged themselves with all the means
at their disposal for the suppressed. Similarly, it was only a
fraction of the enlightened French aristocracy that participated actively in the liberation of the "Third Estate" and
assisted the Revolution of 1789. Certainly the degree of participation of German Jews in developing the theory of socialism
and in the leadership of the workers' movement was far
greater than corresponded their proportion in the population,
not to mention the class level of the Jewish socialists, who
usually had their origin among the ranks of the well-to-do
bourgeoisie.

In another context we will discuss how these German-
Jewish sympathies for the causes of the left, which existed
among more than merely a few individuals, contrasted with
the mass of indifferent, at most moderately liberal German
Jews, along with a few Jewish right-wingers. Here, however,
we are concerned with the nature of the impulses emanating
from sections of the German-Jewish intelligentsia and contributing strongly to the development of a specifically German,
or even German-Jewish, form of communism.

One illustrative example is the case of Ludwig Börne, one
of the leaders of "Young Germany." In the seventy-fourth
letter of his *Letters from Paris*, written on February 7, 1832,
he aptly describes the basic position.

> It is remarkable! Experienced time and again, it always
> hits me anew. Some reproach me for being a Jew, some
> forgive me for it, the third praises me for it, but they all
> think of it. . . . The poor Germans. Living in the lowest
> basement under pressure from seven upper stories of
> the higher ranks, it affords them a measure of relief to
> speak of people who are living even lower down than
> they themselves, and in a cellar. Not being a Jew com-

forts them for the fact that they are not even "privy councillors." I know how to value the undeserved good fortune of being a German and a Jew. . . . Yes, having been born in servitude I love freedom more than you do.

Many of the young German-Jewish intellectuals of the nineteenth century may have felt the same. But the sentiments would hardly have applied to Karl Marx, the "father of socialism"—or at most, only on a subconscious level. In his penetrating study,* Hans Lamm has shown that "subjectively Marx felt little (practically not at all) bound to his ancestors." On the other hand, the man who most shared Börne's sentiments was Moses Hess, the philosopher who was born in Bonn in 1812. He created modern humanist socialism on an ethical basis, broke with his pupils Marx and Engels over their purely materialist views, and was derided by them as an "old fool."

However, let us leave the great and the small prophets of socialism and turn instead to those men and women of the early twentieth century who were reviled as "communists" and presented to their frightened fellow citizens as "advance guards for Bolshevism," "devils in human form," and "bloodthirsty beasts, filled with a satanic lust for destruction."

What kind of peculiar human beings were they—provided that they fell into the category of human beings at all? This question was raised by the philistines, Christian as well as Jewish. Who were these terrible Reds who, despite their birth into such orderly conditions, were proclaiming the fight against their own class, the bourgeoisie? Although by no means proletarian themselves, they espoused the proletarian cause in speeches, in writings, and occasionally in deeds. They considered revolution a necessity; the very word sounded dreadful in the ears of order-loving citizens who jealously guarded their privileges. They fomented the hate of the oppressed for their oppressors by strongly criticizing both those who held property and power and the conditions that had led to the presumed unjust distribution of wealth and power.

For the benefit of the middle classes these spiritual leaders of the German left, in particular those of Jewish origin,

---

*Hans Lamm, *Karl Marx und die Juden* (Munich, 1969).

were—and to some extent still are—depicted in this light.
There are still a considerable number of well-meaning people
who assign a large share of blame to the German-Jewish
"Communists and fellow travelers" for the fate that overtook
the whole Jewish community of Germany beginning in
1933 and thereafter in practically all of Europe. And they are
blamed as well for the subsequent expansion and excesses of
Communism.

To counter this view, we intend to put forward the
hypothesis—and to test its validity—that it was precisely the
German leaders of the left of Jewish origin who were critical
of Communism insofar as it developed totalitarian, inhumane,
and undemocratic traits. These were the people, who, had they
not been killed or driven out, would have helped to bring about
the victory of liberal, humanitarian, and pacificist socialism.

Among these, Rosa Luxemburg deserves to be listed first.
She was the daughter of a Polish Jewish merchant who had
been educated in Germany and belonged to the cultured
upper middle class that was passionate about German Romanticism. This class sent its children to German secondary schools
and universities, largely motivated by the awareness of their
ancestors' origin in the western sections of Germany. The
Luxemburg family came from the city of that name, which
expelled its Jewish citizens in the thirteenth century.

In his work *Gottes erste Liebe* [God's First Love] the
Austrian Catholic Friedrich Heer movingly described how in
1917–1918 the Jewish intelligentsia, and in particular Leon
Trotsky, put their hopes in Germany and expected the German
workers to "rise and take over the leadership of the world
revolution." Heer continues:

> Germany could count on some highly gifted Jewish commu-
> nists suited to this task, Karl Liebknecht* and Rosa
> Luxemburg in the forefront. . . . Though small of stature,
> the Polish Jew, Rosa Luxemburg, wrote letters while in
> prison that are among the most important documents of
> this epoch's political humanism. This "little Jewess" was
> the first who dared oppose Lenin in 1917. Her criticism
> of the beginnings and early developments of Leninist

*Karl Liebknecht's wife was Jewish. He himself was not of Jewish
origin, as Heer and other writers mistakenly believed.

Bolshevism already reveal the whole future drama of the Revolution's becoming engulfed in terror and murder and the stifling of Red hopes.

This is the view of a militant Catholic of non-Jewish origin, and certainly not suspected of having any sympathy for Bolshevism. Heer merely wished to do justice to the majority of Jewish Communists, and Rosa Luxemburg in particular.

The letters written in prison by Rosa Luxemburg and praised by Heer aroused contrary reactions at the time, as was pointed out by her biographer, Peter Nettl. He notes,

A letter from Innsbruck is typical of the implacable hostility and complete lack of understanding on the part of the middle-class spectators of postwar disorganization. Innsbruck was the bastion of Catholic reaction, the exact opposite of "Red" Vienna. The letter was addressed to *Die Fackel* [The Torch], a literary-political magazine that manifested sympathy for aims of a leftist-revolutionary nature. According to her own account, the anonymous letter writer grew up on a large Hungarian estate and took amiss the compassionate description Rosa Luxemburg gave of the mistreatment of captured buffaloes in Germany during the [First World] War. The letter addressed to Sonja Liebknecht containing this description* was copied and printed in *Die Fackel*. The letter writer declared that buffaloes were dull animals, barely capable of feeling, and from time immemorial had been used as draft animals for heavy loads. "Surely, if only she could, Luxemburg would like to preach revolution to the buffaloes and to found a buffalo republic for them. . . . There are many hysterical women who like to stick their noses into everything and always enjoy turning people against each other. If they have any spirit and style, they are readily listened to by the masses and do a lot of harm in the world. We should not be surprised if such a one, who has so often preached violence, comes to a violent end."

---

*Rosa Luxemburg, *Briefe aus dem Gefängnis* [Letters From Prison], 5th edition (Berlin, 1961), pages 57–59. See Appendix for the relevant portion of the letter.

Karl Kraus, publisher of *Die Fackel*, himself of Jewish origin, had great sympathy with the revolutionary left as long as it stuck to humanitarian aims and did not degenerate into terrorism. Kraus, certainly not a Marxist, responded to the letter with a glowing declaration of sympathy for Rosa Luxemburg and her brand of communism. Even in his most strongly felt indignation, Kraus once again proved himself the great master of the German language he was.

Kraus's passionate declaration, under the title "Credo," began:

> Communism—the devil take its practices, but may God keep it alive for us, as a constant threat over the heads of those who own worldly goods while they would drive all others to the frontiers of hunger and of honor for the fatherland to preserve their own, preaching meanwhile the comforting slogan that life itself is not the highest of possessions to be treasured. My God, keep it alive for us so that this mob, bursting at the seams with effrontery, does not become still more aggressive, and so that the society of the exclusively privileged . . . is at least likely to suffer from nightmares! So that at least they will lose the incentive to preach morality to their victims and the sense of humor to joke about them.

It would be a mistake to view Rosa Luxemburg as only a compassionate woman, who became indignant at the mistreatment of any creature, human or animal. She was also a brilliant theoretician of socialism, possessed outstanding intelligence, and knew how to write devastatingly truthfully.

Much as she herself disapproved of the shedding of blood and of terrorist methods and the means by which the Bolsheviks defended the power they had seized—as she stressed to Lenin—neither did she permit criticism from those who had attained their own power by shedding rivers of blood and had always safeguarded it by applying the most cruel measures.

> The Reventlows, Friedbergs, and Erzbergers, without batting an eyelash, had sent millions of German men and boys to be slaughtered for the annexation of Longwy and Brie, for the sake of the new colonies. The Scheidemanns and Eberts, who for four full years gave their

consent to all means necessary for the greatest bloodletting ever experienced by mankind—they now join the hoarse chorus shouting about the "horror" and the reputed "reign of terror" threatening us, so they say, from the dictatorship of the proletariat! These people should leaf through the pages of their own history.

Rosa Luxemburg ridiculed those spreading rumors:

No sooner does a windowpane break or a tire burst with a loud bang than the philistine looks around, his hackles rising, and his skin turning to goose flesh: "Ah, surely the Spartacus people are on the march." . . . Various people have approached Liebknecht with the touching plea that their spouses, nephews, or aunts be exempted from the slaughter of the innocent planned by the Spartacists. Such things honestly and truly happened in the first year and month of the glorious German revolution! . . . Behind all these whispered rumors, ridiculous fantasies, lunatic cock-and-bull stories, and shameless lies stands a very serious process: there is a method in the madness. . . . The purposeful rumors are manufactured and launched upon the public . . . in order to create an atmosphere conducive to a pogrom. . . . They rail against killings, riots, and similar nonsense, and what they mean is socialism.

On January 15, 1919, Rosa Luxemburg was murdered together with Karl Liebknecht by members of the elite guards cavalry division—as "a service to Germany," as the instigator of the deed, a retired Major Pabst, claims to this day. "Rosa Luxemburg belongs to us," the Socialist Unity Party of East Germany declared on the eightieth anniversary of her birth. "Rosa Luxemburg is one of us," the Social Democratic party of West Germany declared on the fortieth anniversary of her death. Both claim Rosa Luxemburg in the name of the charity implicit in a statement once made by this great fighter for a humane socialism: "A world must be toppled. But every tear that flows is an indictment."

"Still others are enthusiastic about her theory of the revolutionary spontaneity of the masses," Manfred Grunert wrote to commemorate the centennial of Rosa Luxemburg's birth in the Munich newspaper *Abendzeitung.* "Some are fascinated by the tragedy of the politician, in whom they see the frustrated moralist. Others view her as the star witness for the leftist liberals, quoting the sentence, 'Liberty is always the liberty of the dissenters.' A figure such as Rosa Luxemburg cannot be squeezed into a pigeonhole, no matter how it is labeled. She belonged to the party of the working class, to whose cause she deliberately dedicated her life—without allowing the other, the 'private' person in her to wither away. Quite the contrary."

In a letter to Sonja Liebknecht of May 2, 1917, Rosa characterizes herself in a manner that cannot be improved on:

> Sometimes I feel that I am not a real human being but some kind of bird or other animal in human form. You know that I will nevertheless die at my post—at least I hope so: in a street battle or in jail. But my innermost self belongs more to my nuthatches than to the "comrades." This is not because, like so many spiritually bankrupt politicians, I have found in nature a refuge or a resting place. On the contrary. Even in nature I find so much cruelty at every step that I suffer greatly.

Rosa Luxemburg was surely the greatest, but she was by no means the only figure among the bedeviled Jewish theoreticians, leaders, and publicists of the German left to be inspired by humanism.

Gustav Landauer, the scholar, poet, and writer, who published one of the best books on Shakespeare, was another member of this group of outstanding men and women. The hatred of the powerful and wealthy was turned on them perhaps precisely because they were not only "traitors to their 'class'"—emerging from the ranks of the middle class to lead the awakening proletariat—but also because of their decency, their dislike of every form of brutality, and for the humanity with which they belied their detractors.

Friedrich Heer writes about Landauer.

> In 1916 Landauer defended the Eastern Jews streaming to the West, who were received with fear, consternation, and rejection by the established German Jews.

Gustav Landauer, that internationalist, saw in his visions a rejuvenated Germany, a rejuvenated Judaism—through the meeting of Eastern and Western Jews—a reborn mankind.

"Filthy Bolshevik! Finish him off!" Soldiers shoot at him, knock him down. The blood streaming down his face, he addresses them: "I have not deceived you. You yourselves do not know how terribly you have been deceived." A certain Baron von Gagern finally clubbed him to the ground. Gustav Landauer, the apostle of reborn mankind, gave deeper thought to questions of Judaism than many before him. He had a strong influence on his friend, Martin Buber, who collected Landauer's writings. Buber can bear witness to the pure humanity of the martyr Gustav Landauer, the "Jewish Bolshevik."

Why did Landauer have to die as well? He had offered his services to the first Bavarian revolutionary government, headed by the German-Jewish labor leader and fervent idealist Kurt Eisner. For a short time, Landauer served as minister of culture, education, and church affairs in the "people's state." It was only after Eisner had been assassinated that hostages were shot in Munich, although all moderate socialists condemned this action as cowardly and senseless bloodshed. Eisner would never have condoned such revenge; and Landauer—the scholar, aesthete, and humanist—was in no way involved, not even indirectly.

One fine morning Munich's citizens awoke and found, to their surprise, that they were living in a council republic—and furthermore, one founded by "rascals" and "foreign elements" (as nowadays every peasant calls every man born beyond his immediate horizon). There they sat behind their tankards of beer and gazed open-mouthed on the world. It was a bitter period. If today you ask these people what they actually had to put up with in those days, they all tell you the same thing: actually nothing at all. All told, the council republic of Munich cost the lives of fourteen people—those ten hostages in the Luitpold gymnasium (an act of murder for which there are various explanations, but no excuse), and, if we are to keep conscientious count, four other lives, which must be entered in the same column. So much for the revolutionaries.

Once the Munich philistines had been liberated from outside, the "victorious" troops marched into the Bavarian capital—and at the same time one hundred and forty-eight human beings of the opposition lost their lives in a variety of ways: by arbitrarily administered martial law, by bestial acts of murder. (Landauer was struck down by those in uniform more brutally than a dog; his corpse was robbed.) Revenge! Revenge!

The principal revenge was enjoyed calmly. The "rascals" were brought before peoples' courts, actually emergency courts—and the council government of Munich paid for its crime with prison sentences of 519 years and 9 months! Besides which there was one death sentence (Leviné); and three leaders were murdered by the soldiers. (But all the members of the Kapp government are free.)

This description of events in Munich was given in 1921 by Kurt Tucholsky. He then turned sharply against those "democrats" who found a further way to torment the now helpless condemned; they issued a decree to convert the mild fortress detention into more severe jail terms of hard labor.

A scion of the middle classes and a qualified lawyer, Tucholsky was one of those intellectuals of Jewish origin whose sense of justice was outraged by the blatant injustice, the inhuman brutality, the betrayal of ideas, and the complacency with which the vanquishers of the revolution started rubbing their hands and picking up their business that had only been briefly interrupted.

As early as 1919 Tucholsky wrote, "Ludendorff can be satisfied. The revolution? People are reluctant to mention it. And if they do, then only with undisguised contempt. It is the revolution's own fault—for it did not seriously tackle anyone. Should its opponents gain power today, we would see a human slaughterhouse in Germany. . . . The hatred of the propertied classes for the worker has grown out of all bounds to frightening dimensions."

Was Kurt Tucholsky a Communist? His biographer, Klaus-Peter Schulz, addresses the question.

Tucholsky was never a Communist, despite all his sympathy with Communism brought about by circumstances,
not even in his most secret thoughts. The Communists
themselves were most aware of this. . . . A 'mot' by
Peter Panter, [one of Tucholsky's pseudonyms] concerned
the KPD [German Communist Party]: "What a pity you're
not a member of the party—then we could expel you." A
slightly different version might well have been whispered,
and overheard by Tucholsky, in the ranks of the KPD,
about himself. . . . As early as 1928, he objected to the
blatant opportunism of the "splendid fact of the Soviet
Union," when an official Soviet account, called "The
First Days of the Red Army" simply suppressed the
name of Trotsky. "One thing I do know," the incorrupt-
ible man added, "that it is a sign of great weakness, fear,
and slavishness not to remember the man who did so
much for Soviet Russia. If the whole *Wochenbericht*
[Weekly Report] is based on such incomplete statements,
such falsified reports, then it is worth nothing. And does
not merit credence."

Occasionally, Tucholsky himself applied the materialist view
of history and certainly learned a lot from it. At the same
time his critical faculties never deserted him, nor did he ever
fashion a dogma out of history. Once he remarked in his
'mots,' "It is the job of historical materialism to portray how
everything must happen in the future"—to which he added the
ironic postscript—"and when it did not happen that way, to
show why it could not have happened that way."

Early in 1931 Kurt Tucholsky expressed himself most clearly,
though astonishingly in an exceedingly sharp polemic against
a papal encyclical dealing with the sacrament of marriage and
condemning abortion.

How I wish that the workers' daughters were free to
adorn their hair with garlands of flowers, free of the
church, and free of economic slavery, but also free of
Communist theology, which is on the point of widening
its followers' mental horizons only to narrow them
down again, just as the Roman Catholic variety did with
its people.

In Paderborn and Fulda they would have considered him a Jewish anti-Catholic, and they may still hold that opinion—unless they are aware of Kurt Tucholsky's *Briefe an eine Katholikin* [Letters to a Catholic Woman], not published until early 1970. His judgment of that segment of the German-Jewish middle class on which he had turned his back, as given in one of these letters, proves how harshly he dissected non-Catholic philistines as well, and not because of their creed.

If the German nationalists were not saddled with the dull, stable-bred, almost animal intelligence of Pomeranian horsetrainers from the last century, they would long ago have given up their—admittedly effective—appeal to the mob, "Hit the Jews!"—and three-quarters of the German Jews would today be seated where they belong according to their social class with the German Peoples Party [conservatives]. They do not, because anti-Semitism repels them. Even so, some of them do, because they prefer their bank balance to a religion of which they observe only the Christmas celebration and the *Frankfurter Zeitung*. . . . These people are supposed to have plunged the ritual slaughter knife into the back of the German people? Far too cowardly. They never would!

Some German Jews may think of him as a Jewish anti-Semite and mutter something about "self-hatred." But this is not the case. The Mr. Wendriner caricatured by Tucholsky was an urban philistine. Tucholsky's target may be defined as cowardly philistines, filled with resentment and creating fresh resentment, regardless of whether they call themselves Christians or Jews. Those were the only ones he meant.

The right wing of the Social Democrats called Tucholsky an "armchair bolshevik" whose "destructive criticism" was alleged to undermine both their republic and Field Marshal-Reich President Hindenburg, whom they had dug out of the mothballs of the Kaiser's leavings. As if this republic could still have been salvaged if only all criticism had been withheld!

Nor did the dutiful members of the Communist Party know what to do with the "great friend of the working class," as they called Tucholsky with some embarrassment whenever they wished to, or imagined they could use him for their own purposes. Casting suspicion on him as a follower of Trotsky would have been too absurd.

Erich Kästner once characterized him with gentle, loving mockery. "A stout little fellow from Berlin who once tried to prevent a catastrophe by using a typewriter."

Fritz Raddatz' illustrated biography of Tucholsky contains another view.

> He thought about this problem often. If we try to disentangle the many Tucholskys and observe the journalist, the polemical writer over a period of time, one thing stands out clearly: More and more he abstains from reliance on jokes, satire, irony—relying more and more on deeper meaning. True, his literary writings, his feature articles, remain the work of the satirist, of the mocking jester. But his struggle to maintain the purity of the political stage and the last vestiges of decency in this crumbling republic is very direct. He understood long ago where the way was leading. The pollution of spiritual life, as demonstrated by Messrs. Nagel, Soergel, or even Mr. Stauff, who published an anti-Semitic encyclopedia containing "statistics on the Jews, including their thieves' cant, their false names, their secret societies, etc."—these are no longer the most important enemies. Nor the press allied to the *Generalanzeiger*, with its "subsidized front page"—all that is indeed "taken care of," but that's all. The number-one archenemy is German justice. Again and again Tucholsky drums it into his readers: These judges proclaim two kinds of justice, these judges bend the law, they fail as a social instrument, as a caste, as human beings. His poem *Deutsche Richter, 1940*" ["German Judges, 1940"], published in the *AIZ* next to a photograph of dueling German students, contains the line, "These will be your judges in 1940."* This prediction turned out to be shockingly true.

Not all the German middle-class Jews were Kurt Tucholskys or Rosa Luxemburgs, nor were all of them professors or Nobel prize laureates—some of them were not even very intelligent. But all of them, one sort as well as the other,

---

*Translator's note: Tucholsky died in 1935, an exile in Sweden.

were ostracized, expelled, or brutally murdered. The few who thought and acted like Kurt Tucholsky and Rosa Luxemburg, or like Gustav Landauer, represented merely a small, outlawed minority within a somewhat larger minority that conducted itself in complete conformity with the other Germans and was outlawed all the same. Nevertheless, if we hope to establish the heaviest losses the Nazi persecution of the Jews inflicted on Germany, these few must not be forgotten.

Chapter 9

Anti-Semitic Pipe Dreams

At this stage of our research, it has been established beyond a shadow of a doubt that the persecution of the Jews brought to Germany and the German people a number of significant and lasting disadvantages. But, what about the possible profit?

After the bloody, cruel slaughter, even to pose such a question seems frivolous. Frivolous especially after the innumerable horrifying, brutal, and petty acts, devoid of the last shred of humaneness, that were part of the annihilation of the Jews. But because we resolved, at the outset of this investigation to proceed with a clear and unbiased mind, we must allow the question: Did, in fact, the destruction of the German Jews—with their incalculable contributions and ties to German culture—result in even the slightest advantages to Germany and the world?

We are not considering the private gain of all those who profited individually from the persecution of the Jews—passively through the elimination of competition, actively through the takeover of Jewish property at artificially low prices, by violent seizure, by looting, or by robbing corpses. Nor are we considering the surviving Jews—those who are Zionists—and the positive evolution by which the persecutions in Europe led to and crucially influenced the creation of the state of Israel, which had its birth in an era of despair.

We do want to ask and to study the most urgent question— the one that is felt to be unseemly or even dangerous in West Germany, where the issue is taboo. Has the fact that Germany today is practically "cleansed of Jews" at least brought about the fulfillment of all those hopes the anti-Semites themselves had as their objective?

To find a dispassionate answer, we must do a thorough study, since the outcome will also give us the touchstone to determine the truth or falsity of the arguments, theories, and mere prejudices that were used to justify the persecution of the Jews—even, to this day, to "explain" what happened.

Some of these arguments appear at first glance quite harmless, even plausible. In the light of more recent experience, others seem somewhat bizarre, in part grotesque. It seems advisable, therefore, to document them by quoting chapter and verse from the writings of leading anti-Semites and of the once-respected experts in "racial science." And if some of these beliefs appear as fantastic and as filled with superstition as if they had come straight from a medieval witches' manual, then we must remember that less than forty years have passed since the end of the era in which these theses were established by ministers, professors, and influential writers, were proclaimed with official blessing, and were taught in German schools.

One of the chief accusations, especially in Germany, against the Jews was their alleged domination of the business world. In the two volumes of *Mein Kampf*, Adolf Hitler describes in detail how, in his opinion, this situation came about.

> Along with the creation of the first early settlements, the Jew is suddenly there. He turns up as a dealer. , . . Gradually he starts to take a hand in the economy, not as a producer, but exclusively as a go-between. In his agility in wheeling and dealing, acquired over a thousand years' experience, he is far superior to the clumsy but excessively honest Aryans. Within a short period trade threatens to become his monopoly.

In his anti-Semitic *Vom Ghetto zur Macht* [From Ghetto to Power], Otto Kernholt distinguishes between "German production of goods" and "Jewish procurement of goods." Because "generally speaking the Jew lacks creative ability" and seems to be endowed with "a disinclination to the production of goods that is linked with physical labor," one finds him almost "exclusively devoted to commercial activities"—synonymous, for the Kernholt, with "a parasitical life cycle within the body of a hardworking people."

Theodor Fritsch—whose publication *Handbuch der Judenfrage* [Handbook of the Jewish Problem] was recommended in Hitler's Germany as a "manual for courses in racial science" and had sold 104,000 copies in 32 editions as early as 1933—supplied "proof" of the Jewish monopoly in German trade. He did so with a "compilation of Jewish statistics for those Germans who will not listen to reason."

According to these "statistics," 49.7 per cent of the Jewish population of Prussia in 1925 was engaged in the pursuit of "commerce and trade," which included ownership of bars as well as banks and insurance companies.

"What follows from this? That the Jews dominate commerce with 49.7 per cent . . . !" At least this is the conclusion, wrong both in syntax and in logic, drawn by the *Handbook of the Jewish Problem* on the basis of a figure that may—or may not—reflect the occupations of the Jews in Prussia, but certainly does not cover the share of Jewish participation in German business life. In 1925 the number of Prussian Jews engaged in commerce and trade, the ownership of bars, banks, and insurance companies amounted to 0.52 per cent of the total population, and a shade over 3 per cent of all those so occupied in all of the country.

There is a simple explanation for the relatively stronger participation of Jews in "commerce and trade." It is due to the fact that most Jews lived in the large cities, most notably Berlin, and belonged to the middle class. A comparison that allows for these variables would show the percentage of Jews in business to be hardly greater than that of the non-Jews. Few farmers are found in cities, and few laborers in the middle class. This argument also leaves aside historical conditions that imposed severe limitations on German Jews in their choice of profession for centuries.

But let us assume for the moment and the sake of argument that Hitler and Fritsch were correct and that the Jews had actually held a monopoly on German business. Let us further espouse the attitude, seemingly basic to the anti-Semitic assertions, that commerce is somehow harmful and largely undesirable, and that the elimination and expulsion of the Jews would considerably reduce business activity.

How do such assumptions, founded in the anti-Semitic doctrines of the 1920s, compare to the reality of the 1980s in a Germany practically "cleansed of Jews"?

In fact, since Jews stopped being part of it, German commerce has not diminished—it has shown an enormous increase. The Federal Republic of Germany has a far greater volume of trade than the Germany of pre-1933 and is among the leading commercial powers of the world. West Germany can even be said to have secured first place among its competitors if the basis for international comparison is the volume of trade in relation to the population. A similar situation exists in East Germany as compared to the other Iron Curtain countries; it has also risen into the first ranks of those nations listed as having international importance.

Beyond doubt the expulsion and annihilation of the Jews has not had the desired effect, which was proclaimed by the anti-Semites, with Hitler at their head, as a high priority—Germany's withdrawal from commerce and the country's dedication to "higher values," in particular to the "sword and plow" and "blood and soil."

The objection may be raised that anti-Semitism was directed, not against commerce as such, but only against specific excesses of commerce considered to be Jewish. Such hints at differentiation are to be found, for instance, in an essay by Arno Franke in Fritsch's *Handbook*. Franke's title, "Die Warenhäuser" [The Department Stores], alone reveals what was considered an abuse. The actual text claims that the Jewish chain stores "had become an immense danger to the German middle class." Franke continues, "That precious level of the German people is destined to play an equalizing role in the social conflicts of the present day and represents that healthy area of the country's economy which enables the intelligent individual with drive and modest means—even someone without means—to achieve economic independence." Elsewhere the author explains what he considers to be the threat that the department stores allegedly pose to the middle-class merchant. "No one can fail to notice how a newly established department store radiates destruction, wiping out independent businesses."

Here we have a clear distinction between a noxious form of trading, the department stores, said to be "mainly or exclusively in Jewish hands," and the middle-class retail shops, representing a "healthy area of the nation's economy." The latter's "growth is crucial to the health and stability of the body politic and therefore extremely important from the angle of population policy."

It is true that a significant number of German department stores were founded by Jews—though they were by no means "mainly or exclusively in Jewish hands." The Karstadt chain, for example is still the largest German department-store complex. It was founded by a businessman from Wismar, Rudolf Karstadt, who has often been wrongly classified as Jewish. In 1881 he established in his hometown, a drapery, and an "establishment for fabrics and for tailor-mades and ready-mades," which confined itself to doing a retail business "only for cash and at fixed, low prices." A network of branches gradually spread Karstadt stores throughout Germany and soon gave rise to a powerful business concern, which merged in 1920 with the (non-Jewish) Theodor Althoff department-store chain. Althoff was founded in 1885 in Münster, and at the time of the merger it had fifteen stores. In 1926 Karstadt took over the (Jewish) firm of M. I. Emden Söhne in Hamburg, with nineteen stores. This was followed in 1929 by the take-over of the (Jewish) chain of Lindemann & Co. in Berlin, with fifteen stores, so that in 1932 Karstadt had a total of eighty-nine large department stores in every part of the country. Karstadt also established the EPA Einheitspreis-AG, established to compete with the five-and-ten-cent stores of the (non-Jewish) American firm of F. W. Woolworth.

This one example goes far to show that any possible "immense danger to the German middle class," arose neither primarily not exclusively from Jewish enterprises. Furthermore, the department stores can claim in their own defense that their system of fixed prices put an end to the previous system of bargaining between customer and seller. And the establishment of their principle of "large turnover, small profit" worked entirely to the benefit of the general public.

Let us nevertheless assume that the anti-Semitic argument was correct according to which damage was done by the

Jewish department stores and mail-order houses; that Karstadt, Althoff, Woolworth, and EPA represent ("praiseworthy" Aryan exceptions and that most of the large and small competitive enterprises of the middle-class business world were in Jewish hands. This leaves the department stores of Hermann Tietz and Leonhard Tietz, the Berlin firm of Wertheim, the Kaufhaus des Westens founded by Adolf Jandorf, and the thirty or so department stores of Salman Schocken, with headquarters in Zwickau. As for the Köster-Defaka group of Jacob Michael, he did not develop it over the years but bought it on the stock exchange during the 1920s. Starting from the anti-Semitic assumption of pre-Hitler days, events in Nazi Germany present us with a splendid view of the opportunity to correct within the shortest possible time the "immeasurable economic damage" mentioned in the *Handbook* as emanating from "the department store." Today, when there are hardly any Jews in Germany, the individual and chain department stores and the mail-order houses should have disappeared for good, allowing the little shopkeepers to triumph.

Of course we know that the reverse is true. In a flagrant breach of the promises that had won them the loyalty of middle-class businessmen once they had seized power, the Nazis neither destroyed the department stores nor did they lease the space to small traders.* Only the Jewish owners were forced to sell their establishments, mostly below their true value and frequently to people who had no experience in this line, but happened to have good connections to the powerful new overlords. Today, well over thirty years after the end of the "Third Reich," West Germany, with its appetite for consumer goods, can boast of having more thriving department stores, chain stores, and mail-order houses than before.

The list of the fifty largest enterprises of the German Federal Republic immediately shows seven giants of this branch, equal to the giants in the steel, chemical, and electrical industries. They are Karstadt, Kaufhof, Hertie, Horten, Quelle, Neckermann, and C. & A. Brenninkmeyer. Together

---

*The program of the Nazi Party (see Appendix) lists, as point 16: "We demand the creation of a sound middle class and its preservation, and immediate expropriation of all the major department stores and their lease at low rentals to small tradesmen."

they account for an annual turnover of over 20 billion marks, while employing approximately 230,000 people.

Of these concerns, four were previously in Jewish hands. Kaufhof-AG (previously Leonhard Tietz) and its subsidiary, Kaufhalle, are today owned by the Dresdner Bank and the Commerzbank. These two great banks also control the majority of shares in Rudolf Karstadt-AG, which also owns the subsidiaries, the Carl Peters and KEPA department stores, while a further 30 per cent of the Karstadt shares belong to Georg and Fritz von Opel.

Hertie (previously Hermann Tietz)—including Kaufhaus des Westens in Berlin, Alsterhaus in Hamburg, and the majority of Wertheim—was "Aryanized" in 1933 by the former buyer for Jandorf's Kaufhaus des Westens, Georg Karg, acting for a banking consortium; he subsequently assumed sole ownership and expanded the chain. Even today the Hertie concern, which has also acquired the bilka group, is the property of the Karg family.

The fourth giant among chain department stores, the Horten concern, was developed by the former apprentice of Leonhard Tietz and subsequent buyer, Helmut Horten. In 1936 he was able to obtain the banks' assistance in taking over Alsberg, a Jewish store, in Duisburg; then he acquired numerous other chain and department stores, most of which he lost in 1945. In 1948 Horten started over, beginning with a department store in a brand-new building in Duisburg. Some years later he was in a position to take over on favorable terms the Merkur chain of Salman Schocken, who had emigrated to America with his sons and was no longer interested. Eighteen months later Horten was offered the shares of the Köster-Defaka concern, and he acquired them at 7.5 times their par value. Until then, Köster-Defaka had been in Jewish hands but had escaped "Aryanization" during the "Third Reich" because their owner, Jacob Michael, had emigrated to the United States in 1932 and there incorporated his holdings into an American firm.

Of the three remaining major concerns today—C. & A. Brenninkmeyer, Quelle, and Neckermann, the former two remained unchanged in the hands of their non-Jewish founders, the Brenninkmeyer family and the mail-order king Gustav Schickedanz respectively. However, the mail-order firm of

Neckermann has its origin in the "Aryanization" of the Carl Joel mail-order house.

In sum, it can be said that the ever-increasing process of consolidation, begun nearly a hundred years earlier, has brought about considerable structural changes in the retail trade, and has deprived a large number of small tradesmen of their independence, when it has not placed them in a competitive position that threatens their livelihood. We leave it an open question whether this is an advantage or a disadvantage to the consumer; but we can conclude that the process was neither slowed nor terminated by the transfer of some large department stores and mail-order houses from Jewish to non-Jewish ownership, as the anti-Semites had hoped. In fact, for whatever reason, the process has flourished and proliferated without any Jewish involvement worth mentioning.

A similar story can be told about advertising, which used to be called a "typically Jewish" invention. According to the anti-Semitic argument, the Jewish manufacturer or dealer would endeavor to deceive the buyer by means of a thousand tricks and artifices. The *Handbook* concludes, "Therefore the German is able to manage with moderate advertising, while for the Jews 'propaganda' is the most important factor, on which they spend enormous sums."

Even if we assume for the moment that Jewish merchants had been the primary movers in introducing large-scale advertising into Germany—though this is not, in fact, the case—it should be noted that commercial advertising did not weaken or vanish with the virtually total elimination of the Jews from the German economy. Exactly the opposite happened. Expenditures on advertising have increased enormously; from slightly over a billion marks for all of Germany in 1925, it rose to 2.5 billion marks in 1965 for West Germany alone. Today these costs have surpassed the 10 billion mark level in Western Germany.

Nor can it be truthfully said that since the expulsion of the Jews advertising has become less aggressive or even slightly more fastidious in its methods—on the contrary! For there is one element that today plays a dominating role in West German advertising. In earlier days, when many businesses owned by Jews were alleged to have embarked on their course of uninhibited, shameless advertising, this element was not completely unknown, but was noticeable only in the most discreet dosages. That element is sex.

This brings us to an area where German anti-Semitism practically indulged in orgies. Nearly all anti-Jewish writings give great prominence to the thesis of the "unbridled sexuality," "complete shamelessness," and also to the "race-destructive lewdness of the Jews" so disastrous to the "Aryan" race.

"A people that no longer feels veneration resembles a fallen woman: it has lost *all*. The demise of spiritual value of necessity leads to physical dissipation." This statement appears in *Judas Schuldbuch* [The Black Book of Judah].* The author continues, "The path described is one Judah has successfully taken with regard to the German people. It has vaccinated the German people with its own historical sin by depriving them of a *sense of shame*."

"If a way of life that focuses on sexuality can be judged corrupt and dissolute among Germans attuned to and respected as Aryans," wrote Herwig Hartner in his *Erotik und Rasse*, published in 1925, "where the Jew is concerned, it can be understood only as the expression of the far greater role sexuality plays in his nature." A later passage reads, "One of the most essential features of Jewish sexuality is that the Jew views women primarily as sex objects." This leads the author to wonder "how Jews manage so easily to ensnare women who are racially different from them, such as German women, how frequently it is precisely the repulsive, uncultured Jews who have the know-how to win over pretty, solidly German girls." He finds the answer in the shocking sensuality—"the sensual ardor" of the Jew whereby he is able "to arouse in the woman especially her sensual quality. In this way the alien race—perhaps even an ugliness that is somehow reminiscent of the animal and a lack of culture—achieves an effect that both rouses and paralyzes the will just as the stare of a snake enthralls its helpless, fatally frightened victim. A major role must be assigned to the quick, passionate, or brutal grasping assault."

---

*[The Black Book of Judah, Wilhelm Meister, *Judas Schuldbuch, Eine deutsche Abrechnung*, A German Statement of Accounts], distributed by the Deutscher Schutz- and Trutzbund (Munich, 1919).

Kernholt begins by an overall accusation of the Jews' "poisoning the souls of our young people." He criticizes the influence of Jewish writers as "quite simply pernicious and abominable," as "truly demoralizing," and therefore as "disastrous." In another passage he laments "a striking feature no doubt connected to Jewish nature"—the fact that Jewish physicians "prefer to specialize in those areas that are somehow associated with sexual affairs. Weininger* believes that "the unchaste concern with matters which the Aryan in the depths of his soul always recognizes as Providence was made part of the natural sciences only by the Jew."

In the *Handbook* one M. Staemmler notes, "The Jew's sexuality is simply different from that of Germanic people; he will not and cannot understand the German. If he tries to transfer his own attitude to the Germans, the only result can be the destruction of the German soul. Whether this is the Jewish aim or whether he is proceeding unconsciously should remain an open question at this stage."

The same author, however, goes on to remark that if a Jewish sexologist has the presumption to declare, "Natural sexual intercourse between young people, provided no coercion is applied from either side, is no sin and nothing dishonorable," one must ask why no father can be found "who shows this Jewish corruptor of youth the door with a riding crop."

Adolf Hitler also dwelled at length on the Jewish danger in matters of sexuality. He viewed it from two angles—"racial pollution," resulting in "mongrelization"; and cultural "deterioration" following "inexorably" on the "desecration" of sexuality.

In *Mein Kampf*, Hitler describes the "terrible way the Jews have intercourse with members of other races."

> "For hours, the black-haired Jew boy, satanic pleasure on his face, lies in wait for the guileless maiden whom he pollutes with his blood, thus robbing the victim's own people. He seeks with every means to undermine the racial foundations of the people to be subjugated. While

*Otto Weininger, whose principal work, *Geschlecht und Charakter* [Gender and Character] is quoted here, was, ironically enough, born a Jew. He put an end to his apostasy by committing suicide at an early age.

systematically corrupting women and girls himself, he
does not hesitate to range far and wide to raise the
barriers of blood for the benefit of others. It was, and is,
the Jews who brought the Negro to the Rhine. . . . So
he is systematically intent on lowering the racial level
through constant poisoning of individuals."

In another passage, Hitler discusses his "transformation into
an anti-Semite."

Soon nothing gave me such pause as the slowly dawning insight into the activity of the Jews in certain
fields. Is there any filth, any kind of shamelessness,
especially in cultural life, where *at least one* Jew has not
participated? . . . It is enough to look at one of the
advertising pillars, to study the names of the spiritual
begetters of those horrid creations extolling moving pictures and plays, to become hardened for some time. This
was the pestilence, the spiritual pestilence, worse than
the Black Death of long ago, with which the people were
being infected . . . !

To be sure, the last quotation indirectly reveals that in the
opinion of the "Führer" himself, many non-Jews participated
in the "shamelessness" of cultural life—how else are we to
understand his qualification, "*at least one* Jew"?

Let us however, presume for the moment that it had been
almost exclusively Jews who had injected a strong erotic taint
or sexual color in the diverse areas noted by the anti-Semites;
had also violated Christian-Germanic taboos; and had indeed
approached unchastely those things "which the Aryan in the
depths of his soul has always perceived as Providence." Let
us forego the privilege of forming our own opinion of such
conduct, and for the sake of argument, let us accept without
contradiction the view that seems to underlie the disquisitions
of all anti-Semitic writers—namely, that such conduct was
highly repulsive, extremely harmful, even life-threatening,
especially in connection with the systematic "mongrelization"
the Jews allegedly practiced.

In that case, since the Jews have practically disappeared
from the public life of Germany, a noticeable improvement

should have set in; perhaps not overnight, but certainly after close to forty years.

But we know only too well that in this period eroticism and overt sexual behavior have greatly increased; that the penetration of traditional "barriers of modesty" is part of our daily business approach, and not only in the area of entertainment and advertising, but also in numerous branches of science; and that the movement to abolish sexual taboos can be called explosive. There can be no question of "improvement" in the sense projected in the statements of the 1920s anti-Semites, who were so concerned for "Aryan" conduct and morality.

A similar view can be taken of "mongrelization," which should at least have come to a standstill after the strict "racial hygiene" education of the "Third Reich"; ten years of the strictest observance of the "blood protection laws"; and the almost total annihilation of the Jews, reputed to be the people who systematically practiced "racial pollution." However, the opposite is the case.

Without entering into a discussion of Nazi racial theories, it can be proved that even the marriages between Germans and members of population groups which the "Third Reich" classified as "racially alien" have greatly increased, especially if we compare the situation since 1945 with the state of affairs before 1914 and between the wars. These figures do not take into account premarital and extramarital relations, about which there are no statistics (though there is ample circumstantial evidence, of a kind that caused yesterday's concerned "racial hygiene experts" to grow pale).

Nor, remarkably enough, can any opposition be found anywhere to the "sex wave" or the marginal phenomenon of the tremendous growth of sexual relations between Germans and foreign nationals, in the wake of increasing promiscuity. Secular and spiritual authorities vie with each other in declaring their understanding for this or that manifestation that they would have harshly condemned only a few years ago. The mass media as well as the consumer-oriented economy are busy with commercial exploitation of the increased pursuit of sex, which in turn accelerates the pursuit. And hardly a voice is raised in any of the magazines to condemn what Hitler once termed "the pestilence, the spiritual pestilence, worse than the Black Death of long ago, with which the people were being infected."

Two reputable German writers belong to the very few exceptions who, like Hitler once upon a time, strongly oppose this modern trend. It is not from prudery, but out of political concern for the German people, whom they believe to be in jeopardy, that the one of them, William S. Schlamm, condemns what he calls the "libertinage of the slums," while the other, Hans Habe, considers himself entitled to warn against the "time bomb of sex," which is already ticking away in the "nursery, having already exploded on children's playgrounds."

However, neither Schlamm nor Habe see the "poisoning through sex" as the "work of Judaism," and therefore neither draws anti-Semitic conclusions from his somber observations. Schlamm believes that such "deterioration" must inexorably lead to the weakening of what he calls "the free West" and thus "plays straight into the hands of Moscow and the masters in the Kremlin."

Habe goes a step further. He views the loosening of morals not only as an advantage to, but actually the handiwork of Moscow. "The formula is basically quite simple," he notes; "the East has not succeeded in subjugating the West by assault from outside. Now they are attempting it from inside!" He cites proof: "Anyone distributing pornographic literature in the Soviet Union is deported to Siberia. . . . China has instituted the death sentence for drug addicts. . . ." However, "in Upper Bavaria, a place called Oberwarmensteinach, boys and girls between the ages of twelve and fourteen demonstrate 'games of love.' When caught in the act, they started chanting Ho-Ho-Ho-Chi-minh. . . . ! The communards in Berlin preach the teachings of Mao and practice group sex. Eighty per cent of the narcotics that is 'enjoyed' in California arrives in the United States from China, some of it below cost."

Since this kind of argument is strikingly reminiscent of the "black-haired Jew boy" whom Hitler saw lying in wait not only out of lust, but also for the purpose of triumphing over the otherwise invincible "Aryan race" by means of systematic "mongrelization," it could offer comfort of a kind to anti-Semites living in a world filled with sex and "deterioration," both of which are meeting with general applause. Their cause, however, is undermined by the fact that Habe, as well as Schlamm (who surpasses his colleague in German nationalism and aggressive anti-Communism), are both Jews. This does not contradict our thesis that Germany is without Jews: Willy Schlamm, born in Przemysl, returned to Europe after the war with United States citizenship. Habe is the son of the publisher Imre Békessy, was born in Budapest, became a United States citizen during his time of emigration, and now lives in Switzerland.

However, their strictly German-nationalistic attitude and their vehement anti-Communism, which no "thaw" in the cold war can diminish, brings us to another anti-Semitic doctrine that gained a position of major importance in the "Third Reich." It was claimed that the German Jews, being invariably on the political left, had undermined and destroyed the imperial realm of the Kaiser, had caused and led the revolution of 1918, and had attempted to convert Germany to Bolshevism, as they had done in Russia.

The *Handbook* states quite simply that Judaism and Marxism are identical, as are Social Democracy and Communism. And when Hitler, in *Mein Kampf*, describes in detail his conversion to anti-Semitism, he gives as one of many rationalizations, "While studying the Marxist teachings in depth and thus subjecting the actions of the Jewish people to a clear and sober scrutiny, fate itself gave me a reply. . . . If the Jew, with the aid of his Marxist creed, is victorious and defeats the peoples of this world, then humanity's Dance of Death will crown his efforts."

If these theses were correct, then, at least in Germany, Social Democracy and Communism should have become practically extinct along with the Jews, while these same political creeds should have been considerably strengthened, wherever the bulk of the surviving Jews of Europe had fled— certainly in the United States. Furthermore, it should follow that where Communism prevailed and held sway for decades, a kind of dictatorship of the Jews—or at least a form where all the key positions are held by Jews—should reign.

The exact opposite has happened. Half of Germany is under Communist rule. But in East Germany the Jews are only an infinitesimal, politically completely insignificant minority. Those who still practice Judaism add up to less than 0.01 per cent of the population. Some few veteran Communists of Jewish origin—most of them intellectuals returned

from Western emigration—have severed all ties with the
Jewish faith.

In Germany—where a strong Social Democratic majority
until recently furnished the president, the prime minister,
and the majority of the cabinet, as well as many of the local
state governments—the anti-Semitic doctrine about the nature of all Marxist movements has been disproved to the
ultimate degree. With very few exceptions, almost all of the
few remaining or returned German Jews—even more so the
foreign Jews who live in Germany—are thoroughly anti-
Communist in their outlook, quite apart from the fact that
scarcely two dozen individuals of Jewish origin play any
part in the political life of the German Federal Republic.
They include the head of the provincial government of
Hamburg, Mayor Herbert Weichmann; the senator for the
interior of Berlin, a post held for many years by Joachim
Lipschitz, who died in 1961; the minister of justice of North-
Rhine Westphalia, Josef Neuberger; Hamburg's chairman of
the Christian Democrats, Erik Blumenfeld; Marcel Hepp,
who steers an extreme right-wing course as chief editor of
Bayernkurier and who is an adviser to Franz Josef Strauss;
the chairman of the "Trusteeship for an Indivisible Germany,"
Wilhelm Wolfgang Schütz; and Ernst Benda, descendant of
an old Berlin Jewish family, distinguished Christian Democratic politician, and temporary federal minister of the interior.

Conversely, in the United States, the nation with the largest Jewish population and where the political influence of
Jewish organizations and individuals is strongest, the Communists are completely unimportant politically, and the overwhelming majority of the Jews are distinctly anti-Communist
in their attitudes.

Even Hitler himself, were he alive today, would not venture to claim that in the Eastern bloc nations the Jews are in
the saddle. Certainly there are a few notables and celebrities
of Jewish origin, even if the majority of Communists of Eastern European Jewish origin have long since fallen by the
wayside as victims of various "purifications" or have at least
been "shelved." In most countries of the socialistic camp, the
Jews as a group are at best tolerated, frequently subjected to
strong pressure, while the mere suspicion of allegiance to
Zionist ideals usually evokes strong police measures against
them.

Finally, and only for the sake of a complete picture, we should point out the situation in Israel. This is the only state in which it is true that "the Jews rule." And in Israel Communists only form little splinter groups, while the most active enemies of the Jewish state, the Arab countries, enjoy strong support from the Eastern bloc.

Although all anti-Semitic theses and prognoses that equate Judaism with Communism have proved to be false, we must address the claims according to which the German Jews always supported the left, had been the instigators and beneficiaries of the revolution of November 1918, and had spearheaded all Communist revolts during the early years of the Weimar Republic even as they were the actual overlords of this "Jew republic." The contention continues along the lines that even if the German right-wing followers had not been on principle opposed to the Jews, they would have been justified in looking on the Jews as particularly dangerous enemies for purely political reasons, even if not on "racial" grounds.

In contradicting these assertions, we will limit ourselves to the critical fifteen years between the summer of 1918 and 1933. This limitation may rob us of the opportunity of clarifying certain historical trends; but there remain an abundance of examples to prove that the few German Jews who actively participated in the radical left were countered by a corresponding number of Jewish sympathizers and active supporters on the extreme right. It was—and is—seldom noted that such German nationalists and right-wing extremists of Jewish origin existed. The one or the other is occasionally exhumed from his anonymity and introduced to the astonished public as a curiosity, like a two-headed calf. Understandably enough, such Jewish drumbeaters for Hitler did not fit—nor do they fit today—into the anti-Semites' constructs or into the cliches advanced with an excess of goodwill by present-day pro-Semites endeavoring to overcome the past.

In actual fact most of the German citizens of the Jewish faith (or Jewish origin) held a national-liberal, loyally patriotic view, they were profoundly opposed to Communism, and frequently they were only slightly more in favor of the moderate parties on the left than of those on the right, because the burgeoning anti-Semitism on the part of the middle-class right-wing parties kept them from giving them their full support. However, there were some who did not take offense even at the overt anti-Semitism of the German National Party and the right-wing extremists, because these people saw such anti-Semitism directed, not against themselves, but perhaps against certain of their fellows who had made themselves objects of dislike. Consciously or subconsciously they endeavored to compensate for alleged or actual offenses to the feelings of the German right wing committed by others— particularly Jewish immigrants from the East—by espousing an emphatically nationalist attitude, occasionally by extreme nationalism and antisocialism. In exceptional cases they themselves became militant anti-Semites.

So it is that in the early years of the Weimar republic we do find, as claimed by the anti-Semites, some figures of Jewish origin among the prominent revolutionaries (as discussed in the previous chapter). Just as many, if not more Jews allied themselves with the advocates of "law and order."

A typical example of this can be found in the circumstances of the murder of Rosa Luxemburg. In January 1919 she and Karl Liebknecht were arrested in Berlin by the "forces of law and order," who had assembled as protection against a Spartacist revolt. The two victims were brutally beaten and shot. The corpses were found later in the waterway known as the Landwehrkanal.

Even though it still cannot be said with absolute certainty who shot Rosa Luxemburg, there can be no question about the group of responsible instigators. The murder was planned and the actual command given by some officers of the guards cavalry rifle division, including two of Jewish origin—Liepmann and Grabowsky. Though the principal active culprit behind the scenes, Major Waldemar Pabst, was not a Jew, another man in the background was the Jewish head of the executive committee of the right-wing German National Party, Consul Salomon Marx. Early in 1919, in his capacity as chairman of the "Berlin citizens' council" Marx had issued an appeal for the fight against the Spartacists, and he had financed propaganda and enlistment efforts, partly out of his own pocket and partly from donations he had collected. The incitement to murder, so funded, was expressed in a poster put up all over Berlin: "Workers, citizens! The Fatherland is threatened! Save it! The danger comes not from outside but from inside! From the Spartacist group! Kill their leaders! Kill Liebknecht! Then you will have peace, work, and bread!"

The right-wing German National Party had been happy to
have the expenses of its 1919 election campaign financed by
the Baroness Mathilde von Rothschild and the—also Jewish—
industrialist and owner of race horses Arthur von Weinberg—
Weinberg had served at the front as a cavalry major, and had
subsequently held a post in the ministry of war. These circumstances did not prevent this political party from forcing Consul Marx soon afterward to relinquish all his posts on the
governing board of the party—because he was Jewish.

The great legal scholar, Otto von Gierke, had been one of
the showpieces of the German National Party—that is, until
the elections for the national parliament, in which both he
and his daughter, Anna von Gierke, were successful candidates.
Both were forced out of the party. The reason: Otto von
Gierke was married to the daughter of a colleague of similar
standing, Professor Edgar Loening, lecturer in Halle and a
member of the Prussian upper chamber. And the Loenings
were Jews.

Other leading Jewish German National Party members
include the head of the "Stahlhelm," Theodor Duesterberg. In
1932 he figured as a candidate for the presidency of the
country on behalf of the right-wing parties and was discussed
above. The party leader, Hugenberg, had a special confidential councillor in the person of Reinhold Georg Quaatz, who
was a member of the board of governors of the Dresdner
Bank and was only "shelved" after Privy Councillor Hugenberg
became minister for commerce in Hitler's first cabinet.

A fully Jewish German National Party member of the right
wing was George Gottheiner, a representative to the national
parliament and an official in the ministry of the interior. He
was temporarily retired by the ministry in 1930 because of
his active participation in a public plebiscite engineered by
Hitler and Hugenberg. However, Franz von Papen, Hitler's
henchman, wasted no time after becoming chancellor in re-
calling Gottheiner to the fold of the ministry of the interior
and entrusted him with the management of the political
department. This office had the job of preparing the coup
against the legal Prussian government of the Social Democrat,
Otto Braun.

It was in this same period that another high government
official of Jewish descent, Heinrich von Kaufmann-Asser, in
his capacity as a confidant of Franz von Papen, was promoted

to the rank of ministerial director and head of the press section of the Reich government. Once Hitler himself had become chancellor, von Kaufmann-Asser was appointed German ambassador to Buenos Aires; but soon he was placed on the retired list.

Among the conservative right wing, we must include some men of Jewish origin whose functions were nonpolitical. For instance, Secretary of State Theodor Lewald was from 1919 to 1933 president of the German Reich committee for physical fitness, and Reich commissioner for the Olympic Games. Curt Walter Joel was first secretary of state, then, until 1932, minister of justice in Brüning's cabinet, where he was the specialist for creating emergency decrees. Adolf Grabowsky founded the umbrella organization, "People's Association for Fatherland and Freedom" in 1917 and published the periodical *Das neue Deutschland*, which sought to win the intelligentsia over to the right-wing parties.

A famous physician, Professor Otto Lubarsch, stood even further to the right and was a very active member of the German National Party. Although fully Jewish, he was cofounder of the anti-Semitic "All-German Union."

The closest confidants and principal advisers of the leader of the All-German group also included the fully Jewish Berlin economist Professor Ludwig Bernhard. The press chief of the radical right-wing Kapp insurgents was a Jewish adventurer from Budapest by the name of Ignatz Trebitsch-Lincoln.

However, it was not only intellectuals of Jewish descent who joined the right-wing parties. There were, for instance, a number of Jewish Freikorps fighters who attached themselves to the German National Party and anti-Communistic combat organizations in the Baltic, Upper Silesia, and the Ruhr. In Upper Silesia there was a Jewish Freikorps leader, Lieutenant Alwin Lippmann, while the flag bearer of the Freikorps leader Albert Leo Schlageter, who achieved legendary fame in the "Third Reich," was a Jew by the name of Alfred Badrian.

If we once again dwell upon the short-lived red regime in Bavaria, we find that not only Kurt Eisner—the leader of this revolution of November 7, 1918 and the first prime minister of the new free state—was of Jewish descent (a fact exploited to the utmost by the anti-Semites), but so was his murderer. An ex-cavalry lieutenant, Anton Count von Arco-Valley was a

member of a radical right-wing student fraternity and grandson of a Jewish banker in Cologne who later converted to
Protestantism, Eduard Salomon, Baron von Oppenheim. On
February 21, 1919, Count Arco shot Kurt Eisner just as the
prime minister was about to offer his resignation to the newly
elected parliament. Eisner was greatly revered by the Munich working class and was influenced more by Kant and
Rousseau than by Marx, abhorring all violence.

Eisner's private secretary, Felix Fechenbach, was also Jewish.
Soon a campaign of calumny was directed against him from
circles close to the 'All-German' group, and denunciations
for high treason were lodged against him. The show-trial that
resulted has no parallel in the history of German justice. It
reminds one of the Dreyfus case.

The completely innocent Fechenbach was sentenced to
eleven years in jail. It was claimed that he had revealed "a
highly sensitive political state secret to a foreign country."
Actually the documents in question were only of historical
interest. Fechenbach, covered by a release order from the
Reich government as well as from his boss, had given a copy
to the young Swiss publicist, Frank Arnau. In sentencing
Fechenbach, the court relied on expert opinion and interpreted it "in a contrary sense"—according to the expert—which
means deliberately incorrectly. After strong pressure from
the Reichstag majority, the Munich high court felt obliged to
review the judgment—and to confirm it. To put an end to the
scandal, the Bavarian minister of justice reduced the sentence to a third, and after two years and four months of
imprisonment, the completely innocent Fechenbach was set
free—coincidentally at the same time as Adolf Hitler. After
1933 Feschenbach was immediately arrested again, tortured,
and finally murdered in a transport.

The case of Fechenbach has a little-known background.
The chief conspirator in the concerted campaign against Eisner's
coworker was the publisher of the *Süddeutsche Monatshefte*,
a man closely linked to the 'All-German' group, Paul Nikolaus
Cossmann, who, though himself a Jew, considered it proper
to continue fomenting anti-Semitism.

These examples are, of course, typical for only a very small
segment of the German Jews of that time. Even so, in
view of this attitude, it will come as no surprise that even
after Hitler's seizure of power and after the onset of open

terrorism, some German Jews politically far to the right seriously sought to achieve an alliance with the Nazis. In the forefront of this movement was the conspicuous figure of Max Naumann, a Berlin lawyer and leader of the "Association of National-German Jews," which he had founded. In the spring of 1933 a new political group was founded by Hans Joachim Schoeps under the name "German-Jewish Followers of the German Vanguard."

Even in his 1963 memoirs Schoeps confirms that in the early 1930s it was his "given task to attempt a generational disengagement of the liberal leadership within German Jewry and its replacement by confederate-military forces, as being possibly more suitable as negotiating partners in the eyes of the National Socialists." What he had in mind was to fit some of the old established "Jewish citizenship into a corporate structure of the state," at the expense of "the Eastern Jews of the immigration vintage of 1918 and later" and of "the Zionists insofar as, by their own admission, they do not feel themselves to be Germans but foreign Palestinians." These groups were to be removed as quickly as possible and "until their emigration be placed under the protection of the law regarding the rights of minorities." Schoeps handed a corresponding memorandum "first of all to the state chancellery and requested a personal interview with Hitler."

To this day there are some Jews in West Germany who are prepared to join in the activities of the extreme right wing and to let themselves be used as tokens. This group includes Schoeps, who, after returning from a rather late emigration, was installed as senior lecturer by the Bavarian state government at the University of Erlangen. The sociologist Ludwig Freund, after returning from American exile, also accepted the so-called Adenauer Prize, which the *Frankfurter Allgemeine Zeitung* has called "A prize invented by right-wing radical sectarians to reward third-rate writers and fringe ideologues." These two, along with other journalists of Jewish origin, are not averse to writing for the *Deutschland-Magazin*, an organ of the same foundation that awards the Adenauer Prize. The board of this organization includes Erich Maier, who in the "Third Reich" was the executive editor of a Nazi provincial organ and the author of numerous inflammatory anti-Semitic articles.

At least the Jewish professors, Schoeps and Freund—unlike

other recipients of the Adenauer Prize—have not yet distinguished themselves as writers in the *Deutsche National-Zeitung und Soldatenzeitung*. This radical-right inflammatory rag, however, has other Jewish contributors, such as Martin Kohn, Moshe Menuhin, and Josef Ginsburg, who is also active on behalf of neo-Nazi book publishers, using the pseudonym Josef Burg.

As part of the anti-Semitic doctrine that Judaism and Marxism are identical, the bold assertion is also made that Jewish-Marxist influence weakened Germany's defense capability.

In *Mein Kampf* Hitler wrote: "While Judaism shouted to the world at large the lie concerning German militarism and endeavored thus to incapacitate Germany by all possible means, Jewish-led Marxist and democratic parties refused to countenance any comprehensive build-up of the German people's strength." And in *The Black Book of Judah* Wilhelm Meister commented on the situation of 1918: "Bismarck is being betrayed again, emperor Weissbart with his paladins is once more fast asleep deep down in the Kyffhäuser Mountains, the empire is in ruins, the German economy destroyed, and, a thousand times worse, German idealism and German honor are broken. Judah has crippled us not only physically, but also spiritually, and has turned us into a leper." Some years later, when Germany's "military strength" began to stir again, Herwig Hartner declared, "It is against this belated self-recognition of our German people, against this will of self-assertion that the Jewish and Jewish-Marxist circles are directing their opposition."

As for the claims that Jews had been mainly responsible for paralyzing the "will to defend the fatherland" and had attempted to undermine "military strength"—for instance, through pacifist propaganda and general attacks on increasing armaments and the military—it must be obvious that logically today's almost complete absence of Jews in Germany, coupled with the almost total absence of Jewish influence, provide ideal conditions for verification. We should expect the "will to defend the fatherland" on the part of young Germans to be of the highest order, and eagerness to serve the fatherland immense. However, the contrary is the case, at least in West Germany. Nowhere else in the world are there as many conscientious objectors since rearmament has started. Their numbers are growing steadily. By March 31, 1969, 55,842 applications by conscientious objectors were received; of these, roughly 30,000 were granted. By 1968 the monthly rate showed a maximum of 1,100, and in the first six months of 1969 it exceeded 1,500 per month. Elements of Jewish influence in this phenomenon could not be found.

Anti-Semitic writers named three principal categories concerning the manner in which Jewish influence was exercised in Germany before 1933. First was "international Jewry's financial power." When desirable, this was extended to the concept of "Jewish international finance," subdivided for Germany into the "immense personal wealth" of most Jews and into "banking and stock-exchange power," by means of which the Jews as a group either kept their German victims in bondage "through interest slavery" or "exploited and impoverished the economy." The second was the total "Jewish infestation" of parliament and government. This was considered to be so penetrating in the ministerial posts that they saw the Weimar Republic simply as the "Jew republic." The third item of anti-Semitic propaganda was specified as the "all-pervading power of the Jewish press." This was attributed less to the occupation of seats on editorial boards than to the Jewish newspaper publishers, who were said to have a "press monopoly."

Let us briefly examine the validity of these arguments. First, concerning the individual wealth of the German Jews, it has to be said that the suspicions inspired by bold imagination or pure envy overshot the target to such an extent that no resemblance with reality remains. Among the broad stratum of wealthy Jewish middle-class families, there were a few who were very rich. The bulk of the Jews of Germany had a standard of living that was modest and close to the conditions applying to the lower middle class. A large number were poor. For instance, in 1932 one-third of all Jewish income-tax payers in Germany had an annual income of less than 2,400 Reichsmarks, while in Berlin alone in the winter of 1932-1933 roughly 31,000 Jews were on the dole.

To deal first with the very rich, we find, in examining the established German fortunes before 1914, that the distribution was quite a different one from what the anti-Semites would have us believe. The appropriate data appear in *Jahrbücher der Millionäre* [Annuals of Millionaires] which

Councillor Rudolf Martins compiled from income-tax lists. This source reveals that in the last year of peace only ten people had been assessed for a personal fortune exceeding 100 million marks:

		Mill. Marks
1.	Emperor William II, King of Prussia	394
2.	Grandduke Adolf Friedrich of Mecklenburg-Strelitz	355
3.	Mrs. Bertha Krupp von Bohlen and Halbach	320
4.	Ludwig III, King of Bavaria	300
5.	Guido, Prince Henckel-Donnersmarck	290
6.	Adalbert, Prince of Thurn and Taxis	270
7.	Baroness Mathilde, the widow von Rothschild	163
8.	Prince Hohenlohe-Öhringen, Duke of Ujest	154
9.	Adolf Josef, Prince of Schwarzenberg	119
10.	Max Egon, Prince of Fürstenberg	110

Obviously 2.5 billion gold marks in round figures were in the hands of ten persons. This figure does not take into consideration that the ruling sovereigns used to assess themselves at a particularly low rate, which accounts for the absence of, for instance, the King of Saxony, who was enormously rich. Furthermore, the ridiculously low unit values of the landed properties of the top aristocracy were not replaced by their actual market values. Had this been done, a further three dozen sovereigns and princes would have had to be included as owning property worth over a hundred million marks, such as Prince Hans-Heinrich XV of Pless (now listed at 99 million marks) Franz-Hubert Count Thiele-Winckler (87 million), and Engelbert Herzog of Arenberg (63 million).

Only one estate in the list was in Jewish hands, that of the Rothschilds, represented by the lady previously mentioned, who four years later would so generously support the enemies of the republic and of the Jews, the political group known as the German National Party.

The lists could go on and on. However, among the further, say, two hundred multimillionaires who before 1914 paid taxes exceeding twenty million marks, we would find more than 90 per cent non-Jews, mainly aristocratic owners of great landed estates, along with upper-class citizens, mostly Rhineland merchants and Hanseatic businessmen and industrialists. Most of the eighteen or so families of similar wealth of Jewish origin turn out to be bankers, usually baptized and knighted. As examples we might mention the Barons von Oppenheim, Beit von Speyer, von Mendelssohn, and von Bleichröder, or such successful industrialists as the resoundingly German National von Weinbergs and von Friedländer-Fuld.

Certainly before 1914 there could be no question of a concentration of German wealth in Jewish hands. During the Weimar Republic the picture changed only insofar as inflation consumed the savings of the middle class, and that included the bulk of the Jews. The large-scale estate owners waxed even richer at the expense of the people who went hungry, while heavy industry, greatly expanded because of the war, experienced an unprecedented boom, profiting enormously from the devaluation of currency and increasing the fortunes of the "lords of industry" immeasurably. In those days the top group of German wealthy acquired three new members, each in the multihundred million goldmark range: Fritz Thyssen, the heirs of the Saarland mining industrialist von Stumm, and of course Hugo Stinnes. All three were non-Jews.

As the most successful profiteer from the inflation, Stinnes became the richest man in Germany—according to contemporary records, the fifth-richest man in the world. When his star went into decline, he was succeeded by an even more adroit shark of the stock exchange and creator of large concerns: Friedrich Flick. He, also a non-Jew, has remained the richest man Germany can boast of.

In the 1920s and 1930s, the following multimillionaires joined the fold: the Munich banker and large estate owner, August von Finck; the families Bosch, von Siemens, von Opel, and Henschel; the food manufacturer Oetker; the producers of laundry detergent Henkel; the Werhahns in Neuss; the Quandts from the Uckermark; the potassium king Rosterg; and another two dozen large-scale industrialists. All these men had one feature in common: each and every one of them was not Jewish.

Concerning the second part of the anti-Semitic argument with regard to the financial power of the Jews, their reputed entrenched monopoly in banking and stock-exchange dealings, with the aid of which they had subjugated the total economy and had reduced the "exceedingly honest Aryans" to the level of "interest slaves," two points must be made.

For one, it is true that the Jews played an important role in the structure of German banking, had a crucial share in founding today's great banking institutions, and in their capacity as private bankers—greatly esteemed for both their skill and honesty—contributed greatly to transforming Germany into an industrial power of the first order. They therefore had no reason to be ashamed of their strong position, though it was far from a monopoly within the German banking world.

However, if we follow the line of argument of most anti-Semitic writers in viewing the banking profession, and even more so stock-exchange trading, as something highly disreputable, reprehensible, detrimental to the people, (and therefore typically Jewish and unworthy of an "Aryan,") we should expect the following scenario. Since the Jews were excluded from the world of banking in the "Third Reich" and have remained excluded to the present day with few exceptions, the anti-Semitic argument would lead to current conditions that can be likened only to paradise—a "solid" economy open to easy survey, and an end to the abuses inherent in jobbing and speculation. We should expect currency transactions consonant with the German character, free of "Jewish haste," of unfair tricks and of undignified bargaining. And of course, most important of all, free of all "interest slavery"—whatever that may mean.

In reality, in the capitalist section of Germany the expulsion of the Jews has had the reverse consequence. The power of the great banking institutions, now completely "cleansed of Jews," has grown to gigantic proportions; speculation in stocks and bonds has trickled down to the ranks of middle-class housewives and the better-paid blue-collar workers. The German Federal Republic is not only a first-rank financial power, but is steeped in materialism reaching the remotest corners. Quick and easy earnings are desired, and never before have so many Germans run up such huge debts—coupled with the corresponding interest burden—encouraged as they are on every street corner to buy on the installment plan, to apply for credit, to borrow, and to indulge in overdrafts.

All this has happened and is spreading even though no more than a handful of banks have any Jewish officers or owners. Where the major banks are concerned, there is no Jewish influence whatsoever. Jewish participation in stock-exchange trading is negligible.

Let us assume that once upon a time the Jews really exercised power, or are still doing so—which is certainly not the case—how would they have used it? Against the anti-Semites of the "national right"? To support the interests of the Social Democrats, who were tolerant of them? Or to turn Germany over to "Bolshevism"?

Our examples have allowed us to establish the fact that there were a number of Jews with right-wing leanings, who were in the German National group. These specifically included those who, because of their wealth, would have been most likely to exercise power, such as Baroness Rothschild and von Weinberg. Might these campaign supporters of the "All-German" group have been the exception to the rule, while in reality an alliance between finance capital, press monopoly, and Marxist parties flourished, as claimed by the anti-Semites?

Leaving aside for the moment the question of a Jewish press monopoly, let us take up the assertion, however absurd it may sound, of Jewish-capitalist sympathies for Jewish-Marxist parties. These definitely unnatural leanings were said to have led to a coupling in 1918 that engendered what the extreme right liked to call the "Jew republic."

Was the Weimar Republic really created and wholly dominated by Jews? If so, did the Jewish men in power strive to hand Germany over to Bolshevism?

Let us first establish the fact that the first German republic was the result of the defeat of the German empire. It followed in the wake of the demand on the part of the commanding German generals, Hindenburg and Ludendorff, to accept the armistice conditions immediately. It was subsequent to, and linked with, the cowardly flight across the border, first of Kaiser William II, then of Ludendorff, into neutral territory, coupled with the despair of the population, which had been misled for years. The people had to recognize the futility of the immense sacrifices, deprivations, and efforts they had made. This first German republic was an attempt to bring order into the chaos left behind by the collapsed monarchy, to save a Reich that was falling apart, and to terminate the senseless war that the Kaiser's Germany had started and lost.

Two possibilities seemed to offer themselves. The German Social Democrats, as the strongest party and the least compromised political group, could have endeavored to create a socialist state in an alliance with the extreme left. The chances for its success would have been no worse than, say, in Russia. But, realization of such an idea would have required, as it did in Russia, revolutionary will and drive, a radical break with the past, brutal measures leading to the expropriation and divestment of power of all potential counterrevolutionaries, bloody suppression of the resistance to be expected in the interior, and a years-long struggle against American-British-French attempts at intervention.

The other possibility, the one the Social Democrats decided to embrace, was an alliance with the middle classes and the old forces, and preservation and modest reform of the surviving structures. This course entailed assuming responsibility for liquidating the previous regime's insolvency, for which they were not to blame, with all the consequences that were bound to follow. It also entailed a harsh struggle against the revolutionary left. This was necessary in order to gain credibility with the many members of the middle class who were suspicious and basically antirepublican. It also meant a very mild resistance to interference from the extreme right.

The decision to choose an alliance with the middle class is termed "a foregone conclusion" by Friedrich Stampfer, chronicler of the Weimar Republic, for many years editor in chief of the Social Democrats' national organ, *Vorwärts*, and himself of Jewish origin. The radical left called it "an act of treason by the majority of socialists," for which they blamed Ebert and Otto Landsberg.

In his work *Die vierzehn Jahre der ersten deutschen Republik* [The Fourteen Years of the First German Republic], Stampfer writes about Landsberg: "Thanks to his achievements as a jurist, his encyclopedic knowledge, and his active work for the Party over several decades, he was held in the highest esteem. In view of his emphatically nationalist attitude during the war, he was all the more suspect as far as the radical left was concerned."

In fact the leaders of the left vilified him as Ebert's "gray eminence" and "Mephistopheles of the revolution." From their point of view, they may have been right, since he was by conviction a supporter of parliamentarian democracy and of cooperation with the middle-class parties, opposed to any violent overthrow, any radical change, and especially any attempt to realize socialism by force, bloodshed, and dictatorship.

Dr. Otto Landsberg took on the ministry of justice in the new republic's first cabinet. This government was formed in February 1919 by the prime minister, Philipp Scheidemann. Along with Ebert and Scheidemann, Landsberg had earlier been a member of the provisional government that called itself the "Council of the People's Delegates."

This interim solution of November 9, 1918 owed its inception to another Social Democrat of Jewish origin, Dr. Hugo Haase, a lawyer from Königsberg. Before 1914 he had been joint chairman of the Social Democratic Party with Ebert; he also headed the Party in the Reichstag. Opposed to war by conviction, he had left the Social Democratic Party and had become the leader of the Independent Social Democratic Party, founded in 1917.

On the critical November 9, 1918, Haase led the majority of his party into a coalition with the Social Democrats who opposed socialist experiments and were in favor of cooperation with the middle-class parties. This move met with embittered resistance from the left wing of the Independents and even more from the Spartacists under the leadership of Rosa Luxemburg and Karl Liebknecht. The coalition lasted only seven weeks and ended with the resignation of Haase and his friends, while Ebert and Landsberg retained, along with the "purely socialist" Council of the People's Delegates, the old administrative departments and added insult to injury by filling them with either middle-class politicians or with their department heads from the old order. Furthermore, they sent for "regular" troops, commanded by an aristocratic general and a Kaiser loyalist, to come to Berlin and deployed them against the leftist radicals.

Even so, during the seven weeks of "truce" and coalition between the Social Democrats and the Independents, guidelines were set in the direction of cooperation with all shades of middle-class groups and the military, and away from a socialist overthrow of the old system. This decision would not have been feasible without Haase's cooperation. Yet the German right wing showed its gratitude for Haase's choice of peace and order in a nasty way; as early as 1919 Haase was assassinated by a deranged man who had been incited to commit the deed. His Independents split in 1920. The bulk— under the leadership of Rudolf Hilferding, an outstanding economist of Jewish origin—returned to the fold of the Social Democrats. The remainder joined the Communists.

A number of people of Jewish origin were among the middle-class politicians heading administrative departments during the period of the Council of the People's Delegates. The same situation existed in the government formed by Scheidemann after the national assembly elections, which remained in office until the middle of 1919. Dr. Otto Landsberg was Minister of Justice; Dr. Hugo Preuss, Dr. Eugen Schiffer, and Dr. Georg Gothein, all members of the Democratic Party, were also among the leaders. In April 1919 Schiffer was replaced by his party colleague and friend, Dr. Bernhard Dernburg.

Who were these men whom Hitler and his followers later derisively labeled "Jewish-Marxist-November criminals"?

Dr. Bernhard Dernburg's father, Friedrich Dernburg, was a renowned editorial writer on the *National-Zeitung* during the Bismarck era and a National Liberal delegate to the Reichstag. Bernhard himself had been active in banking and was already director of a major bank when the Kaiser's chancellor, Prince Bülow, called on him in 1907 to become head of the colonial department of the foreign office. Against the intentions of the Reichstag, he successfully waged an energetic colonial policy in accordance with the wishes of the Kaiser. After the dissolution of parliament and the government's election victory, to which Dernburg had contributed considerably, an independent colonial office was created with Dernburg as its first head. After popularizing the colonial idea in Germany, he relinquished his post in 1909. As discussed elsewhere, in 1914 he organized the German propaganda effort in the United States. Near the end of 1918 he joined the right wing of the newly founded Democratic Party, was elected to the National Assembly, and served as minister of finance from April to June 1919, replacing his party colleague Eugen Schiffer, who retired. Dernburg refused to agree to signing the Versailles Treaty and resigned as well.

Dr. Eugen Schiffer, born in Breslau, was a jurist and had initially adopted a judicial career. Under the monarchy he was a superior court councillor in Berlin and then attained the rank of judge at the Royal Prussian higher administrative court. It was still in the days of the Kaiser in 1917 that he was appointed undersecretary of state in the treasury department.

In 1918 he took over as its chief and continued as minister of state for finance in the Scheidemann cabinet. He was also a member of the National Liberals, and later on belonged to the right wing of the middle-class Liberal Democratic Party. From October 1919 to March 1920, and again from May 1920 to October 1921, he was minister of state for justice. Thereafter he was the leader of the German delegation for the Upper Silesia negotiations with the Allies in Geneva, and there he made the best possible settlement for Germany.

Dr. Georg Gothein, the third minister of Jewish origin in the first elected government of the Weimar Republic was head of the state treasury. The career of this Silesian began with the post of chief secretary of the Upper Silesian Mining and Foundry Association in Kattowitz. Next he took on the jobs of district official, councillor for mines, and corporate lawyer of the chamber of commerce in Breslau. As a liberal politician, he sat in the prewar Reichstag and the Prussian house of deputies. He joined the Democratic Party in 1918, and in 1919 he retired from office because he would not agree to the signing of the Versailles Treaty.

Finally there was Dr. Hugo Preuss. Born in Berlin, in 1918 he was appointed secretary of state of the ministry of the interior; he then became the first minister of state for the interior. He was a distinguished jurist, a pupil of Otto von Gierkes, as well as a political philosopher and historian. In his capacity as municipal deputy, he devoted himself to community affairs; after 1900 he became an unpaid town councillor in Berlin. During the First World War, at the suggestion of army headquarters, he designed a liberal state constitution, the wording of which was kept secret from the public but was much discussed in political circles. When, in November 1918, the Council of the People's Deputies replaced the monarchy, Preuss spoke out against any kind of dictatorship in a sensational editorial in the *Berliner Tageblatt*; he demanded the institution of democratic conditions and offered the Social Democrats an equal working partnership with the liberal middle classes. The very same day Ebert called him in; the result of this conversation, which included Landsberg, was the appointment of middle-class experts from the liberal camps as heads of the state departments. Preuss himself took on the department of the interior and accepted a mandate to draft a constitution for the future democratic republic, which the Na-

tional Assembly still to be elected would have to adopt.
Although in this way he became the father of the Weimar
Republic, he soon resigned from his ministerial post, in
protest against the Versailles Treaty. He vigorously opposed
the Treaty, not least because of the clause prohibiting the
annexation of the Austrian Republic by Germany.

A further Jewish politician deserves to be mentioned—the
first ambassador of Austria to Germany after the end of the
monarchy, Ludo Hartmann. He was an adviser to the men
who prepared for the National Assembly and, like his father,
Moritz Hartmann in the Frankfurt National Assembly of 1848,
he endeavored with energy until the end, to achieve the
inclusion of the German part of Austria in the Weimar Republic.
He may be considered the chief initiator of the final decision
to reintroduce the old state colors—black, red, and gold—as
a symbol of the idea of Greater Germany.

Summing up, then, it can be said that some German politicians of Jewish descent had a strong, some even a decisive,
influence on developments during the foundation phase of
the Weimar Republic. This situation was soon to change.
Nineteen cabinets followed Scheidemann's, with well over 200
ministerial posts to bestow. In them can be found very few
department heads of Jewish origin. The Jewish Social Democrat Dr. Rudolf Hilferding, who in 1920 led the Independents back into the Social Democratic Party, has already
been briefly mentioned. In Gustav Stresemann's first government in 1923, Hilferding headed the ministry of finance for a
few months, as he did again in Hermann Müller's second
cabinet. In 1929 he resigned under pressure after an extremely unsavory campaign against him, one of the principal
instigators of which was the German National president of his
Reichsbank, Hjalmar Schacht. In 1941 Hilferding committed
suicide in prison after the French government of Marshall
Pétain handed him over to the Gestapo, in violation of his
right to asylum.

For a few months in 1920 the long-time chairman of the
Democratic Party, Dr. Erich Koch-Weser, held the post of
vice chancellor and minister of the interior in Hermann Müller's
first cabinet. In the Germany of the Kaiser, he had been
mayor of the cities of Delmenhorst, Bremerhaven, and Kassel.
He had a reputation as an outstanding administrative jurist,
and in October 1919 he took over as minister of the interior

from the non-Jewish Social Democrat Dr. Eduard David, in Bauer's government. Koch-Weser returned to government as minister of justice in Müller's last coalition government under Social Democratic leadership, which was ousted in March 1930. In August of that year, Koch-Weser effected the short-lived merger of the Democratic Party and the Young German Order in the newly formed German State Party and then relinquished active participation in politics. In April 1933 the "Aryan" paragraph deprived him of the right to practice law. It required the intervention of the aged Hindenburg to re-verse the professional ban imposed on "this man of great merit, imbued with the national spirit, and greatly esteemed by his excellency, the Reich President [Hindenburg]." In 1934 Dr. Koch-Weser emigrated to Brazil. Before then, his daughter had committed suicide because her Jewish descent barred her from taking the teachers' qualifying exam.

Curt Walter Joel has been briefly mentioned as belonging to the conservative right wing. He was minister of justice in the first two Marx cabinets and the last Brüning cabinet after long service as secretary of state in the ministry of justice.

The politically colorless career diplomat and orientalist, Friedrich Rosen, scion of a well-known Jewish family of scholars, held the post of foreign minister for a few months during 1921 in the first Wirth government, while the depart-ment of the interior of this transition government was in the hands of Dr. Georg Gradnauer. This right-wing Social Demo-crat was the first prime minister of Saxony after the 1918 revolution. Working with the middle-class parties and the military, he had kept the radical left under control. During the "Third Reich" Gradnauer was sent to the Theresienstadt concentration camp because of his Jewish origins.

The last, and presumably most outstanding, German-Jewish politician to attain ministerial rank in the Weimar Republic was Dr. Walter Rathenau. Within the cabinet he was first head of the newly created ministry for reconstruction; in the second Wirth cabinet he was head of the state department for foreign affairs.

As the son of the founder of AEG, Emil Rathenau, Walther Rathenau was a member of a very wealthy family, but he struck out on an independent course soon after he finished his engineering studies. He became prominent both as a leader in economic affairs, but also as a theoretician and writer on economic theory. During the First World War the ministry of war entrusted him with establishing and running the department responsible for the supply of raw materials. His organizational talent, his tough energy, and not least, his patriotism, coupled with his great sense of duty, enabled him to achieve the seemingly impossible. His planning, seizure, and allocation of all available raw materials allowed Germany to hold out economically for four years.

Politically, Rathenau should be listed rather further to the right than to the left—in sharp contrast to the scurrilous calumnies the extreme right wing was to shower on him. During the war he belonged with the superpatriots and annexationists. In October 1918 he published a startling article in the *Vossische Zeitung* in which he advocated the rejection of unacceptable armistice conditions and a mass uprising of the German people to repulse invading enemy armies. After the debacle, which could not be averted, Rathenau offered his services to the new government. He participated in the preparations for the German peace delegation, was the expert at the conference at Spa, and in 1921 took part in the preliminary work for the London reparation conference, among other services. He began by opposing the acceptance of the London ultimatum. After the government had been formed again under the Catholic Center Party member Wirth, however, he reconciled himself to joining the cabinet as minister for reconstruction.

When the League of Nations partitioned Upper Silesia, he resigned in protest, though he continued to act as adviser to and negotiator for the government. In the five months that remained during which he was Germany's foreign minister in 1922, he was able to realize very noteworthy successes for Germany, in particular the treaty of Rapallo with Russia. Equally important, he managed to reassure the Western nations, which had viewed the German-Russian economic agreements with a great measure of distrust.

His successful endeavors to improve Germany's hopeless position after the defeat of 1918 did not endear him with or win the thanks of the German Nationals and the People's Party. Rathenau, himself by conviction a Nationalist and fervent patriot, was slandered and threatened as being a "Jewish appeasement politician." A very popular song made the rounds of the right-wing extremists and the Freikorps with a recurring refrain that crudely suggested that he should be assassinated. Although Rathenau knew how seriously this incitement to assassination had to be taken, he refused to be intimidated and absolutely rejected any protective measures. On June 24, 1922, the state minister for foreign affairs was murdered as he was being driven in an open car from his home outside Berlin to the foreign office. The perpetrators of this foul deed were ex-officers and Freikorps members armed with pistols.* Ernst von Salomon, one of the participants in the plot against Rathenau, effectively described the circumstances in his novel *Die Geächteten* [The Outlaws].

Besides these few Jewish or half-Jewish ministers, a few other notables of Jewish descent played a role in the political life of the Weimar Republic. Let us cite merely a few typical examples. Apart from the few on the extreme left—such as Ruth Fischer, who was expelled from the Communist Party and turned anti-Stalinist—or Heinz Neumann—who from 1928 on was at the head of the Communist Party together with the non-Jewish Ernst Thälmann and belonged to the group of German Communists "liquidated" by Stalin—the historical facts reveal that most of the Jews were more comfortable in the ranks of the middle-class parties that proclaimed "law and order."

Hermann Reincke-Bloch (1867-1928), for instance, was one of the leaders of the German People's Party, which belonged in the moderate right wing. After his return from the First World War as a captain of the reserve, he became head of the coalition government in conservative Mecklenburg-Schwerin, and subsequently minister of education. Erich Kuttner, a noncommissioned officer who was severely wounded at Verdun, took an active part in repressing the Spartacist revolt. Subse-

*Translator's note: After Rathenau's death, his mother wrote the following letter to the mother of Ernst Techow, one of the surviving assassins: "In nameless sorrow do I proffer you my hand, you poorest of all women. Tell your son that I forgive him in the name and in the spirit of the one he murdered, as God may forgive him, when he renders full and open confession before earthly justice and repents in front of the Divine. Had he known my son, the noblest on earth, he would sooner have poised the murder weapon against himself than against him. May these words grant peace to your soul.
Mathilde Rathenau." (Reprinted from *The Star*. Johannesburg, Jan. 21, 1960.)

quently he was a member of the Social Democrats in the Prussian parliament. In 1933 he fled to Holland, where, after the occupation by the Nazis, he was tracked down by the Gestapo and killed in the Mauthausen concentration camp in 1942.

Jakob Riesser was a nephew of the renowned Gabriel Riesser who—as previously discussed—made a name for himself for his 1849 speech in Frankfurt and, on behalf of the National Assembly offered King Frederick William IV of Prussia the German imperial crown. As the founder of the Central Union of German Banks and Banking Trade, as well as of the Hansa League, Jakob Riesser is certainly not suspect of Marxist leanings. Furthermore, in his capacity as president of the League, in November 1918 he appealed for the establishment of "citizens' councils" as a counterweight to the "workers' and soldiers' councils" and to finance the fight against the Spartacists. From 1906 to 1928 Riesser was a member of the Reichstag, first as a National-Liberal delegate, then as a member of the German People's Party, a group of moderate conservatives. From 1921 on he was one of the vice presidents of parliament; the national citizens' council he had initiated in 1925 nominated the old Field Marshal Paul von Hindenburg as candidate for the office of president. Just before he turned eighty, Riesser died in 1932.

Dr. Georg Solmssen, like his father before him chairman of the board of the Deutsche Bank and Diskontogesellschaft, succeeded Riesser as president of the governing board of the Central Union of German Banks and Banking Trade. Solmssen was an economic leader with a conservative, strongly anti-socialist bent. On such occasions as bankers' conventions, his speeches were well received and in their conservative bias were almost indistinguishable from those of a Hugenberg or a Schacht. Solmssen died in 1957 in Lugano, where he had been able to retire during the "Third Reich" because he was also a Romanian counsul general.

Another man who sided with the right wing, although he was a member of the Catholic Center Party, and exerted a strong influence on the Social Democrats, was a highly controversial figure in the political life of the Weimar Republic—Secretary of State Robert Weismann, the closest adviser to the Prussian prime minister, Otto Braun, a Social Democrat. Originally Weismann had been state prosecutor. During the revolutionary turmoil of 1918–1919 he used all the means at his disposal to preserve public order and to foil attempted coups from the radical left. In 1920 he was appointed state commissioner for public security.

One other figure on the political scene of the Weimar Republic became a target for the most violent anti-Semitic attacks—Dr. Bernhard Weiss, whose last post was that of vice president chief of police in Greater Berlin. The son of a wealthy Jewish merchant, he studied law and then risked entering the Prussian service as an administration lawyer. In the First World War he volunteered for frontline duty and was promoted to the rank of cavalry captain in a Bavarian regiment; he received the Iron Cross First Class for personal bravery. In 1918, still under the Kaiser's empire, he entered the police service and served as head of the political police of Berlin from 1920 to 1924. An attack on the Soviet trade mission cost him his position and caused his temporary retirement. In 1927 he returned to police headquarters as vice president.

Dr. Bernhard Weiss could have been popular with the German right, since he was a decorated veteran with nationalist sentiments and since, as a Prussian official, he had been publicly disciplined for overzealousness in his proceedings against Soviet officials. He would have been—but for his Jewish faith. He had the added misfortune of looking somewhat like what anti-Semites imagined Jews to look like. Hitler's "regional leader of Greater Berlin," Dr. Joseph Goebbels, editor of the Nazi *Der Angriff*, nicknamed him "Isidor" and every week showered him with personal insults, calumnies, and malicious insinuations. After Franz von Papen's coup on July 20, 1932 against the legitimate Prussian government, Weiss was forced to resign. In late January 1933 he managed at the last moment to escape seizure by his mortal enemies. He fled the country and died in London in 1955.

The Weimar Republic cannot by the wildest stretch of the imagination be described as a "Jew republic." And there is no proof of a significant influence in its political life that can be ascribed to figures of Jewish origin—rendering the term "a Jewish-Bolshevik conspiracy" ludicrous. The reputed domination of Germany by a "Jewish press monopoly" is even more fantastic, and perhaps a deliberate lie with a specific purpose.

Presumably the attribution was intended to conceal the fact that the principal influence on the German press was in fact exercised by the large industrial concerns and associations, who were adept at veiling their highly self-seeking interests in German National garb.

Unlike, for example, the situation in England, no mass-circulation newspapers existed in prewar or postwar Germany that were read throughout the country. The capital city did have its gutter press, such tabloids as *BZ am Mittag*, the *8-Uhr Abendblatt*, and the *Nachtausgabe*. But the circulation of these and all other Berlin papers was infinitesimal compared to the major English newspapers.

Not only Berlin, but almost all the larger cities of Germany issued newspapers with international reputations. Since there was no financial link among them, a monopoly was out of the question. In the Weimar Republic there were only two newspaper publishing concerns of importance that could be considered Jewish in that they belonged to publishers of Jewish origin—Ullstein and Mosse.*

The only papers owned by these publishers that carried any political weight and were quoted internationally were the *Vossische Zeitung* (Ullstein; largest issue ever achieved, 80,000 copies) and the *Berliner Tageblatt* (Mosse; highest circulation, 310,000 copies). There was one further politically important daily paper in Berlin, the *Deutsche Allgemeine Zeitung* which during its period of influence belonged to Stinnes and was alternately subsidized by heavy industry and by the state.

Ullstein's *Vossische Zeitung* was a newspaper of distinction and high reputation but required large annual subsidies because of its small circulation. Ullstein also brought out less prestigious morning papers, tabloids, weeklies, and other periodicals, among them the *Berliner Morgenpost* with an average circulation of more than 500,000 copies, the largest German daily, and the *Berliner Illustrierte*, the illustrated periodical with the largest circulation in the country.

Apart from the *Berliner Tageblatt*, two further papers issued by the publishing house of Rudolf Mosse were the *Berliner Volks-Zeitung* and the *8-Uhr-Abendblatt*. However,

---

*The *Frankfurter Zeitung*, founded by Leopold Sonnemann (1831–1909) another such newspaper. Not only was it highly regarded internationally, but it also stood out in its choice and presentation of subject matter.

the financial source of the corporation was the advertising agency known as Annoncen-Expedition Rudolf Mosse, an address-book publishing branch, and the "Rudolf Mosse Code," which was an internationally established popular means of communication.

Both Ullstein and Mosse pursued a middle-class liberal policy. Learnings of a leftist nature, let alone Communist learnings, were not tolerated. When, in 1932, Mosse met with financial reverses, the publishers tried to rescue the business by opening the *Berliner Tageblatt* to moderately German-National opinion.

Ullstein may possibly claim some "power of the press," since in 1928 it could claim with pride that every seventh German was a regular reader of one or another of its publications. But these included such unpolitical periodicals as *Dame*, *Bauwelt Verkehrstechnik*, the guide to radio programs called *Sieben Tage*, *Der heitere Fridolin*, and *Grüne Post*, which expressed homey, patriotic sentiment and was much read by farmers and Germans abroad.

No, politically the power of Ullstein and Mosse hardly extended beyond Berlin, if we except the national and occasionally international attention frequently paid to the editorials appearing in the *Berliner Tageblatt* and the *Vossische Zeitung*.

However, there was a third great publishing house in the nation's capital that wielded genuine power and that exerted a strong influence on public opinion, both directly and indirectly. Since it was not in Jewish hands, little attention was given to its concentration of power. Only a few experts were aware of the immensely large and powerful "opinion factory" behind it. This publishing house went under the name of its founder, August Scherl. As early as the First World War it had changed hands. It was rumored that the new owners were closely connected with the heavy industry of the Rhine. Very few understood the practical implications of this alliance.

All the major corporations along the Rhine and Ruhr belonged to the Association for Mining Interests; for many years this institution had represented the political interests of heavy industry. Shortly before the First World War its chairman of those days suggested to the members, and obtained their full consent to a new policy. All major fund-raising appeals from private sources, most especially from newspaper publishers, would be examined and evaluated by a controlling body of the association, who would oversee any binding commitments made or any money given to the applicants. Such a controlling body was immediately established and, not unexpectedly, immediately came under the control, in its turn, of the association's chairman. Privy Councillor Dr. Alfred Hugenberg was also chairman of the board of the largest concern allied with the heavy industry, not only of Germany, but of the whole of Europe—none less than Krupp's top director (and leader of the All-Germans).

Within very few years, and using the Ruhr industries, Hugenberg was able to construct a press empire that he alone controlled. In 1919 he left Krupp's board of directors to devote himself exclusively to politics. This meant that the "silver fox"—as he was called in Essen—had the use of an immense apparatus for influencing public opinion. From then on he no longer had any need of support from heavy industry, but the magnates along the Rhine, Ruhr, and Saar still needed him, the secret ruler of the mass media. Subsequently he managed to elevate his position by taking on the chairmanship of the German National Party—a key political position.

At the height of his power Hugenberg presided over his own international news agency Telegraphen Union (TU); the largest German advertising agency, Allgemeine Anzeigengesellschaft (Ala); and a network of printing-die and correspondence services concentrated in the Wirtschaftsstelle der Provinzpresse (Wipro). The last gained great political importance because it supplied hundreds of medium-size and small daily papers, which were given articles and even whole pages of material in matrices ready for printing. The result was a situation in which the customers—allegedly "independent" editorial offices—could make decisions only on the local sections of their publications. Hugenberg's own "newspaper bank," the Mutuum Darlehens-AG (a savings-and-loan institution) and the Vera publishing house enmeshed a number of provincial German papers in a camouflaged relationship of dependency on Hugenberg and his cohorts. In addition, he held large blocks of shares in a total of fourteen important newspapers in large and medium-sized cities. And he owned the Scherl publishing house in Berlin, which brought out the *Berliner Lokalanzeiger,* a newspaper with a large circulation and much advertising revenue, as well as the illustrated weekly *Die Woche*, founded to serve as competition to Ullstein's *Berlin Illustrierte*. Apart from Hugenberg's press empire, which dominated large sections of the German provincial and local press by providing ads, articles, news items, matrix services, and loans and investments, there was also Hugenberg's film fiefdom, the Universal Film-AG, known as "UFA." It owned its own production sites and studios, distribution firms, and movie theaters. This structure completed the "opinion factory" wholly controlled by the German National party leader, furnishing not only its own UFA weekly newsreel but also a number of "patriotic" films that glorified war and endeavored to sabotage Gustav Stresemann's policy of reconciliation.

After Hitler entered the government, staunchly helped by Hugenberg to climb into the saddle, Hugenberg became the first minister of state for commerce. The "silver fox" gradually relinquished all his press and movie interests; in 1944 he even stepped away from the Scherl publishing house. It is interesting to note that, in contrast to the "Aryanized" Mosse and Ullstein, the Scherl establishment was grotesquely overvalued, despite the fact that a paper shortage placed it on the brink of bankruptcy at the time of sale. For only these remnants of his empire Hugenberg received roughly 64 million marks—not in devalued cash, but in blocks of shares held by the state that secured for Hugenberg a substantial investment in two of Germany's greatest industrial concerns.

But in spite of its proliferation and enormous potential for exerting influence, even the Hugenberg concern was by no means the largest press establishment in the history of German newspapers. Hitler himself can lay claim to setting the record here, with the aid of Max Amann and a few straw men. Even if they did not achieve the absolute monopoly they aimed for, in the end, 82.5 per cent of the whole German press was in the hands of Amann and thus of Hitler.

It was Hugenberg and Hitler, not the Jews, who destroyed the German local and provincial press. They forced respectable publishing houses, owned by one family for generations, to give up their autonomy, to stop publishing locally rooted papers, and finally to sell them. In the end Hugenberg was even swallowed up in the consolidation process and had to throw in the towel—though he was the only one to be excessively compensated. However, the man who had promised with his party," his life "if necessary to give their lives" to use all means at his disposal to create a sound middle class and to prevent the formation of trusts,* seized for his own gain, at the expense of middle-class entrepreneurs, far more than any other German before or after him.

One more objection might be raised against our contradiction of the anti-Semitic assertions with regard to "Jewish press domination." It could be said that Hugenberg had taken possession of or put into trusteeship those concerns offered for sale only to prevent even stronger Jewish influence on the German press of the Kaiser's Germany and of the Weimar Republic, so as to preserve them for the "national cause" and to prevent their "falling into Jewish hands." It could also be objected that Hitler was only practicing a kind of nationalization, viewing himself as the personification of the state in line with the old principle of absolute monarchs, *l'état c'est moi.*

It is not worth going into the matter of Hitler's alleged altruism. It is true that nationalization would have been quite feasible; but that was not his procedure. He preferred buying up all the Jewish and non-Jewish presses through front men, so that not even the sellers knew to whom they were handing over their newspapers. The argument was actually frequently used about Hugenberg's later acquisitions that anything was fine that prevented one or another "national" newspaper from falling into Jewish hands. It was this trick—or to be precise, the (fraudulent) assertion of having received a higher bid from Mosse—that allowed, for instance, August Scherl in 1913 to assemble a group of conservative financial donors that gradually bought his investments at a very high price in order to cede them later to the gallant Privy Councillor Hugenberg. Paradoxically, the financial consortium that saved a German-National anti-Semitic publishing house from alleged seizure by Berlin's "newspaper Jews" was headed by the Cologne banker, Simon Alfred, Baron von Oppenheim, along with two bankers, who were several degrees more Jewish—Louis Hagen and Eduard Beit von Speyer, of the banking house of Lazard Speyer-Ellissen.

Even in the "Third Reich" no one dared seriously to claim that the decline and demise of newspapers, which started in

---

*See Appendix for the Nazi party program.

the last years of the Weimar Republic, was due to Jewish influence (or at least traceable to the overwhelming competition offered by Ullstein and Mosse). Today such a statement concerning the situation in West Germany and West Berlin would be even more absurd. There is now not one Jewish owner of, or partner in any of the ten largest press conglomerates. The consolidation process, however, started again some time ago. And the process continues and accelerates, despite the interesting fact that, after 1945, a hopeful fresh start was made, resulting in the reappearance of many newspapers that were extinguished in the "Third Reich" alongside the blossoming of many new papers.

The correct assessment of today's situation may also have applied to pre-1933 Berlin. Such an assessment focuses on the method by which Jews influence the press—provided that they do so at all—not financially, but editorially, to determine a political line. We have already mentioned and quoted, William S. Schlamm and Hans Habe. Apart from them, a number of respected journalists of Jewish origin are engaged in the Federal Republic and West Berlin. Although numerically they form a negligible minority of the total of significant journalists, some of them occupy positions of extraordinary influence. The direction taken by the papers under their influence will dispel without fail the last lingering vestiges of doubt as to the truth of the allegation about the identity of Jewish and Marxist-Bolshevik influence on the press and will reveal that this claim was and still is purely and simply an anti-Semitic invention.

A single example will suffice—the largest and most powerful Continental press empire that belongs to Axel Springer, a man most certainly not suspect of any sympathy for the doctrines of Marx or even for the Soviet system. It is said that the publications' political line is determined by the "newspaper czar," Springer himself. However, he has by his side a kind of advisory council formed by the grand dukes and barons of his empire. A clause in the concern's constitution of 1963 spoke of a journalistic advisory council for "planning in publishing matters and development of all objectives on behalf of the corporation's various enterprises." It seemed at first glance to refer to something "casually professional," as Hans Dieter Müller puts it in his critical study *Der Springer-Konzern*, published in 1968. Müller continues, "they may still be talk-

GERMANY WITHOUT JEWS

ing the same way. However, the small executive panel became politicized following the appointment, on January 1, 1968, of the new executive officer, Dr. Horst Mahnke, formerly editor in chief of *Kristall*. In the cultured serenity of the twelfth floor, housed right next to the offices of the publisher himself, he became a kind of one-man "politbureau."

Hans Dieter Müller also names the members of the 1968 "editorial advisory council" who, "for a special remuneration of DM 2,500 a month, meet once a week to discuss with the owner and his close advisers general editorial problems." They are Hans Blum for *Hör zu*, Peter Boenisch for *Bild* and *Bild am Sonntag;* Julius Hollos for the Springer Foreign Bureaus Service (he has since become a kind of editorial director for *Die Welt* as well); Malte Till Kogge and Heinz Köster, alternating for the Berlin newspapers; Bernhard Menne (since deceased) for *Welt am Sonntag;* Martin Saller for the *Hamburger Abendblatt;* and Dr. Hermann F. G. Starke, Hans-Wilhelm Meidinger, and Dr. Heinz Pentzlin for *Die Welt*. Members who are not also editors in chief are Ernst J. Cramer, Otto Siemer, Adam Vollhardt and Karl Andreas Voss. Of course, Mahnke is also a member of this illustrious circle.

Among these fifteen advisers who, jointly with their boss, established the "political guidelines" for the Springer empire in 1968, two were known to have been previously active Nazis. Voss was a deputy Reichsleiter and Mahnke himself is a former functionary in Heydrich's Reich security headquarters. However, a further three—or 20 per cent—are of Jewish origin. Both Julius Hollos and Ernst J. Cramer returned from emigration as press officers with the Allies. Kogge is a grandson of Privy Councillor Dr. Oscar Cassel, the distinguished liberal politician and son of a rabbi who did so much for the municipal government of the nation's former capital.

Among other leading Jewish associates at Springer, William S. Schlamm—already mentioned and politically far to the right—contributes to *Welt am Sonntag,* while Willy Haas ("Caliban"), the most distinguished critic and editorial writer is worth listing for his achievements in the cultural columns of *Die Welt*.

These few names suffice to show that the remnants of what the anti-Semites called "Jewish power of the press" are found precisely where a distinctly right-wing bias—not only of an antisocialist character, but with a distinctly reactionary flavor—is practiced to influence the masses. No more than a scattered handful of journalists of Jewish origin are found in the left-leaning press. And none of West Germany's left-wing papers can be even faintly described as wielding power.

This leaves the question of how it is that the few prominent journalists of Jewish origin who still work in West Germany are allied with the political right and feel professionally comfortable in a publishing house that condones strange practices. Although Springer made the "reconciliation between Jews and Germans" one of the four fundamental principles of its publishing policy, it nevertheless—to cite one example—employs a political caricaturist such as Hicks on *Die Welt*. This old hand in his field now attacks Walter Ulbricht and Sebastian Haffner in the same manner he once upon a time made fun of the flight of the Jews from the "Third Reich" and the misery of emigrants. It also tolerates the caption "Eradicate!" on the front page of one of its major tabloids, referring to a new unpopular minority and awakening terrible associations. Its columnists, such as Wilfried Hertz-Eichenrode, preach a new nationalism. According to Hans Dieter Müller, there is a deliberate attempt "to interpret the power shift in Europe as a consequence of Communism and not the consequence of explosive German nationalism." And he recalls, "It was not the racial doctrines that brought Hitler to power, but his militant anti-Communism, which had its covert forerunners in middle-class anxiety and the Freikorps mentality, in the neoconservative factions and associations, in Hugenberg's German-National press and in the unaltered reactionary ideologies of business, the judicial system, and the army, all calling for a savior and finding him."

This analysis and reminder also answers our question. The German Jews—some caught up in "civil fear" of chaos and expropriation, some trapped in the same "reactionary ideologies" that ensnared their "Aryan" competitors, partners, colleagues, and friends in "business, the judicial system, and the army"—by and large took a stand in the middle-class conservative camp. They thought themselves far to the left if they so much as voted for the German State Party, the successor of the Democratic Party. And the only thing that has changed is the fact that there are hardly any Jews in Germany today. Every other view of the situation—in particular the story that the German Jews had "promoted Bolshevism" or even, as its originators and secret leaders, are identical with it, is the brainchild of anti-Semitic minds.

And so we return to our main question: whether, apart from all the disadvantages we are so clearly aware of, there is evidence of those genuine or alleged advantages the anti-Semites hoped would accrue for Germany once the Jews were eliminated—such as the recovery of German love of "inner values" connected with soil and plow, racial inheritance, and Germanic chastity; withdrawal from materialism, from trading, and from the shopkeepers' mentality; a rise in zeal for the armed forces; the repression of "pernicious" influences in the plastic arts, theater, film, and literature, to be replaced by the development of purely Germanic conceptions; delivery of the wage-earning middle class from the clutches of department stores, variety stores, supermarkets, and mail-order firms; the abolition of "interest slavery"; the smashing of monopolies and the supremacy of the banks; the reduction of competition back to Aryan norms; the end of blatant and misleading advertising; and most important of all, an end to the "unchaste concern with matters which the Aryan in the depths of his soul always recognizes as Providence"; the elimination of the "species-alien" mentality from all fields of science and the retreat from all purely theoretical thought; the recovery of agriculture; and the abolition of the international Bolshevik menace.

Today, much more than a quarter-century after the enormous persecution of the Jews, we know that nothing of the kind has happened, that not one of the effects the anti-Semites had fervently believed would follow in the wake of the complete elimination of all Jewish influence has occurred—none at all!

Even the innocent victims had not expected such an outcome. Even they occasionally were not completely immune to the poison of "racial" agitation. Even they sometimes considered one or the other symptom they saw in negative terms to be "typically Jewish." A few Jews felt certain that new tendencies in art, literature, or even science were "corrosive," and they fearfully looked to see whether any fellow Jews might be involved. They also waxed indignant whenever a coreligionist uttered a statement that deviated from the middle-class norm; frequently they judged such an utterance, not as the belief of an individual but as a "racially conditioned" misdemeanor. They even cultivated racial attitudes by emphasizing—analogous to the Nazi ideology of the "Nordic master race"—the distinctive differences between highly civilized, neatly dressed, possibly even academically trained Central Europeans of Jewish origin and the unkempt proletariat "Eastern Jews" struggling to keep their heads above water, predestined, as they appeared to be, for the role of the "racially inferior." This difference was amplified by the fact that the Eastern group had never before come into contact with a modern industrial state that embodied civil liberties. Nor did it give the German Jews pause that this mass of millions of suppressed, half-starved Jews from Eastern Europe, cut off from modern life, cried out for education in a plea that was even louder than their clamor for bread.

There is one lesson to be learned by Jews, non-Jews, anti-Semites, Zionists, as well as other fanatics of each and every "race" and religion. It was not the people, the objects of the racial madness, who became suddenly transfigured and turned upside down all that was popularly believed about them and about the consequences of their destruction. No, it was the racial madness itself which, built on completely wrong premises, had of necessity to lead to completely wrong, totally unexpected, and wholly undesirable results, from the point of view of the partisans and purveyors of their own lying doctrine.

However, the wish that this lesson be taken to heart probably presupposes more insight and common sense than can be expected from people who somehow combine dull-witted prejudice, fear of competition, sexual neurosis, intolerance, and primitive feelings of hatred, into an ideology that allows them to consider themselves "the master race." It also gives them free rein to classify as an "inferior race" any group that is weaker because it is smaller or less able to defend itself, to torment them to their hearts' content, and eventually to slaughter them.

Chapter 10

Balance Sheet for an Extermination

We have been unable to show any advantages to Germany from the expulsion and destruction of German Jewry—not even the very dubious ones that the anti-Semites hoped for, much less others that, viewed in hindsight, might seriously have been considered. The only benefit from the widespread persecution of the Jews in the 1930s and early 1940s in no way accrues to the persecutors—the greatly accelerated pace in the creation of the state of Israel.

All that remains for us to do is to draw a heavy line under the empty columns marked "profit"—unless, that is, we were cruel enough to take a leaf out of the book of the "SS-WVHA"* and regard as profit the slave labor of those who were harried to their deaths, their corpses systematically utilized. Were that disgrace registered as a benefit, our ledgers, kept with the usual German thoroughness, would have to record much else that was a seeming gain for the Reich, such as the gradual—and eventually complete and thorough—confiscation of all Jewish property. Even within the old fron-

---

*SS-WVHA = Economic and Administrative Headquarters of the SS, responsible for the thoroughgoing economic exploitation of all concentration camp inmates.

tiers of the Reich, this procedure netted an estimated 12 billion marks. Experts would also have to establish whether—and if so, to what extent—the forced special labor of Jewish girls—tattooed with a number and the identification "frontline whore"—should be included in the balance sheet. And then there was the unpaid use of countless thousands of men, women, and children as living experimental objects for cruel pseudoscientific research.

Even if we continued the list of such dubious "benefits," the sum total would still be disappointing. The total looting from, and enslavement of, millions brought in nothing but deep abhorrence from all of civilized humanity. The fact that individuals are still profiting from their grabs made during the bargain sales of the Third Reich cannot be considered a profit item in the total economic calculation; it is a further loss in the column registering the moral accounts of East and West Germany, but just a drop in the bucket in the total debit balance.

No, from any point of view the almost complete destruction of the Jews in the areas dominated by the Nazis has brought in no profit, not even such dubious advantages as the inveterate anti-Semites had hoped for. But what about losses and disadvantages?

The material reparations—totaling roughly 30 billion marks—that the German Federal Republic has largely paid or still intends to pay represents a trifle in every respect, an item not worth mentioning in our balance sheet. (Austria was also liable for a far more modest contribution, while the East German Democratic Republic took the line of complete abstention.) In the framework of the total German war obligations of roughly 400 billion marks, the financial reparations are a very modest share compared with the remaining 94 per cent. A part of the reparations has also been absolved collectively, and in the form of goods for Israel. From the German point of view, this solution was more than just a friendly gesture, since it actually meant subsidizing certain branches of the German industry that needed a shot in the arm (such as shipbuilding); such subsidies, granted for development, are expected in the long run to yield many economic and political gains.

Incomparably greater is the loss incurred by the current two Germanies from the fact that, together with the Jews, a very considerable segment of what can only imperfectly be described as the "middle class" and the "intelligentsia", was expelled, exterminated, or completely alienated.

We have tried to arrive at some quantitative and qualitative assessment of the approximate losses through selected examples from medicine, physics, chemistry, drama, film, and literature. Our results may have been insufficiently precise. But one thing we can say with certitude: the Germans drove out and murdered precisely that segment of the population that had made the most significant contributions, in almost every field, to the benefit of what is generally called civilization.

It was those Germans who, despite their relatively small numbers, achieved at least one-fifth of the total in international medical research over the last 150 years, contributing considerably to Germany's worldwide reputation in this area.

It was those Germans who helped to assure a prestigious place in the world for German chemical research and the German chemical industry. They brought about this position with twenty to thirty times more scientists of international repute than would have been warranted by their proportion within the total population.

It was also those Germans from whose group the most outstanding physicists, mathematicians, and engineers emerged—once more a multiple of what might have been expected from the proportion of Jews in the total German population. And, it was precisely the German-Jewish physicists and mathematicians who contributed most decisively in the Second World War by helping to prevent the world's domination by Hitler's Germany.

The enormous contribution of German Jews to every aspect of the arts—as theatrical managers, producers, actors, singers, librettists, and composers; as movie producers and writers; as painters, sculptors, architects, and illustrators; and most importantly as writers of fiction, nonfiction, and poetry—this we established, not only by a single playbill and the window displays of a large bookshop of the early 1930s; the demonstration is threaded through our survey of these totally different areas. The numerous criss-crossing links between the realms of art and science, not to mention their patrons, and leaders of industry and commerce, merited special emphasis on elements that further increased the cultural loss.

Naturally not all German citizens of Jewish origin were outstanding scientists, philosophers, writers, artists, or patrons. Most of them were ordinary men and women of the German middle class—merchants, artisans, shopkeepers, professionals, civil servants, soldiers, farmers. Yes, even Jewish farmers existed—in spite of all assertions to the contrary by the Nazis— and in spite of all the limitations governing the acquisition of arable land applied to keep Jews out until well into the nineteenth century. We have only to look at the little community of Rexingen in the former Duchy of Württemberg, where in 1937 the 262 Jews, all old settlers, were forced to give up their farms. They emigrated to Israel where they founded the village Shave Zion. According to *Der Spiegel* magazine, only one—a butcher—went back to live in Rexingen after 1945.

Of course this German-Jewish group also included some anti-social and criminal elements. But in speaking of Roman Catholic or Protestant imposters, confidence tricksters or drug dealers from a middle-class background, it would occur to no one to stress or even mention their religion or origin; the situation was quite different when it came to Jewish lawbreakers. The German middle-class newspapers—and frequently the courts—smugly noted the "species-alien" origin of Jewish malefactors. At the same time it escaped their attention—and when it did not, they cited Jewish cowardice—that such crimes of violence as murders, homicides, rapes, and aggravated assault were hardly ever committed by Jewish criminals. Nor, strangely enough, were the courts called upon to deal with Jews brought up on charges of drunkenness, child abuse, wife-battering, cruelty to animals, sodomy, refusal to pay alimony, and sundry others. They would have to admit that criminal convictions of Jewish Germans was slightly higher than for Protestants, but considerably lower than among Catholics. Most of the sentences were for such crimes as fraud and for "gentlemanly" felonies, such as tax evasion. We are not trying to make light of these negative aspects, but they must be described for what they were—an unavoidable manifestation, which in its own odd way only further confirmed the clearly preponderant affinity of the German Jews to the middle-class intelligentsia.

And this was also the outcome of our examination: There can be no doubt that the German Jews—and, along with them, the Jewish masses of Eastern and Southeastern Europe—

were in large part the descendants of the very residents of
the medieval German towns who distinguished themselves
from most other inhabitants of the state in only two respects—
their refusal to depart from their customary form of worship
and their higher level of civilization, culture, and education.
What the Germans of the Middle Ages succeeded to a large
extent in suppressing, expelling, and killing was a considerable segment of their own intelligentsia. The Jews had, until
then, been the culturally significant stratum of Central Europe,
a large percentage of those who had come with the Romans to
settle the land.

A certain period of recovery lasted from the age of Enlightenment to the collapse of the German parliamentary system
in 1933. This period—with considerable participation by the
German Jews, who were at long last emancipated again—
saw the national unification of Germany, the rise of the
Reich to the status of a world power, enormous industrial
development, growing democratization and tolerance, and
the greatest revival of science and technology, theater and
literature, ever experienced.

Subsequently the Christian lower middle classes completed
the work started by the first crusaders from France with their
marauding camp followers, and continued by the medieval
Inquisition. Employing the far more effective methods of a
modern state, these forces thoroughly destroyed everything
that did not seem to them to be "truly German." Being petty
pedants as well, requiring a bureaucratic system for the out-
pourings of the hatred born of feelings of inferiority, they
manufactured deeply illogical "racial" laws. The observance
of these forced them to extend their work of destruction to
sections of the population they did not hate at all. Other
categories that they abhorred they were now unable to reach
directly. For this reason the "sound feelings of the people"
led them to search for possibilities enabling them to specify
as "white Jews" and to exterminate, like "non-Aryans," the
following: non-Jewish intellectuals, pure theoreticians, avant-
garde artists, jazz fans, modern composers, bookish people,
overcivilized aristocrats, pacifists, cosmopolitans, and all other
unpopular "Aryans," among them priests, soldiers, liberal
civil servants, and unrepentant democrats.

They were not disturbed by the fact that their definition of
a "white Jew"—really not a Jew at all—depended on a prem-

ise that did not exist: the stereotype of the "true"—presumably "black"—Jew, paralleling the ideal of a fair-haired, blue-eyed Viking athlete. Only three of the top Nazi functionaries could be said to come close to resembling this type. On the grounds of their appearance it excludes Hitler, Hess, Göring, Goebbels, Röhm, Ley, Bormann, Himmler, Funk, Rust, Streicher, Frick, Daluege, Frank, to name a few. The three leaders who were more fortunate in their looks happened to be Speer, Milch, and Heydrich—especially the last. As we know today, Heydrich was burdened with Jewish descent, and it was known in the "Third Reich" that Milch, made a field marshal by Hitler, had a Jewish father.

We have been more or less astonished to see the details of the immense stubborn stupidity with which the "racial" laws were interpreted, perfected, and applied. The process went so far that some people, who were "Aryan" beyond doubt according to the Nazis' own theories, were declared to be "racially inferior" only because, although originally baptized, they had converted to Judaism temporarily during a brief marriage to a Jewish partner. Conversely, some of the deceased, from Johann Strauss to Max Bruch, were posthumously "Aryanized." All was done according to the faulty principle that the end justifies the means.

This principle—eminently sound where overriding state interests are concerned—was not ever, or only rarely, applied where it would have been most appropriate to the widely advertised "common weal," as in the case of indispensable scientists. One preferred, as Hitler actually put it, to manage for the next hundred years without chemists and physicists.

When exceptions were permitted—such as exempting citizens of Jewish origin from laws barring them from practicing their professions—it was done ("down to the operetta," as Goering liked to put it) rarely out of humanitarian considerations or even genuine utilitarian motives, but only to oblige the masses once in a while by not depriving them of a star popular with "the little man."

The "racial" laws were manipulated in this manner, and as could hardly be expected otherwise, they had catastrophic consequences. In other nations—not only in the United States, but also, for instance, in Turkey—additional professorships were established and even new universities and institutions founded. These measures were intended to take advantage of the unique opportunities to acquire cheaply figures of international renown who under normal circumstances would have been out of reach. By the same token, the "nation of poets and thinkers" stripped itself of its most capable minds and expelled nearly half of its university teachers, institution deans, and research leaders, including many "white Jews," such as Max Planck, Petrus Debye, and Erwin Schrödinger.

When Schrödinger came to Berlin in 1927, he was enthusiastic about the "unparalleled population density of first-class physicists" who worked not only at the university, the engineering college, and the Kaiser Wilhelm Institute, but also at the physical-technical state institute and at the research centers of the great industrial concerns, such as Siemens and AEG, and who met weekly at a colloquium. Schrödinger was mistaken, however; the little town of Göttingen was another center for scientific scholars, with an even greater "population density of first-class physicists," not to mention mathematicians and philosophers. After 1933, however, Göttingen, like Berlin, became a desolate wasteland at least as far as science was concerned. Not only there, but at all the other German universities, other scientists, mostly of the second or third rank, took over the vacancies, created overnight, in the positions previously occupied by "black" and "white" Jews in every department. Our investigation, limited to random spot checks, did not do justice to the German judicial scholars of Jewish descent, to the many secondary-school teachers, judges, journalists, and especially lawyers. Let us mention only one of them, as a representative of them all. Max Alsberg, born in Bonn in 1877, was Berlin's outstanding defense lawyer in the 1920s and early 1930s. In 1931 he became honorary professor at the University of Berlin. He was a distinguished jurist, whose court pleas were famous for the way in which they combined the factual and the judicial. Alsberg not only gained prominence for his legal and philosophical writings, such as *Die Philosophie der Verteidigung*. [The Philosophy of Defense], but was also very successful with his novels and plays. His stage work written in collaboration with Otto Ernst Hesse, *Voruntersuchung* [Preliminary Investigation] which deals with the problematic nature of circumstantial evidence, was filmed in 1931 by Robert Siodmak for the UFA with Albert Bassermann in the lead.

This brings us to a point that recurred in our investigation which is of interest in three respects. First, there is the close link among science, the professions, art, and literature as they functioned in those cultural middle-class groups that had not yet been "cleansed of Jews." Max Alsberg offers a typical example. Second, there are the no less close personal and intellectual ties between Jewish and non-Jewish members of this particular stratum. The "non-Aryan" Alsberg writes a play with the "Aryan" Hesse; the "Aryan" actor Albert Bassermann is married to a "non-Aryan" woman—these examples could be continued endlessly.

The third aspect is difficult to capture. It has to do with something colorful, irridescent, something that fascinated those who cared about culture and creativity and frequently irritated the underlings, the prejudiced, the stupid, and the small-minded. It was this atmosphere at which Goebbels might have looked with envy but which he venomously defined as "a society polluted with Jews from top to bottom." It was an atmosphere of spirit and humor, tolerance and humaneness, and, despite all its business acumen and occasional superficiality, full of noblesse. A strangely old-fashioned word, noblesse—but it goes to the heart of the matter. The fact that the word sounds dusty and unused only demonstrates that those to whom it applied and who applied it to themselves are no longer present in sufficient numbers. For instance, it fitted a scientist like James Franck, an artist like Max Liebermann, and a political satirist as uncompromising as Kurt Tucholsky, who did not hesitate to engage himself on behalf of his adversaries when they were subjected to disgraceful injustice. This observation is not intended, as reverse racism, to claim that all men of noble stature were German Jews or all German Jews of noble stature. Instead of James Franck, we could just as easily have named Max von Laue or Max Planck—in other words, one of the "white Jews."

This breathtaking, exciting, extraordinarily fruitful atmosphere was evident not only in the western section of Berlin during the Wilhelmenian era and even more so during the 1920s and early 1930s, though it flourished there most particularly, in the political, intellectual, and artistic center of the nation. It would be impossible to visualize that Berlin without the many artists and scientists, writers and musicians, doctors and lawyers, journalists, critics, painters, architects, even merchants and bankers of Jewish origin—though no one, least of all they themselves, would have agreed unreservedly to the truth of this phenomenon. Because it would mean that a very considerable proportion of the following achievements would have been due to the Jewish contribution: the vigorous revival of German theater and film; musical life; the fine arts and German literature; the country's leading position in international medicine, physics, and chemistry; the worldwide standing in research and technology of modern German architecture; of progressive education, of cultured hospitality and the exemplary patronage of the arts and science by the wealthy; and the proverbial honesty of civil servants, wholesalers, and bankers!

Indeed, we have been forced to acknowledge that this is precisely the case. And it is therefore just as clear that the loss is immeasurable and what has been lost can never be replaced.

With the destruction of the German Jews, everything else was also destroyed that was open to and related to them. And what is more, all opportunities for regeneration are gone. Most of the millions of Jews of the European East, mainly of German descent, were slaughtered, and the pitiful remnant has little longing for its old home on the Rhine. And the attempt to reassemble and guide homeward those dispersed all over the world was neglected, though right after the war such an effort would have been possible.

"It is true that a few universities addressed a request to their erstwhile faculty for renewed collaboration, while Adolf Arndt,* in his capacity as Berlin senator for education, appealed to the emigrants to return," Jürgen Boettcher noted in the spring of 1967 in a series on Radio Free Berlin entitled *Um uns die Fremde* [Around Us, Foreign Territory]. "*However, an appeal to return was never issued by the government itself.*"

In 1964 Theodor W. Adorno wrote that "this form of reparation, which was omitted as far as the badly impaired intellectual life was concerned, is irresponsible not only to the

---

*Arndt, Social Democratic politician and legal counsel to his party, was born in Königsberg in 1904, the son of the constitutional lawyer Professor Adolf Arndt, and was therefore of Jewish origin.

victims, but even more so to what on other occasions likes to present itself as being representative of German interests."

Those German politicians responsible during the first twenty years of the Federal Republic of Germany not only for what was done, but also for what was left undone, have often prided themselves on the enormous voluntary material reparations they—in contrast to others—granted the Jews. A further source of pride was that this policy had been followed in spite of the misery and poverty that resulted from Germany's total military, economic, and political collapse and in spite of Germany's own refugee problem, with its attendant misery and starvation. Without detracting from the moral—as well as economic—value of the monetary reparations, we should note that the German politicians by no means paid these billions out of their private fortunes. Their payment was meant to atone "at least morally" for the murder of nearly a million children, to single out merely one item in that truly macabre accounting. To be truthful, we must recognize that the payment did no more than to return some of the illegally seized booty to its owners.

Having said all this, there remain three aspects related to the West German reparations. First, there was a clear lack of imagination and goodwill that kept them from thinking of any other means than money to make amends for the immeasurable injury and injustice that cried to heaven; they gave money and valuables—and a few polite platitudes. Second, a shop-keeper mentality and obsession with appearances was demonstrated in dealing with individual claims to restitution. Third, the procedure was so steeped in crass materialism and obstinate stupidity that in the attention to all the calculations and petty haggling, it was clean forgotten to offer, as a self evident matter of course, a return trip to those to whom henceforth they were prepared to grant a modest pension. No thought was given to offering a return, not only under escort and at government expense, not only to homes and an environment as closely as possible matching the requirements of those exiled for so long, but also to their old station in society.

The enormous injury inflicted, not only on the Jews, but also on all Germans by the all-encompassing destruction of a culture, or at least of the middle class that supported it, would have been only minimally ameliorated by such a measure for the benefit the nation as a whole, which has become impoverished—greatly impoverished.

No, not impoverished as far as material goods are concerned. Here we come face to face with the sad irony of the German persecution of the Jews. It did not paralyze German commerce, as anti-Semitic theories would have had us believe. It did not bring the workings of the stock exchange to a halt. And it did not rout the forces of international capital. Today West Germany, the largest of the successor states of the "Third Reich," is a very wealthy nation. Commerce is flourishing, its bank vaults can hardly contain the wealth, and even the so-called little man leads a comfortable existence. As for material goods, with which most of the people are blessed, the ideals of the petit bourgeois have been very nearly realized.

At the same time in the Federal Republic of Germany, and to some extent in the other successor states—and this fact has been noted by many others, chiefly Americans, British, and French—a frightful spiritual poverty prevails, a shockingly poor educational system, a distressing lack of general and specific knowledge, a provincialism hardly less pronounced in the large cities, and a general petty narrow-mindedness even where it is not immediately visible because it is obscured by an exaltation of sexuality introduced to stimulate consumption. Most important is the attitude of those particular people who acted against their own better judgment, and only because they considered the persecution of the Jews an "unavoidable side effect" of what they found desirable—the construction of a "bulwark against Bolshevism." Their attitude, born in petty-minded fear, allowed Hitler and his henchmen a free hand; they refused to see and hear, and enabled the leadership to pursue its own highly profitable business deals without batting an eyelash. Today these same people are moved to sentimental pro-Semitism whenever they happen to meet a "Jewish fellow citizen," as they like to phrase it. This kind of pro-Semitism—a mixture of troubled conscience, opportunism, and lack of critical thinking based on an inertia of heart and mind, is annually blown up into a "brotherhood week," where celebrities with some integrity, idealists, and visionaries join with a few survivors of persecution and resistance to give a sheen of credibility to the confessions of remorse issuing from armament profiteers and careerists.

Of course there are many isolated events that qualify this picture. Occasionally a play is stirring enough to penetrate the lethargy; a movie is inventive and creative; but most important, and at long last, the younger generation is beginning to realize the prevailing condition and is becoming more demanding in line with their growing insight. A considerable number of intellectuals, even some of the older ones—mainly poets, novelists, artists, and some scientists—act in solidarity with the younger group. The president's palace in Bonn finally had a resident head of state who was of unblemished integrity and who, unlike his predecessor, had not participated in constructing the concentration camps. Finally the chancellor's chair was occupied by a man who actively fought against the "Third Reich," voluntarily went into exile with the other emigrants, and who did not, like his predecessor, help to pave the way for the "final solution" by means of propaganda. Finally there was a secretary of state in the federal chancellery who had not, like his predecessor Hans Maria Globke, made the effort to refine the hare-brained "blood protection" laws by providing them with judicial embroidery and increased their severity by particularly crafty interpretation. Instead, the office was filled by an intellectual of noticeable standing, who, because he had a "non-Aryan" grandmother, himself suffered under the yoke of "racial" madness.

Gustav Heinemann, Willy Brandt, Egon Bahr, and some of their associates, as well as progressive professors and students, writers, journalists, and television editors, the courageous individualists and outsiders who make themselves vulnerable by their independent opinions—they are the "white Jews" of today. They are looked upon with scowls and just a little revulsion by the "moderates" of the political right as well as by the Stalinists and by those who still wave the swastika flag. They must feel very lonely and grief-stricken when they think how thin are the ranks of a great people in the heart of Europe as it marches into the twenty-first century— and how it might have been.

No attempt to establish the actual losses to Germany that resulted from the expulsion and extermination of the Jews could define them so clearly as a comparison, holding up the cultural richness of the nineteenth and early twentieth centuries against the current cultural barrenness of today's two Germanies.

And the worst of it is: most German people hardly seem to notice.

Appendix

The Earliest Nazi Program

In 1919 Hitler joined a small, insignificant political group that called itself the German Worker's Party (Deutsche Arbeiterpartei, or DAP). He became a popular member because he was never averse to public speaking, and his rabble-rousing speeches were very popular. But when the Party called for a mass meeting on February 24, 1920, Hitler's name was not even on the posters that advertised it.

At the meeting, however, Hitler took the podium after the night's principal speaker. It had been his idea that a program be written down, and this he now read out to the audience of nearly two thousand. Even without completely accepting Hitler's own apocalyptic version of this historic night, we can agree that the twenty-five-point program marked the beginning of the powerful Nazi movement. Certainly most of the points became embodied in "Third Reich" policy.

The program of the German Workers' Party was limited in time. The leaders refused to enunciate new goals once those aimed at in the program had been achieved, for no other purpose than to insure the continuation of the Party by artificially stimulating dissatisfaction among the masses.

1. We demand the unification of all Germans into a Greater Germany on the basis of the right of self-determination of all peoples.

2. We demand the equality of the German people in relation to other nations, the annulment of the peace treaties of Versailles and St. Germain.

3. We demand land and soil (colonies) for the feeding of our people and for the settlement of our surplus population.

4. Only national comrades [Volksgenossen] can be citizens of the state. Only carriers of German blood can be national comrades, regardless of religious faith. No Jew can therefore be a national comrade.

5. Whoever is not a citizen of the state may live in Germany only as a guest and must be subject to legislation concerning foreigners.

6. The right to decide leadership and legislation of the state can only belong to citizens of the state. We therefore demand that every public office of any description, whether on the national, provincial, or local level, be filled only by citizens of the state.

We are fighting against the corrupt parliamentary procedure that makes appointments in accordance only with partisan considerations, without regard to character and capabilities.

7. We demand that in the first instance the state pledge itself to provide the citizen with work and housing. If it is not possible to feed the total population of the state, then the subjects of foreign nations (noncitizens) are to be expelled from the Reich.

8. Any additional immigration of non-Germans is to be prevented. We demand that all non-Germans who immigrated into Germany after August 2, 1914, be forced to leave the Reich immediately.

9. All citizens of the state must be given equal rights and obligations.

10. The first duty of every citizen has to be to perform mental or physical work. The activity of the individual must not violate the interests of the whole, but must be within the framework of the whole and for the benefit of all. We therefore demand:

11. Abolition of income without work and effort, *breaking interest serfdom*.

12. In view of the immense sacrifices in wealth and life that every war exacts as its toll from the people, personal enrichment from war must be designated a crime against the people. We demand the complete confiscation of all war profits.

13. We demand the nationalization of all trusts that have already been incorporated.

14. We demand profit sharing in the large concerns.

15. We demand generous expansion of care for the aged.

16. We demand the creation of a sound middle class and its preservation, immediate exportation of all the major department stores, and their lease at low rentals to small tradesmen. We demand the strictest consideration to be given to all small tradesmen in matters of deliveries to the State, the counties, or the communities.

17. We demand land reform in line with our national needs, a law allowing confiscation without compensation of land for the common weal, abolition of interest on land, and the prevention of all property speculation.

18. We demand ruthless repression of those whose actions damage the common interest. Common criminals, usurers, racketeers, etc., should be punished by means of the death penalty, regardless of religion or race.

19. We demand the replacement of the Roman Law which serves the materialistic world order with a German common law.

20. In order to enable every competent and industrious German to be eligible for higher education and therefore to enter into leading positions, the state must engage in a thorough expansion of our whole public-school system. The curriculums of all educational institutions are to be aligned with the requirements of a practical life. An understanding of the idea of statehood and citizenship must be acquired in the early years of schooling. We demand the education and training of particularly gifted children of poor parents at state expense, regardless of the parents' class or profession.

21. The state is to be responsible for improving the health of the people by protection for mother and child, by forbidding child labor, by achieving physical fitness through legislation stipulating compulsory gymnastics and sport, and by maximum support of all those societies devoted to the physical training of youth.

22. We demand the abolition of mercenaries and the formation of an army of the people.

23. We demand legal action against the *conscious* political lie and its spread by the press. To enable the creation of a German press, we demand that:

a) all editors and workers of German-language newspapers must be national comrades;

b) non-German papers be subject to explicit state license to be published. They may not be printed in the German language;

c) it be legally forbidden for non-Germans to have a financial share in ownership of any German paper or any influence appertaining to it. Contravention should be punished through closing such a newspaper establishment, as well as the immediate expulsion from the Reich of the non-Germans involved.

Papers violating the common weal are to be banned. We demand legal steps be taken in the struggle against an artistic and literary trend that has a destructive influence on the life of our people, and we demand the shutting down of performances that transgress with regard to these demands.

24. We demand freedom for all religious denominations within the state insofar as they do not endanger its continued well-being or violate the ethical and moral precepts of the Germanic race.

The Party as such espouses a positive Christianity without committing to any specific denomination. It is against the Jewish materialistic mentality *inside* and *outside* and is convinced that permanent recovery of our people can only take place from *inside*, on the principle of:

Common Weal Before Self-Interest.

25. To bring about all the above, we demand: Creation of a strong central authority for the Reich, unconditional authority of the political central parliament over the whole of the Reich and its organizations in general, and the formation in the various federal states of class and professional chambers for implementing the laws framed by the Reich.

The leaders of the Party promise, if necessary, to give their lives for the absolute implementation of the above points.

Munich, February 24, 1920.

The Illogic of the "Racial" Laws

When one grandparent is a full-blooded German who, because of marriage to a Jew converted to Judaism, the full-blooded German grandparent will be deemed to be fully Jewish . . . in the racial classification of the grandchildren. Evidence to the contrary is not admissible. This ruling greatly facilitates racial classification. . . . It does not matter for how long the grandparent adhered to the Jewish religion. For the purposes of our classification, even temporary membership is sufficient.

This ruling would appear to be reasonable enough; as a rule, adherence to the Jewish religion must be seen as an avowal of Judaism sufficiently strong to justify the assumption that the descendants will also be contaminated with Judaism. It does not matter for how long the grandparent adhered to the Jewish religion. Even one's uncontested listing as a member of a congregation or unrepudiated payment of the Jewish religious tax, must in themselves be considered sufficient evidence.

From Stuckart-Globke, commentary on the "Law for the Protection of German Blood and German Honor" and the "Reich Citizen Law," Berlin, 1935.

The Haber Case

LETTER OF RESIGNATION FROM THE NOBEL PRIZE WINNER IN CHEMISTRY, PROF. FRITZ HABER, APRIL 30, 1933

To the Minister for Science, Art, and the People's Education,
Berlin

My dear Minister!
I herewith request permission to retire as of October 1, 1933, both from my principal position in Prussia as Director of the Kaiser Wilhelm Institute and from my secondary post in Prussia as professor in ordinary at the University of Berlin. According to the regulations of the official law

of April 7, 1933, the application of which has been decreed for the Institute of the Kaiser Wilhelm Society, I am entitled to retain my post despite my descent from Jewish grandparents and parents. However, I do not wish to make use of this permission any longer than is necessary for the orderly winding up of the scientific and administrative activity inherent in my spheres of responsibility.

In substance, my request is identical with the applications put forward by Professors H. Freundlich and M. Polanyi, scientific members and department heads of the Kaiser Wilhelm Institute for Physical Chemistry and Electrochemistry in the employ of the Kaiser Wilhelm Society, and addressed by them to that association. I have recommended acceptance of their applications.

My decision to resign derives from the contradiction between the tradition regulating research that I have observed until now and the changed conceptions that you, Minister, and your Ministry, represent as followers of the present great National movement. In my scientific post my tradition requires me to consider only the professional qualifications and the character of the applicants in selecting my associates, and I do not ask about their racial background. You will not expect that a man of sixty-five will change the way of thinking that has guided him through the past thirty-nine years of university life.

You will also understand that the same pride with which he has served his German homeland all his life now obliges him to request his retirement.

Yours faithfully,
F. Haber.

THE ATTEMPT BY THE HITLER GOVERNMENT TO PREVENT A MEMORIAL SERVICE FOR THE LATE FRITZ HABER, NOBEL PRIZE LAUREATE FOR CHEMISTRY, WHO DIED IN EXILE IN 1935

The Minister of State for Science, Culture, and the People's Education,
Berlin W 8,
January 24, 1935.

To the President of the Kaiser Wilhelm Society for the
Advancement of Science,
Privy Counsellor, Prof. Dr. Planck,
Berlin C 2, Schloss

My dear Mr. President!

With regard to your letter of January 18, 1935, I
most respectfully wish to inform you of the following. If
on June 28, 1934, the Prussian Academy for Science took
it upon itself to deliver a special commemorative speech
in remembrance of Fritz Haber, this could possibly be
the more readily overlooked because noted thinkers and
scientists from both Germany and *abroad* have joined
together in the Prussian Academy of Science, irrespec-
tive of nationality or race.

However, the Kaiser Wilhelm Society represents one
of the most prominent institutes of *German* research,
and the German public expects it to act in conformity
with the principles of the National Socialist state every
time the Society takes a public stand.

I am happy to acknowledge that you, Mr. President,
are always prepared to give proof in word and deed of
your positive attitude toward the State and toward the
Führer. I regret, however, that the planned memorial
service for Fritz Haber could convey the opposite
impression. On April 30, 1933, Prof. Haber relinquished
his appointment because he placed himself in opposition
to the National Socialist state.

After all that, I cannot expect any official of the
National Socialist state or any NSDAP members to participate in the service planned by the Kaiser Wilhelm Society.
Greatly esteemed Mr. President, I therefore find myself
quite unable to annul the decree in question.

On the other hand, since the attention of the national
and the foreign press has already been drawn to this
matter, and since foreign participants are expected to
attend the service, and finally, since the Kaiser Wilhelm
Institute has private members among its ranks, I would
suggest to you, Mr. President, that you permit the service
to take place as a purely internal and private ceremony
of the Kaiser Wilhelm Society which, for obvious
reasons, may not be reported in the press. In case you

should decide to follow my suggestion, may I request
that you provide me immediately with a list of those
professors who have indicated that they may attend,
whether in their capacity as members of the Kaiser
Wilhelm Society, the German Chemical Society, or the
German Physical Society. It then is up to me to grant
these professors a dispensation with regard to the decree
if it is of great importance to them. I would be pleased, if
you, Mr. President, would call on me in the next few
days.

Heil Hitler!
Yours,
(Signed) Rust

THE KAISER WILHELM SOCIETY
FOR THE ADVANCEMENT OF SCIENCE

in conjunction with the German Chemical Society
and the German Physical Society,
has the honor
to invite you to a
MEMORIAL SERVICE FOR FRITZ HABER
on Tuesday, January 29, 1935, at 12 noon
in the Harnackhaus, Berlin-Dahlem, Ihnestrasse 16–20.

1. *Andante con moto (Theme with Variations)*
from the Quartet No. 14 by Franz Schubert

2. *Introduction, Privy Councillor Prof. Dr. Max Planck, Presi-*
dent of the Kaiser Wilhelm Society for the Advancement of
Science

3. *Commemorations*
Prof. Dr. Otto Hahn, Director of the Kaiser Wilhelm
Institute of Chemistry,
Colonel (Retired) D.Sc. (Eng.) (honoris causa) Josef Koeth,
Prof. Dr. Karl-Friedrich Bonhoeffer, nonresident scien-
tific member of the Kaiser Wilhelm Institute for Physical
Chemistry and Electrochemistry.

4. *Cavatina (adagio molto espressivo)*
from the Quartet Op. 130 by Ludwig van Beethoven.

The members of the Philharmonic Orchestra:
Concert master Siegfried Borries (1st violin), Karl Höver
(2nd violin), Reinhard Wolf (viola), Wolfgang Kleber (cello).

Uniforms or dark suits.

The service was dignified and impressive. Unfortunately
Prof. Bonhoeffer was unable to deliver his speech in person;
it would have cost him his appointment as University lecturer
in Leipzig. At his request, I read his address. Having resigned from the faculty in 1934, I myself was not endangered.
(Otto Hahn)

Association of German Chemists (Reg. Ass.)
Berlin W 35,
Potsdamerstr 103A

According to a decree
of the President of the RTA, Dr. Eng. Todt,
participation in the memorial service for Fritz Haber
on January 29, 1935, at the Harnackhaus
is prohibited for all members of the Association of
German Chemists (registered association).

Final instructions from the Ministry were: There will be no
reports of this service, and the speeches are not to be
published. This commemoration for Haber shows that during
the early years of the Hitler regime it was still possible to
offer at least slight resistance, a situation that was not available later. (Otto Hahn)

"White Jews" in Science

*The following article appeared on July 15, 1937, in
the official organ of the SS, Das Schwarze Korps.
The entire article is probably the work of an old
party member and a Nobel Prize laureate for physics,
Johannes Stark, who certainly signed the postscript,
and can be assumed to be the instigator of the whole.
His heirs, however, have disputed his authorship.*

There is a primitive type of anti-Semitism limited to fighting the Jews as such. Its adherents content themselves with drawing a clear line of demarcation between Germans and Jews. They consider the problem solved once the mixing of the blood has been stopped and the Jews are no longer allowed to participate in the political, cultural, and economic life of the nation. The most extreme solution they visualize is a Jewish emigration from Germany to Palestine or elsewhere. Once Germany is thus purified, freed from Jewish pollution, the end of anti-Semitism would consequently be at hand.

This perspective is attractive because it is simple, but it is weakened by a fallacy. If we were to fight the Jews on the strength of the old—not even completely reliable—characteristics of their hooked noses and kinky hair, we would be tilting at windmills. But the fact that we had to combat Jewish influence on politics and cultural life, and must continue to fight Jewish influence on the German economy proves that it is not a matter concerning the Jews "as such." What is at stake is the spirit or the antispirit they spread—precisely what we term influence.

We will, unfortunately find that after the ideal solution of a Jewish emigration, we will still have to fight Jewish influence. A wide field of action will still be open to anti-Semitism even after the last hooked nose has left Germany. It is a regrettable fact that the dreadful danger that our public life will become polluted with Judaism and the power of Jewish influence which National Socialism had to curb, was not due solely to the numerically weak Jewish community. It must also be laid to an equal degree at the door of those people of Aryan origin who proved receptive to the Jewish mentality and became enslaved by it.

The victory of racial anti-Semitism can therefore be seen as only a partial victory. We cannot limit ourselves to implementing the Nuremberg laws and to insisting on the solution of the remaining problems of "Jews in the economy." We must also eradicate the Jewish mentality, which today flourishes more luxuriantly than ever now that its representatives can present the most impeccable proofs of "Aryanism."

The racial Jew as such has never been a danger to us but the spiritual aura emanating from him has. If the proponent of this mentality is not a Jew but a German, we must see him as the target of our fight, twice as dangerous as the original culprit, the racial Jew who is unable to hide the origin of his mentality.

JEWS BY PROXY

The common language has coined the term "white Jew" for such carriers of the germ. This is highly suitable, because it extends the concept of the Jew over and above the racial concept. In the same sense one could also speak of Jewishness of spirit, Jewishness of alignment, or Jewishness of character.

They have willingly adopted the Jewish mentality because they lack one of their own. They worship a hair-splitting intellect because they lack natural instincts and those character traits that force human beings to develop capabilities of their own and if need be, to make do with them. There is one area in particular where the Jewish mentality of the "white Jews" confronts us in its purest form and where the spiritual link of the white Jews with their Jewish exemplars and instructors can always be clearly demonstrated—science. To cleanse science of the Jewish mentality is our primary task. We can handle the "white Jews" we meet in everyday life with police power and stricter laws. But a science contaminated with Jewishness is a key position from which the Jewish spirit can always regain dominating influence over all levels of the nation's life.

For instance, it is characteristic that in our time, when German medicine is faced with totally new problems and medical research has to come up with crucial discoveries in the fields of congenital biology, race hygiene, and health measures for the people, the medical press published in a single year 2,183 articles, of which 1,085 were of foreign authorship, including 116 from the Soviet Union. These hardly address the problems that ought to be in the forefront of research. Under the guise of "exchange of knowledge" we find lurking the well-known doctrine of the internationalism of science, which the Jewish mentality has always upheld and propagated because it established the precondition for uncontrollable, autocratic self-glorification.

It is in the realm of physics that the Jewish mentality is most evident. In Einstein it has produced its most "important" representative. It is the particular skill on the part of

Germanic scientists to concentrate on patient, industrious, and constructive observations of nature, which has given us all the great discoveries and new insights in the natural sciences. It is also established that the Germanic scientist always recognizes so-called theory only as an aid that may possibly facilitate observation of nature, but is never an end in itself. Knowledge that penetrates genuine reality is the only objective of his research. To this end he is willing to sacrifice his own theory, if it proves to be faulty or insufficient. Conversely, the Jewish mentality that has pushed its way to the fore within recent decades has known how to boost and turn the spotlight on theory, dogmatically hailed but devoid of reality. The total hegemony of such theories was brought about by hair-splitting generalizations from existing facts, by cunning juggling of mathematical formulas, and by obfuscating ambiguities. These theories correspond so closely to the Jewish mentality and Jewish "research methods" because they make industrious, patient, constructive observation of nature appear superfluous.

THE DICTATORSHIP OF GRAY THEORY

The Jewish professor Leo Grätz, in Munich, made the characteristic statement that in future the experimental physicist would sink to the level of a good mechanic as compared to the theoretician, who will give him instructions for experimental research. Einstein himself, during a lecture in 1922, made the pronouncement, "It is to be expected that theory will soon be in a position to calculate in advance the qualities of chemical atoms and their reactions. This will obviate the need for the troublesome and time-consuming experimental work of the chemists."

This tendency to push into the background the research scientist, with his link to reality, soon became the prevailing practice.

The Jews Einstein, Haber, and their comrades in spirit, Sommerfeld and Planck, were almost unhampered in deciding the succession to the German university professorships. Sommerfeld for one was able to boast of having placed ten of his students in such posts. The literature of the Jewish theoreticians and their propagandists swelled in barely fifteen years to 50,000 printed pages. That generation of students was trained practically exclusively in their "spirit." Given free reign, this would have led in a few decades to the demise of the type of scientist we know as a productive research worker in touch with reality. Speculating, sterile theoreticians would have replaced them.

The seizure of power by National Socialism has banished this danger but has not yet rooted it out. With all the means as its disposal the Jewish mentality seeks to preserve its positions, at least in those branches of science such as physics, that are not subject to a manifest imprint of a philosophical slant. Thereupon these positions can one day be used as starting points for a new advance.

EINSTEIN AS CORNERSTONE

Professor Warner Heisenberg, professor for theoretical physics in Leipzig, is an example and proof of how secure the "White Jews" deem themselves in their strongholds. He actually managed in 1936 to smuggle a paper into an official party organ in which he declared Einstein's theories of relativity to be "the self-evident basis for further research" and saw "one of the primary tasks of young German scientists to be the quest for further development of theoretical concepts." At the same time he endeavored stenuously to make an impression on the authorities by arranging a vote among German physicists concerning the value of the theory and to silence his critics.

This chief representative of Einstein's "spirit" within the new Germany was made a professor in Leipzig in 1928, having been Sommerfeld's prize pupil. At the then tender age of twenty-six, he can hardly have had time to carry out serious research. He began by dismissing the German assistant of his Institute and replacing him first of all with the Viennese Jew Beck, followed by the Zurich Jew Bloch. Until 1933 his seminar was mainly frequented by Jews. Even today, the inner circle of his students is made up of Jews and foreigners.

THE "OSSIETZKY" OF PHYSICS

In 1933 Heisenberg received the Nobel Prize together with the Einstein disciples Schrödinger and Dirac—a demon-

stration of the Nobel Prize's being awarded under Jewish
influence and directed against National Socialist Germany, on
a par with the distinction conferred on Ossietzky. Heisenberg
requited himself by refusing to sign, in August 1934, a proclamation of the German Nobel Prize laureates in support of the
German leader and Reich Chancellor. At the time his reply
was, "Although I personally vote 'yes,' political manifestos by
scientists appear to me to be misplaced and have not been done
in the past. Therefore, I will not sign."

This reply reflects the Jewish mentality of its author,
who considers the bond linking the people and national responsibility on the part of the "scientists" to be "misplaced."

Heisenberg is only one example of many. They are all
representatives of Judaism within German spiritual life, and
they must disappear just like the Jews themselves.

The urgency of this demand and its importance to the
future of German scientific research that attaches to the problem under discussion has induced *Das Schwarze Korps* to
request a statement from Professor Johannes Stark, President
of the Physical-Technical Reich Institute.

The personality of the scientist we have appealed to should
open everyone's eyes to the fact that German science and its
faithful guardians face an unavoidable decision. Stark is not only
a pioneer of National Socialism, but also a Nobel Prize winner,
who was honored at a time when its distribution was uninflu-
enced by political motives of hate and revenge.

"SCIENCE" HAS LET US DOWN POLITICALLY

Professor Stark wrote to us as follows:

The foregoing article is fundamentally to the point and
so complete that any addition would seem redundant. However,
following the invitation of the editors, I will append the
following remarks.

It is widely recognized that the majority of professors at
German universities and technical colleges failed miserably
during the period of National Socialism's struggle. They showed
a complete lack of understanding for Hitler and his movement,
and some even displayed a hostile attitude. At several universities sharp conflicts arose between the student body of National Socialist persuasion and the hierarchy of professors

linked to the black-red system. Reich Minister Rust was fully justified when in 1933, he bitterly reproached the professors at the University of Berlin in this respect. The crucial reason for the majority of the German professors' failing politically in the National Socialist struggle for German freedom was because of the dominant Jewish influence at German universities.

Its strength lay not only in the fact that in numerous universities 10 to 30 per cent of the faculty were either Jewish or closely related to Jews. It was also largely due to the support given by the Aryan fellow travelers of Jews and the disciples of Jews.

The political influence of the Jewish mentality at the universities was obvious. The influence was less obvious but just as damaging in scientific respects. It hampered Germanic research focused on reality by imposing Jewish intellectualism, dogmatic formalism, and propagandistic methods. It sought to train the student body, and especially the younger generation of teachers, in Jewish ways of thinking.

A CHANGE OF TACTICS

Indeed, in 1933 teachers and assistants of the Jewish race had to relinquish their jobs. Furthermore, at the moment, Aryan professors with Jewish wives are being dismissed. However, the great number of Aryan Jewish sympathizers and disciples of Jews, who used to support the Jewish dominance at German universities, either openly or covertly, have kept their positions. They retain the influence of the Jewish mentality at German universities.

Until the election of the Führer as Reich President, they were naive enough to foresee a quick end to the National Socialist government, and therefore they withheld proclaiming allegiance to the Führer. In the last two years they have changed their tactics. Outwardly they now behave as if they had a national attitude; earlier pacifists are joining military service, and disciples of Jews seek to obtain links with the administrative departments of Party and State—the very same people who published numerous scientific works in collaboration with German and foreign Jews, and who as late as 1929 participated in professional meetings with Soviet Jews.

Apart from their national or even National Socialist participation, they have used the following arguments to gain influence in authoritative quarters. As scientific experts, they and their candidates would be indispensable to the implementation of the Four Year Plan. Furthermore, they claim to be acknowledged abroad as great German scientists and that it would therefore be in the interest of German scientific prestige for them to keep a strong influence in international circles. In putting forward this bluff, they believe that they can count on the authorities' being unaware of the fact that their "celebrity" abroad is an inflated consequence of their cooperation with foreign Jews and fellow travelers.

The following fact is significant indication of continued Jewish influence in German academic circles: Not long ago an influential German physician declared in a conversation with me, "I simply cannot imagine a medical science without Jews."

THE NEW JEWISH DELUGE

Recently a large university's science faculty proposed three disciples of Jews to fill a teaching vacancy. Two of them have published numerous scientific works in collaboration with German and foreign Jews. Especially in physics the German scientific market is again being flooded with books written by German and foreign Jews and their disciples. The principal perpetrator is the publisher Julius Springer with offices in Berlin and Vienna. The firm used to be entirely Jewish and now claims to be 50 per cent Aryan.

While the influence of the Jewish mentality has been eliminated from the German press, literature and art, and German justice, it has found in German science a champion at the universities and a successor in the Aryan fellow travelers and disciples of Jews. Hiding behind a smoke screen of scientific objectivity and referring to international recognition, it continues unabated and even seeks to strengthen its hold and dominance through tactical influential links among the authorities.

In this situation a measure of thanks is due to the *Schwarze Korps* that it has drawn public attention to this damaging infiltration with its courageous and crucially important presentation outlining the menace inherent in the "White Jews" to a section of German spiritual life and to the training of our young academics.

(Signed) Stark

Correspondence on the Atomic Bomb

LETTER OF TRANSMITTAL, SZILARD TO DR. ALEXANDER SACHS, AUGUST 15, 1939

Dear Dr. Sachs:

Enclosed I am sending you a letter from Prof. Albert Einstein, which is addressed to President Roosevelt and which he sent to me with the request of forwarding it through such channels as might appear appropriate. If you see your way to bring this letter to the attention of the President, I am certain Prof. Einstein would appreciate your doing so; otherwise would you be good enough to return the letter to me?

If a man, having courage and imagination, could be found and if such a man were put—in accordance with Dr. Einstein's suggestion—in the position to act with some measure of authority in this matter, this would certainly be an important step forward. In order that you may be able to see of what assistance such a man could be in our work, allow me please to give you a short account of the past history of the case.

In January this year, when I realized that there was a remote possibility of setting up a chain reaction in a large mass of uranium, I communicated with Prof. E. P. Wigner of Princeton University and Prof. E. Teller of George Washington University, Washington, D. C., and the three of us remained in constant consultation ever since. First of all it appeared necessary to perform certain fundamental experiments for which the use of about one gram of radium was required. Since at that time we had no certainty and had to act on a remote possibility, we could hardly hope to succeed in persuading a university laboratory to take charge of these experiments, or even to acquire the radium needed. Attempts to obtain the necessary funds from other sources appeared to be equally hopeless. In these circumstances a few of us physicists formed an association, called the "Association for Scientific Collaboration," collected some funds among ourselves, rented about one gram of radium, and I arranged with the Physics Department of Columbia University for their permission to carry out the proposed experiments at Columbia. These experiments led early in March to rather striking results.

At about the same time Prof. E. Fermi, also at Columbia, made experiments of his own, independently of ours, and came to identical conclusions.

A close collaboration arose out of the coincidence, and recently Dr. Fermi and I jointly performed experiments which make it appear probable that a chain reaction in uranium can be achieved in the immediate future.

The path along which we have to move is now clearly defined, but it takes some courage to embark on the journey. The experiments will be costly since we will now have to work with tons of material rather than—as hitherto—with kilograms. Two or possibly three different alternatives will have to be tried; failures, set-backs and some unavoidable danger to human life will have to be faced. We have so far made use of the Association for Scientific Collaboration to overcome the difficulty of persuading other organizations to take financial risks, and also to overcome the general reluctance to take action on the basis of probabilities in the absence of certainty. Now, in the face of greater certainty, but also greater risks, it will become necessary either to strengthen this association both morally and financially, or to find new ways which would serve the same purpose. We have to approach as quickly as possible public-spirited private persons and try to enlist their financial cooperation, or, failing in this, we would have to try to enlist the collaboration of the leading firms of the electrical or chemical industry.

Other aspects of the situation have to be kept in mind. Dr. Wigner is taking the stand that it is our duty to enlist the co-operation of the Administration. A few weeks ago he came to New York in order to discuss this point with Dr. Teller and me, and on his initiative conversations took place between Dr. Einstein and the three of us. This led to Dr. Einstein's decision to write to the President.

I am enclosing a memorandum which will give you some of the views and opinions which were expressed in these conversations.

I wish to make it clear that, in approaching you, I am acting in the capacity of a trustee of the Association for Scientific Collaboration, and that I have no authority to speak in the name of the Physics Department of Columbia University, of which I am a guest.

Yours sincerely,

MEMORANDUM, SZILARD TO THE PRESIDENT, AUGUST 15, 1939

Much experimentation on atomic disintegration was done during the past five years, but up to this year the problem of liberating nuclear energy could not be attacked with any reasonable hope for success. Early this year it became known that the element uranium can be split by neutrons. It appeared conceivable that in this nuclear process uranium itself may emit neutrons, and a few of us envisaged the possibility of liberating nuclear energy by means of a chain reaction of neutrons in uranium.

Experiments were thereupon performed, which led to striking results. One has to conclude that a nuclear chain reaction could be maintained under certain well defined conditions in a large mass of uranium. It still remains to prove this conclusion by actually setting up such a chain reaction in a large-scale experiment.

This new development in physics means that a new source of power is now being created. Large amounts of energy would be liberated, and large quantities of new radioactive elements would be produced in such a chain reaction.

In medical applications of radium we have to deal with quantities of grams; the new radioactive elements could be produced in the chain reaction in quantities corresponding to tons of radium equivalents. While the practical application would include the medical field, it would not be limited to it.

A radioactive element gives a continuous release of energy for a certain period of time. The amount of energy which is released per unit weight of material may be very large, and therefore such elements might be used—if available in large quantities—as fuel for driving boats or airplanes. It should be pointed out, however, that the physiological action of the radiations emitted by these new radioactive elements makes it necessary to protect those who have to stay close to a large quantity of such an element, for instance the driver of the airplane. It may therefore be necessary to carry large quantities of lead, and this necessity might impede development along this line, or at least limit the field of application.

Large quantities of energy would be liberated in a chain reaction, which might be utilized for purposes of power production in the form of a stationary power plant.

In view of the development it may be a question of national importance to secure an adequate supply of uranium. The United States has only very poor ores of uranium in moderate quantities; there is a good ore of uranium in Canada where the total deposit is estimated to be about 3000 tons; there may be about 1500 tons of uranium in Czechoslovakia, which is now controlled by Germany; there is an unknown amount of uranium in Russia, but the most important source of uranium, consisting of an unknown but probably very large amount of good ore, is Belgian Congo.

It is suggested therefore to explore the possibility of bringing over from Belgium or Belgian Congo a large stock of pitchblende, which is the ore of both radium and uranium, and to keep this stock here for possible future use. Perhaps a large quantity of this ore might be obtained as a token reparation payment from the Belgian Government. In taking action along this line it would not be necessary officially to disclose that the uranium content of the ore is the point of interest; action might be taken on the ground that it is of value to secure a stock of the ore on account of its radium content for possible future extraction of the radium for medical purposes.

Since it is unlikely that an earnest attempt to secure a supply of uranium will be made before the possibility of a chain reaction has been visibly demonstrated, it appears necessary to do this as quickly as possible by performing a large-scale experiment. The previous experiments have prepared the ground to the extent that it is now possible clearly to define the conditions under which such a large-scale experiment would have to be carried out. Still two or three different setups may have to be tried out, or alternatively preliminary experiments have to be carried out with several tons of material if we want to decide in advance in favor of one setup or another. These experiments cannot be carried out within the limited budget which was provided for laboratory experiments in the past, and it has now become necessary either to strengthen—financially and otherwise—the organizations which concerned themselves with this work up to now, or to create some new organization for the purpose. Public-spirited private persons who are likely to be interested in supporting this enterprise should be approached without delay, or alternatively the collaboration of the chemical or the electrical industry should be sought.

The investigations were hitherto limited to chain reactions based on the action of *slow* neutrons. The neutrons emitted from the splitting uranium are fast, but they are slowed down in a mixture of uranium and a light element. Fast neutrons lose their energy in colliding with atoms of a light element in much the same way as a billiard ball loses velocity in a collision with another ball. At present it is an open question whether such a chain reaction can also be made to work with *fast* neutrons which are not slowed down.

There is reason to believe that, if fast neutrons could be used, it would be easy to construct extremely dangerous bombs. The destructive power of these bombs can only be roughly estimated, but there is no doubt that it would go far beyond all military conceptions. It appears likely that such bombs would be too heavy to be transported by airplane, but still they could be transported by boat and exploded in port with disastrous results.

Although at present it is uncertain whether a fast neutron reaction can be made to work, from now on this possibility will have to be constantly kept in mind in view of its far-reaching military consequences. Experiments have been devised for settling this important point, and it is solely a question of organization to ensure that such experiments shall be actually carried out.

Should the experiments show that a chain reaction will work with *fast* neutrons, it would then be highly advisable to arrange among scientists for withholding publications on this subject. An attempt to arrange for withholding publications on this subject had already been made early in March but was abandoned in spite of favorable response in this country and in England on account of the negative attitude of certain French laboratories. The experience gained in March would make it possible to revive this attempt whenever it should be necessary.

NIELS BOHR'S MEMORANDUM
TO PRESIDENT ROOSEVELT, JULY 1944

The project of releasing, to an unprecedented scale, the energy bound in matter is based on the remarkable development of physical science in our century which has given us the first real insight in the interior structure of the atom.

This development has taught us that each atom consists of a cluster of electrified corpuscles, the so-called electrons, held together by the attraction from a nucleus which, although it contains practically the whole mass of the atom, has a size extremely small compared with the extension of the electron cluster.

By contributions of physicists from nearly every part of the world, the problems of the electron configuration within the atom were in the course of relatively few years most successfully explored and led above all to a clarification of the relationship between the elements as regards their ordinary physical and chemical properties.

In fact all properties of matter like hardness of materials, electric conductivity and chemical affinities, which through the ages have been exploited for technical developments to an ever increasing extent, are determined only by the electronic configuration and are practically independent of the intrinsic structure of the nucleus.

This simplicity has its root in the circumstance that by exposure of materials to ordinary physical or chemical agencies, any change in the atomic constitution is confined to distortion or disrupture of the electron cluster while the atomic nuclei are left entirely unchanged.

The stability of the nuclei under such conditions is in fact the basis for the doctrine of the immutability of the elements which for so long has been a fundament for physics and chemistry. A whole new epoc of science was therefore initiated by the discovery that it is possible by special agencies, like the high speed particles emitted by radium, to produce disintegrations of the atomic nuclei themselves and thereby to transform one element into another.

The closer study of the new phenomena revealed characteristic features which differ most markedly from the properties of matter hitherto known, and above all it was found that nuclear transmutations may be accompanied by an energy release per atom millions of times larger than the energy exchanged in the most violent chemical reactions.

Although at that stage no ways were yet open of releasing for practical purposes the enormous energy stored in the nuclei of atoms, an immediate clue was obtained to the origin of the so far quite unknown energy sources present in the interior of the stars, and in particular it became possible to explain how our sun has been able through billions of years to emit the powerful radiation upon which all organic life on the earth is dependent.

The rapid exploration of this novel field of research in which international cooperation has again been most fruitful led within the last decenniums to a number of important discoveries regarding the intrinsic properties of atomic nuclei and especially revealed the existence of a non-electrified nuclear constituent, the so-called neutron, which when set free is a particularly active reagent in producing nuclear transmutations.

The actual impetus to the present project was the discovery made in the last year before the war, that the nuclei of the heaviest elements like uranium, by neutron bombardment, in the so-called fission process, may split in fragments ejected with enormous energies, and that this process is accompanied by the release of further neutrons which may themselves effect the splitting of other heavy nuclei.

This discovery indicated for the first time the possibility, through propagation of nuclear disintegrations from atom to atom, to obtain a new kind of combustion of matter with immense energy yield. In fact a complete nuclear combustion of heavy materials would release an energy 100,000,000 times larger than that obtainable by the same amount of chemical explosives.

This prospect not only at once attracted the most widespread interest among physicists, but of its appeal to the imagination of larger circles I have vivid recollections from my stay in the U.S.A. in the spring of 1939 where, as guest of the Institute of Advanced Studies in Princeton, I had the pleasure to participate together with American colleagues in investigations on the mechanism of the fission process.

Such investigations revealed that among the substances present in natural ores, only a certain modification of uranium fulfills the conditions for nuclear combustion. Since this active substance always occurs mixed with a more abundant, inactive uranium modification, it was therefore realized that in order to produce devastating explosives, it would be necessary to subject the available materials to a treatment of an extremely refined and elaborate character.

The recognition that the accomplishment of the project would thus require an immense technical effort, which might even prove impracticable, was at that time, not least in view of the imminent threat of military aggression, considered as a great comfort since it would surely prevent any nation from staging a surprise attack with such super weapons.

Any progress on nuclear problems achieved before the war was, of course, common knowledge to physicists all over the world, but after the outbreak of hostilities no further information has been made public, and efforts to exploit nuclear energy sources have been kept as military secrets.

During my stay in Denmark under the German occupation nothing was therefore known to me about the great enterprise in America and England. It was, however, possible, due to connections originating from regular visits of German physicists to the Institute for Theoretical Physics in Copenhagen in the years between the wars, rather closely to follow the work on such lines which from the very beginning of the war was organized by the German Government.

Although thorough preparations were made by a most energetic scientific effort, disposing of expert knowledge and considerable material resources, it appeared from all information available to us, that at any rate, in the initial, for Germany, so favorable stages of the war, it was never by the Government deemed worthwhile to attempt the immense and hazardous technical enterprise which an accomplishment of the project would require.

Immediately after my escape to Sweden in October 1943, I came on an invitation of the British Government to come to England where I was taken into confidence about the great progress achieved in America and went shortly afterwards together with a number of British colleagues to the U.S.A. to take part in the work. In order, however, to conceal my connection with any such enterprise, post-war planning of

international scientific cooperation was given as the object of
my journey.

Already in Denmark I had been in secret connection with
the British Intelligence Service, and more recently I have had
the opportunity with American and British Intelligence Officers to discuss the latest information, pointing to a feverish
German activity on nuclear problems. In this connection it
must above all be realized that if any knowledge of the
progress of the work in America should have reached Germany,
it may have caused the Government to reconsider the possibilities and will not least have presented the physicists and
technical experts with an extreme challenge.

Definite information of preparations elsewhere is hardly
available, but an interest within the Soviet Union for the
project may perhaps be indicated by a letter which I have
received from a prominent Russian physicist with whom I
had formed a personal friendship during his many years stay
in England and whom I visited in Moscow a few years before
the war, to take part in scientific conferences.

This letter contained an official invitation to come to Moscow
to join in scientific work with Russian colleagues who, as I
was told, in the initial stages of the war were fully occupied
with technical problems of a immediate importance for the
defense of their country, but now had the opportunity to devote
themselves to scientific research of a more general character. No
reference was made to any special subject, but from pre-war
work of Russian physicists it is natural to assume that nuclear
problems will be at the center of interest.

The letter, originally sent to Sweden in October 1943, was
on my recent visit to London handed to me by the Counsellor of the Soviet Embassy who in a most encouraging manner
stressed the promises for the future that understanding between
nations entailed in scientific collaboration. Although, of course,
the project was not mentioned in this conversation I got
nevertheless the impression that the Soviet officials were
very interested in the effort in America about the success of
which some rumors may have reached the Soviet Union.

Even if every physicist was prepared that some day the
prospects created by modern researches would materialize, it
was a revelation to me to learn about the courage and fore-
sight with which the great American and British enterprise

had been undertaken and about the advanced stage the work
had already reached.

What until a few years ago might have been considered a
fantastic dream is at the moment being realized in great
laboratories erected for secrecy in some of the most solitary
regions of the States. There a group of physicists larger than
ever before assembled for a single purpose, and working
hand in hand with a whole army of engineers and technicians
are producing new materials capable of enormous energy release and developing ingenious devices for their most effective use.

To everyone who is given the opportunity for himself to
see the refined laboratory equipment and the huge production machinery it is an unforgettable experience of which
words can only give a poor impression. Truly no effort has
been spared and it is hardly possible for me to describe my
admiration for the efficiency with which the great work has
been planned and conducted.

Moreover it was a special pleasure to me to witness the
complete harmony with which the American and British
physicists, with almost everyone of whom I was intimately
acquainted through previous scientific intercourse, were de-
voting themselves with the utmost zeal to the joint effort.

I shall not here enter on technical details, but one cannot
help comparing them with the alchemists of former days, grop-
ing in the dark in their vain efforts to make gold. Today physicists and engineers are on the basis of well established knowledge directing and controlling processes by which substances
far more precious than gold are being collected atom by atom
or even built up by individual nuclear transmutations.

Such substances must be assumed to have been abundant
in the early stages of our universe where all matter was
subject to conditions far more violent than those which still
persist in the turbulent and flaming interior of the stars. Due,
however, to their inherent instability the active materials
now extracted or produced have in the course of time become
very rare or even completely disappeared from the household
of nature.

The whole enterprise constitutes indeed a far deeper interference with the natural course of events than anything ever
before attempted and its impending accomplishment will bring
about a whole new situation as regards human resources.

Surely, we are being presented with one of the greatest triumphs of science and engineering destined deeply to influence the future of mankind.

It certainly surpasses the imagination of anyone to survey the consequences of the project in years to come, where in the long run the enormous energy sources which will be available may be expected to revolutionize industry and transport. The fact of immediate preponderance is, however, that a weapon of an unparalleled power is being created which will completely change all future conditions of warfare.

Quite apart from the questions of how soon the weapon will be ready for use and what role it may play in the present war, this situation raises a number of problems which call for the most urgent attention. Unless, indeed, some agreement about the control of the use of the new active materials can be obtained in due time, any temporary advantage, however great, may be outweighed by a perpetual menace to human security.

Ever since the possibilities of releasing atomic energy on a vast scale came in sight, much thought has naturally been given to the question of control, but the further the exploration of the scientific problems concerned is proceeding, the clearer it becomes that no kind of customary measures will suffice for this purpose and that especially the terrifying prospect of a future competition between nations about a weapon of such formidable character can only be avoided through a universal agreement in true confidence.

In this connection it is above all significant that the enterprise, immense as it is, has still proved far smaller than might have been anticipated and that the progress of the work has continually revealed new possibilities for facilitating the production of the active materials and of intensifying their effects.

The prevention of a competition prepared in secrecy will therefore demand such concessions regarding exchange of information and openness about industrial efforts including military preparations as would hardly be conceivable unless at the same time all partners were assured of a compensating guarantee of common security against dangers of unprecedented acuteness.

The establishment of effective control measures will of

course involve intricate technical and administrative problems, but the main point of the argument is that the accomplishment of the project would not only seem to necessitate but should also, due to the urgency of mutual confidence, facilitate a new approach to the problem of international relationship.

The present moment where almost all nations are entangled in a deadly struggle for freedom and humanity might at first sight seem most unsuited for any committing arrangement concerning the project. Not only have the aggressive powers still great military strength, although their original plans of world domination have been frustrated and it seems certain that they must ultimately surrender, but even when this happens, the nations united against aggression may face grave causes of disagreement due to conflicting attitudes towards social and economic problems.

By a closer consideration, however, it would appear that the potentialities of the project as a means of inspiring confidence just under these circumstances aquire most actual importance. Moreover the momentary situation would in various respects seem to afford quite unique possibilities which might be forfeited by a postponement awaiting the further development of the war situation and the final completion of the new weapon.

Although there can hardly be any doubt that the American and British enterprises is at a more advanced stage than any similar undertaking elsewhere, one must be ready to accept that a competition in the near future may become a serious reality. In fact, as already indicated, it seems likely that preparations, possibly urged on by rumors about the progress in America, are being speeded up in Germany and may even be under way in the Soviet Union.

Further it must be realized that the final defeat of Germany will not only release immense resources for a full scale effort within the Soviet Union, but will presumably also place all scientific knowledge and technical experience collected in Germany at the disposal for such an effort.

In view of these eventualities the present situation would seem to offer a most favorable opportunity for an early initiative from the side which by good fortune has achieved a lead in the efforts of mastering mighty forces of nature hitherto beyond human reach.

Without impeding the importance of the project for immediate military objectives, an initiative, aiming at forestalling a
fateful competition about the formidable weapon, should serve
to uproot any cause of distrust between the powers on whose
harmonious collaboration the fate of coming generations will
depend.

Indeed, it would appear that only when the question is
taken up among the United Nations of what concessions the
various powers are prepared to make as their contribution to
an adequate control arrangement, it will be possible for any
one of the partners to assure themselves of the sincerity of
the intention of the others.

Of course, the responsible statesmen alone can have the
insight in the actual political possibilities. It would, however,
seem most fortunate that the expectations for a future harmonious international cooperation which have found unanimous
expression from all sides within the United Nations, so remarkably correspond to the unique opportunities which, unknown to the public, have been created by the advancement
of science.

Many reasons, indeed, would seem to justify the conviction
that an approach with the object of establishing common
security from ominous menaces without excluding any nation
from participating in the promising industrial development
which the accomplishment of the project entails will be
welcomed, and be responded to with a loyal cooperation on the
enforcement of the necessary far reaching control measures.

Just in such respects helpful support may perhaps be afforded by the worldwide scientific collaboration which for
years has embodied such bright promises for common human
striving. On this background personal connections between
scientists of different nations might even offer means of establishing preliminary and noncommittal contact.

It needs hardly be added that any such remark or suggestion implies no underrating of the difficulty and delicacy of
the steps to be taken by the statesmen in order to obtain an
arrangement satisfactory to all concerned, but aims only at
pointing to some aspects of the situation which may facilitate
endeavors to turn the project to lasting advantage for the
common cause.

Should such endeavours be successful, the project will

surely have brought about a turning point in history and this wonderful adventure will stand as a symbol of the benefit to mankind which science can offer when handled in a truly human spirit.

THE FRANCK REPORT

1. Preamble

The only reason to treat nuclear power differently from all the other developments in the field of physics is its staggering possibilities as a means of political pressure in peace and sudden destruction in war. All present plans for the organization of research, scientific and industrial development, and publication in the field of nucleonics are conditioned by the political and military climate in which one expects those plans to be carried out. Therefore, in making suggestions for the postwar organization of nucleonics, a discussion of political problems cannot be avoided. The scientists on this Project do not presume to speak authoritatively on problems of national and international policy. However, we found ourselves, by the force of events, the last five years in the position of a small group of citizens cognizant of a grave danger for the safety of this country as well as for the future of all the other nations, of which the rest of mankind is unaware. We therefore felt it our duty to urge that the political problems, arising from the mastering of nuclear power, be recognized in all their gravity, and that appropriate steps be taken for their study and the preparation of necessary decisions. We hope that the creation of the Committee by the Secretary of War to deal with all aspects of nucleonics, indicates that these implications have been recognized by the government. We feel that our acquaintance with the scientific elements of the situation and prolonged preoccupation with its world-wide political implications, imposes on us the obligation to offer to the Committee some suggestions as to the possible solution of these grave problems.

Scientists have often before been accused of providing new weapons for the mutual destruction of nations, instead of improving their well-being. It is undoubtedly true that the discovery of flying, for example, has so far brought much more misery than enjoyment and profit to humanity. However in the past, scientists could disclaim direct responsibility for the use to which mankind had put their disinterested discoveries. We cannot take the same attitude now because the success which we have achieved in the development of nuclear power is fraught with infinitely greater dangers than were all the inventions of the past. All of us, familiar with the present state of nucleonics, live with the vision before our eyes of sudden destruction visited on our own country, of Pearl Harbor disaster, repeated in thousandfold magnification, in every one of our major cities.

In the past, science has often been able to provide adequate protection against new weapons it has given into the hands of an aggressor, but it cannot promise such efficient protection against the destructive use of nuclear power. This protection can come only from the political organization of the world. Among all arguments calling for an efficient international organization for peace, the existence of nuclear weapons is the most compelling one. In the absence of an international authority which would make all resort to force in international conflicts impossible, nations could still be diverted from a path which must lead to total mutual destruction, by a specific international agreement barring a nuclear armaments race.

II. Prospectives of Armaments Race

It could be suggested that the danger of destruction by nuclear weapons can be prevented—at least as far as this country is concerned—by keeping our discoveries secret for an indefinite time, or by developing our nucleonic armaments at such a pace that no other nations would think of attacking us from fear of overwhelming retaliation.

The answer to the first suggestion is that although we undoubtedly are at present ahead of the rest of the world in this field, the fundamental facts of nuclear power are a subject of common knowledge. British scientists know as much as we do about the basic wartime progress of nucleonics— with the exception of specific processes used in our engineering developments—and the background of French nuclear physicists plus their occasional contact with our Projects, will enable them to catch up rapidly, at least as far as basic scientific facts are concerned. German scientists, in whose discoveries the whole development of this field has originated, apparently did not develop it during the war to the same extent to which this has been done in America; but to the last day of the European war, we have been living in constant apprehension as to their possible achievements. (The knowledge that German scientists were working on this weapon and that their government certainly had no scruples against using it when available, was the main motivation of the initiative which American scientists have taken in developing nuclear power on such a large scale for military use in this country.) In Russia, too, the basic facts and implications of nuclear power were well understood in 1940, and the experience of Russian scientists in nuclear research is entirely sufficient to enable them to retrace our steps within a few years, even if we would make all attempts to conceal them. Furthermore, we should not expect too much success from attempts to keep basic information secret in peacetime, when scientists acquainted with the work on this and associated Projects will be scattered to many colleges and research institutions and many of them will continue to work on problems closely related to those on which our developments are based. In other words, even if we can retain our leadership in basic knowledge of nucleonics for a certain time by maintaining the secrecy of all results achieved on this and associated Projects, it would be foolish to hope that this can protect us for more than a few years.

It may be asked whether we cannot achieve a monopoly on the raw materials of nuclear power. The answer is that even though the largest now known deposits of uranium ores are under the control of powers which belong to the "western" group (Canada, Belgium and British Indies); the old deposits in Czechoslovakia are outside this sphere. Russia is known to be mining radium on its own territory; and even if we do not know the size of the deposits discovered so far in the USSR, the probability that no large reserves of uranium will be found in a country which covers 1/5 of the land area of the earth (and whose sphere of influence takes in additional territory), is too small to serve as a basis for security. Thus, we cannot hope to avoid a nuclear armament race, either by keeping secret from the competing nations the basic scientific facts of nuclear power, or by cornering the raw materials required for such a race.

One could further ask whether we cannot feel ourselves safe in a race of nuclear armaments by virtue of our greater industrial potential, including greater diffusion of scientific and technical knowledge, greater volume and efficiency of our skilled labor corps, and greater experience of our management—all the factors whose importance has been so strikingly demonstrated in the conversion of this country into an arsenal of the Allied Nations in the present war. The answer is that all that these advantages can give us, is the accumulation of a larger number of bigger and better atomic bombs—and this only if we produce those bombs at the maximum of our capacity in peace time, and do not rely on conversion of a peace time nucleonics industry to military production after the beginning of hostilities.

However, such a quantitative advantage in reserves of bottled destructive power will not make us safe from sudden attack. Just because a potential enemy will be afraid of being "outnumbered and outgunned", the temptation for him may be overwhelming to attempt a sudden unprovoked blow—particularly if he would suspect us of harboring aggressive intentions against his security or "sphere of influence." In no other type of warfare does the advantage lie so heavily with the aggressor. He can place his "infernal machines" in advance in all our major cities and explode them simultaneously, thus destroying a major part of our industry and killing a large proportion of our population, aggregated in densely populated metropolitan districts. Our possibilities of retaliation—even if retaliation would be considered compensation for the loss of tens of millions of lives and destruction of our largest cities—will be greatly handicapped because we must rely on aerial transportation of the bombs, particularly if we would have to deal with an enemy whose industry and population are dispersed over a large territory.

In fact, if the race of nuclear armaments is allowed to develop, the only apparent way in which our country could be protected from the paralyzing effects of a sudden attack is by dispersal of industries which are essential for our war effort and dispersal of the population of our major metropolitan cities. As long as nuclear bombs remain scarce (this will be the case until uranium and thorium cease to be the only basic materials for their fabrication) efficient dispersal of our industry and the scattering of our metropolitan population will

considerably decrease the temptation of attacking us by nuclear weapons.

Ten years hence, an atomic bomb containing perhaps 20 kg
of active material, may be detonated at 6% efficiency, and
thus have an effect equal to that of 20,000 tons of TNT. One
of these may be used to destroy something like 3 square
miles of an urban area. Atomic bombs containing a larger
quantity of active material but still weighing less than one ton
may be expected to be obtainable within ten years which
could destroy over ten square miles of a city. A nation which
is able to assign 10 tons of atomic explosives for the preparation of a sneak attack on this country, can then hope to
achieve the destruction of all industry and most of the population in an area from 500 square miles upwards. If no choice of
targets, in any area of five hundred square miles of American
territory, will contain a large enough fraction of the nation's
industry and population to make their destruction a crippling
blow to the nation's war potential and its ability to defend
itself, then the attack will not pay, and will probably not be
undertaken. At present, one could easily select in this country a hundred blocks of five square miles each whose simulta-
neous destruction would be a staggering blow to the nation.
(A possible total destruction of all the nation's naval forces
would be only a small detail of such a catastrophe.) Since the
area of the United States is about six million square miles, it
should be possible to scatter its industrial and human resources in such a way as to leave no 500 square miles important enough to serve as a target for nuclear attack.

We are fully aware of the staggering difficulties of such a
radical change in the social and economic structure of our
nation. We felt, however, that the dilemma had to be stated,
to show what kind of alternative methods of protection will
have to be considered if no successful international agreement is reached. It must be pointed out that in this field we
are in a less favorable position than nations which are either
now more diffusely populated and whose industries are more
scattered, or whose governments have unlimited power over
the movement of population and the location of industrial
plants.

If no efficient international agreement is achieved, the race
of nuclear armaments will be on in earnest not later than the
morning after our first demonstration of the existence of

nuclear weapons. After this, it might take other nations three or four years to overcome our present headstart, and 8 or 10 years to draw even with us if we continue to do intensive work in this field. This might be all the time we have to bring about the re-groupment of our population and industry. Obviously, no time should be lost in inaugurating a study of this problem by experts.

III. Prospectives of Agreement

The prospect of nuclear warfare and the type of measures which have to be taken to protect a country from total destruction by nuclear bombing, must be as abhorrent to the other nations as to the United States. England, France, and the smaller nations of the European continent, with their congeries of people and industries, are in an entirely hopeless situation in the face of such a threat. Russia, and China are the only great nations which could survive a nuclear attack. However, even though these countries value human life less than the peoples of Western Europe and America, and even though Russia, in particular, has an immense space over which its vital industries could be dispersed and a government which can order this dispersion, the day it is convinced that such a measure is necessary—there is no doubt that Russia, too, will shudder at the possibility of a sudden disintegration of Moscow and Leningrad, almost miraculously preserved in the present war, and of its new industrial cities in the Urals and Siberia. Therefore, only lack of mutual *trust*, and lack of *desire* for agreement, can stand in the path of an efficient agreement for the prevention of nuclear warfare. The achievement of such an agreement will thus essentially depend on the integrity of intentions and readiness to sacrifice the necessary fraction of one's own sovereignty, by all the parties to the agreement.

From this point of view, the way in which the nuclear weapons, now secretly developed in this country, will first be revealed to the world appears of great, perhaps fateful importance.

One possible way—which may particularly appeal to those who consider the nuclear bombs primarily as a secret weapon developed to help win the present war—is to use it without warning on an appropriately selected object in Japan. It is doubtful whether the first available bombs, of comparatively low efficiency and small size, will be sufficient to break the will or ability of Japan to resist, especially given the fact that the major cities like Tokyo, Nagoya, Osaka and Kobe already will largely be reduced to ashes by the slower process of ordinary aerial bombing. Certain and perhaps important tactical results undoubtedly can be achieved, but we nevertheless think that the question of the use of the very first available atomic bombs in the Japanese war should be weighed very carefully, not only by military authority, but by the highest political leadership of this country. If we consider international agreement on total prevention of nuclear warfare as the paramount objective, and believe that it can be achieved, this kind of introduction of atomic weapons to the world may easily destroy all our chances of success. Russia, and even allied countries, which bear less mistrust of our ways and intentions, as well as neutral countries, will be deeply shocked. It will be very difficult to persuade the world that a nation which was capable of secretly preparing and suddenly releasing a weapon, as indiscriminate as the rocket bomb and a thousand times more destructive, is to be trusted in its proclaimed desire of having such weapons abolished by international agreement. We have large accumulations of poison gas, but do not use them, and recent polls have shown that public opinion in this country would disapprove of such a use even if it would accelerate the winning of the Far Eastern war. It is true, that some irrational element in mass psychology makes gas poisoning more revolting than blasting by explosives, even though gas warfare is in no way more "inhuman" than the war of bombs and bullets. Nevertheless, it is not at all certain that the American public opinion, if it could be enlightened as to the effect of atomic explosives, would support the first introduction by our own country of such an indiscriminate method of wholesale destruction of civilian life.

Thus, from the "optimistic" point of view—looking forward to an international agreement on prevention of nuclear warfare—the military advantages and the saving of American lives, achieved by the sudden use of atomic bombs against Japan, may be outweighed by the ensuing loss of confidence and wave of horror and repulsion, sweeping over the rest of the world, and perhaps dividing even the public opinion at home.

From this point of view a demonstration of the new weapon may best be made before the eyes of representatives of all United Nations, on the desert or a barren island. The best possible atmosphere for the achievement of an international agreement could be achieved if America would be able to say to the world, "You see what weapon we had but did not use. We are ready to renounce its use in the future and to join other nations in working out adequate supervision of the use of this nuclear weapon."

This may sound fantastic, but then in nuclear weapons we have something entirely new in the order of magnitude of destructive power, and if we want to capitalize fully on the advantage which its possession gives us, we must use new and imaginative methods. After such a demonstration the weapon could be used against Japan if a sanction of the United Nations (and of the public opinion at home) could be obtained, perhaps after a preliminary ultimatum to Japan to surrender or at least to evacuate a certain region as an alternative to the total destruction of this target.

It must be stressed that if one takes a pessimistic point of view and discounts the possibilities of an effective international control of nuclear weapons, then the advisability of an early use of nuclear bombs against Japan becomes even more doubtful—quite independently of any humanitarian consideration. If no international agreement is concluded immediately after the first demonstration, this will mean a flying start of an unlimited armaments race. If this race is inevitable, we have all reason to delay its beginning as long as possible in order to increase our headstart still further. It took us three years, roughly, under forced draft of wartime urgency, to complete the first stage of production of nuclear explosives— that based on the separation of the rare fissionable isotope U_{235}, or its utilization for the production of an equivalent quantity of another fissionable element. This stage required large-scale, expensive construction and laborious procedures. We are now on the threshold of the second stage—that of converting into fissionable material the comparatively abundant common isotopes of thorium and uranium. This stage requires no elaborate plans and can provide us in about 5-6 years with a really substantial stockpile of atomic bombs. Thus it is to our interest to delay the beginning of the armaments race at least until the successful termination of this second stage. The

324 GERMANY WITHOUT JEWS

benefit to the nation, and the saving of American lives in the future, achieved by renouncing an early demonstration of nuclear bombs and letting the other nations into the race only reluctantly, on the basis of guesswork and without definite knowledge that the "thing does work," may far outweigh the advantages to be gained by the immediate use of the first and comparatively inefficient bombs in the war against Japan. At the least, pros and cons of this use must be carefully weighed by the supreme political and military leadership of the country, and the decision should not be left to considerations, merely, of military tactics.

One may point out that scientists themselves have initiated the development of this "secret weapon" and it is therefore strange that they should be reluctant to try it out on the enemy as soon as it is available. The answer to this question was given above—the compelling reason for creating this weapon with such speed was our fear that Germany had the technical skill necessary to develop such a weapon without any moral restraints regarding its use.

Another argument which could be quoted in favor of using atomic bombs as soon as they are available is that so much taxpayers' money has been invested in those Projects that the Congress and the American public will require a return for their money. The above-mentioned attitude of the American public opinion in the question of the use of poison gas against Japan shows that one can expect it to understand that a weapon can sometimes be made ready only for use in extreme emergency; and as soon as the potentialities of nuclear weapons will be revealed to the American people, one can be certain that it will support all attempts to make the use of such weapons impossible.

Once this is achieved, the large installations and the accumulation of explosive materials at present earmarked for potential military use, will become available for important peace time developments, including power production, large engineering undertakings, and mass production of radioactive materials. In this way, the money spent on war time development of nucleonics may become a boon for the peace time development of national economy.

IV. Methods of International Control

We now consider the question of how an effective international control of nuclear armaments can be achieved. This is a difficult problem, but we think it to be soluble. It requires study by statesmen and international lawyers, and we can offer only some preliminary suggestions for such a study.

Given mutual trust and willingness on all sides to give up a certain part of their sovereign rights, by admitting internaional control of certain phases of national economy, the control could be exercised (alternatively or simultaneously) on two different levels.

The first and perhaps simplest way is to ration the raw materials—primarily, the uranium ores. Production of nuclear explosives begins with processing of large quantities of uranium in large isotope separation plants or huge production piles. The amounts of ore taken out of the ground at different locations could be controlled by resident agents of the international Control Board, and each nation could be allotted only an amount which would make large scale separation of fissionable isotopes impossible.

Such a limitation would have the drawback of making impossible also the development of nuclear power production for peace time purposes. However, it does not need to prevent the production of radioactive elements on a scale which will revolutionize the industrial, scientific and technical use of these materials, and will thus not eliminate the main benefits which nucleonics promises to bring to mankind.

An agreement on a higher level, involving more mutual trust and understanding, would be to allow unlimited production, but keep exact bookkeeping on the fate of each pound of uranium mined. Certain difficulty with this method of control will arise in the second stage of production, when one pound of pure fissionable isotope will be used again and again to produce additional fissionable material from thorium. These could perhaps be overcome by extending control to the mining and use of thorium, even though the commercial use of this metal may cause complications.

If check is kept on the conversion of uranium and thorium ore into pure fissionable materials, the question arises how to prevent accumulation of large quantities of such materials in the hands of one or several nations. Accumulations of this kind could be rapidly converted into atomic bombs if a nation would break away from international control. It has been suggested that a compulsory denaturation of pure fissionable isotopes may be agreed upon—they should be diluted after production by suitable isotopes to make them useless for military purposes (except if purified by a process whose development must take two or three years), while retaining their usefulness for power engines.

One thing is clear: any international agreement on prevention of nuclear armaments must be backed by actual and efficient controls. No paper agreement can be sufficient since neither this or any other nation can stake its whole existence on trust into other nations' signatures. Every attempt to impede the international control agencies must be considered equivalent to denounciation of the agreement.

It hardly needs stressing that we as scientists believe that any systems of controls envisaged should leave as much freedom for the peace development of nucleonics as is consistent with the safety of the world.

Summary

The development of nuclear power not only constitutes an important addition to the technological and military power of the United States, but also creates grave political and economic problems for the future of this country.

Nuclear bombs cannot possibly remain a "secret weapon" at the exclusive disposal of this country, for more than a few years. The scientific facts on which their construction is based are well known to scientists of other countries. Unless an effective international control of nuclear explosives is instituted, a race of nuclear armaments is certain to ensue following the first revelation of our possession of nuclear weapons to the world. Within ten years other countries may have nuclear bombs, each of which, weighing less than a ton, could destroy an urban area of more than five square miles.

In the war to which such an armaments race is likely to lead, the United States, with its agglomeration of population and industry in comparatively few metropolitan districts, will be at a disadvantage compared to the nations whose population and industry are scattered over large areas.

We believe that these considerations make the use of nuclear bombs for an early, unannounced attack against Japan inadvisable. If the United States would be the first to release this new means of indiscriminate destruction upon mankind, she would sacrifice public support throughout the world, precipitate the race of armaments, and prejudice the possibility of reaching an internaional agreement on the future control of such weapons.

Much more favorable conditions for the eventual achievement of such an agreement could be created if nuclear bombs were first revealed to the world by a demonstration in an appropriately selected uninhabited area.

If chances for the establishment of an effective international control of nuclear weapons will have to be considered slight at the present time, then not only the use of these weapons against Japan, but even their early demonstration may be contrary to the interests of this country. A postponement of such a demonstration will have in this case the advantage of delaying the beginning of the nuclear armaments race as long as possible. If, during the time gained, ample support could be made available for further development of the field in this country, the postponement would substantially increase the lead which we have established during the present war, and our position in an armament race or in any later attempt at international agreement will thus be strengthened.

On the other hand, if no adequate public support for the development of nucleonics will be available without a demonstration, the postponement of the latter may be deemed inadvisable, because enough information might leak out to cause other nations to start the armament race, in which we will then be at a disadvantage. At the same time, the distrust of other nations may be aroused by a confirmed development under cover of secrecy, making it more difficult eventually to reach an agreement with them.

If the government should decide in favor of an early demonstration of nuclear weapons it will then have the possibility to take into account the public opinion of this country and of the other nations before deciding whether these weapons should be used in the war against Japan. In this way, other nations may assume a share of responsibility for such a fateful decision.

To sum up, we urge that the use of nuclear bombs in this war be considered as a problem of long-range national policy

rather than military expediency, and that this policy be directed
primarily to the achievement of an agreement permitting an
effective internaional control of the means of nuclear warfare.

The vital importance of such a control for our country is
obvious from the fact that the only effective alternative method
of protecting this country, of which we are aware, would be a
dispersal of our major cities and essential industries.

A Document of Eastern-Jewish Sympathy for Germany

*"Hoch der Keiser!" by Morris Rosenfeld appeared in
the February 1916 issue of* Süddeutsche Monatshefte.

Morris Rosenfeld, the most notable of the Yiddish poets, who
has lived in the United States for many years, is of Russian
origin. This poem is taken from a Yiddish paper published in
the United States. It will serve as a barometer for the mood
of the Russian Jews living in America and as a sample of the
Yiddish language.

In Rußland is main Wieg gestannen,
Dort hot men mich zum Schlof gesungen . . .
Es hot im Land von die Tyrannen
Main Wieglied trauerig geklungen.

Von Anfang hot gewejnt main Mutter,
Nochdem hob ich gegossen Trähren;
Mich hot gepeinigt der Nit-Guter
Un nit gewollt main Jammer hören.

Der Frühling pflegt far mir nit grünen,
Dos Leben sein far mir verschlossen;
'ch hob nit gekennt dem Ssoine dienen,
Denn wos wollt ich dervun genossen?

In Weh gewacht, in Schreck geschlofen,
Hob ich in jenem Land vun Klogen;
Ich hob gesüfzt und bin entloffen,
Entloffen, wo die Ejgen trogen.

'ch hob in der waiten Welt vernummen
Die Gwalten vun dem groben Schikker

Gehört vum Bär den wilden Brummen,
Wenn er zerreißt main Volk in Stücker.

'Wet Risches ejbig, ejbig siegen?
Ihr bejser Dunner ejbig rollen?
Wet Jowon mehr sain Psak nit kriegen?
Wet Rußland mehr ihr Schuld nit zohlen?"

Gefrägt hob ich dos mit Varzogen,
Ich hob gezittert noch Nekome.
Itzt hör ich, as sie werd geschlogen,
Un Freud füllt über main Neschome.

Far jeden Schmitz, wos sej derlangen,
Begleit mit der Geschichte Bejser,
Ruf ich mit fröhlichen Gesangen:
Hurra far Daitschland! Hoch der Kejser!

A literal English translation reads:

My cradle stood in Russia,
That's where I heard my lullabies;
And in the land of tyrants
It was a mournful song.

At first it was my mother's weeping,
Then I shed the tears.
I was tortured by the fiend,
And no one wished to hear my moans.

Spring would not bloom for me,
Life would not open for me;
I could not serve the enemy,
For what good would it have done me?

Awake in grief, asleep in fear,
That's how I lived in that land of sorrow;
I sighed and ran away—
Ran wherever my eyes led me.

All over the wide world I heard
The cruel deeds of the rough drunkard,
Heard the bear's wild growls
As he tore my people to pieces.

"Will wickedness win out forever?
Their wicked thunder ever roll?
Will the Russian never get his punishment?
Will Russia never pay for its deeds?"

That's what I asked in my despair,
I trembled with my thirst for vengeance.
Now I have heard that they've been beaten
And joy overcomes my soul.

For every blow that they receive,
Accompanied by history's rage,
I shout, with cheerful song:
Hurray for Germany! Three cheers for the Kaiser!

Jews of Poland!

> Proclamation of the General Command of the Joint
> Armies of Germany and Austro-Hungary at the be-
> ginning of the First World War. (Translated into
> English from the German translation of the origi-
> nal Yiddish.

With the help of God, the victorious armies of the Allied
Great Powers, Germany and Austro-Hungary, have advanced
into Poland.

We wage war, not against the people, but against *Russian
tyranny*. Russian despotism has collapsed under the weight of
the powerful thrusts inflicted on it by our brave armies.

Jews of Poland! *We come to you as friends and saviors!*
Our flags herald justice and freedom for you: *Equal and full
civil rights, genuine freedom of religion, freedom to work in
all economic and cultural fields*. For too long you have suffered under Moscow's iron yoke. We come to you to liberate
you. The tyranny of foreign rule has been broken. A new
epoch has dawned for Poland; we will use all our might to
support and secure the liberation of the entire Polish
population. On a safe footing, guaranteed by law, we will
introduce the equality of the Jews in Poland, in conformity
with the Western European model.

Don't be misled by the false promises of the Russians! In
1905 Russia gave its sacred pledge promising you equality.

Do we have to remind you how the Muscovite kept his promise? Think of Kichinev, Homel, Bialystok, Odessa, Siedlce, and a hundred of other bloody pogroms! Remember the mass expulsions and deportations. Without any pity for human suffering, the tormentor hunted and harrassed you with wife and child, as if you were wild animals.

Do not forget the Beilis trial and other blood accusations, when the Russian government itself, and acting officially, leveled the infamous, false accusation of ritual murder.

The portals of life were shut in the face of the Jews, the portals of education were closed to Jewish children. Your sons and daughters have been chased out of Russian schools, Russian cities, and Russian villages. They were permitted to live in Russia only as prostitutes with yellow passports. That is how Russia kept its sacred promise—given at a time when the country was in trouble.

Now Russia is in trouble again, and it has begun to feed you with new promises.

Jews in Poland! Your hour of vengeance has come. The brave armies of the Great Powers, Germany and Austro-Hungary, are in Poland. With the help of God Almighty they will settle accounts with your oppressors and tormentors. You, however, have the sacred duty to do all in your power to support the work of deliverance. All the potential of the people—your youth, your communities, your associations— all of you must be placed as one man in the service of the sacred cause. Every one of you must help us with everything at his disposal. By helping us, you are helping yourselves. Our enemy is also your enemy. The ranks of our common enemy must be destroyed by perpetual vigilance. We expect you to prove by deeds what you are capable of achieving by intelligence and zeal.

You have nothing to fear from our soldiers. They will not touch a hair on your heads. We will pay generously, in cash, for whatever you supply us. If you have a request, do not hesitate confidently to approach the officers in charge, the commanders of our troops.

Help in defeating the enemy and work toward the victory of freedom and justice!

The General Command of the Joint Armies of Germany and Austro-Hungary.

Rosa Luxemburg's Letter from Prison

This letter, addressed to Sonja Liebknecht, incited a reader's letter to Die Fackel, *cited in the text, along with Karl Kraus's reply with his "credo."*

Oh, Sonitschka, I've felt a terrible pain here. The yard where I walk is often entered by military wagons. They are loaded with sacks of old soldiers' uniforms and shirts frequently bloodstained. They are off-loaded here, distributed among the cells, patched, re-loaded, and returned to the military. The other day such a wagon arrived, harnessed to buffaloes instead of horses. For the first time I saw these animals close up. They are stronger and more compact than our cattle, have flat heads and horns flattened out at an angle. Their faces are similar to those of our sheep, completely black and with large gentle eyes. They represent war booty from Rumania. . . . The soldiers driving these wagons report that it was quite laborious catching these wild animals and even more difficult to utilize them as beasts of burden, seeing they were used to liberty. They were terribly beaten until the word: "vae victis" was applicable. . . . In Breslau there are said to be no less than 100 of these animals and they are fed miserably after being accustomed to luxuriant Rumanian meadows. They are relentlessly exploited for lugging all kinds of heavy trucks and are inclined to perish quickly. A few days ago a wagon, laden with sacks, came driving in with its load packed so high that the buffaloes were unable to cross the threshold of the entrance to the gate. The soldier driving them, a brutal fellow, began hitting the animals with the thick end of the whip handle to such an extent that the female warden asked him, full of indignation, whether he had no pity for the poor animals! "Nobody pities us humans either," he answered with a malicious smile and hit even harder. Finally the animals pulled and surmounted the rise, however, one was bleeding. . . . Sonitschka, a buffalo hide is proverbial for its thickness and toughness and this one was torn. During off-loading the animals stood there, completely quiet, exhausted. The bleeding one had an expression in its black face and gentle dark eyes like a weeping child. It was the expression of a child that has been severely punished and does not know what for, nor how to escape the torment and brutal violence. . . . I stood in front of it; the animal looked at me and my tears started rolling, they were its tears. One cannot wince on behalf of a beloved brother more painfully than I did in my impotence over this silent suffering. How far away, unattainable and lost, are the free fertile green meadowlands of Rumania! How differently would the sun be shining there, the wind blowing, the happy sounds of birds and the melodious calls of shepherds reverberating. Here, this strange, gruesome town, the stuffy stable, the nauseating musty hay, intermingled with rotten straw—the strange terrible humans, the beatings and the blood from the fresh wound . . . Oh, my poor buffalo, my poor beloved brother, the two of us are standing here, so impotent and so dumb, united only in pain, helplessness, and longing. Meanwhile, the prisoners got busy around the wagon, unloaded the heavy bags and carried them into the house. Moreover, the soldier stuck his hands into his pockets, stalked with large steps across the yard, smiled, and whistled softly to himself some vulgar tune. At that moment the whole magnificent war passed in front of me. . . .

Men and Women of Medicine

A selection of notable Jewish—chiefly German-Jewish—physicians of the nineteenth and early twentieth century, grouped by specialties:

	Principal location	Year of Birth	Primary specialty, discoveries, etc.
ANATOMY AND PATHOLOGY			
Askanazy, Max	Geneva	1865	Formation of tumors, blood-forming organisms
Auerbach, Leopold	Breslau	1828	Mesenteric plexus
Benda, Carl	Berlin	1857	Tissue theory, atlas of histology
Born, Gustav Jacob	Breslau	1851	Embryology
Christeller, Erwin	Berlin		Total organ incisions
Cohnheim, Julius	Leipzig	1839	Theory of origin of tumors, Cohnheim fields

Epstein, Albert	New York	1880	Lipoid nephrosis
Erdheim, Jacob	Vienna	1874	Ailments of the pituitary gland
Fishbein, Morris	Chicago	1889	President of American Medical Association
Fränkel, Eugen	Hamburg	1853	Welch-Fränkel bacillus
Gärtner, Gustav	Vienna	1855	Ergometer
Gluge, Gottlieb	Brussels	1812	First to describe "the influenza, or grippe"
Goldblatt, Harry	Cleveland	1891	Blood pressure
Guttmann, Ludwig	Breslau	1899	Diseases of the spinal cord, war injuries
Heidenhain, Martin	Tübingen	1864	Discovered microsomes within the cell nucleus
Henle, Jakob	Göttingen	1809	Epithelial tissue
Herxheimer, Gotthold	Wiesbaden		Liver disease, malformations, benign tumors
Klemperer, Paul	New York	1877	Lupus erythematosus
Kohn, Alfred	Prague		Discovered the epithelial corpuscle
Landau, Max	Vienna, Frankfurt am Main, Freiburg		Cholesterol metabolism
Levin-Jacobson, Ludwig	Copenhagen	1873	Anastomosis, etc., comparative anatomy, embryology
Liebow, Averill	New Haven	1911	Pathology of the thoracic cavity
Lubarsch, Otto	Düsselsorf, Kiel, Berlin	1860	Textbook of pathology, anatomy, tumors, and infectious diseases
Olitsky, Peter	New York	1886	Viral research
Pick, Ludwig	Berlin	1868	Pathology of bone diseases
Poll, Heinrich	Hamburg	1877	Heredity theory
Pribram, Alfred	Prague	1841	Heart diseases, rheumatism, infections
Remak, Robert	Berlin	1815	Embryology
Rezek, Philipp	Vienna, New York, Baltimore	1895	*Autopsy pathology*
Rich, Arnold	Baltimore	1893	Tuberculosis
Rothberger, Carl J.	Vienna	1871	Pathological physiology of circulation
Schwartz, Philipp	Istanbul	1894	Pathology of the central nervous system in newborns
Sternberg, Carl	Vienna	1872	Description of Hodgkin's disease
Stricker, Salomon	Vienna	1834	Tissue anatomy

Tandler, Julius	Vienna	1869	*Konstitutionslehre*
Weichselbaum, Anton	Vienna	1845	W. meningocossus, W. reagent
Weigert, Karl	Frankfurt am Main	1845	Introduction of dye technology in histology and bacteriology
Wolbach, Simon	Cambridge	1880	Cancer research, typhoid fever
Zuckerkandl, Emil	Vienna	1849	Z. *Corpuscles*
Zuckerman, Sir Solly	Birmingham	1904	*A New System of Anatomy*

BACTERIOLOGY AND SEROLOGICAL RESEARCH

Adler, Sol	Jerusalem	1895	Parasitology
Bergel, Salo	Berlin	1868	Lymphocytosis in pathology
Besredka, Alexander	Paris	1870	Anaphylaxis, local immunity
Blumenthal, Fred	Berlin	1870	Cancer
Caspari, Wilhelm		1872	Tumor immunity
Chain, Sir Ernst B.	Berlin, Oxford, Rome	1906	Microbiology, Nobel Prize
Cohn, Ferdinand J.	Breslau	1828	Bacteriology
Ehrlich, Paul	Frankfurt	1854	Developer of chemotherapy, Salvarsan, Nobel Prize
Felix, Arthur	London	1887	Diagnosis of typhoid fever
Flexner, Simon	New York	1863	Dysentery bacillus
Fraenkel, Karl	Halle	1861	Cholera, recurrent fevers
Freund, Ernst Friedrich Franz	Vienna	1863	Blood-sugar in cancer, serum research, blood clotting
Friedmann, Ulrich	Frankfurt, Berlin	1877	Scarlet fever
Friedmann,	Berlin	1876	Tuberculosis research
Georgi, Felix	Breslau	1893	Syphilis, Georgi-Sachs test
Gerstenfeld, Louis	Philadelphia	1895	Pharmacology, immunology
Haffkine, Waldemar	Bombay	1860	Inoculation against cholera and bubonic plague
Kafka, Victor	Hamburg	1881	Serochemical diagnosis
Kahn, Reuben L.	Ann Arbor	1887	K. test in syphilis
Klopstock, Alfred	Heidelberg	1896	Methoden der Blutuntersuchung
Kraus, Rudolf	Sao Paolo	1868	Precipitin, polio
Levinthal, Walter	Berlin		L.'s agar, parrot fever
Löwenstein, Ernst	Vienna	1878	Proof of TB bacilli in the blood
Luria, S. Edward	Boston	1912	Viral research, Nobel Prize
Marmorek, Alexander	Paris	1865	Streptococci and TB serum
Metschnikoff, Ilja	Paris	1845	Phagocytosis, Nobel Prize
Morgenroth, Julius	Berlin	1871	Chemotherapy

Neisser, Max	Frankfurt	1869	Staining process for diphtheria bacilli
Neufeld, Fred	Berlin	1869	Bacteriology
Olitski, A. Leo	Jerusalem	1898	Fever vaccines, immunology
Plaut, Hugo Carl	Hamburg	1858	Described Plant-Vincent's angina
Pribram, Ernst	Chicago	1879	Classification of bacilli
Rabinowitsch-Kempner, Lydia	Berlin	1871	Research on TB
Sabin, Albert	Cincinnati	1906	Oral polio vaccine
Sachs, Hans	Heidelberg, Dublin	1877	Syphilis, S. Georgi-Sachs test
Salk, Jonas Edward	Pittsburgh	1914	Polio vaccine
Scherago, Morris	Lexington	1895	Allergies, immunology
Schnitzer, Robert J.	Berlin	1894	Chemotherapy of bacteria and protozoa
Sobernheim, Georg	Berlin, Bern	1865	Anthrax and other infectious diseases
Solomonsen, Carl J.	Breslau, Copenhagen		Pioneer in bacteriology, proved infectiousness of TB in 1878 (four years before Koch)
Waksman, Selman A.	New Brunswick	1888	Streptomycin, Neomycin, Nobel Prize
Wassermann, August von	Berlin, New Jersey	1866	Syphilis (Wassermann test)
Weichbrodt, Raphael	Frankfurt	1886	Proof of globulin in solution
Weil, Edmund	Prague	1879	Weil-Felix bacillus and test
Widal, Georges F.	Paris	1862	Typhoid-fever vaccine, Widal test

PHYSIOLOGY AND PHYSICAL CHEMISTRY

Ascher, Leon	Berne	1865	*Praktische Übungen in der Physiologie*
Bechhold, Heinrich	Frankfurt	1866	Colloidal research
Bernstein, Julius	Halle	1839	Electrical impulses in nerves and muscles
Cori, Gerty Theresa	St. Louis	1896	Cori cycle, Cori tumors, Nobel Prize
Embden, Gustav	Frankfurt	1874	Metabolism
Erlanger, Josef	St. Louis	1874	Highly differentiated function of individual nerve fibers, Nobel Prize
Fleischl v. Marxow, Ernst	Vienna	1846	Hemoglobin measurement

Frank, Alfred Erich	Breslau, Istanbul	1884	Physiology of the blood and the autonomic nerve system, diabetes
Freundlich, Herbert	Braunschweig, Berlin	1880	Colloidal and capillary chemistry
Funk, Casimir	Warsaw	1884	Discoverer of Vitamin B
Gaertner, Gustav	Vienna	1855	Inventor of blood-pressure gauge, of the ergometer and of the electrical two-cell bath
Hamburger, H. J.	Groningen	1859	Studies in osmosis, described chloride shift
Heidenhain, Rudolf	Breslau	1834	Physiology of muscles, digestion, kidneys
Hermann, Ludimar	Zurich, Königsberg	1838	Metabolic processes in the muscles
Jacob, Francois	Paris	1920	Molecular biology
Katchalski, Ephraim	Rehovot	1916	Biochemistry of protein
Kestner, Otto	Heidelberg, Hamburg	1873	Chemistry of proteins and enzymes
Krebs, Sir Hans Adolf	Sheffield, Oxford	1900	Citric acid cycle, Nobel Prize
Kronecker, Hugo	Berne	1839	Physiology of the heart muscle, Kronecker's inhibitory center
Laqueur, Ernst	Ghent, Amsterdam	1880	*Endokrinologie*
Lipmann, Fritz A.	Berlin, New York	1899	Coenzyme A, Nobel Prize
Loeb, Jacques	New York	1858	Artificial insemination
Loewy, Adolf	Berlin, Davos	1862	High-altitude research
Lwoff, André	Paris	1902	Microphysiology, Nobel Prize
Mayer, Sigmund	Prague	1842	M's cell masses and growth end globules
Meyerhof, Otto	Heidelberg, Philadelphia	1884	Energy transformation in muscles, Nobel Prize
Michaelis, Leonor	Berlin, New York	1875	Cell staining
Mislowitzer, Ernst	Berlin	1895	Protein enzymes
Monod, Jacques	Paris	1910	Heredity, Nobel Prize
Munk, Hermann	Berlin	1839	Physiology of the brain
Munk, Immanuel	Berlin	1852	Nutrition research
Necheles, Heinrich	Hamburg, Chicago	1897	Experimental and clinical physiology
Neuberg, Carl	Berlin, New York	1877	Intermediate and protein metabolism, enzymes, biochemical effect of light

Rona, Peter	Berlin	1871	Proof of enzymes in the body
Rosenthal, Isidor	Erlangen	1836	*Lehrbuch der allgemeinen Physiologie*
Schiff, Moritz	Geneva	1823	Founder of hormone therapy
Semon, Richard	Berlin	1859	Comparative morphology, general and experimental biology
Shelesnyak, Moses	Rehovot	1909	Ergocornine as birth-control agent
Spiro, Karl	Strasbourg, Basel	1867	Colloidal chemistry, hemolysis
Steinach, Eugen	Vienna	1861	Comparative physiology, rejuvenation doctrine
Traube, Isidor	Berlin	1860	Theory of general anesthesia, disinfectants
Valentin, Gabriel	Berne	1810	Named nucleolus of cell nucleus, diastasis
Warburg, Otto H.	Berlin	1883	Cellular physiology, Nobel Prize
Wertheimer, Ernst	Jerusalem	1893	Diabetes, metabolism
White, Abraham	New York	1911	Biochemistry
Willstätter, Richard	Berlin	1872	Biochemistry of cholesterines, Nobel Prize
Winterstein, Hans	Breslau, Istanbul		Physiology of the nervous system
Zuntz, Nathan	Berlin	1847	Measurement of oxygen consumption

BLOOD GROUP RESEARCH, GENETICS, ANTHROPOLOGY

Boas, Franz	New York	1858	Anthropology and ethnology
Cohn, Edwin C.	Cambridge (USA)	1892	Fractioning of blood components
Damescheck, William	Boston	1900	Chemotherapy of leukemia
Friedenthal, Hans	Berlin	1870	Anthropology and physiology
Goldschmidt, Richard	Berlin	1878	Genetics
Gurevitz, Josef	Jerusalem	1898	Blood groups of platelets
Heller, Harry	Tel Haschomer	1899	Genetics of recurrent fevers
Kornberg, Arthur	Palo Alto	1918	DNA as basis of gene, Nobel Prize
Landsteiner, Karl	New York	1868	Established basis of blood grouping, Nobel Prize
Lederberg, Josua	Madison	1925	Gene mutations, Nobel Prize

Levine, Philip	Newark	1900	Rh-factor in blood transfusions
Levy, Fritz	Berlin	1887	Experimental embryology, parthenogenesis
Loeb, Jacques	Chicago	1859	Tropisms
Loeb, Leo		1869	Artificial fertilization
Müller, Herman J.	New York	1890	Mutation of genes through X-rays, Nobel Prize
Nelken, David	Jerusalem	1921	Blood groups of blood platelets
Pappenheim, Arthur	Berlin	1870	Pappenheim method of staining
Peretz, Max	Vienna, Cambridge	1914	Spiral structure of globulin
Poll, Heinrich	Berlin	1877	Anatomical study of twins
Rachmilewitz, M.	Jerusalem	1899	Hematology
Strassburger, Eduard	Bonn	1841	Fundamental contribution to cytology
Weidenreich, Frans	Heidelberg	1873	Research on leucocytes
Wiener, Alexander	New York	1907	With Landsteiner discovered Rh-factor
Wintrobe, Maxwell	Utah	1901	Manual of diseases of the blood

GYNECOLOGY

Adler, Ludwig	Vienna	1879	Fundamental studies in diagnosis and therapy of malignant tumors of the uterus
Aschermann, Joseph	Tel Aviv, Jerusalem	1899	Maternity
Ascheim, Selmar	Berlin, Paris	1878	Hormone research, Ascheim-Zondek test
Aschner, Bernhard	Vienna		Relation of the blood glands with regard to gynecology and midwifery
Cohnstein, Isidor	Heidelberg	1841	Muscle tone and innervation of uterus; manual of obstetrics
Fraenkel, Ernst	Breslau	1844	Extrauterine pregnancies, sterility
Fraenkel, Ludwig	Breslau	1870	Manual of the sexual psychology of women
Freund, Wilhelm A.	Strassburg	1833	Hysterectomy
Guttmacher, A. F.	New York	1898	*Life in the Making*
Halban, Josef	Vienna	1870	Manual of the biology and pathology of women
Hirsch, Max	Berlin	1877	Social gynecology
Hofbauer, Isidor	Vienna, Baltimore	1891	Hofbauer cell
Jarcho, Julius	New York	1880	Gynecological X-ray technology

Kristeller, Samuel	Berlin	1820	Kristeller's maneuver
Landau, Leopold	Berlin	1848	Vaginal surgery
Landau, Theodor	Berlin	1861	Surgical gynecology
Lee, Joseph B. de	Chicago	1869	Obstetrics
Liepmann, Wilhelm	Berlin, Istanbul	1878	Gynecological psychotherapy
Novak, Josef	Prague, Vienna	1869	Internal secretions
Rubin, Isidore	New York	1883	Rubin test for sterility
Saenger, Max	Prague	1853	Obstetrics
Strassmann, Paul	Berlin	1866	Head of internationally famous gynecological hospital
Theilhaber, Adolf	Munich	1854	Cancer in women
Wertheim, Ernst	Vienna	1864	Wertheim's operation
Zondek, Bernhard	Jerusalem	1892	Ascheim-Zondek test

PEDIATRICS

Abt, Arthur	Baltimore	1867	Editor of pediatrics annual
Amberg, Samuel	Baltimore	1874	Basic contributions to pediatrics
Baginsky, Adolf	Berlin	1843	Manual of children's diseases
Dorfman, Albert	Chicago	1916	Rheumatism in children
Epstein, Alois	Prague	1849	Epstein's pearls, bleeding and diarrhetic vomiting in infants
Epstein, Berthold	Prague	1890	Infant tuberculosis
Finkelstein, Heinrich	Berlin	1865	Finkelstein's albumin milk
Gross, Robert E.	Boston	1905	Pediatric cardiac surgery
Henoch, Heinrich	Berlin	1820	Henoch's purpura
Hirschsprung, H.	Copenhagen	1850	Hirschsprung's disease
Hochsinger, Karl	Vienna	1860	Hochsinger's sign for tetanus
Jacobi, Abraham	New York	1830	Invented the laryngoscope
Kassowitz, Max	Vienna	1842	Syphilis and rickets
Knöpfelmacher, Wilhelm	Vienna	1861	Director of the Caroline Hospital
Koplik, Henry	New York	1857	Koplik's sign in measles
Kugelmass, Newton	New York	1896	Nutrition for children
Langstein, Leopold	Berlin	1876	Nutrition and metabolism in infants
Leiner, Karl	Vienna	1871	Leading pediatrician; L.'s test, L. disease
Levins, Samuel Z.	Ithaca	1895	Pediatrician at Cornell University
Meyer, Ludwig F.	Berlin, Tel Aviv	1879	Hospitalization, infant nutrition

Moll, Leopold	Vienna	1871	Author of numerous works on pediatrics
Nassau, Erich	Berlin, Tel Aviv	1888	Nutritional disfunctions, in infants
Neumann, Hugo	Berlin	1858	Child welfare
Rosenbaum, Schimon	Leipzig, Israel	1890	Numerous contributions to pediatrics
Schick, Bela	New York	1877	Schick test for diphtheria
Schiff, Erwin		1891	Diseases of the heart and kidneys, pediatric eczema, pathogenesis of nutritional problems in infants
Scholossmann, Arthur	Düsseldorf	1867	Handbook of pediatric diseases
Taussig, Helen	Baltimore	1898	With Blalok, surgery for blue babies

INTERNAL MEDICINE

Adlersberg, David	Vienna, New York	1897	Diabetes, lipoid metabolism
Albu, Albert	Berlin	1867	Digestive diseases
Bamberger, Heinrich v.	Vienna	1822	Diseases of heart and kidneys
Barron, Moses	Minneapolis	1898	Diabetes
Basch, Siegfried. J. v.	Vienna	1837	First usable sphygmomanometer
Bauer, Julius	Vienna, Los Angeles	1877	Constitutional theory
Berenblum, Izaak	Rehovot	1903	Cancer research
Bettelheim, Karl	Berlin	1840	Phosphorous poisoning, pneumonia
Blumgart, Hermann	Cambridge	1895	Heart
Boas, Ismar	Berlin	1858	Gastroenterology
Brieger, Ludwig	Berlin	1849	Described the Brieger bacillus, toxins, and ptomaines
Conn, Jerome W.	Ann Arbor	1907	Described Conn's disease
Ebstein, Wilhelm	Göttingen	1836	Albumin diet for obesity
Einhorn, Max	New York	1862	Gastroenterology
Fishberg, Arthur	New York	1898	Kidney diseases
Fraenkel, Albert	Berlin	1848	Described action of diplococcus pneumoniae
Fraenkel, Albert	Heidelberg	1864	Developed strophantin therapy
Frank, Erich	Breslau, Istanbul	1884	Internal secretions, metabolism

Goldenberg, Marcel	Vienna, New York	1901	Described some aspects of the adrenal gland
Goldschneider, Alfred	Berlin	1855	Pathology of pain
Groedel, Franz	Frankfurt	1881	Physical therapy for circulation disorders
Gruby, David	Paris	1834	Discoverer of trypanasoma protozoa
Hayem, George	Paris	1841	Muscular atrophy, cholera, count of blood platelets
Herxheimer, Herbert	Berlin	1894	Measurement of heart involvement during physical activity
Hirschfeld, Hans	Berlin	1879	Cancer research
Jacobson, Heinrich	Berlin	1826	Hemodynamics
Kisch, Bruno	Cologne, New York	1890	Electromicroscopic circulation research
Kleeberg, I. Julius	Frankfurt, Jerusalem	1894	Experimental formation of gall stones
Klemperer, Felix	Berlin	1866	Publisher *Neue deutsche Klinik*
Klemperer, Georg	Boston	1865	Metabolism
Kuttner, Leopold	Berlin	1866	Diet treatment of stomach ailments, court physician to Empress Augusta Victoria
Lazarus, Adolf	Frankfurt	1867	Close collaborator of Ehrlich
Lazarus, Julius	Berlin	1847	Larynx, lung, heart ailments
Lazarus, Paul	Berlin	1873	Cancer treatment
Lebert, Hermann	Zurich, Breslau	1833	First atlas of pathological anatomy, hospital of chest diseases
Levine, Rachmiel	New York	1910	Diabetes
Levine, Samuel	Cambridge	1891	Cardiac disorders
Lichtwitz, Leopold	Berlin, New York	1876	Clinical chemistry, metabolism
Liebmann, Emanuel	New York	1872	Liebmann-Sachs syndrome
Litten, Moritz	Berlin	1845	Litten's endocarditis, Litten's sign, Litten's theory
Luzatto, Benjamino	Padua	1850	Tuberculosis, heart murmur
Mannaberg, Julius	Vienna	1860	Kidney and malaria research, M.'s symptoms
Mendes, Guido	Rome, Gedera	1876	Established lung sanatorium in Gedera
Meyer, Erich	Göttingen	1874	*Mikroskopie und Chemie am Krankenbett*
Minkowski, Oskar	Breslau	1858	Significance of the pancreas in diabetes

Oser, Leopold	Vienna	1839	Pyloric innervation
Ossermann, Kermit	New York	1909	Diabetes, myasthenia gravis
Pappenheim, Arthur	Berlin	1870	Blood research, Pappenheim's lymphocyte stains, staining method
Perutz, Max Ferdinand	Vienna	1914	Spiral structure of proteins, chemistry Nobel Prize
Pick, Alois	Vienna	1859	Stomach and intestinal disorders
Pick, Friedel	Prague	1867	Described pseudocirrhosis (Pick's disease), Pick's syndrome
Pletsch, Johann		1878	Leukemia
Rombert, Ernst von	Munich	1865	Circulatory disorders
Rosenbach, Ottomar	Breslau	1851	Rosenbach's nodes, R.'s reflexneurosis, Rosenbach's law, Rosenbach's test
Rosenstein, Samuel S.	Leiden	1832	Kidney diseases, epilepsy, meningitis, diabetes
Rosin, Heinrich	Berlin	1863	Trousseau-Dumontpallier-Rosin test
Scherf, David	Vienna, New York	1899	Cardiac arrhythmias
Senator, Hermann	Berlin	1854	Metabolism and kidney diseases
Snapper, Isidore	New York	1889	Bone diseases
Soffer, Louis	New York	1904	Adrenal gland, manual of endocrinology
Strauss, Hermann	Berlin	1868	Sigmoidoscopy for intestinal examinations
Thannhauser, Siegfried	Boston	1885	Lipoid metabolism
Traube, Ludwig	Berlin	1818	Digitalis for heart disease
Winterbeg, Heinrich	Vienna	1867	Heart disease
Winternitz, Wilhelm	Vienna	1835	Founder of hydrotherapy
Wolff, Max	Berlin	1844	Tuberculosis
Zondek, Hermann	Jerusalem	1887	Disorders of internal secretions
Zondek, Samuel G.	Tel Aviv	1894	Significance of electrolytes for treatment of cardiac disorders

SURGERY

Baruch, Simon	New York	1840	US pioneer of appendectomy
Berg, Albert A.	New York	1872	Abdominal surgery

Borchardt, Moritz	Berlin	1868	Brain and spinal-cord surgery
Davidoff, Leo Marx	New York	1898	Brain surgery
Donati, Mario	Milan	1879	Ulcers, abdomen
Garlock, John H.	New York	1896	Esophagus
Gersuni, Robert	Vienna	1844	Plastic surgery
Heidenhain, Max	Griefswald	1860	*Das Problem maligner Tumoren*
Kerewski, Ferdinand	Berlin	1858	Hernia surgery
Katzenstein, Moritz	Berlin	1872	Experimental surgery, stomach tumors
Küttner, Hermann	Breslau	1870	Chief naval physician, authority on military surgery
Lewisohn, Richard	New York	1875	Pioneer of blood transfusion, inventor of the blood bank
Lilienthal, Howard	New York	1861	Chest surgery
Mandel, Felix	Vienna	1892	Cancer, novocaine blockers
Marcus, Max	Tel Aviv	1892	Traumatology
Melchior, Eduard	Breslau	1893	*Grundriss der allgemeinen Chirugie*
Mühsam, Richard	Berlin	1872	Spleen, abdomen, kidneys
Nissen, Rudolf	Berlin, Basel	1895	Lung resection
Rosenstein, Paul	Berlin	1875	Abdominal surgery
Schnitzler, Julius	Vienna	1865	Stomach and intestinal surgery
Stilling, Benedikt	Kassel	1810	Pioneer of modern surgery, central nervous system
Thorek, Max	Chicago	1880	Pioneer of thoracic surgery
Wachsmann, Siegfried	New York	1865	Professor at Columbia University
Wölfler, Anton	Vienna	1850	Gastroenterostomy

ORTHOPEDICS

Bayer, Hans von	Heidelberg, Basel	1875	Neurophysiology, mechanology
Haffa, Albert	Berlin	1859	*Handbuch der orthopädischen Chirugie* (with Joachimsthal and Wolff)
Joachimsthal, Georg	Berlin	1863	*Handbuch der orthopädischen Chirugie* (with Haffa and Wolff)
Mayer, Leo	New York	1884	Physiological sinew transplants

| Wolff, Julius | Berlin | 1836 | *Handbuch der orthopädischen Chirugie* (with Haffa and Joachimsthal) |
| Zabludowski, Isidor | Berlin | 1851 | Established medical massage |

PHARMACOLOGY

Ellinger, Alexandre	Frankfurt	1870	Metabolism
Filehne, Wilhelm	Breslau	1844	Discovered antipyrins
Fröhlich, Alfred	Vienna, Cincinnati	1871	Potentiation of cocaine with adrenalin, Fröhlich's syndrome
Gottlieb, Rudolf	Heidelberg	1864	Experimental pharmacology
Jaffe, Max	Königsberg	1840	Metabolism procedures
Koller, Carl	New York	1857	First local anesthesia with cocaine
Lewis, Louis	Berlin	1850	Discovered *Anhalonium Lewini*
Liebreich, M.E.O.	Berlin	1839	Discovered soporific qualities of chloral hydrate, lanolin as basic ingredient for salves, produced evidence of phosphorus in the brain
Loewe, Siegfried	Göttingen, Dorpat		Anesthesia, urine colloids in mental illness
Loewi, Otto	Graz, New York	1873	Chemical transmission of nerve impulses, albumin synthesis, Nobel Prize
Macht, David	Baltimore	1882	Toxicological test with plant seeds
Magnus, Rudolf	Utrecht	1873	Pharmacology of internal tract and central nervous system
Meltzer, Samuel L.	New York	1851	Endotracheal anesthesia (with Auer)
Meyer, Jacques	Strasbourg	1895	Morphology
Pick, Ernst Peter	Vienna, New York	1872	Studies in biochemistry, serology, immunology
Reichstein, Thadeus	Basel	1879	Isolation of cortisone, Nobel Prize
Starkenstein, Emil	Prague	1884	Relation of pharmacology to inflammation and hydroequilibrium

UROLOGY

| Bürger, Leo | New York | 1879 | Bürger's Disease |
| Casper, Leopold | Berlin | 1859 | Invented urethrocatherization |

Cohn, Theodor	Königsberg	1867	TB of the kidneys
Israel, James	Berlin	1848	Renal surgery
Joseph, Eugen	Berlin	1879	Chromocytoscopy
Lichtenberg, Alex v.	Berlin	1880	Pyelography
Posner, Karl	Berlin	1854	Diagnosis and therapy of urinary diseases
Zuckerkandl, Otto	Vienna	1861	Prostate hypertrophy

RADIOLOGY

Bucky, Gustav	Berlin, New York	1880	Bucky's diaphragm
Buschke, Franz	Berlin, Berkeley	1902	Radiation therapy of tumors
Ellinger, Fr. Ph.	Washington	1900	Biological basis for radiation therapy
Felson, Benjamin	Cincinnati	1913	Exploratory radiation of the chest
Freund, Leopold	Vienna	1868	Founder of radiation therapy
Halberstädter, Ludwig	Jerusalem	1870	Ovary sterilization by radiation
Kaplan, Ira	New York	1887	Radiation therapy for tumors
Lenz, Maurice	New York	1890	Therapy for tumors and tuberculosis
Levy-Dorn, Max	Berlin	1863	Pioneer of radiation treatment
Marks, Hirsch	New York	1892	Filter method of depth radiation
Poppel, Maxwell	New York	1903	Signs of radiation in pancreatic diseases
Rigler, Leo G.	Minneapolis	1896	Abdominal tumors in children
Schatzki, Richard	Cambridge	1901	Exploratory radiation of stomach and intestinal tract
Uhlmann, Erich M.	Chicago	1901	Introduction of linear accelerator for treatment of cancer

DERMATOLOGY

Auspitz, Heinrich	Vienna	1835	Auspitz sign in psoriasis
Bettmann, Siegfried	Heidelberg	1869	Introductory to dermatology
Biberstein, Hans	Breslau, New York	1889	Tropical diseases
Bloch, Bruno	Zurich	1878	Pigment formation, skin cancer
Blumenthal, Franz	Berlin, United States	1878	Eczema and idiosyncracy

Bruck, Carl	Altona	1879	Serodiagnosis of syphilis, uticaria, medication-induced eruptions, tuberculosis
Buschke, Abraham	Berlin	1868	Described European blastomycosis (with Busse)
Delbanco, Ernst	Hamburg	1869	Leprosy, skin tuberculosis, discovered prevalence of free sebaceous glands on the foreskin
Dostrovsky, Arieh	Jerusalem	1887	Border-ray therapy of Oriental sores
Ehrmann, Salomon	Vienna	1854	Skin stains, syphilis prophylaxis
Frei, Wilhelm	Berlin	1885	Frei test for venereal lymphogranuloma
Gans, Oskar	Berlin	1888	Histology of skin diseases
Haber, Henry	London	1900	Histopathology of the skin
Hebra, Ferdin v.	Vienna	1816	Classification of skin diseases
Heller, Julius	Berlin	1864	Disorders of the nails
Herxheimer, Karl	Frankfurt	1861	Jarisch-Herxheimer reaction for syphilis
Jadassohn, Joseph	Breslau	1863	Skin allergies (platelet test)
Jessner, Max	Breslau	1887	Skin allergies
Joseph, Max	Berlin	1860	Histologist, teacher, and therapist
Kaposi, Moritz	Vienna	1837	*Pathologie und Therapie*, and *Handatlas der Hautkrankheiten*
Köhner, Heinrich	Breslau	1838	Köhner signs
Königstein, Hans	Vienna, Israel	1878	Lecturer on skin and venereal diseases
Lassar, Oskar	Berlin	1849	Lassar's paste
Lesser, Edmund	Berlin	1852	*Lehrbuch der Haut- und Geschlechtskrankheiten*
Lipschütz, Benjamin	Austria	1878	Described acute vulvar ulcer
Meirowsky, Emil	Cologne	1876	Research on pigmentation
Müller, Rudolf	Vienna	1876	Müller-Oppenheim reaction
Neisser, Albert	Breslau	1855	Discovered gonococcus
Neumann, Isidor	Vienna	1832	Neumann's disease
Noble, Gabor	Vienna	1864	Classical description of venereal pathology
Oppenheim, Moritz	Vienna, Chicago	1876	*Praktikum der Haut- und Geschlechtskrankheiten*
Pick, Philipp J.	Prague	1834	President of German dermatologists' society

Pinkus, Felix	Berlin	1868	Pathologist, therapist, described Lichen nitidus
Rothman, Stephan	Chicago	1894	Physiology and biochemistry of the skin
Sagher, Felix	Jerusalem	1908	Diagnosis of leprosy
Schnitzer, Robert	Berlin, United States	1893	Chemotherapy of bacteria and protozoa
Sulzberger, Marion B.	New York	1895	Allergies, Sulzberger-Block disease
Unna, Paul G.	Hamburg	1850	Unna's disease
Urbach, Erich	Vienna, Philadelphia	1893	Classical works on dermatology and allergies
Wertheim, Gustav	Vienna	1822	Diagnostic work
Zeissel, Hermann v.	Vienna	1817	*Lehrbuch der konstitutionellen Syphilis*
Zeissl, Maximilian v.	Vienna	1853	Research on syphilis

PUBLIC HEALTH

Baehre, Georg	New York	1887	Public-health affairs
Baer, Abraham Adolf	Berlin	1834	Social and prison hygiene
Behrend, Friedrich Jakob	Berlin	1803	Syphilis countermeasures, canalization
Blaschko, Alfred	Berlin	1858	Cofounder of the society to combat venereal diseases
Fraenken, Karl	Marburg, Halle	1861	Biological purification of sewage
Friedberger, Ernst	Berlin	1875	Domestic hygiene
Goldberger, Joseph	New York	1874	Discovered cause of pellagra
Gottstein, Adolf	Berlin	1857	School hygiene
Hahn, Martin	Berlin	1871	Vocational hygiene
Hirsch, August	Berlin	1817	Cofounder of the German society for public health, pioneer in asepsis
Horwitz, Abraham	Santiago	1910	Epidemiology
Keigler, Israel J.	Jerusalem	1889	Malaria countermeasures, discovered carrier of one kind of typhoid fever
Loewy, Julius	Berlin	1885	Professional diseases, carbon monoxide poisoning
Neisser, Max	Frankfurt	1869	Diphtheria and serological problems, head of hygiene institute

Neumann, Salomon	Berlin	1819	Social hygiene, statistics
Prausnitz, Carl	Breslau	1876	Prausnitz-Küstner reaction, member of Hygiene Panel of the League of Nations
Proskauer, Bernhard	Berlin	1851	*Enzyklopädie der Hygiene*
Rosenau, M.J.	Cambridge	1869	*Preventive Medicine and Hygiene*
Seligmann, Erich	Berlin	1880	Director of the central health administration, Berlin
Sobernheim, Georg	Berlin, Berne	1865	Anthrax, cholera
Strauss, Walter	Berlin, Jerusalem	1895	Industrial hygiene

OPHTHALMOLOGY

Axenfeld, Emil	Freiburg	1867	Axenfeld-Monax bacillus
Berliner, M.L.	New York	1891	Biomicroscopy
Bernheimer, Stephan	Innsbruck	1861	Intersection of optical nerves
Bielschowsky, Alfred	Breslau	1871	Physiology and pathology of eye movement
Cohn, Hermann	Breslau	1838	Color blindness, school hygiene
Deutschmann, Heinrich	Göttingen	1852	Cataract formation, tuberculosis of the eye, ophthalmia, treatment of detached retina
Fehr, Oskar	Berlin, London	1871	Treatment of detached retina
Feigenbaum, Ariel	Jerusalem	1885	Founder of antitrachoma center in Israel
Friedenwalt, Jonas	Baltimore	1897	Anatomy and pathology of the eye
Fuchs, Ernst	Vienna	1851	Manual of ophthalmology
Goldmann, Hans J.	Bern	1899	Head of the Bern eye clinic
Hays, Isaac	Philadelphia	1796	Founder of the American Medical Association
Hirschberg, Julius	Berlin	1843	Removal of foreign bodies by means of electromagnet
Hirschmann, Leonhard	Charkow	1839	Myosis, myoriasis, trachoma, color sense
Igersheimer, Joseph	Frankfurt, Boston	1879	Toxicology and neurology of the eye
Jacobson, Julius		1828	Surgical treatment of cataracts and trachoma

Jakob, Salomon	Schleswig	1790	Research on penetration of the eyeball by foreign bodies
Javal, Louis E.	Paris	1839	Strabismus
Kaufmann, Herbert E.	Boston	1931	Keratitis
Kestenbaum, Alfred	Vienna, New York	1890	Neuro-ophthalmology
Koller, Karl	New York	1857	Cocaine anesthesia
Landolt, Edmond	Paris	1846	Landolt's bodies
Laquer, Ludwig	Strasbourg	1839	Glaucoma
Magnus, Hugo	Breslau	1842	Ophthalmascopic atlas
Mauthner, Ludwig	Prague	c. 1845	Relationship between brain and eye
Michaelson, Isaac	Jerusalem	1903	Circulation of the retina
Sachs, Moritz	Vienna	1865	Physiological and pathological movements of the eyeball
Salzmann, Max	Graz	1862	Invention of the gonioscope
Schnabel, Isidor	Innsbruck	1842	Schnabel's cavities
Sichel, Julius	Tübingen, Berlin, Paris	1802	Pioneer in ophthalmology
Sorby, Arnold	London	1900	Genetics
Ticho, Abraham	Jerusalem	1883	Trachoma

EAR, NOSE, AND THROAT

Alexander, Gustav	Berlin	1873	Description of the anatomy of the vestibular ganglia
Baginsky, Benno	Berlin	1848	Lecturer in laryngology
Bárány, Robert	Uppsala	1876	Disorders of the equilibrium, Nobel Prize
Flatau, Theodor	Berlin	1860	Phonetics and physiology of the vocal chords
Fränkel, Bernhard	Berlin	1836	Cancer of the larynx, cross sections of the frozen nasal cavity
Fröscheles, Emil	Vienna, United States	1886	Mechanics of speaking and singing, Fröscheles' symptom of deafness
Gottstein, Jakob	Breslau	1832	Manual of laryngial diseases
Hajek, Max	Vienna, London	1861	Laryngorhinologist
Hirsch, Oskar	Vienna	1877	Hirsch's septum operation, pioneer in the endonasal operation of the pituitary
Leidler, Rudolf	Prague, Vienna	1880	Important writer on otic therapy

Lembert, Julius	New York	1891	Operation for otosclerosis
Moos, Salomon	Heidelberg	1831	Pathology of the inner ear
Moses, Paul J.	San Francisco	1879	Neurosis of the voice
Neumann, Heinrich	Vienna	1873	Method for inner-ear surgery
Politzer, Adam	Vienna	1835	*System der Ohrenheilkunde*
Rosen, Samuel	New York	1897	Mobility of the stapes
Ruttin, Erich	Vienna	1880	Researcher, writer, and lecturer in otology
Semon, Felix	London	1849	Laryngologist
Stoerk, Karl	Vienna	1832	Laryngoscopy, oseophagopathy
Tuerck, Ludwig	Vienna	1810	Introduced the laryngial mirror into general practice
Wodak, Ernst	Prague, Israel	1891	Physiology of the labyrinth, plastic facial surgery

NEUROLOGY AND PSYCHIATRY

Adler, Alfred	New York	1870	Founder of individual psychology
Aschaffenberg, Gustav	Baltimore	1866	Criminal psychopathology
Beck, Samuel J.	New York	1896	Rorschach Test
Benedikt, Moritz	Vienna	1835	Electrotherapy
Bernfeld, Siegfried	Vienna	1892	Pedagogy
Bernheim, Hyppolyte	Paris	1837	*Hypnose, Suggestion und Psychotherapie*
Bielschowsky, Max	Berlin	1869	Structure of the interbrain
Bing, Paul Robert	Basel	1878	Localization of brain lesions
Birnbaum, Karl	Berlin	1878	Criminal anthropology
Brill, Abraham A.	New York	1874	Pioneer of psychoanalysis in the United States
Bychowski, Zygmunt	Warsaw	1865	Neurologist
Cassirer, Richard	Berlin	1865	Neurosis, sclerosis, spinal cord
Dattner, Bernhard	Vienna, New York	1887	Syphilis of the nervous system
Edinger, Ludwig	Frankfurt	1853	Neuroanatomy
Elsberg, Charles	New York	1871	Heart and brain anatomy
Eulenburg, Albert	Berlin	1840	Heat centers in the brain, publisher of *Realenzyklopädie der gesamten Heilkunde* in 26 volumes
Federn, Paul	Vienna	1871	*Psychoanalytisches Volksbuch*

Flatau, Eduard	Warsaw	1868	Neurologist
Frankl v. Hochwart, L.	Vienna	1862	Neurologist
Freud, Sigmund	Vienna, London	1856	Founder of psychoanalysis
Goldflam, Samuel	Warsaw	1852	Neurologist
Goldstein, Kurt	Berlin, New York	1878	Brain damage and character changes
Holland, Henry	London	1788	Pre-Freudian psychiatrist
Homburger, August	Frankfurt	1873	Psychopathology of children
Kallmann, Franz	Berlin, New York	1878	*The Genetics of Schizophrenia*
Kline, Nathan S.	New York	1916	Experimental psychopharmacology
Kronfeld, Arthur	Berlin	1886	Psychiatrist
Lichtheim, Ludwig	Königsberg	1845	Lichtheim's disease
Liepmann, Hugo Karl	Berlin	1863	Apraxia
Lombroso, Cesare	Turin	1836	*Genius and Lunacy*
Mayer-Gross, Willy	Heidelberg, London	1889	Discovered multiple sclerosis
Mendel, Emanuel	Berlin	1839	Progressive paralysis and mania
Mendel, Kurt	Berlin	1874	Mendel-Bechterew reflex
Minkowski, Eugen	Paris	1885	Founder of existentialist psychiatry
Minkowski, Mechislaw	Zurich	1884	Editor of the Swiss archives for neuropsychiatry
Moll, Albert	Berlin	1862	Hypnosis, magnetism
Myerson, Abraham	Boston	1881	Clinical psychiatry
Neumann, Heinrich	Breslau	1814	Father of psychiatry
Oppenheim, Hermann	Berlin	1858	Oppenheim's disease, handbook of neurology
Pannenheim, Martin	Vienna, Tel Aviv	1881	Professor of neurology and psychiatry
Pick, Arnold	Prague	1851	Cerebral atrophy
Rabinowitch, Reuben	Montreal	1908	Professor at McGill University
Reich, Wilhelm	Vienna	1897	Psychopathology of sexuality
Reik, Theodor	Vienna	1888	Psychology of religion
Remak, Robert	New York, Berlin	1815	Founder of electrotherapy
Rickman, John	London	1891	Pioneer of psychoanalysis in England
Romberg, Moritz, H.	Berlin	1795	One of the founders of neurology
Rosenthal, Moritz	Vienna	1833	Pioneer in electrotherapy

Rotschild, S.F.	Göttingen, Jerusalem	1899	*Neue Psychiatrie der Selbstentwicklung*
Sachs, Bernard	New York	1858	Tay-Sachs disease and pediatric neurology
Sakel, Manfred J.	New York	1900	Insulin shock for schizophrenia
Schilder, Paul	Vienna, New York	1886	*Gehirn und Persönlichkeit*
Slavson, Samuel R.	New York	1891	Group therapy
Spiegel, Ernst	Vienna, Philadelphia	1895	Experimental neurology
Steiner, Gabriel	Heidelberg, United States	1885	Neurologist, Steiner's tumor
Stekel, Wilhelm	Vienna, London	1868	Psychopathology of sexuality
Tramer, Moritz	Bern	1882	Child psychiatry, Tramer's test
Voronoff, Serge	Paris	1866	Rejuvenation with implanted reproductive glands of animals
Wallenberg, Adolf	Danzig	1862	Wallenberg's syndrome
Wechsler, Israel	New York	1886	*Textbuch der klinischen Neurologie*

Bibliography

Arendt, Hannah, *Elemente und Ursprünge totaler Herrschaft*, Frankfurt a.M., 1962.

Baum, Vicki, *Es war alles ganz anders*, Frankfurt, 1962.

Bentwich, Norman, *The Rescue and Achievement of Refugee Scholars*, The Hague, 1953.

bin Gorion, Emanuel, et. al., eds., *Philo-Lexikon—Handbuch des jüdischen Wissens*, Berlin, 1934.

Boberach, Heinz, ed., *Meldungen aus dem Reich, Auswahl aus den geheimen Lageberichten des SD der SS 1939–1944*, Neuwied, 1965.

Böhm, Franz, and Walter Dirks, eds., *Judentum—Schicksal, Wesen und Gegenwart von Hendrik G. van Dam*, Wiesbaden, 1965.

Bronder, Dietrich, *Bevor Hitler kam*, Hanover, 1964.

Coudenhove-Kalergi, Heinrich Graf von, *Das Wesen des Antisemitismus*, Leipzig, 1923.

Dam, Hendrik G. van, *Jüdische Gemeinschaft in Deutschland—Jahresbericht 1966/67*, Düsseldorf, 1967.

Dam, Hendrik G. van, *Jüdische Gemeinschaft in Deutschland—Ergänzungsbericht . . . vom 23. Mai 1968*, Düsseldorf, 1968.

Dam, Hendrik G. van, *Die Unverjährbarkeit des Völkermordes*, Mainz, 1969.

Deschner, Karlheinz, ed., Das Jahrhundert der Barbarei, Munich, 1966.

Durieux, Tilla, Eine Tür steht offen, Erinnerungen, Berlin, 1954.

Elbogen, Ismar, Geschichte der Juden in Deutschland, Berlin, 1935.

Fahrenhorst, Karl, "Juden in Politik und Wehrverband," in Der deutsche Roland, Mitteilungsblatt des Vereins für deutschvölkische Sippenkunde zu Berlin, vol. 7/9, Berlin, 1932.

Feilchenfeld, Alfred, trans. and ed., Denkwürdigkeiten der Glückel von Hameln, a. d. Jüdisch-Deutschen, Berlin, 1923.

Fermi, Laura, Illustrious Immigrants, The Intellectual Migration from Europe 1930–41, Chicago, 1968.

Fest, Joachim C., The Face of the Third Reich, New York, 1972.

Fischer, Fritz, Griff nach der Weltmacht, Die Kriegszielpolitik des kaiserlichen Deutschland 1914/18, Düsseldorf, 1964.

Fischer, Horst, Judentum, Staat und Heer in Preußen im frühen 19. Jahrhundert, Publications of the Leo Baeck Institute, Tübingen, 1968.

Fleming, Donald, and Bernard Bailyn, eds., The Intellectual Migration—Europe and America, 1930–1960, Cambridge, Mass., 1969.

Ford, Henry, Der internationale Jude, trans. into German by P. Lehmann, Leipzig, n.d.

Frank, Herbert, Enthüllte Geheimnisse jüdischer Geschichte— Grundlagen jüdischer Weltherrschaft, Munich, n.d.

Friehe, Albert, Was muß der Nationalsozialist von der Vererbung wissen?, Frankfurt, 1936.

Fritsch, Theodor, ed., Handbuch der Judenfrage, 29th ed., Leipzig, 1923.

Fritsch, Theodor, ed., Handbuch der Judenfrage, 32nd rev. ed., Leipzig, 1933.

Ganther, Heinz, ed., Die Juden in Deutschland—1951/52, 1958/59—Ein Almanach, Hamburg, n.d.

Gläser, Ludwig, "Eduard Magnus," Ein Beitrag zur Berliner Bildnismalerei des 19. Jahrhunderts, Berlin, 1963.

Göppinger, Horst, Der Nationalsozialismus und die jüdischen Juristen, Villingen, 1963.

Goldschmidt, Hermann Levin, Das Vermächtnis des deut_ Judentums, Frankfurt, 1957.

Gröning, Karl and Werner Kliess, Friedrichs Theaterlexikon, ed. by Henning Rischbieter, Velber near Hanover, 1969.

Grossmann, Kurt R., Emigration, Die Geschichte der Hitler-Flüchtlinge 1933–1945, Frankfurt, 1969.

Groves, Leslie R., Now It Can Be Told, The Story of the Manhattan Project, New York, 1962.

Habel, Walter, ed., *Wer ist wer?, Das deutsche Who's who,* 14th ed. of *Degeners Wer ist's?* Vol. 1, *Bundesrepublik Deutschland und Westberlin,* Berlin, 1962.

Hahn, Otto, Vom Radiothor zur Uranspaltung—Eine wissenschaftliche Selbstbiographie, Braunschweig, 1962.

Hamburger, Ernest, Juden im öffentlichen Leben Deutschlands, Regierungsmitglieder, Beamte und Parlamentarier in der monarchischen Zeit 1848–1918, Scientific Publications of the Leo Baeck Institute, Tübingen, 1958.

Hartmann, Hans, Lexikon der Nobelpreisträger, Berlin, 1967.

Hartner, Herweg, Erotik und Rasse—Eine Untersuchung über gesellschaftliche, sittliche und geschlechtliche Fragen, Munich, 1925.

Heer, Friedrich, Gottes erste Liebe, Munich, 1967.

Hensel, Sebastian, Die Familie Mendelssohn, Berlin, 1880.

Hermann, Hans H., Weimar—Bestandsaufnahme einer Republik, Reinbek near Hamburg, 1969.

Herrlinger, Robert Die Nobelpreisträger der Medizin, Munich, 1963.

Herrmann, Klaus J., Das Dritte Reich und die deutsch-jüdischen Organisationen 1933–1934, Publications of the Institute for Political Science, Munich, 1969.

Herz, Ludwig, Spaziergänge im Damals, Aus dem alten Berlin, Berlin, 1933.

Hewlett, Richard G., and Oscar E. Anderson, Jr., The New World 1939–1946, Pennsylvania State University, 1962.

Hieronimus, Ekkehard, Bedeutende Juden in Niedersachsen, Theodor Lessing, Otto Meyerhof, Leonard Nelson, Hanover, 1964.

Adolf, Mein Kampf, Munich, 1934.

Walther, ed., *Der Nationalsozialismus—Dokumente 1945,* Frankfurt, 1957.

The Virushouse, London, n.d.

Hanns, Johann Strauß, der Walzerkönig und tie, Vienna, 1965.

Jungk, Robert, Heller als tausend Sonnen—Das Schicksal der Atomforscher, Munich, n.d.

Katcher, Leo, Post Mortem—The Jews in Germany—Now, London, 1968.

Kaufmann, David, Die letzte Vertreibung der Juden aus Wien und Niederösterreich, ihre Vorgeschichte (1625–1670) und ihre Opfer, Vienna, 1889.

Kaznelson, Siegmund, ed., Juden im deutschen Kulturbereich, Ein Sammelwerk, 3rd. rev. ed., Berlin, 1962.

Keller, Werner, Und wurden zerstreut unter alle Völker, Munich, 1966.

Kempner, Robert M.W., Eichmann und Komplizen, Zurich, n.d.

Kernholt, Otto, Vom Ghetto zur Macht, Leipzig, 1923.

Kesten, Hermann, Ich lebe nicht in der Bundesrepublik, with essays by Max Brod, Richard Friedenthal, Hans Habe, Werner Helwig, Jakov Lind, Walter Mehring, Robert Neumann, Kurt Pinthus, and others, Munich, 1964.

Klass, Gert von, Aus Schutt und Asche, Krupp nach fünf Menschenaltern, Tübingen, 1961.

Kogon, Eugen, Der SS-Staat, Das System der deutschen Konzentrationslager, Frankfurt, 1946.

Lamm, Hans, Karl Marx und die Juden, Munich, 1969.

Leiber, Bernfried, and Theodor Olbert, Die klinischen Eponyme, Medizinische Eigennamenbegriffe in Klinik und Praxis, Munich, 1968.

Mann, Thomas, Sieben Manifeste zur jüdischen Frage 1936–1948, ed. by Walter A. Berendsohn, Darmstadt, 1966.

Marx, Karl, and Friedrich Engels, Deutsche Geschichte im 19. Jahrhundert, ed. by Iring Fetscher, Frankfurt, 1969.

Massing, Paul W., Vorgeschichte des politischen Antisemitismus, trans. and revised by F. J. Weil, Frankfurt, 1959.

Meister, Wilhelm, Judas Schuldbuch, Eine deutsche Abrechnung, Munich, 1919.

Mendelssohn, Peter de, Zeitungsstadt Berlin, Berlin, 1959.

Miles, Eine Welt im Umbruch, Zurich, 1961.

Morse, Arthur D., Die Wasser teilten sich nicht, trans. by N. Wölfl, Berne, 1968.

Müller, Hans Dieter, Der Springer-Konzern, Eine kritische Studie, Munich, 1968.

Nettl, Peter, Rosa Luxemburg, Oxford University Press, 1965.

Neumann, Carl, Curt Belling, and Hans-Walther Betz, Film-Kunst, Film-Kohn, Film-Korruption, Berlin, 1937.

Nissen, Rudolf, Helle Blätter, dunkle Blätter, Erinnerungen eines Chirurgen, Stuttgart, 1969.

Olenhusen, Albrecht Goetz von, Die NS-Rassenpolitik und die jüdischen Studenten an der Universität Freiburg 1933–1945, Freiburg, 1964.

Oppenheimer, John F., ed., Lexikon des Judentums, Gütersloh, 1967.

Passarge, Siegfried, Das Judentum als landschaftskundlich-ethnologisches Problem, Munich, 1929.

Pohl, J., Juden in der Sowjetunion zu Beginn der Herrschaft Stalins, Statistische Angaben aus jiddisch-sowjetischen Quellen, Tilsit, 1942.

Pross, Helge, Die deutsche akademische Emigration nach den Vereinigten Staaten 1933–1941, Berlin, 1955.

Pschyrembel, Willibald, Klinisches Wörterbuch mit klinischen Syndromen, rev. ed., Berlin, 1969.

Pulzer, Peter G. J., Die Entstehung des politischen Antisemitismus in Deutschland und Osterreich 1867–1914, trans. by J. u. T. Knust, Gütersloh, 1966.

Raddatz, Fritz J., Tucholsky, Eine Bildbiographie, Munich, 1961.

Rohling, August, Der Talmudjude—Zur Beherzigung für Juden und Christen aller Stände, Munster, 1873.

Rosa, Franz, Wieder Weltkrieg um Juda?, Berlin, 1939.

Rosenstein, Paul, Narben bleiben zurück, Munich, 1954.

Schilling, Konrad, ed., Monumenta Judaica, 2000 Jahre Geschichte und Kultur der Juden am Rhein, Cologne, 1963.

Schlamm, William S., Wer ist Jude?, Ein Selbstgespräch, Stuttgart, 1964.

Schoenberner, Gerhard, Der gelbe Stern, Die Judenverfolgung in Europa 1933 bis 1945, Hamburg, 1960.

Schoeps, Hans-Joachim, Rückblicke, 2nd rev. ed., Berlin, 1963.

Schoeps, Hans-Joachim, Barocke Juden, Christen, Judenchristen, Berne, 1965.

Schulz, Klaus-Peter, Tucholsky, Kurt Tucholsky in Selbstzeugnissen und Bilddokumenten, dargestellt von, Reinbek near Hamburg, 1959.

Schwaiger, Egloff, Laser—Licht von morgen, Munich, 1969.

Schwarz, Dieter, Das Weltjudentum—Organisation, Macht und Politik, Berlin, 1944.

Shirer, William L., The Rise and Fall of the Third Reich, New York, 1960.

Smyth, Henry D., Atomic Energy for Military Purposes, Princeton, N.J., 1945.

Söhn, Gerhard, Heinrich Heine in seiner Vaterstadt Düsseldorf, Düsseldorf, 1966.

Sombart, Werner, Die Juden und das Wirtschaftsleben, Munich, 1928.

Speer, Albert, Inside the Third Reich, trans. by Richard and Clara Winston, New York, 1970.

Spuler, Minister-Ploetz, Regenten und Regierungen der Welt, Bielefeld, 1953.

Stampfer, Friedrich, Die vierzehn Jahre der ersten deutschen Republik, Offenbach, 1947.

Stengel, Theo and Herbert Gerigk, Lexikon der Juden in der Musik, Berlin, 1940.

Stern, Desider, Werke jüdischer Autoren deutscher Sprache, Eine Bio-Bibliographie, 3rd ed., Munich, 1970.

Strecker, Reinhard-M., ed., Dr. Hans Globke, Aktenauszüge, Dokumente, Hamburg, 1961.

Theilhaber, Felix A., Jüdische Flieger im Weltkrieg, Berlin, 1924.

Trietsch, Davis, Juden und Deutsche—Eine Sprach- und Interessengemeinschaft, Vienna, 1913.

Tucholsky, Kurt, Deutschland, Deutschland über alles, Berlin, 1929.

Tucholsky, Kurt, Briefe an eine Katholikin, Reinbek near Hamburg, 1970.

Tucholsky, Kurt, Gesammelte Werke, 4 vols. ed. by Mary Gerold-Tucholsky and Fritz Raddatz, Hamburg, 1961.

Ullmann, Arno, Israels Weg zum Staat, Munich, 1964.

Ullstein, Heinz, Spielplatz meines Lebens, Erinnerungen, Munich, 1961.

Ullstein, Hermann, The Rise and Fall of the House of Ullstein, London, n.d.

Willstätter, Richard, Aus meinem Leben, Weinheim, 1949.

Zechlin, Egmont, Die deutsche Politik und die Juden im ersten Weltkrieg, Göttingen, 1969.

Zuckermann, Sir Solly, Scientists and War, London, 1966.

Zweig, Friderike M., Stefan Zweig, Eine Bildbiographie, Munich, 1961.

Works Without Authorship

Antisemiten-Spiegel, Die Antisemiten im Lichte des Christen-thums, des Rechtes und der Wissenschaft, Danzig, 1900.

Der Orden pour le mérite für Wissenschaft und Künste von 1842 bis 1963, nebst Ergänzungen bis 1968, (Bundesministerium des Innern, Bonn), n.d.

Die Juden als Soldaten, ed. by Comité zur Abwehr antisemitischer Angriffe in Berlin, Berlin, 1897.

Die jüdischen Gefallenen des deutschen Heeres, der deutschen Marine und der deutschen Schutztruppen 1914–1918, A commemorative volume issued by Reichsbund jüdischer Frontsoldaten, Berlin, 1932.

Göttinger Gedenktafeln, Ein biographischer Wegweiser, Göttingen, 1962.

Juden als Erfinder und Entdecker, Publication of Henriette Becker-Stiftung, Berlin, 1913.

Jüdisches Archiv, Mitteilungen des Komitees jüdisches Kriegsarchiv, Vienna, May 1915.

Jüdische Familien-Forschung, Mitteilungen der Gesellschaft für jüdische Familienforschung, no. 27, vol. VII, September 1931, Berlin.

Süddeutsche Monatshefte, Rußland, Munich, February 1915.

Süddeutsche Monatshefte, Ostjuden, Munich, February 1916.

Trial of Major War Criminals Before the International Military Tribunal, 42 vols., Nuremberg, 1947–1949.

Unseren gefallenen Kameraden, published by the Munich office of the Reichsbundes jüdischer Frontsoldaten, 1929.

Abwehr-ABC, ed. by Verein zur Abwehr des Antisemitismus, 2nd rev. ed., Berlin, n.d.

Semigothaisches Genealogisches Taschenbuch ari(st)okratisch-jüdischer Heiraten, Munich, 1914.

Auszug des Geistes—Bericht über eine Sendereihe (Radio Bremen), Bremen, n.d.

Um uns die Fremde, Die Vertreibung des Geistes 1933–1945, No. 9, Radio Free Berlin, Berlin, n.d.

Index

363

ABOUT THE AUTHOR

BERNT ENGELMANN was born in Berlin in 1921 and completed high school in 1938. In World War II he was in the Luftwaffe, stationed in France, where he acted as a contact with the French resistance and worked with German anti-Nazi groups. As a result, he was arrested twice by the Gestapo, sent to prison without trial, and then to Dachau concentration camp until April 1945, when the U.S. Army liberated the camp.

Engelmann began his career as a writer and journalist in 1949. He served as a correspondent, editor, and special correspondent for the German magazine *Der Spiegel*, and then as a special correspondent for German television. His first book, *My Friends the Millionaires*, was published in 1962 and has sold over 500,000 copies. Engelmann retired from active journalism in order to write full-time. His thirty books have nearly eight million copies in print worldwide and have been translated into many languages.

Bernt Engelmann has four children and lives with his wife, Kirsten Wedemann, in Rottach-Egern, West Germany.

Here are the Books that Explore

Fiction

the Jewish Heritage-Past and Present.

☐	24352	**Karpov's Brain** Gerald Green	$3.95
☐	24160	**Mila 18** Leon Uris	$4.50
☐	22536	**Dawn** Elie Wiesel	$2.95
☐	20807	**Night** Elie Wiesel	$2.95

Non-Fiction

☐	24445	**Germany Without Jews** Bernt Engelmann	$4.95
☐	23653	**The Last Jews in Berlin** Leonard Gross	$3.95
☐	34003	**The Jewish Almanac** Siegel & Rheins, eds.	$10.95
☐	01369	**Seasons of Our Joy** Arthur Waskow	$8.95
☐	22500	**Children of the Holocaust** Helen Epstein	$3.95
☐	23477	**The War Against the Jews** Lucy S. Dawidowicz	$4.95

Prices and availability subject to change without notice.

Buy them at your local bookstore or use this handy coupon for ordering:

We Deliver!
And So Do These Bestsellers.

SPECIAL MONEY SAVING OFFER

Now you can have an up-to-date listing of Bantam's hundreds of titles plus take advantage of our unique and exciting bonus book offer. A special offer which gives you the opportunity to purchase a Bantam book for only 50¢. Here's how!

By ordering any five books at the regular price per order, you can also choose any other single book listed (up to a $4.95 value) for just 50¢. Some restrictions do apply, but for further details why not send for Bantam's listing of titles today!

Just send us your name and address plus 50¢ to defray the postage and handling costs.